FERDINAND CHRISTIAN BAUR

FERDINAND CHRISTIAN BAUR

A Reader

Edited by
David Lincicum and Johannes Zachhuber

LONDON • NEW YORK • OXFORD • NEW DELHI • SYDNEY

T&T CLARK

Bloomsbury Publishing Plc

50 Bedford Square, London, WC1B 3DP, UK
1385 Broadway, New York, NY 10018, USA
29 Earlsfort Terrace, Dublin 2, Ireland

BLOOMSBURY, T&T CLARK and the T&T Clark logo are trademarks of
Bloomsbury Publishing Plc

First published in Great Britain 2022
Paperback edition published 2023

Copyright © David Lincicum and Johannes Zachhuber and translators, 2022

David Lincicum and Johannes Zachhuber have asserted their right under the Copyright,
Designs and Patents Act, 1988, to be identified as Editors of this work.

For legal purposes the Acknowledgments on p. viii constitute an
extension of this copyright page.

Cover design: Charlotte James
Cover image: Ferdinand Christian Baur © Universitätsbibliothek Tübingen (UBT)

All rights reserved. No part of this publication may be reproduced or transmitted
in any form or by any means, electronic or mechanical, including photocopying,
recording, or any information storage or retrieval system, without prior
permission in writing from the publishers.

Bloomsbury Publishing Plc does not have any control over, or responsibility for, any
third-party websites referred to or in this book. All internet addresses given in this
book were correct at the time of going to press. The author and publisher regret
any inconvenience caused if addresses have changed or sites have ceased
to exist, but can accept no responsibility for any such changes.

A catalogue record for this book is available from the British Library.

Library of Congress Cataloging-in-Publication Data
Names: Baur, Ferdinand Christian, 1792-1860, author. | Zachhuber,
Johannes, editor. | Lincicum, David, 1979- editor.
Title: Ferdinand Christian Baur : a reader / edited by David Lincicum
and Johannes Zachhuber.
Description: London ; New York : T&T Clark : 2022. | Includes bibliographical references. |
Summary: "Brings together the key writings of Ferdinand Christian Baur across
theology, biblical studies, early Christian history, and philosophy, showing his crucial
role in the development of 19th-century thought"– Provided by publisher.
Identifiers: LCCN 2021057939 (print) | LCCN 2021057940 (ebook) |
ISBN 9780567694485 (hardback) | ISBN 9780567706515 (paperback) |
ISBN 9780567694492 (pdf) | ISBN 9780567694515 (epub)
Subjects: LCSH: Religion–Philosophy. | Theology, Doctrinal. |
Protestantism. | Church history–Primitive and early church, ca. 30-600.
Classification: LCC BL51 .B3813 2022 (print) | LCC BL51 (ebook) |
DDC 230.01–dc23/eng/20220201
LC record available at https://lccn.loc.gov/2021057939
LC ebook record available at https://lccn.loc.gov/2021057940

ISBN:	HB:	978-0-5676-9448-5
	PB:	978-0-5677-0651-5
	ePDF:	978-0-5676-9449-2
	eBook:	978-0-5676-9451-5

Typeset by Integra Software Services Pvt. Ltd.

To find out more about our authors and books visit www.bloomsbury.com
and sign up for our newsletters.

CONTENTS

Preface	vii
Acknowledgments	viii
Note on Text and Translations	ix
List of Abbreviations	xi
Introduction	1

PART ONE: PHILOSOPHY OF RELIGION

1	Mythology, History, and the Philosophy of Religion	17
2	Gnosis as Christian Philosophy of Religion	25
3	On the Idea of a Philosophy of Religion	45

PART TWO: HISTORY OF DOGMA

4	Introduction to the History of Dogma	53
5	On the Doctrine of Reconciliation in Its Historical Development	65
6	On the History of Trinitarian and Christological Doctrine	77

PART THREE: NEW TESTAMENT CRITICISM

7	Prolegomena to New Testament Studies	95
8	Critical Investigations of the Canonical Gospels	101
9	Paul, the Apostle of Jesus Christ: His Life and Works	129

PART FOUR: CHURCH HISTORY

10	On the History of Ecclesiastical Historiography	143
11	Christianity in Its First Three Centuries	157

PART FIVE: BAUR IN THE CONTROVERSIES OF HIS TIME

12 Baur on Baur and His School — 185

13 On Protestantism and Catholicism — 191

14 In Defense of Critical Exegesis — 203

BIBLIOGRAPHY — 214
GENERAL INDEX — 228
INDEX OF ANCIENT SOURCES — 232
INDEX OF MODERN AUTHORS — 233
INDEX OF BIBLICAL PASSAGES — 236

PREFACE

Composing a *Reader* for an author as prolific and versatile as Ferdinand Christian Baur is both rewarding and challenging.

Baur's published oeuvre runs to *c*. 25,000 pages and thus encompasses approximately 7.5 million words. He wrote on New Testament criticism, church history, the history of religions, and the philosophy of religion. In addition, he was also an active participant in academic and political developments of the time. He engaged in debates about the "essence" of Protestantism and its relationship to other manifestations of Christianity, notably Catholicism.

Few if any will have the opportunity, the ability, or indeed the desire to read it all. It is therefore arguable that Baur like few other writers offers himself to the effort of the compiler. And yet, to this date no *Reader* with excerpts from Baur's many publications exists in any language. We are, consequently, excited to offer the present book as a first attempt to introduce those with an interest in Baur's work to his writings through a collection of excerpts from his most important texts.

That said, we are conscious that any attempt to select from the wealth of texts Baur penned cannot but be partial and must, to an extent, reflect the concerns and specializations of those who have put it together. The present *Reader* probably says something about the viewpoints of its editors with their interests in the origin of modern New Testament Studies and theological historicism. Some might wish that Baur's texts on Greek religion, on Platonism and Christianity, on mysticism or the principle of Protestantism would be more strongly represented. Without denying that there is more to be discovered, however, we feel confident that Baur's main areas of scholarly activity are well represented in the *Reader*. Even most of his minor interests come to the fore here or there, and those whose interest is kindled by what they find here can, of course, always explore what else there is beyond the confines of the present book.

We both have spent many years with Baur's works, but the process of selecting from the breadth of his oeuvre and the ensuing opportunity to look concurrently at such a wide variety of texts has been highly illuminating for both of us. Underlying concerns that extend through and structure Baur's many fields of academic interest become visible, putting into relief the remarkable coherence of a scholarly oeuvre whose contours can easily get lost in the extraordinary amount of text dedicated to such a variety of specialist topics.

In publishing this volume, we hope that others will have the same experience. F. C. Baur is more often cited than read. He has often been pigeonholed in one way or another. If those who are inclined to critique or dismiss him will in the future first make an effort to read him in his own words, this *Reader* will have reached its purpose.

David Lincicum and Johannes Zachhuber
South Bend/Oxford, August 2021

ACKNOWLEDGMENTS

We could not have produced this *Reader* without support from various sides. Beata and Matthew Vale translated Baur's texts for chapters 1, 2, 3, 5, 6, 7, 8, and 13. Without their enormous effort at what can be a rather impenetrable original, this project would have been impossible to complete.

The other chapters reproduce previously published translations. Here too we need to acknowledge the generous support that made our own work possible.

Oxford University Press kindly gave permission to reprint chapter 4 from F. C. Baur, *The History of Christian Dogma*, trans. Robert F. Brown and Peter C. Hodgson (Oxford: OUP, 2014); and chapter 10 from F. C. Baur, *On the Writing of Church History*, ed. and trans. Peter C. Hodgson (Oxford: OUP, 1968).

Wipf and Stock kindly gave permission to reprint chapter 9 from F. C. Baur, *Paul, the Apostle of Jesus Christ*, trans. Robert F. Brown and Peter C. Hodgson (Eugene, OR: Cascade, 2021); chapter 11 from F. C. Baur, *Christianity and the Christian Church of the First Three Centuries*, trans. Robert F. Brown and Peter C. Hodgson (Eugene, OR: Cascade, 2019); and chapter 12 from F. C. Baur, *Church and Theology in the Nineteenth Century*, trans. Robert F. Brown and Peter C. Hodgson (Eugene, OR: Cascade, 2018).

Fortress Press kindly permitted reprinting chapter 14 from Christophe Chalamet (ed.), *The Challenge of History: Readings in Modern History* (Minneapolis, MN: Fortress, 2020).

Prof. Peter Hodgson supplied editable files for all his translations we are here reprinting. He also gave invaluable advice on the selections from Baur's huge oeuvre. We feel privileged that in this enormously difficult task we had the guidance of the grand master of Baur studies.

We furthermore gratefully acknowledge the support of the Institute for Scholarship in the Liberal Arts, College of Arts and Letters, and of the Nanovic Institute for European Studies, both of the University of Notre Dame.

NOTE ON TEXT AND TRANSLATIONS

The present *Reader* combines new and existent translations. Chapters 1, 2, 3, 5, 7, 8, and 13 have been translated for this volume and, with the exception of Chapter 2, have never been rendered into English before. By contrast, Chapters 4, 9, 10, 11, 12, and 14 reproduce translations that have previously been published. As for the latter, the editors have not changed the translated texts except for the correction of obvious errors. For the new translations on the other hand, which were prepared by Beata and Matthew Vale, the editors bear full responsibility.

The different provenance of the translations has inevitably led to a certain heterogeneity in the principles of rendering Baur's text. These differences, which careful readers will be able to observe across the volume, seemed a small price to pay, however, when compared with the benefit of drawing on the outstanding scholarship of those whose translations the editors were able to use.

Regarding annotations, similar divergences have been accepted by the editors. In the newly translated texts, the editors have generally omitted Baur's own notes, whereas previously published translations have mostly incorporated them. Overall, the editors have, again, accepted this inconsistency. The editors have, however, checked all annotations carefully, modified them, or added to them as appropriate. As the procedure varied throughout the book, the reader will find an indication of what notes to expect at the beginning of each chapter.

The editors have consistently added references to Baur's original pagination as well as the pagination of published English translations where they were reprinted here. The former are given in square brackets ([]), the latter in angled brackets (< >).

All translators of Baur's German are faced with some difficult decisions. Baur's sentences often run on for too many lines and include parentheses that are hard to follow for the most attentive reader. He was also no friend of regular paragraph breaks. Many of his texts contain few or no subheadings to give orientation in chapters that can go on for dozens of pages.

The editors have followed precedent by breaking up Baur's paragraphs into accessible units. Where appropriate, they have also inserted additional headings. For those, Baur's often extensive, analytic tables of contents have sometimes been helpful. Where this is the case, this will be indicated in the text.

A further problem consists in Baur's vocabulary which includes terms with no perfect correspondence in English. Annotations are used to explain some of the more difficult decisions taken by the translators.

For some recurrent cases, the following Glossary may also be helpful. Annotations throughout the volume will refer back to it.

Concept (*Begriff*): For Hegel and Baur this is an ontological as much as an epistemological term. Using the language of *Begriff* permits Baur to conceive of "intellectual history," for example, the history of dogma, as real, objective, historical evolution.

Consideration (*Betrachtung*) is the term Baur typically uses for critical, scientific (*wissenschaftlich*) historical method. It has both an empirical and a speculative (reflective) component (cf. CCC, 3, n. 1).

In itself/for itself (*an sich/für sich*): When Baur refers to something as it is "in itself," this does not normally signify its true being (unlike Kant's famously elusive "thing-in-itself"). Rather, being in itself is only the first step in a process which subsequently has to involve the acquisition of full self-awareness, being "for itself." In Hegel's language, the full truth about a thing is its being in-and-for-itself (*an und für sich*). This conceptual and ontological movement from "in itself" to "for itself" to "in-and-for-itself" is often found in Baur's language, especially in his writings from 1835 to 1847.

Science (*Wissenschaft*): The German *Wissenschaft* has retained the broader meaning of Latin *scientia* which in English has been lost from the mid-nineteenth century. Science can thus be employed for humanities disciplines such as history or philosophy as much as for the natural sciences. In addition, Baur sometimes uses *Wissenschaft* in an emphatic sense for philosophy in the Hegelian sense. Hegel often employed the term as a conscious derivative of *Wissen* (knowledge) and could, in fact, use *Wissenschaft* and *Wissen* interchangeably. Later, under the influence of Strauss, Baur employs *Wissenschaft* in a more positivistic sense for the "presuppositionless," methodologically driven examination of empirical sources.

Spirit or mind (*Geist*): It is crucial for all idealist systems of thought that the German *Geist* is both a philosophical and a theological term. The transition from a discussion of the mind and of mental faculties to the biblical language of the Holy Spirit is thus easy in a way that is difficult to render into English. Generally, where Baur uses the Hegelian language of *Geist* as a fundamentally ontological category, the English "spirit" (not capitalized) is used. "Spirit" (capitalized) is employed where the predominant reference is to the third Person of the Trinity.

Sublate (*aufheben*): In the German term, three meanings coalesce: (1) cancel out, abolish; (2) retain; (3) lift up. The (rather artificial) English term "sublate" is often employed to convey the fluctuation between these meanings which in Baur is often intentional.

System of Doctrine (*Lehrbegriff*): *Lehrbegriff* was a popular theological term in nineteenth-century German without an obvious English equivalent. It denotes a coherent body of teaching central for a religious tradition.

ABBREVIATIONS

1. Baur's main works

AE "Abgenöthigte Erklärung gegen einen Artikel der evangelischen Kirchenzeitung, herausgegeben von Dr. E. W. Hengstenberg, Prof. der Theol. an der Universität zu Berlin. Mai 1836." *Tübinger Zeitschrift für Theologie* 1836, Issue 3: 179–232.

BdR "Über den Begriff der Religionsphilosophie." *Zeitschrift für speculative Theologie* 2 (1837): 368–73.

CCK *Das Christenthum und die christliche Kirche der ersten drei Jahrhunderte.* Tübingen: Fues, 1853; 2nd ed. 1860.

CCC *Christianity and the Christian Church in the First Three Centuries*, ed. Peter C. Hodgson; trans. Robert F. Brown and Peter C. Hodgson. Eugene, OR: Cascade, 2019.

CG *Christian Gnosis*, ed. Peter C. Hodgson; trans. Robert F. Brown. Eugene, OR: Cascade, 2020.

CKA *Die christliche Kirche vom Anfang des vierten bis zum Ende des sechsten Jahrhunderts in den Hauptmomenten ihrer Entwicklung.* Tübingen: Fues, 1859.

CKM *Die christliche Kirche des Mittelalters in den Hauptmomenten ihrer Entwicklung*, ed. Ferdinand Friedrich Baur. Tübingen: Fues, 1861.

CLV *Die christliche Lehre von der Versöhnung in ihrer geschichtlichen Entwicklung von der ältesten Zeit bis auf die neueste.* Tübingen: Osiander, 1838.

CPKG "Die Christuspartei in der korinthischen Gemeinde, der Gegensatz des petrinischen und paulinischen Christenthums in der ältesten Kirche, der Apostel Petrus in Rom." *Tübinger Zeitschrift für Theologie* (1831), no. 4: 61–206.

CTNC *Church and Theology in the Nineteenth Century*, trans. Robert F. Brown and Peter c. Hodgson. Eugene, OR: Cascade, 2018.

DCG *Die christliche Gnosis oder die christliche Religions-Philosophie in ihrer geschichtlichen Entwiklung.* Tübingen: Osiander, 1835.

ECH	*The Epochs of Church Historiography*, trans. Peter C. Hodgson, in: *Ferdinand Christian Baur on the Writing of Church History*, ed. Peter Hodgson. Oxford: Oxford University Press, 1968.
EkG	*Epochen der kirchlichen Geschichtsschreibung*. Tübingen: Fues, 1852.
ENT	"Die Einleitung in das Neue Testament als theologische Wissenschaft." *Theologische Jahrbücher* 9 (1850): 463–566; 10 (1851): 70–94, 222–52, 291–328.
HCD	*History of Christian Dogma*, trans. Robert F. Brown and Peter C. Hodgson. Oxford: Oxford University Press, 2014.
KGNJ	*Kirchengeschichte des neunzehnten Jahrhunderts*, ed. Eduard Zeller. Tübingen: Fues, 1862.
KGNZ	*Kirchengeschichte der neueren Zeit, von der Reformation bis zum Ende des achtzehnten Jahrhunderts*, ed. Ferdinand Friedrich Baur. Tübingen: Fues, 1863.
KUKE	*Kritische Untersuchungen über die kanonischen Evangelien, ihr Verhältniss zu einander, ihren Charakter und Ursprung*. Tübingen: Fues, 1847.
LD	*Lehrbuch der Dogmengeschichte*. Stuttgart: Becher, 1847.
LDM	*Die christliche Lehre von der Dreieinigkeit und Menschwerdung Gottes in ihrer geschichtlichen Entwicklung*, 3 vols. Tübingen: Osiander, 1841–3.
NTT	*Lectures on New Testament Theology*, ed. Peter C. Hodgson; trans. Robert F. Brown. Oxford: Oxford University Press, 2016.
PAJC	*Paulus, der Apostel Jesu Christi. Sein Leben und Wirken, seine Briefe und seine Lehre: Ein Beitrag zu einer kritischen Geschichte des Urchristenthums*. Stuttgart: Becher und Müller, 1845.
PAJC(E)	*Paul the Apostle of Jesus Christ*, ed. Peter C. Hodgson; trans. Robert F. Brown and Peter C. Hodgson. Eugene, OR: Cascade, 2021.
PAP	*Die sogenannten Pastoralbriefe des Apostels Paulus aufs neue kritisch untersucht*. Stuttgart and Tübingen: Cotta, 1835.
SuM	*Symbolik und Mythologie oder die Naturreligion des Alterthums* 2 vols. Stuttgart: Metzler, 1824–5.
VNT	*Vorlesungen über neutestamentliche Theologie*, ed. Ferdinand Friedrich Baur. Leipzig: Fues's Verlag, 1864; reprint Darmstadt: Wissenschaftliche Buchgesellschaft, 1973, with an introduction by W. G. Kümmel.

2. Other abbreviations

ThJb(T) *Theologische Jahrbücher* (Tübingen), ed. Eduard Zeller. Tübingen: Fues, 1842–57.

TZTh *Tübinger Zeitschrift für Theologie*, ed. Members of the Evangelical-Theological Faculty. Tübingen: Osiander (later Fues), 1828–40.

ZWT *Zeitschrift für wissenschaftliche Theologie*, ed. Adolf Hilgenfeld. Jena, Halle, Leipzig, Frankfurt/M: Hauke, 1858–1914.

Introduction

DAVID LINCICUM AND JOHANNES ZACHHUBER

Ferdinand Christian Baur was, without a doubt, one of the giants of nineteenth-century Christian theology. In his influential *History of Protestant Theology in the Nineteenth Century*, Karl Barth called him "the greatest theologian since Schleiermacher."[1] Baur was not only extremely prolific—his entire published oeuvre runs to approximately 25,000 pages—he was also remarkably versatile even for a time when scholars were generally less specialized than they are now. He must be considered as one of the founders of modern New Testament studies, contributed in major ways to the history of dogma and church history in general, but wrote also on the history of religion and the philosophy of religion. In addition, Baur was also an active participant in major scientific and religious controversies of the time. He mastered the controversialist's sharp, witty, and polemical style as much as the reflective diction of the scholar.

Despite his indubitable merits, however, Baur is considerably less well known than comparable nineteenth-century figures, such as Friedrich Schleiermacher, Albrecht Ritschl, or Ernst Troeltsch. In 2017, Peter C. Hodgson could write that "in the Anglophone world, Baur is still the most neglected and least appreciated of the major German theologians of the nineteenth century."[2] There may be more than one reason for this state of affairs. Baur reached the apogee of his scholarly productivity just at the point when political life in Germany turned decisively against any form of liberalism. Some of his most gifted students were either altogether prevented from attaining university posts, such as David Friedrich Strauss, or pushed into neighboring disciplines, such as Baur's son-in-law, Eduard Zeller, who was officially banned from teaching theology and instead became an influential scholar of ancient philosophy.[3]

It is, however, arguable that the reasons for the limitations of Baur's reception were not purely extraneous. Baur wrote constantly, but many of his publications were not accessibly written, not even by the standards of the German academy in the nineteenth century. He published extensive monographs on an almost yearly basis, but most of them never saw more than a single edition. Other important ideas appeared in journal articles which often ran to more than one hundred pages in length. The reader can be forgiven for suspecting that the price Baur paid for his productivity was the absence, more or less, of an editorial process. Many of his publications read as if they were

---

[1] Karl Barth, *History of Protestant Theology in the Nineteenth Century: Its Background and History*, new edn. (London: SCM, 2001), 485.
[2] Peter C. Hodgson, "Translator's Introduction," in *Ferdinand Christian Baur and the History of Early Christianity*, ed. Martin Bauspieß, Christof Landmesser and David Lincicum (Oxford: OUP, 2017), v. The most important existing portrayal of Baur in English remains Hodgson's own *The Formation of Historical Theology: A Study of Ferdinand Christian Baur* (New York: Harper & Row, 1966). Cf. also Horton Harris, *The Tübingen School* (Oxford: OUP, 1975); Johannes Zachhuber, *Theology of Science in Nineteenth-Century Germany: From F. C. Baur to Ernst Troeltsch* (Oxford: OUP, 2013); and the studies collected in Martin Bauspieß, Christof Landmesser, and David Lincicum (eds), *Ferdinand Christian Baur and the History of Early Christianity* (Oxford: OUP, 2017).
[3] Zachhuber, *Theology of Science*, 21–2.

printed as he put them originally to paper. Even a fast and diligent reader will not always find it easy to keep track of Baur's ideas and arguments.

If his productivity may, ironically, have been a factor hampering Baur's reception, his very versatility was arguably another one. Baur is today known and discussed for his scholarly contributions to New Testament studies or his Hegelian leanings, or as the author of a polemical critique of Johann Adam Möhler's *Symbolik*. Such discussions, however, provoke the question of what his underlying theological vision was. Is there any coherence between these various and rather different aspects of his work? The absence of a single work summarizing his ideas makes this kind of question difficult to answer, but without some awareness of the unity behind Baur's work, his overall contribution to theology and the study of religions more broadly is impossible to adjudicate.

The present *Reader* is aimed at beginning to fill this lacuna. Texts have deliberately been chosen from across Baur's work, including his exegetical and historical writings as much as his more philosophical or polemical ones. The overall purpose is to facilitate access to Baur's thought through his own words. While individual readers may, of course, choose to focus on the sections of the book which are close to their own specific interests, the editors hope to encourage a perception of Baur's thought in its broader contours. It is the task of this introduction to offer some guidelines for such an approach. After some biographical information, therefore, we will comment briefly on Baur's major areas of scholarship and their interrelation.

BAUR'S LIFE

Baur was born on June 21, 1792, in Schmiden, a village near Stuttgart in the Duchy of Württemberg (now Baden-Württemberg, Germany), where at the time his father, Jakob Christian Baur, was the Lutheran Pastor.[4] He was educated at home until the age of fourteen, then sent to the lower theological seminaries of Blaubeuren and Maulbronn. In 1809, Baur entered the University of Tübingen to study philosophy and theology. His most influential teacher there was Ernst Gottlieb Bengel (1769–1826), the leading theologian in Tübingen. Bengel was known for his attempt to modernize supranaturalism by injecting it with Kantian ideas. Baur also encountered other ideas in Tübingen, however. In 1812, for example, he attended a lecture course by Carl August Eschenmayer (1768–1852) who was a follower of F. W. J. Schelling.

Baur graduated from Tübingen in 1814 as the first of his class. He initially went through a succession of smaller preaching and teaching posts until, in 1817, he was appointed to a professorship at the seminary in Blaubeuren. Despite the grand title, Baur was effectively a schoolmaster there with teaching responsibilities in classical literature and history. A lecture manuscript on ancient history (*Die Geschichte des Althertums*) is extant from this time.[5] While in Blaubeuren, Baur married, in 1821, Emilie Becher (1802–39). The couple had two sons and three daughters of which one, Emilie Caroline, went on to marry Baur's student, Eduard Zeller (1814–1908).

Baur remained at Blaubeuren until 1826. In that year, Bengel died, and Baur was made his successor as Professor Ordinarius of Evangelical Theology at his *alma mater*. In connection with

---

[4]The fullest account of Baur's biography is Gustav Fraedrich, *Ferdinand Christian Baur der Begründer der Tübinger Schule als Theologe, Schriftsteller und Charakter* (Gotha: Perthes, 1909).
[5]F. C. Baur, *Geschichte des Alterthums*, unpublished lecture manuscript, undated [prior to 1826], Tübinger Universitätsbibliothek, Mh II 166q.

INTRODUCTION

his professorial appointment, he wrote, as was common, a brief Latin dissertation. Baur's essay was entitled *Primae rationalismi et supranaturalismi historiae* and contained an attempt to overcome the theological opposition of rationalism and supranaturalism through a historical study of Gnosticism. The small work was, in many ways, programmatic for Baur's work in subsequent years. Theologically, he identified with the goal of tracing a path beyond the staid opposition between (orthodox) supranaturalism and (enlightened) rationalism.[6]

Characteristically, Baur identified the key to this conundrum in the application of a philosophically informed history to theological questions. Hence, his study of Gnosticism was both an exercise in historical theology and a systematic argument supposedly relevant in his own time. The latter point is underscored by Baur's attempt, in a second part of his dissertation, to draw a parallel between one variant of Gnosticism and the theology of Friedrich Schleiermacher. For Baur, who had read the *Glaubenslehre* soon after it was first published, this was his way of showing his appreciation of what he thought was the most important theological work in a long time,[7] but Schleiermacher could be forgiven for taking it as censure. His two *Letters to Lücke on the Glaubenslehre* contained a sharp repudiation of Baur's interpretation.[8]

This was neither the first nor the last time that Baur miscalculated the personal effect his scholarly work could have. His *Symbolik und Mythologie* was intended as an emphatic endorsement of Friedrich Creuzer's position on the matter for which the latter had come under heavy fire, but Creuzer bluntly and publicly rejected Baur's overtures.[9] In his controversy with Johann Adam Möhler, too, Baur arguably underestimated how much his expressions of estimation would be drowned out by the sharp tone of his scholarly critique.

Baur remained professor in Tübingen until his death, on December 2, 1860. In these almost thirty-five years, his life was of legendary regularity. He did not travel and rarely changed his daily routine. The latter was described in the following words by his son-in-law, Eduard Zeller:

> Through summer and winter, he got up at four o'clock. In the winter, he normally worked for some hours in the unheated room to spare the servants, even though, as would happen in particularly cold nights, the ink in his inkpot might freeze. From then, his regular walks after lunch and in the evening were the only lengthy interruptions of his learned pursuit.[10]

Baur seems to have spent the first four or five years of his professoriate mostly on his teaching duties. Lecture manuscripts that are extant among his papers have been prepared with the utmost diligence. Baur wrote these notes in continuous text not, as was common, in short paragraphs on which the lecturer would extemporaneously comment. In fact, these "notes," fully annotated, looked more like book manuscripts ready for publication.

---

[6] For a similar agenda, cf. Philipp Marheineke, *Die Grundlehren der christlichen Dogmatik als Wissenschaft*, 2nd edn. (Berlin: Duncker & Humblot, 1827), xi–xxvii.
[7] F. C. Baur, "Letter to Friedrich August Baur of July 26, 1823," in *Briefe*, part 1: *Die frühen Briefe (1814–1835)*, ed. Carl E. Hester (Sigmaringen: Thorbecke, 1993), 31–6, esp. 33–4.
[8] F. D. E. Schleiermacher, "Über die Glaubenslehre: Zwei Sendschreiben an Lücke (1829)," in *Kritische Gesamtausgabe*, vol. I/10, ed. Hans-Friedrich Traulsen and Martin Ohst (Berlin: de Gruyter, 1990), 307–94, here: 314, 11–28; 362, 12–18.
[9] Friedrich Creuzer, *Symbolik und Mythologie der alten Völker, besonders der Griechen*, 3rd edn., vol. 1 (Leipzig/Darmstadt: Leske, 1837), xv.
[10] Eduard Zeller, "Ferdinand Christian Baur (1861)," in *Vorträge und Abhandlungen geschichtlichen Inhalts* (Leipzig: Fues, 1865), 354–434, here: 363.

As a result of this punctilious approach, Baur did not publish much until the early 1830s, but from that point onwards, his productivity grew continuously for at least the next fifteen years. Only in the last decade of his life, from around 1847, did he become more concerned to gather his ideas into their final, summary form, most notably through the publication of his multi-volume *Church History* including his celebrated account of the early Church in *Christianity and the Christian Church of the First Three Centuries* (first published in 1853).

The great external caesura in Baur's life occurred in the year 1835. By that time, Baur had gathered around himself a growing crop of promising, young scholars—from the 1840s they would be called the Tübingen School.[11] One of them was David Friedrich Strauss (1808–74). The precocious Strauss published in 1835, aged only twenty-eight, *The Life of Jesus* (*Das Leben Jesu kritisch bearbeitet*), in two volumes.[12] The book, which argued for an interpretation of the gospel story as myth and used Hegelian ideas to compensate for the historical critique, caused one of the fiercest public controversies in nineteenth-century Germany.[13] Strauss' own academic career could not be salvaged, and soon enough Baur himself became implicated in the attacks of Strauss' opponents as well.

Baur's self-defense was complicated by the fact that he did not, in fact, agree with Strauss' mythical interpretation.[14] Whether in the ensuing controversy he always chose the right nuance of expression has been variously assessed.[15] There is, however, no doubt that the consequences for Baur himself were severe. While he could not be deprived of his professorial post, he was now, for much of traditional German Christianity, tainted as the mentor of a radical detractor of the gospel truth. He had no sway outside Tübingen and could not support any of his students in finding appointments. At the end of his life, Baur appears as a lone voice in an ecclesiastical and theological world that had decidedly and aggressively turned away from the ideas he embodied. None of his former students held a chair in a Theological Faculty. The only seeming exception to this rule, Albrecht Ritschl (1822–89), had publicly terminated his attachment to his former academic teacher.[16]

THEOLOGY AND THE HISTORY OF RELIGIONS

In 1819, F. C. Baur published his first known text, a lengthy review of a *Biblical Theology* by a certain G. P. C. Kaiser.[17] Despite the title, Kaiser's book was an attempt to inscribe the biblical stories into the broader frame of a history of religion. Baur disagreed with most details of Kaiser's

---

[11] KGNJ, 398–9; CTNC, 367–8.
[12] David Friedrich Strauss, *Das Leben Jesu kritisch bearbeitet*, 2 vols. (Tübingen: Osiander, 1835/6). English translation: *The Life of Jesus Critically Examined*, trans. Maryann Evans [= George Eliot] 3 vols. (London: Chapman brothers, 1846). NB: The English text translates the fourth German edition.
[13] Baur's own account of this controversy remains one of the best: CTNC, 333–50.
[14] Zachhuber, *Theology as Science*, 92.
[15] Ulrich Köpf, "Ferdinand Christian Baur and David Friedrich Strauss," in *Ferdinand Christian Baur and the History of Early Christianity*, ed. Martin Bauspieß, Christof Landmesser, and David Lincicum (Oxford: OUP, 2017), 3–44; esp. 19–22.
[16] Johannes Zachhuber, "Theology and History in the Controversy between Albrecht Ritschl and Eduard Zeller," in *Theology, History and the Modern University*, ed. Michael DeJonge and Kevin Vander Schel (Tübingen: Mohr Siebeck, 2021), 125–47, here: 128–30.
[17] F. C. Baur, "G. P. C. Kaiser, *Die Biblische Theologie, oder Judaismus und Christianismus nach der grammatisch-historischen Interpretationsmethode, und nach einer freimüthigen Stellung in die kritische-vergleichende Universalgeschichte der Religionen und in die universale Religion* (Erlangen: Palm, 1813–14)," in *Archiv für die Theologie und ihre neueste Literatur*, ed. Ernst Gottlieb Bengel, 2:3 (1818): 656–717.

account, but he emphatically *endorsed* the principle that Christian theology can only proceed from the recognition that Christianity as historical reality must be understood as embedded in a history that began long before its emergence in first-century Palestine. In 1853, toward the end of his career, Baur opened his pivotal *Christianity and the Church of the First Three Centuries* by restating this same principle:

> The historian who enters upon the object of his presentation with the faith of the church is confronted at the very outset with the miracle of all miracles, the primal fact of Christianity—that the only-begotten son of God descended to earth from the eternal throne of the Godhead and became human in the womb of the Virgin. Whoever regards this as simply and absolutely a miracle immediately steps completely outside the nexus of history. [...] Therefore a truly historical examination or reflection [*die geschichtliche Betrachtung*] very naturally is concerned to draw the miracle of the absolute beginning into the historical nexus and to resolve it, insofar as possible, into its natural elements.[18]

This basic continuity is central for understanding the main, internal impulse of Baur's work. The historical perspective, he observed, required contextualization, but this requirement clashes with religious intuitions at the very heart of the Christian faith. How can this faith be unique and uniquely true as a religion if it cannot be insulated from the "historical nexus" of history and its "natural elements"?

Kaiser's response to this question was typical for the theological rationalism predominant in Protestant faculties at the turn of the nineteenth century. According to him, the absolute religion of, as he called it, "universalism" was not historic Christianity. Rather, it was the religion of reason which had only fully come to the fore in enlightened Europe but could, in its essentials, be discovered across the entire history of religions.[19]

Baur disagreed with this solution for at least two reasons. First, insofar as Christian theology had the task of providing an intellectual justification of Christianity's uniqueness, Enlightenment theology with its ideal of rational religion was essentially bad theology. Second, rationalism also lacked rigor in its understanding of history. If religion as such had to be understood in a historical framework, how could the absolute religion of reason somehow exist outside history?[20]

In many ways, Baur's subsequent work can be understood as a series of attempts to find alternative answers to what he found unsatisfactory in theological authors such as Kaiser. His guiding assumptions in these attempts seem to have been the same from the very beginning:

1. The historical study of Christianity has to follow the same principles as historical study in general. In his earliest lecture course of Church History, written probably in 1827, Baur noted blandly that Church History had to work by the same method "that is valid for history as such, since Church History is merely one part of general world history."[21]

---

[18] CCK, 1; CCC, 3.
[19] Baur, "Kaiser Review," 660.
[20] In his later work, Baur occasionally went further to claim that rationalism was fundamentally "ahistorical." Cf. Zachhuber, *Theology as Science*, 55.
[21] F. C. Baur, *Kirchengeschichte*, unpublished lecture manuscript, undated [1827?], Tübinger Universitätsbibliothek, Mh II 166 h, 19.

2. Principle no. 1 is misunderstood, however, if it is taken to imply the absence of philosophical reflection. Historical facts need interpretation, and the use of philosophical methods to this end (we might use the word "hermeneutical" here) is no violation of the historical approach.
3. The most fundamental concepts in religious history are nature and spirit (*Geist*). Religions either identify the divine with nature or juxtapose the two. The former is generally the case in "paganism" (nature religion), the latter in Judaism (spirit religion). As both have their partial truth, they can only be truly overcome in a religion that affirms both God's identity with spirit *and* his intimate connection with nature, that is, the religion of the Incarnation, Christianity.
4. Religious history, thus understood, reveals itself as the gradual progression from nature religion (*Naturreligion*) via spirit religion (*Geistreligion*) to absolute religious truth which is reached in Christianity. Historical study can thus reaffirm traditional Christian beliefs albeit not without transforming their older, dogmatic form.

These ideas underlay Baur's *Symbolik und Mythologie oder die Naturreligion des Alterthums* (1824/5). As indicated by the study's subtitle, Baur's twist to the continuing debate about mythology was its identification as the "nature religion of antiquity" which, he explained in his preface, could only be understood from its contrast with Christianity (see Chapter 1 in this *Reader*).[22]

When his research turned to Gnosticism, from the late 1820s, his fundamental set of ideas remained the same. Gnosticism, he argued, became so important to Christianity because it is the "Christian philosophy of religion"—the subtitle to Baur's *Christian Gnosis* (1835). As such, however, it is thoroughly historical. Gnostics are only philosophers of religion insofar as they are, at the same time, historians of religion. They gain their understanding of religious truth from a comparison of pagan, Jewish, and Christian ideas. Christianity's absoluteness is established insofar as it brings together nature and spirit in the Incarnation.[23]

Christian Gnosis, however, also displays a stubborn problem Baur himself was unable to solve. While he saw the Gnostics as following his own script of a historically inflected philosophy of religion, he also diagnosed their fundamental failure in doing so. Their Christology, after all, was docetic; Christ's Incarnation did not *really* take place. The savior was the spiritual principle smuggled under cover into the material world to bring home those held captive there against their will.[24]

Christianity, then, did not gain an appropriate philosophy of religion at the outset. Or perhaps it did, but not in those heretical groups? Baur clearly did not think that orthodox Christianity in the Patristic period had better answers to offer; instead, it developed into an institution whose members were duty-bound to accept the dogmatic claims of their Church. What would happen, however, once this authoritarian shell cracked? This, Baur believed, had occurred in modernity whose descent into rationalism and supranaturalism—one as indefensible as the other—only served to highlight the intellectual insufficiency of traditional theology.

The main task, then, was still to be accomplished, and Baur—at least in his early years—was evidently optimistic that Christianity stood at the cusp of a major new, doctrinal breakthrough.

---

[22]SuM, vi–vii.
[23]DCG, 21; CG, 9.
[24]DCG, 260–1; CG, 154–5. On the broader problem see Zachhuber, *Theology as Science*, 47–50.

Its signs were everywhere but particularly in the emergence of a slate of new philosophies which, he thought, offered to theology conceptual tools promising substantive progress in tackling the issues it had never before been able to solve.

THEOLOGY AND PHILOSOPHY

It may surprise some that Baur's relationship to the philosophies of his time is only broached at this point. After all, it is one of the most abiding clichés about the theologian that he was the major representative of Hegelianism within historical theology. There is some truth to such an assessment. As we have seen, Baur was insistent that historical analysis was incomplete without a philosophical element. "Without philosophy, history remains to me forever dead and dumb," as he confessed at the outset of *Symbolik und Mythologie*.[25] It is also the case that Baur looked to philosophers for guidance. He was always conscious that his own vocation was not the independent development of philosophical insight but its critical use within historical theology.

"Critical," however, is the operative word here. Baur was never beholden to any particular philosophy, however much such a caricature suited his many detractors. As for Hegel, Baur seems to have been unaware of his philosophy until the posthumous publication, in 1832, of his *Lectures on the Philosophy of Religion*.[26] As we have seen, however, the principal outlines of his thought had been fixed at that time for at least a decade.

The root of Baur's fascination for the contemporaneous, idealist philosophies followed directly from his analysis of theology's predicament. Overcoming the staid opposition of rationalism and supranaturalism required a new interpretation of history. Precisely such an interpretation of history, however, had been at the center of philosophical activity in Germany since the final decade of the eighteenth century. Kant notoriously left behind a tension between the rigid dualism of phenomenon and noumenon as established in the *Critique of Pure Reason* on the one hand, and the absoluteness of his moral metaphysics as contained in his writings on practical philosophy, on the other. Insofar as "can implies ought," however, the latter had to impact the empirical world as well in a way that seemed to violate the dualisms of the first critique.

Kant himself intimated in some later writings that this tension could be mitigated through a philosophy of history, which would show how humankind's development would successively transform nature in accordance with the principles of practical reason.[27] These cautious hints were eagerly adopted by the following generation of thinkers including F. W. J. Schelling and Friedrich Schleiermacher. Both introduced history into philosophy as the medium in which the dualities of natural determination and spiritual freedom would come together. In this connection, religion and especially Christianity played a crucial part.

---

[25] SuM, xi.
[26] G. W. F. Hegel, *Vorlesungen über die Philosophie der Religion, nebst einer Schrift über die Beweise vom Dasein Gottes*, ed. Philipp Marheineke, in *G. W. F. Hegel's Werke, herausgegeben durch einen Verein von Freunden des Verewigten*, vols. 11–12 (Berlin: Duncker & Humblodt, 1832).
[27] Cf. Emil Fackenheim, "Kant's Concept of History," in *The God Within: Kant, Schelling, and Historicity*, ed. J. W. Burbidge (Toronto: University of Toronto Press, 1994), 34–49.

In his *Lectures on Academic Study* (1803), Schelling identified theology as the meeting ground of philosophy and history:

> Since it [sc. theology], as the true centre of the objective realization of philosophy, deals chiefly in speculative ideas, it is also the highest synthesis of philosophical and historical knowing.[28]

The reason for this particular significance of theology does not only lie in the fact that Christianity like all religions is historical in character. Rather, Schelling perceived another, "absolute relationship" between Christianity and history:

> The absolute relation of theology is that in Christianity the world is looked upon as history, as the realm of morals, and that this general intuition constitutes its fundamental character.[29]

Christianity, Schelling claimed, is not merely historical in an incidental sense, it is emphatically historical because it raises history to the level of the Absolute. While Greek religion was nature religion, Christianity is religion of the spirit, of morality, and thus of history. It is the religion in which "the divine principle has ceased to reveal itself in nature, and is recognised only in history."[30]

We know from an early letter that Baur was deeply impressed by Schelling's philosophy at this point in his career.[31] His writing in *Symbolik und Mythologie* is deeply infused with terms and concepts of a Schellingian ring. At the same time, it is not difficult to see that he could not, in the long run, be content with Schelling's approach which consciously stopped short of endorsing a speculative philosophy, let alone a theology of history in the sense Baur intuited it, namely, as integrating the plurality of historical events into a single, progressive narrative.[32] History, to Schelling, always remained empirical and thus incapable of being synthesized in support of theological principles.

The same could be said for Schleiermacher, whose *Christian Faith* Baur read soon after its first publication. A letter to his brother from 1823 speaks of the profound impression this text made on him. Yet even at that early point, Baur averred that Schleiermacher did not go far enough in that he merely inscribed Christianity into the history of religions without offering proof that it *was* the absolute religion. Crucially, in his Christology, Schleiermacher retained the dualism of (intra-mental) self-consciousness and the external reality of history, thus foregoing the opportunities offered by a speculative interpretation of the Incarnation.[33]

Hegel's thought is first referenced in Baur's literary engagement with Johann Adam Möhler,[34] but it is *Christian Gnosis* which shows the full effect it had on Baur's thought. There is no doubt

---

[28]F. W. J. Schelling, "Vorlesungen über die Methode des akademischen Studiums (1803)," in *Sämmtliche Werke*, vol. I/5, ed. K. F. A. Schelling (Stuttgart: Cotta, 1859), 207–311, here: 286; English translation: *Lectures on University Study*, trans. Ella S. Morgan, in *The Journal of Speculative Philosophy* 12 (1878), 205–13, here: 205.
[29]Schelling, *Lectures*, 287; English Text: 206.
[30]Schelling, *Vorlesungen*, 289; English Text: 208.
[31]F. C. Baur, "Letter to Ludwig Bauer of November 2, 1822," in *Frühe Briefe*, 26–7.
[32]Cf. Christian Danz, "Geschichte als fortschreitende Offenbarung Gottes: Überlegungen zu Schellings Geschichtsphilosophie," in *System als Wirklichkeit: 200 Jahre Schellings "System des Transzendentalen Idealismus,"* ed. Christian Danz, C. Dierksmeier and C. Seysen (Würzburg: Königshausen & Neumann, 2001), 69–82.
[33]Baur, "Letter to Friedrich August Baur."
[34]Cf. GKP, 431–2. See Chapter 13 in this volume.

that Baur here discovered the conceptual tools for which he had long been searching.[35] Hegel's "objective" interpretation of history as the process of spirit unfolding itself in and through historical development was, so to speak, the key to the lock Baur had been trying to open. There is no doubt, furthermore, that this Hegelian inspiration only enabled Baur's subsequent, decisive advances in the history of dogma.

Yet Baur's appropriation of Hegel's philosophy was never uncritical. In *Christian Gnosis*, he is clear that the principal problem diagnosed in ancient Gnosticism, the separation of the historical and the spiritual saviour, remained unsolved in Hegel's philosophy. Consequently, he never lost the suspicion that Hegel's philosophy led to a level of speculation for which history would, once again, become insignificant. He observes that, according to Hegel,

> Christ is God-man only by the mediation of faith. [The question of] what lies behind faith, however, as the historically given, objective reality which was the basis from which the merely external, historical view could turn into faith, remains shrouded in a mystery which we ought not [attempt to] penetrate.[36]

Baur's work has often been divided into three phases: an early one prior to his acquaintance with Hegel; a second, Hegelian one; and a third one, beginning in the mid-forties, during which Hegel's influence once again recedes.[37] Such a scheme, however, is misleading. Baur's fundamental concerns remained the same throughout much of his career. Hegel's philosophy was *adopted* into the service of an agenda that had been set a decade earlier. While it propelled forwards Baur's work in several areas, it never came to total domination. For that reason, too, the waning of Hegel's influence—in line with his overall eclipse in German intellectual life from the mid-1840s—is less of a sharp caesura than often claimed.

HISTORY OF DOGMA

After publishing *Christian Gnosis*, Baur was confronted with the obvious question of what, exactly, the Christian philosophy of religion conducted in a historical framework wider than Christianity itself had to do with theology. Baur sought to clarify the problem in a lengthy essay, "On the Concept of the Philosophy of Religion" (Chapter 3 in this volume). According to his argument, the philosophy of religion must always proceed through historical comparison, but theology can turn more exclusively to the Christian dogma. The latter, he held, was the Christian religion looked at from the insight; its study, we might say, considered the architecture of Christianity.[38]

Yet dogma, too, has its history; when it comes to the study of this history, the scholar is once again in a field much closer to the history of religion. In fact, Baur seems to suggest that the history of dogma really is a subdiscipline of the history of religion and treated separately mostly because of its more specific subject matter.

---

[35]On Hegel's influence on Baur, cf. Martin Wendte, "Ferdinand Christian Baur: A Historically Informed Idealist of a Distinctive Kind," in *Ferdinand Christian Baur and the History of Early Christianity*, ed. Martin Bauspieß, Christof Landmesser and David Lincicum (Oxford: OUP, 2017), 67–80.
[36]DCG, 712; CG, 442. See below, Chapter 2.
[37]Horton Harris, *Tübingen School*, 158; Fraedrich, *Baur*, xiv.
[38]BdR, 372.

History of dogma at the time was still a young discipline. While Baur was conscious of seventeenth-century pioneers, notably the Jesuit Denys Pétau,[39] he felt the development of this discipline was part and parcel of theology's novel mission in his own time. It is arguable that no other discipline, with the exception of New Testament studies, bears the lasting imprint of Baur's work as much as the history of dogma.

Baur's main writings in the field cover the decade from 1838, when *The Doctrine of Reconciliation* appeared, to 1847, which saw the first edition of *History of Christian Dogma*, intended as the authoritative summary treatment of the discipline. His relevant publications from that period cover over 4,000 pages—3,000 alone in the three volumes of his *Doctrine of the Triune God*—indicating the sheer amount of primary material Baur incorporated into his studies. More important than these impressive figures, however, is Baur's ability to weave the disparate historical facts into a more or less coherent narrative.

This narrative flowed directly from *Christian Gnosis*. Religion had there been defined as culminating in the idea of the reconciliation of nature and spirit. Christianity was the absolute religion because it offered this reconciliation in the idea—and the historical reality—of the God-man. Yet the precise understanding of this truth was not immediately given. The history of dogma, then, is the process by which Christianity came to consciousness of its deepest principle. From this it followed that the first object of Baur's study was the doctrine of atonement or reconciliation itself. Immediately connected with it, however, were the doctrines of the Trinity and the Incarnation which Baur, interestingly, saw as twin doctrines and, therefore, treated in a single work.

There is no doubting the significance of Hegel's philosophy for this entire area of Baur's work. From Hegel he learned to think of dogma in its "objective" reality, that is, to identify the vanishing point from which the perspective of the various theologians and their doctrinal topics becomes one and the same. The history of dogma is thus really what the name suggests, the historical unfolding of Christian doctrine, rather than the enumeration of opinions held by authors across the centuries. Even in *History of Christian Dogma*, where the Hegelian orientation overall recedes more into the background, Baur is adamant about this point:

> It is dogma itself that in its various specifications sets out its content and positions the content over against itself, splitting itself up internally, so that the concept, which is its substantial being itself, may be released into the distinction of its moments and then drawn back into its unity. A choice must be made: if the changes portrayed by the history of dogma are not simply a contingent and arbitrary fluctuation, then this history can only be viewed as an intellectual or spiritual process in which the essential nature of spirit itself is revealed, for dogma itself is essentially intellectual or spiritual in nature. Thus the method of the history of dogma can only be the objective nature of the subject matter itself.[40]

Few if any later students of the discipline were willing to adopt this perspective *tout court*. Baur's noted colleague, Isaak August Dorner, and his sometime student, Albrecht Ritschl, fundamentally diverged from Baur's insistence that dogma only moves toward its perfection during the course of Christian history by insisting that Christian perfection existed in the original period of "primitive

---

[39]Baur, *Vorlesungen über die christliche Dogmengeschichte*, vol. 1., ed. Ferdinand Friedrich Baur (Leipzig: Fues, 1865), 112. Cf. LD, 30–4; HCD, 70–2.

[40]LD, 7–8; HCD, 53. See Chapter 4 in this volume.

Christianity." Adolf Harnack, the most influential Ritschlian historian, saw the emergence of dogma from the outset as a problematic, albeit inevitable development and, consequently, envisaged an undogmatic future for the Church. Despite these sharp disagreements, however, none of Baur's successors could fully escape from the long shadow cast by his work on the history of dogma. Both his overall vision and the impressive extent of his treatment of the sources ensured Baur's abiding influence over the subsequent development of the discipline.

NEW TESTAMENT STUDIES

As we have seen, Baur was adamant that theology could not insulate itself from history. He was under no illusion that the most neuralgic point in this regard, especially within Protestantism, was the history recorded in the Bible and, especially, the New Testament. He early on decided that theology could make biblical studies an exception to its general historicization only at the peril of losing its credibility. In his exchange with Möhler, he was explicit that abandoning the rigid Scripture principle was as necessary on the Protestant side as the Catholic departure from extraneous authoritarianism.[41]

Yet while he published important works in the field from the early 1830s, it took him longer to gain his own, definitive perspective. With hindsight, he wrote that he was unable to take a more determined stance in the controversy about Strauss' *Life of Jesus* because at that point he had not yet achieved his own, considered view of the matter.[42] Whether or not this was partly said to deflect the criticism that he failed to stand up for his former student, there is no doubt that Baur's major, monographic publications in New Testament Studies fall in the 1840s.

Beginning already in the early 1830s, Baur demonstrated the hallmarks of the approach that was to mark his contribution to New Testament scholarship. In his 1831 essay on the "Christ party" at Corinth, he undertook a patient, critical sifting of the received sources as he puzzled at length over the identification of the nebulous group seemingly referred to in 1 Cor 1:12.[43] Dissatisfied with previous approaches, but taking up elements of their solutions, Baur found behind Paul's description of parties at Corinth the reflection of a rift in earliest Christianity: between Pauline, Gentile-friendly, law-free Christianity on the one hand, and Petrine, Jewish-Christian, law-observant Christianity on the other. The conviction that tensions not only marked early Christianity but also drove its development became a key insight in Baur's interpretative work.

Alongside his discovery of the productive nature of disagreement, Baur also became convinced that criticism could not simply be a "negative" exercise, discrediting traditional views about the authenticity, integrity, or historical accuracy of a canonical text. Rather, criticism worthy of the name needed to offer a positive conception of a text's place in the totality of early Christianity.[44] Schleiermacher had called into question the authenticity of 1 Timothy in 1807,[45] but Baur's own

---

[41] KGP, 424–9; partly in Chapter 13 in this volume.
[42] KGNJ, 397; see Chapter 12 in this volume.
[43] CPKG.
[44] See Chapters 7 and 14 in this volume.
[45] F. D. E. Schleiermacher, *Über den sogenannten ersten Brief des Paulos an den Timotheos. Ein kritisches Sendschreibung an J.C. Gass* (Berlin: Realschulbuchhandlung, 1807) [= F. D. E. Schleiermacher, *Schriften aus der Hallenser Zeit (1804–1807)*, ed. Hermann Patsch and Kritische Gesamtausgabe, vol. I/5 (Berlin: de Gruyter, 1995), 153–242].

investigations into Christian Gnosticism convinced him that, not only was 1 Timothy not written by the apostle Paul (the negative judgment), but also that it belonged, together with the other Pastoral Epistles, to the period of the church's fight against "what is falsely called knowledge" in the second century (the positive judgment).[46]

This attempt to determine the theological position, or what Baur referred to as the "tendency" (*Tendenz*), of the writings, marked Baur's most significant contributions to New Testament study. A series of long articles on Pauline matters culminated in his magisterial book on *Paul the Apostle* in 1845, in which he reduced the number of certifiably genuine letters to four, the so-called *Hauptbriefe* of Galatians, 1 and 2 Corinthians, and Romans, and discounted the evidentiary value of Acts for reconstructing the apostle's life and thought.[47] All of Paul's genuine letters, on Baur's view, are marked by his struggle for a universalizing mission to the Gentiles, over against the claims of Jewish particularism advanced by James and also, to a slightly lesser degree, Peter and those who followed them. Baur then read the remaining letters and Acts as writings that reflect various points along the way to a resolution of the tensions between Gentile and Jewish-Christian forms of faith.

If Baur was unprepared to offer an evaluation of Strauss's *Life of Jesus* when it first appeared in 1835/6, over the subsequent decade he undertook the sort of detailed study of the four gospels and their individual tendencies that would enable him to render his own independent verdict on their historical quality. Baur gathered up his studies into his 1847 *Critical Investigations of the Canonical Gospels*, in which he concluded decisively in favor of the historical reliability of the synoptic gospels, particularly Matthew, over against the Gospel of John. Baur held to the chronological priority of Matthew even over against Luke and Mark (the so-called Griesbach theory of synoptic relations) because this enabled him to locate Matthew, with its Jewish-Christian character, at the earliest stage of Christian literary development.[48]

These studies of the individual tendencies of the canonical writings enabled Baur to construct a total view of early Christian history. Rather than the placid agreement among the apostles that the book of Acts portrays, this history is marked by rifts and division, propelled forward by thesis and antithesis, before achieving a resolution. The early Jewish-Christian mission, with its particularistic insistence on the Jewish nation and her law, confronted the Pauline law-free mission to the Gentiles. Concessions and further developments on each side eventually produced a resolution in the emergence of "early Catholicism." The Gospel of John, with its stark emphasis on the deity of Jesus and its assumption that the Christian movement is almost entirely Gentile, hardly knows of the lively conflict that preceded it.[49]

Not all of Baur's concrete judgments have aged well, particularly those tied to problematic conceptions of Judaism. But his insistence on the critical freedom of the interpreter, his attempt to grasp the totality of early Christian development, and his attention to conflicts and divisions as engines of history have all left an indelible mark on the study of the New Testament.

---

[46]PAP.
[47]PAJC, Chapter 9 in this volume.
[48]See Chapter 8 in this volume.
[49]See Chapter 8 in this volume.

CHURCH HISTORY

Baur lectured on Church History from the time of his appointment at Tübingen. Throughout his career, he continued to publish in the field, but it was the final decade of his life during which Church History took center stage in his work. At this point, he apparently decided to collect his various studies into a full presentation of Christian history from its inception to his own time. Yet only two of the anticipated volumes appeared during Baur's lifetime; a third was prepared for publication when he died.[50] Two more were published posthumously from his lecture notes.[51] Of these five, two are most remarkable albeit for different reasons. The first volume, *Christianity and the Christian Church in the First Three Centuries*, has often been considered one of Baur's single most important books. It is the unique summary of a lifetime of research into the origins of Christianity beginning from the New Testament period.

Then there is the (posthumous) *Church and Theology in the Nineteenth Century*. Based on Baur's regular lectures on the topic, this book is mainly of interest as a historical source. Baur closely and astutely observed major developments in his own time. He writes with precision, wit, and often passion, sometimes with barely concealed frustration.

In 1852, Baur published *Epochs of Church Historiography*, meant as an introduction to his actual church history. That Baur writes such an introduction as a history of the historiographical approaches of theologians through the ages makes the book nearly unique simply in terms of its genre. In the concluding chapter of the book, Baur addressed the task of the church historian in his own time. He did not think of this task primarily in terms of detailed or specialist research. In fact, he opined that there was a good amount of such detailed research available already.[52]

Instead, it is the question of history's overall coherence which seemed to Baur of predominant significance. There continues to be, he wrote, "a mismatch between idea and phenomena." The idea "soars indefinitely and at a great distance" above the phenomena with which it should be connected.

> It is not yet strong and vital enough to penetrate and vivify the historical material as the soul penetrates the body, or to become, through such an organic unity, the moving principle of the entire series of phenomena in which the history of the Christian church takes its course.[53]

Once again, then, Baur sees his own vocation in a reflection on the intelligibility of the historical process. How can individual people and events be more than fragments detached from their greater context? How can the many stories make up the one history?

Baur's own comments may provide a surprisingly fair and judicious assessment of his role as a historian. It would be difficult to credit him with too many specific insights, except in his specialist field of earliest Christian history. His contemporary and rival, August Neander, undoubtedly had much more to offer in this regard. Baur never wrote historical monographs the way Neander did, covering specific, historical individuals or epochs. Central to him was the internal nexus of history including the problem of periodization and its justification which he repeatedly discussed. That

---

[50]CCK (1853, 2nd edn. 1860); CKA (1859). CKM was still prepared by Baur and appeared in 1861.
[51]CKM and KGNJ.
[52]EKG, 247. Chapter 10 in this volume.
[53]EKG, 247–8. Chapter 10 in this volume.

he saw these questions as urgent desiderata in the 1850s, when historical research had decidedly turned in the much more specialist and positivist direction associated with the term historicism, may appear anachronistic. Half a century later, however, Wilhelm Dilthey and others would return to the very question of historical hermeneutics that had been central to Baur.

CONCLUSION

As this brief introduction has tried to suggest, Baur is a fascinating, complex thinker whose vast productivity threatens to obscure the fundamental coherence of his thought. His neglect has probably owed much to the diffusion of his writings, to shifts in philosophical and theological fashions, and, in the Anglophone world, to the persistent stereotypes about Baur and his work that have functioned as convenient excuses not to engage him. Baur, however, is well worth engaging—not because he was correct in everything he wrote or because time has vindicated his every position, but because we find in his restless mind a striving to grasp the totality of history as a realm of theology, as the self-revelation of the Spirit.

This *Reader* excerpts Baur's work under five main headings: philosophy of religion; history of dogma; New Testament criticism; church history; and Baur in the controversies of his time. As should be clear by this point, these are only heuristic divisions. To understand Baur's New Testament work, one needs also to grasp his philosophical convictions. Or again, it would be foolhardy to approach his church historical work without a sense of his punchy engagement with his own contemporaries. We hope the actual readers of this volume will enjoy Baur's invitation to overrun our customary sub-disciplinary specializations and think synthetically and boldly about larger theological projects.

English-speaking readers captivated by Baur find themselves in a fortunate position. The past few years have witnessed a flurry of excellent translations of Baur's sometimes-difficult German. Peter Hodgson and Robert Brown together have produced, as of this writing, expertly edited translations of several of Baur's most important books, including his *Lectures on the History of Christian Dogma, Lectures on New Testament Theology, Church and Theology in the Nineteenth Century, Christian Gnosis, Christianity and the Christian Church of the First Three Centuries*, and *Paul the Apostle*.[54] This *Reader* can do no more than offer a taste of Baur's larger corpus, but it is our hope that it demonstrates why a deeper engagement with Baur is worthwhile.

---

[54] HCD; NTT; CTNC; CG; CCC; PAJC(E).

PART ONE

Philosophy of Religion

CHAPTER ONE

Mythology, History, and the Philosophy of Religion

EXTRACT FROM: SUM, VOL. 1, III–XIV
TRANSLATION: BEATA AND MATTHEW VALE

Baur published *Symbolik und Mythologie oder die Naturreligion des Alterthums* in 1824–5. At the time, he was teaching at the Protestant Seminary in Blaubeuren.[1] The book came out in two parts, the latter divided into two volumes. Baur's aim in producing such an ambitious work must have been, at least in part, to present himself as a suitable candidate for a university post. His professorial appointment to the Tübingen Faculty in 1826 shows that this hope was not in vain. Baur's main teaching duties at Blaubeuren were in the classics rather than theology, and his professional need to engage with ancient literature and history is evident from the textual basis of his presentation in *Symbolik und Mythologie*. Yet the thrust of his argument prefigures some of his most important later ideas.

Throughout the work, Baur presents three main, interlocking arguments. First, he analyzes the mythical texts extant from classical civilization in order to demonstrate their internal, historical relationship. Second, he interprets mythology in this reconstructed form as the characteristic form in which humanity at an early stage of its development had expressed its deepest philosophical and religious insights. Third, he inscribes this early, mythological worldview into a historical succession of religious ideas which ultimately leads to Christianity as its fulfillment.

In none of these attempts was Baur without precedent. Historical studies into the origin and interconnectedness of mythical texts were widespread at the time, and Baur himself acknowledges various sources of inspirations. The project of a philosophical interpretation of myths, too, had been popular at least since J. G. Herder's impactful work. At the beginning of the nineteenth century, it was advanced mainly by Friedrich Creuzer and F. W. J. Schelling, two thinkers Baur held in high regard. The notion, finally, that an interpretation of Christianity within the history of religions could vindicate its truth had been adumbrated by Schelling and F. D. E. Schleiermacher. Baur particularly claims the latter in support of his own construction.

In writing his book, Baur boldly entered into controversial territory. Creuzer's work had provoked furious reactions from classicists who felt it was too theological. Baur clearly liked it for that reason, but his embrace proved too much for Creuzer, who coolly disowned Baur's self-consciously Christian approach protesting that he was a mere historian. Not for the last time in his life, Baur found himself rather isolated. There is little evidence that his book exerted a major influence on the continuing debate on mythology in Germany, and Baur's own work soon moved into different directions.

---

[1] See the editors' Introduction: 1. Baur's life.

The following extract offers the full text of Baur's Preface which contains his famous confession that without philosophy, history to him remained "forever dead and dumb."

SYMBOLISM AND MYTHOLOGY OR NATURE RELIGION OF ANTIQUITY

[iii] Preface

For a number of years [now], mythology[2] has attracted the attention of the learned public in a way which in itself can be seen as proof for a certain universality by which this field distinguishes itself.[3] In fact, it has gained pre-eminence among related disciplines in the study of antiquity, even though, in its more recent form, it is the youngest of them all.[4] Going forward, this priority will, it seems, increasingly make the science[5] of classical antiquity as a whole dependent on mythology and even endow the latter with a more general recognition beyond its proper [academic] sphere.

Mythology owes this [success] to a fortunate union of efforts which—precisely through their differences—were most suited to illumine its true essence. For if we might be allowed to transfer onto itself one of mythology's own images, what can better describe this essence than that oft-recurring creature called Maia, Thetis, or Proteus—a character which, in general, even though it is pleased to appear in a multitude of beautiful and charming shapes, [iv] does not allow itself to be grasped in a single one of these, but only in all of them taken together? For this reason, it might be the case that precisely in this domain of knowledge—where the hope of seizing the individual is just as great as the danger of seeing the whole escape—everyone who is either attracted by the allure of the characters presenting themselves, or who feels strong enough to subdue those deceptive and reluctant [appearances], is all the more furnished with the freedom to try their fortune and prove their strength.

The way in which the present work, now passing into the public's hands, is linked in continuity with the *oeuvres* of its predecessors I have indicated in its title, which names the science treated here not only as antiquity's symbolism and mythology, but also as its nature religion.[6] In what sense this science is to be considered from this perspective in general terms is the object of the investigations contained in this first part [of the study].[7]

I was drawn to mythology by an early inclination and became more familiar with it through Creuzer's famous and classic work,[8] which gave mythology a meaning [I had] hardly suspected

---

[2] "Mythology" here and in what follows translates Baur's "*Mythologie*" by which he means the academic study of myths.
[3] For the early-nineteenth-century interest in and study of mythology, cf. George S. Williamson, *The Longing for Myth in Germany: Religion and Aesthetic Culture from Romanticism to Nietzsche* (Chicago: Chicago University Press, 2004), chs. 1–4.
[4] Baur is here taking sides in the bitter controversy following the publication of Creuzer's *Symbolik und Mythologie der alten Völker, besonders der Griechen*, 4 vols. (Leipzig and Darmstadt: Leske, 1810–12). Creuzer's critics, including classical philologists Gottfried Hermann (1772–1848) and Johann Heinrich Voss (1751–1826), accused him of betraying the ideals of the Enlightenment reassimilating classics "into an intellectual framework dictated by Christian theology" (Williamson, *Longing for Myth*, 138). Baur apparently applauded Creuzer for precisely that reason.
[5] *Wissenschaft*. See Note on Text and Translations.
[6] *Naturreligion*. On Baur's view of paganism as nature religion, see the Introduction to this volume.
[7] The present text is the preface to volume 1. Baur published a second volume in two parts a year later (1825).
[8] Friedrich Creuzer (1771–1858), *Symbolik und Mythologie*. See note above.

before, and first claimed for it the dignity of a science. Since then, mythology has awakened in me an ever-mounting interest, above all because, in it and through it, I believed I was coming closer to the idea of the oneness of knowledge which, prefigured as it is in the organism of the human spirit, must be the true goal [v] of every judicious scientific endeavor. The more I came to know, through my thorough study of the sources of mythology, the animated and wonderful life which it comprises, the depth of its ideas, as well as the richness of its forms, the more the conviction was confirmed in me that mythology could not be a merely random aggregate of atoms which have come together by coincidence. Rather, in the entire range of its appearances, which is a whole that can only [ever] be dismembered by gratuitous arbitrariness and restriction of one's standpoint, mythology represented a philosophy which was developing in an organic context. This philosophy was at a higher level than any individual philosophical system, just as the species stands at a higher level than the individual.

If world history in general in its widest and most dignified sense is a revelation of the Godhead[9] and the most animated expression of divine ideas and purposes, then world history, as the unity of spiritual life, can only be considered as the development of a consciousness, since wherever there is spiritual life, there also is consciousness. And this development, although it can only be conceived in a way analogous to the development of individual consciousness, must not be measured by the limited standard of individual consciousness. Just as the consciousness of individuals rests in the consciousness of the nations to which they belong—in a living union which is certainly not that of the abstract concept—so the consciousness of the nations is in turn borne by the higher, collective consciousness of [vi] humanity, whose living unity is the image and the mirror of the divine spirit itself.

The inner coherence binding all world-historical phenomena of human life and human spirit into a unity can only be intuited in analogy to the identity that lies at the basis of all the varying phenomena within the individual consciousness. The higher consciousness objectivized in world history is a philosophy, which, if any, justly merits the name "the divine philosophy." It can therefore only be reconstructed from the perspective of the individual by turning back to the inner organism and to the laws of spirit itself since it is spirit that reveals itself in its various capacities and activities as the living original source, from which alone this philosophy can have sprung. And where should such an attempt, if it is ever to be made, bear more fruit than in the place where the spiritual life in its most immediate and greatest expression presents itself of its own accord: in the history of religious faith?

I have sought to understand the mythology of the nations of antiquity as a world-historical phenomenon belonging to the domain of religion and religious history, one which can only be grasped as a unity. In that attempt, mythology presented itself, as of its own accord, as the antithesis to Christianity. And just as Christianity, precisely because it is not a human system but divine revelation, [vii] can only truly be appreciated from the highest standpoint of world history, so it seemed that it was only possible to know mythology, or nature religion, in its inner essence by placing it in an appropriate relation to Christianity.

---

[9]In passages such as this, Baur's debt to F. W. J. Schelling is evident. Cf. his *System of Transcendental Idealism*, trans. Peter Heath (Charlottesville, VA: University of Virginia Press, 1978), where he calls history the "progressive, gradually self-disclosing revelation of the Absolute" (p. 211).

To a significant degree, I have to thank for the development of this idea Schleiermacher's *Christian Faith*, a work which more than any other in the history of theology has been epoch-making.[10] The more determinedly its brilliant and sharp-witted author presents the specific character of Christianity in this work, the greater are the gains for the reconstruction of any other form of religion, particularly for the one most immediately opposed to Christianity. But [Schleiermacher's] reconstruction of the Christian faith itself was, of course, only made possible by considering Christianity from the perspective of the philosophy of religion. The general indications in this connection found in [*The Christian Faith*] are primarily what I have in mind in the second chapter of the first section,[11] and I have tried to follow these indications further and to draw them out in service of my purposes.

The reader who is familiar with Creuzer's work will be able to see in the present text to what degree my treatment of mythology, based on the above-mentioned philosophical stance, [viii] partly concurs with and partly departs from this book.[12] But as much as the form and layout of the whole might seem to differ from Creuzer's, I believe I have, precisely through those differences, come that much closer to the true spirit of his work as it expresses itself with abundant clarity both in its general tendencies and in individual passages. If mythology is at all what it is supposed to be according to the idea established by Creuzer, then at some point an attempt has to be made to carry out a system in the way the present work has undertaken to do. As far as I am from thinking that my attempt at discharging this task has been completely successful, I am still convinced that in it I have taken a path through which mythology will come closer to its scientific goals. Just how much, by the way, Creuzer's symbolism and mythology has left to successive philosophical treatment is already evident especially in the fact that one cannot even find a firmly determined and dialectically developed definition of the two main concepts of symbol and mythos in his entire great *oeuvre*. This deficiency had a profound effect on the scientific *modus operandi* of the work, however lively and gripping the truly philosophical spirit which so completely pervades it.

In approximately the same way I distance myself from Creuzer in a philosophical respect, [ix] I also distance myself from him in the historical part of mythology. It seems to me that there is no place that could be more disadvantageous than Egypt's narrow and isolated Nile valley for

---

[10] F. D. E. Schleiermacher, *Der christliche Glaube. 1821/22*, 2 vols., ed. Hermann Peiter (Berlin: de Gruyter, 1984). Baur read the work soon after its publication. In a letter of July 26, 1823, he reports to his brother on the deep impression the work has made on him: C. Hester, *Ferdinand Christian Baur: Briefe*. Part 1: *Die frühen Briefe (1814–35)* (Sigmaringen: Thorbecke, 1993), 31–6 (with notes on pp. 152–5). In Schleiermacher, Baur found a theory of religion that was profoundly historical in character. This theory, he believed, had the potential to overcome the dogmatism of supranaturalism and the ahistorical rationalism of Enlightenment theology. Yet even at this early point, Baur did not think that Schleiermacher's theory accomplished this result because it retained the dualism of (intra-mental) self-consciousness and the external reality of history.

[11] Baur, *Symbolik und Mythologie*, vol. 1, 103–216. But cf. Hester's observation that "the first chapter of *Symbolik und Mythologie* was already complete before Baur had read Schleiermacher's *Glaubenslehre*" (*Briefe*, 154).

[12] While Baur saw his work as complementary to Creuzer's work, the latter disagreed. When Baur sent him his work, he responded coolly (Hester, *Briefe*, 55–6), but in the third edition of *Symbolik und Mythologie*, vol. 1 (Leipzig/Darmstadt: Leske, 1837), Creuzer bluntly disowned Baur's claim: "Das gleichmäßig betitelte Werk von F. Chr. Baur erschien bald nach der zweiten Ausgabe des meinigen. Es würde mir wenig anstehen, die Lobsprüche zu wiederholen, die er ihm besonders in der Vorrede ertheilt, und ich muss selbst den ablehnen, dass es in 'ächtphilosophischem Geiste' geschrieben sey (Vorrede S. VIII), hingegen aber auch seine Ausstellungen auf sich beruhen lassen; wobei er mir aber auch verzeihen wird, wenn ich sein aus den Schriften von Karl Ritter und den meinigen über ein Schleiermachersches Fachwerk aufgebautes System zu künstlich finde" (p. xv).

the kind of universal system which is called for here.¹³ Even now, after I have all but finished my investigations in the specialized part [of this work], the opinion at which I arrived in this first part has completely confirmed itself to me, namely, that not even Greece can be placed in a subordinate position to Egypt. Instead (and rather than weaken the formulation this argument receives in the first part [of my book], I would rather like to strengthen it), Egypt and Greece should only be regarded as diverging radii which issued from one center, from the collective unity located in higher Asia.¹⁴ By that I do not want to say that Creuzer does not also acknowledge this to be the case, but the entire way in which he makes the Egyptian system the basis of the structure seems to me to bestow on this system a significance and a universalism it does not merit.

I will gladly admit how much the historical part of my text is indebted to the enlightening investigations of Hammer¹⁵ and Ritter,¹⁶ and particularly to the latter's *Vorhalle*,¹⁷ which is truly of an incomparably higher value than any temple hall excavated from the sands of Egypt or of Nubia. May these heroes of the German spirit and of German scholarship recognize their ideas and intimations (even in the extensions [x] I have undertaken to give them here) as [still] worthy of the spirits from which they originated as fruitful seeds!

Just how little agreement, by the way, has been achieved even today in the historical treatment of mythology is attested to by the most recent writings on mythology, which have only just become available to me.¹⁸ How little they still take account of and appreciate investigations such as Ritter's! In contrast, there are always new voices that can be heard on how the religions of individual nations can only be treated separately and have to be unveiled each on its own terms with the greatest possible certainty—a claim which can be advanced only where that intimate interrelation, in which philosophy and history touch and interpenetrate each other precisely in mythology, has been misunderstood. One would indeed be better off, then, not to speak of religion at all in [the context of] mythology; and what sort of statements are liable to result from this approach? Of course, mostly the kind which have little, or nothing at all, to do with religion. Yet the relationship [sc. between religion and mythology] is not only an extrinsic (as such, by the way, it is plain as day), but much rather an intrinsic one. The idea always determines individual phenomena. Without the idea of religion, the essence of [p. xi] individual forms of religion cannot be understood, and how, in turn, can the principle and character of a specific form of religion be correctly understood unless all phenomena, which belong together as members of the same class, are considered in their mutual connection?

In saying this, we do not in the least want to deny the value of individual mythological research of this kind; these kinds of investigations indeed offer much that is beautiful and relevant. But

---

¹³The origins of mythology were controversial among scholars of the time. Cf. on these differences and Creuzer's approach: Williamson, *Longing for Myth*, 127–45.
¹⁴Baur's detailed argument for this position is found in *Symbolik und Mythologie*, vol. 1, 217–94.
¹⁵Joseph Freiherr von Hammer-Purgstall (1774–1856), Austrian orientalist, poet, and historian. Cf. Werner Welzig, "Hammer-Purgstall, Joseph Freiherr von," *Neue Deutsche Biographie* 7 (1966): 593–4. Online: https://www.deutsche-biographie.de/pnd118545426.html#ndbcontent. Accessed on August 19, 2021.
¹⁶Carl-Georg Ritter (1779–1859), one of the founders of modern, scientific geography. Cf. Lindgren, Uta, "Ritter, Carl," *Neue Deutsche Biographie* 21 (2003): 65–6. Online: https://www.deutsche-biographie.de/pnd11860130X.html#ndbcontent. Accessed on August 19, 2021.
¹⁷Carl Ritter, *Vorhalle der europäischen Völkergeschichten vor Herodotus um den Kaukasus und um die Gestade des Pontus: Eine Abhandlung zur Altertumskunde* (Berlin: Reimer, 1820).
¹⁸Baur may here be referring to Karl Otfried Müller's *Geschichte hellenischer Stämme und Städte*, 3 vols. (Breslau: Max, 1820–4). Cf. Williamson, *Longing for Myth*, 145–8.

when it comes to the principle underlying the historical treatment of mythology, scholarship seems already to have reached a much higher level; it seems unlikely that it could bear this kind of fretful [self-]limitation for much longer. I can only see two paths here: either the path of separation and individuation, which, if pursued consistently, by necessity must eventually lead to atomism, fatalism, and atheism, or the path on which, to the degree that the spiritual life of the nations in its majestic interconnection is recognized as one great whole, a purer and higher consciousness of the divine arises in this field [that is, mythology]. There are no real middle ways between the two, and halfway procedures, if they are permissible anywhere, are surely the least permissible in that science which sets for itself the task of the absolute. I do not fear the well-known accusation of mixing philosophy with history: without philosophy, history remains forever dead and dumb to me. But whether in the reconstruction of an individual mythos or of an entire religious system a subjective, arbitrarily limited philosophical perspective has been mixed in—that, of course, can only be demonstrated [p. xii] in the midst of the reconstruction and with historical reasons.

What I would add vis-á-vis etymology is basically only an application of what has just been said.[19] It is also my conviction that etymology ought rightly to be considered a very important aid for mythology. For how else would language be the living expression of spirit? And where else does the recognition of a collective consciousness, exalted above all individuality—a consciousness just of the kind we must presuppose in mythology in general—more strongly impose itself than in the wondrous edifice of speech forms, which are no invention of the individual, but the *opus* of the constructive human spirit itself? Etymology is for that reason, just as mythology, the interpretation of that same primordial philosophy veiled in signs. But what results does etymology yield if here, too, we make it a law to separate one language from another as much as possible? Its results only acquire a higher measure of truth if we follow the same manner of appearance through several languages, while continuously relating the forms of words to their relevant concepts. In the etymological comments found especially in the second part, I sought to hold fast to this perspective [on language] as much as possible.

The fact that my work is in certain respects not equipped with the scholarly apparatus one is probably accustomed to in works of this kind partly has its reasons in the individual limitations of my circumstances,[20] but partly it was done on purpose. Convinced as I was that the essential ideas of the ancient Greek religion did not depend on the dubious authenticity of this passage or the other, or on [scholarly] reports[21] accessible only to a few, but that, rather, they must have found

---

[19]On German linguistics in the early nineteenth century and its broader significance cf. Tuska Benes, *In Babel's Shadow: Language, Philology, and the Nation in Nineteenth-Century Germany* (Detroit: Wayne State University Press, 2008).

[20]Baur wrote the book while teaching at the Lutheran Seminary Maulbronn and thus without access to a university library.

[21]*Notizen*. Baur may be referring here to the practice in the emerging nineteenth-century fields of oriental studies and classics of publishing brief reports or transcriptions of manuscript fragments, inscriptions, monuments, or other artifacts. For instance, the 1824 issue of the *Transactions of the Royal Asiatic Society of Great Britain and Ireland* (vol. 1, no. 1) includes contributions like "Inscriptions upon Rocks in South Bihar" (pp. 201–6), "Three Grants of Land, Inscribed on Copper, Found at Ujjayani" (pp. 230–9), "An Account of Greek, Parthian, and Hindu Medals, Found in India" (pp. 313–42), and "Extract from the Akhlak e Naseri, a Work Written by Naser ud Din about the Middle of the Thirteenth Century" (pp. 514–19). In Egyptology, the celebrated *Description de L'Égypte* (whose twenty-three-volume first edition was completed in 1818) devoted the first four volumes, along with five volumes of plates, to "descriptions" and "mémoires" of antiquities. The equally famed *Mémoires sur l'Égypte* (1798–1801) includes "rapports," "descriptions," and "notices" of such antiquities as Pompey's column (part 1, vol. 1 [reprint, 1799 = year VIII of the French Republican calendar], pp. 59–64). In the German-speaking sphere, Baur may have in mind publications like the multi-volume *Corpus Inscriptionum Graecarum*

their most natural and purest expression in the properly classic writings of the ancients, I mainly kept to those passages which for mythology in particular have still been too little put to use. And I generally sought to provide throughout a presentation as simple, clear, and straightforward as possible. I only took into account outside opinions where it seemed to me necessary for the sake of the *res* [under investigation]. What I could use on oriental religions is not much, but it is tried and proven, and I believe that with this approach I have found all the more how rich and fruitful that little bit can become. I have purposely made almost no use of any works of art, since what I wanted to consider under the aegis of mythology is not art but science.

[...]

With that, I now trustingly deliver my work into the public's hands. May it find the same reception with others that I gladly give to writings which have issued from serious scientific effort, and may it awaken in many, especially in young minds, the same love with which the study of this science has seized me—a science which more than any other is able to enliven the spirit's youth and open up for it a freer and more capacious prospect.

---

headed by August Boeckh (begun in 1815; first volume, 1828), which reported transcriptions of all known inscriptions in ancient Greek. See Hans Kippenberg, *Discovering Religious History in the Modern Age*, trans. Barbara Harshav (Princeton: Princeton University Press, 2002), 18. The editors wish to express their gratitude to Mr. Matthew Vale for providing the information contained in this note.

CHAPTER TWO

Gnosis as Christian Philosophy of Religion

FROM: DCG, EXTRACTS
TRANSLATION: BEATA AND MATTHEW VALE

Published in 1835, *Die christliche Gnosis* is indisputably one of Baur's most important works. Many ideas that had dominated his earlier research culminate here, while the book's results foreshadow the succession of monographs Baur was to publish over the subsequent decade.

Baur's interest in Gnosticism went back at least to 1827, when he presented, in Latin, a brief historical analysis of ancient Gnosticism together with an argument for Schleiermacher's theology as a modern variety of Gnosis. In 1831, he published a full monograph on Manichaeism. Another factor was his engagement with the thought of Johann Adam Möhler who had argued in his *Symbolik* that Protestantism was a modern renewal of Gnosticism, an idea Baur subsequently made his own in only slightly modified form. Finally, *Gnosis* also stands in continuity with the philosophical interpretation of mythology and the embrace of the history of religions first expressed in *Symbolik und Mythologie*.

Notwithstanding these continuities, *Gnosis* is a work of striking originality. Baur powerfully weaves together his own, earlier ideas, thorough textual research, and a clear philosophical and theological vision. Gnostic thought, as he would have it, is an early form of a comparative history of religions, conducted in a philosophical key. Gnosticism is thus "syncretistic" but only in the sense that it seeks religious truth in the correct relationship between paganism, Judaism and Christianity.

Despite their shortcomings, therefore, the ancient Gnostics set the tone for the subsequent history of the Christian philosophy of religion, which Baur seeks to demonstrate through a full analysis of Jacob Boehme, F. W. J. Schelling, F. D. E. Schleiermacher, and, especially, G. W. F. Hegel. *Gnosis* is the first major work in which Baur's new-found fascination for Hegel's philosophy of religion comes to the fore. Yet Baur retains a critical edge arguing that the most fundamental problems identified in ancient Gnosticism are still also characteristic of Hegel's system.

Baur's Hegelian orientation is one aspect of *Gnosis* that points forward to his subsequent works. Yet it is not the only one. In *Gnosis*, Baur classifies the historic religions based on their views on the relationship of the infinite and the finite, spirit and matter. In this perspective, the reconciliation of the two becomes key for the history of religious ideas. How this has worked out in the history of Christianity will be the topic of his subsequent books *Die Lehre von der Versöhnung* (1838) and *Die Lehre von der Dreieinigkeit* (1841–3).

The following extract seeks to provide a sense of Baur's argumentative sweep across the whole volume. It therefore consists of selections from three of the four main parts of the book.

CHRISTIAN GNOSIS OR THE CHRISTIAN PHILOSOPHY OF RELIGION IN ITS HISTORICAL DEVELOPMENT

The Relation of Gnosis to Religion: History of Religion and Philosophy of Religion as Its Main Elements[1]

[18] Among all the peculiarities which present themselves to us in Gnosis,[2] possibly none stands out more clearly, and there is none other that so obviously and to such a profound degree penetrates to its essence than the relationship it has with religion. Religion is the proper object Gnosis deals with, but not, in the first instance, religion as an abstract idea, but rather religion in the concrete shapes and positive [19] forms in which it historically objectivized itself at the time when Christianity came into existence.

Paganism, Judaism, and Christianity are the integrating elements that make up the material content of Gnosis in all its major forms. And—however negative and brusque the posture particular Gnostic systems took vis-à-vis one or the other [of these three] religious form[s]—the task at hand is nonetheless to determine the relationship in which the three forms of religion named above stand to one another according to their character and inner value and, in this way, to arrive at the true concept[3] of religion by considering them from a critically comparative perspective. Thus, whenever the essence of Gnosis is located in philosophical or theological speculation—as is often the case—this determination needs to be corrected in the following point: the speculative [idea] must not be considered the object of Gnosis in and of itself, [that is,] in the manner in which philosophy is engaged with it; rather, it may only be considered the object [of Gnostic thought] insofar as it is given in the content of the positive religions to which Gnosis relates itself.

From this perspective we can also easily judge the accuracy of the claim, already found among the ancients and, on the basis of their authority, often repeated by the moderns: [namely,] that the central task which Gnosis attempted to discharge was the question of the origin of evil.[4] [20] It is true that the content of the Gnostic systems can for the most part be traced back to this question. Since the Gnostics took evil not merely in a moral but especially in a metaphysical sense—so that evil is the finite, that which is different and separate from the absolute—this question comes to encompass nothing other than the great problem of how the finite emerges from the Absolute, how the world emerges from God. And since the fall from the Absolute cannot be thought without a future return and resumption into the original principle of being, this one question encompasses both sides of the sphere around which all Gnostic systems revolve on larger or smaller orbits.

But if it were, above all, this question alone whose attempted solution had called forth the Gnostic systems, the character they exhibit could not be satisfactorily explained. They would have to appear much more in the form of philosophical systems, just as the question itself with which they are dealing is a purely philosophical one. And in that case, one would not really be able to

---

[1]Section headings are adapted from Baur's table of contents.
[2]Baur uses "Gnosis" and "Gnosticismus" interchangeably. The present translation renders them as "Gnosis" and "Gnosticism," respectively, without reference to the distinction that more recent researchers have sought to draw between these terms. Cf. Christoph Markschies, *Gnosis: An Introduction*, trans. John Bowden (London: Bloomsbury, 2003), 13–16.
[3]*Begriff.* See Note on Text and Translations.
[4]For dualism as a characteristic of Gnosticism, cf. Kurt Rudolph, *Gnosis: The Nature and History of Gnosticism*, trans. Robert McLachlan Wilson (Edinburgh: T&T Clark, 1983), 59–67. Rudolph cites ancient authors, such as Plotinus, who foregrounded this aspect in their critique of Gnosticism.

grasp why, for this [philosophical] end, they positioned themselves in such an exact relationship with the positive, historically given religions. After all, these religions can only be an authority in answering such a question if they are regarded—from a more general perspective—as the necessary mediation of what is to be known as truth in philosophy and religion.

[21] Now, following from what we have just noted above, while the three forms of religion, which came into contact with each other at the time when Gnosticism emerged, are the elements which constitute its given basis and its material content—so that [Gnosis] needs to be considered from the perspective of the history of religion—this [aspect] is nevertheless only one side of its essence, to which another one, which [also] belongs essentially to it, must immediately be connected. For Gnosis is only history of religion insofar as it is, at the same time, philosophy of religion, and the characteristic way in which these two elements and tendencies—the historical and the philosophical—have mutually penetrated each other and bound themselves into a whole also provides us with the proper concept of its essence. Every Gnostic system contains pagan, Jewish, and Christian elements. But in each of these systems, these elements appear to stand in a particular relationship with one another, so that the position given to them in the order of the whole defines the character of the religious form to which they belong.

Above merely historical consideration stands philosophical, reflective consideration,[5] which in the historically given religions glimpses the associated parts of an organic whole. In this organic whole, one and the same living idea moves in its concrete configuration through a series of forms and stages of development. All religions are one in the idea of religion. They relate to this idea just as appearance and form relate to essence, as the concrete relates to the abstract, and as the mediating relates to the immediate: the entire history of religion is nothing but the living concept of religion unfolding itself and driving forward, and precisely in doing so, realizing itself; or [better], religious knowledge does not become [22] absolute, a knowledge *about* absolute religion, until it is also conscious of its mediation.

This is the point of view from which Gnosis considers the historically given religions in their relationship to each other. At the same time, however, the idea of religion coincides for Gnosis with this [idea's] essential and necessary content, which is the idea of the Godhead. For Gnosis, therefore, the history of religion is not merely the history of divine revelations, but these revelations are simultaneously the process of development in which the eternal essence of the Godhead itself goes forth from itself, manifests itself in a finite world, and splits itself from itself in order to return into an eternal union with itself through this manifestation and this self-bifurcation.[6] This explains the strict opposition found in all Gnostic systems between the absolute God and the self-revealing God. The richer the unfolding of life in which the divine manifests itself, and the more manifold the succession of divine powers into which the eternally One separates itself, the greater also is the effort to retain the idea of the absolute in its pure abstractness, and the Gnostics never tire of finding expressions to describe the essence of the Godhead which is closed and hidden in itself, nameless and unnameable, absolutely elevated above every imagination and description.

---

[5]*Betrachtung*. See Note on Text and Translations.
[6]*Selbstentzweiung*. Here, Baur's language betrays the influence of G. W. F. Hegel's philosophy which the author acknowledged in his Preface (DCG, vii–ix). Baur first encountered Hegel's thought when he read his *Lectures on the Philosophy of Religion*, published posthumously by Philipp Marheineke: G. W. F. Hegel, *Vorlesungen über die Philosophie der Religion, nebst einer Schrift über die Beweise vom Dasein Gottes*, ed. Philipp Marheineke, in *G. W. F. Hegel's Werke, herausgegeben durch einen Verein von Freunden des Verewigten*, vols. 11–12 (Berlin: Duncker & Humblot, 1832). Cf. Michael Inwood, *A Hegel Dictionary* (Oxford: Blackwell, 1992), 35–8.

But if the divine is determined to egress from itself, then a cause determining the Godhead must be conceivable as well. This cause is matter, and for this reason, it is the opposition between spirit and matter which conditions and determines divine self-revelation in its different moments. Divine revelation and the development of the world in their entirety become a battle between two opposing principles, in which it is the ultimate task [23] of the Godhead, or absolute spirit, to overcome and sublate[7] the antithesis constituted by matter.

Matter can, it is true, stand in different relationships to God. Either it is conceived as a principle external to God and co-eternal to him, or it is posited as being within the divine essence itself, or it is nothing really substantial at all, but rather the principle of negation, which—as soon as the Godhead reveals itself and the opposition between the infinite and the finite arises—as the principle which limits and restricts the perfection of the divine essence cannot be separated from the finite world in which the divine reveals itself. But even in this case, where the concept of matter is reduced to only this minimum, the opposition between spirit and matter, in itself, remains the same. If matter is conceived as an independent principle over-against God, he can only reveal himself in a struggle whereby his absolute essence is delimited and made subject to finitude. Yet even if matter is not placed in opposition to God as an independent principle, the inexplicable tendency still remains in God to go forth from himself and to reveal himself in a world where the perfection of the divine essence can only present itself as delimited and finite. The same higher necessity which places matter in opposition to God is also at work in God's inability to resist his own inner urge to reveal himself in a world which can only be a material one.

But if in this way, in the creation of the world, matter—however it is conceived—has power over God as a principle which negates the absoluteness of the divine essence, then this is only ever a negation which itself in turn must be negated and sublated. And thus, over against the moment of the world's creation [24]—by which God makes himself finite—there stands the moment of salvation and the return of the finite to God. The spirit which has been delivered over into matter and taken captive by it must once more be freed and redeemed from the power of matter; divine self-revelation returns to the place from where it came.

Nevertheless, the end is not entirely the same as the beginning. Rather, inasmuch as the spirit once more wards off the power of matter, which [threatened to] overwhelm it, has gathered itself within itself and withdrawn itself away from matter and back into itself, it is now for the first time truly conscious of its independence from matter, [and hence] its absolute power. Even if matter as an independent principle once again stands in opposition to spirit, and both principles once again assume their former condition (the Gnostic ἀποκατάστασις[8]), it is no longer the same relationship; rather, as the result of the struggle is won precisely the consciousness of their true relation. These are the chief moments of the self-revelation of the divine essence and of the development of the world which all Gnostic systems, in all their variations, traverse.

Only from this perspective is Gnosis revealed in its high significance which has almost always been recognized, even though it has [hitherto] not been possible to establish a clear concept of its peculiar essence. Gnosis is the remarkable attempt to conceive nature and history, and the entire course of the world with everything it encompasses, as the succession of moments in which the

---

[7]*Aufheben*. This again is Hegel's language. Cf. Inwood, *Hegel Dictionary*, 283–5 and Note on Text and Translations.

[8]*Apokatastasis*: restoration. The term is usually associated with the doctrine of universal salvation as found in Origen and many others. Baur here takes it in its more basic meaning implying that the eschaton is a restoration of the original state.

absolute spirit objectivizes itself and mediates itself to itself. As such, it is all the more notable since there is nothing more akin or analogous to Gnosis in the entire history of philosophical and theological speculation than the most recent philosophy of religion.[9]

[...]

The Origins of Gnosis

[37] It automatically follows from this that Gnosis could only emerge on a terrain where elements from different religions had already come into mutual contact. Thus, if it is possible for us to investigate the origins of Gnosis by going back before the Christian period (inasmuch as its Christian content is only an individual, and not an essentially necessary, element of Gnosis), we are in that case referred all the more, and by the very concept of Gnosis, to the field of Jewish religious history.

The first elements of Gnosis could accordingly only emerge where the Jewish religion developed the sort of relationship with pagan religion and philosophy that people felt pressed to recognize an immanent principle of truth on both sides, and thereby saw themselves presented with the task of bringing into a more precise inner coherence what was recognized as true on both sides, and of reducing it to one principle. This happened, as we know, among those Jews who—outside of their homeland—found themselves in circumstances where they, while always remaining Jews, had to set aside and moderate some aspects which otherwise belonged to the uncompromising, strictly secluded nature of Judaism. [There], they found themselves placed in a milieu in which they could not help but become open to the influence of new ideas and opinions, however little their great reverence for the religion of their fathers would thereby be weakened.

With good reason, then, genetic explanations of the phenomena of Christian Gnosis have given special weight to Philo as the truest representative of Alexandrian philosophy of religion.[10] Philo's ideas and opinions, already highlighted above in connection with Neander's presentation[11]—to which further [material] from Philo's writings could still be added, if one wanted to go [38] into more detail—provide the clearest proof of the close kinship between his standpoint and that of Christian Gnosis. The real reason for this kinship, however, can only be found in the fact that Philo, as a Platonist, took up ideas from pagan religion and philosophy which could not but make the Jewish religion appear to him in a very different light than it did to the typical Jew. The Platonist idea of deity as the absolute spirit, a being elevated in an infinite distance above all that is finite and humanly limited[12]; the closely connected [39] doctrine, fashioned from Platonist elements, of the Logos as the necessary organ of all [40] divine revelations; the opposition—so rigorously

---

[9]By this, Baur means the philosophical development in Schelling, Schleiermacher, and Hegel, prepared by Jacob Boehme. Cf. DCG, 557–635.
[10]Philo of Alexandria (c. 20 BCE–50 CE): Jewish philosopher from Alexandria. Cf. Maren J. Niehoff, *Philo of Alexandria: An Intellectual Biography* (New Haven: Yale University Press, 2018).
[11]Cf. DCG, 12–15.
[12]Here, Baur adds a lengthy note (DCG, 38–41) in which he assesses the relationship between Plato's philosophy and Gnosticism. Overall, his verdict is negative. While Gnostics drew on the notion of an utterly transcendent first principle, they could not find in Plato the ontological dualism of God and matter which, for Baur, is constitutive for all Gnostic systems. Another major difference is Plato's affirmation of freedom against Gnostic determinism. According to Baur, the Neoplatonic rejection of Gnosticism is prefigured in Plato's writings even though they contain ideas and elements which the Gnostics could utilize in their own efforts.

followed through as to determine and condition [one's] entire view of the world and of life—between these two principles, the spiritual [41] and the material, the ideal and the real: these are the ideas which predominantly formed the content of a philosophy of religion in contrast to which Judaism, according to its ordinary, outward meaning, appeared to belong to a subordinate level, from which it had yet to be elevated in order worthily to correspond to the newly achieved religious consciousness.

The accommodation of these two elements, the philosophical and the historical, which from this new perspective together made up the essential content of religious consciousness, was found in allegory, that ingeniously chosen means to breathe into the rigid letter a new spirit. Allegory transformed what at first appeared to be the thing itself into mere form. In this pictorial form the ideas one could no longer give up[13] now appeared as reflecting the true spiritual content of the sacred religious scriptures whose mediation, however, remained necessary to ensure the true possession of those ideas.

There was now a double Judaism, a higher and a lower, a spiritual and a sensual, an esoteric and an exoteric one. Even though the unity of the two was supposed to consist in their relation to one another as spirit and letter, as soul and body, and as content and form, a difference had, nevertheless, been established which had to lead even further. As soon as allegory lost its respected standing—which necessarily had to happen in a situation where people could no longer maintain the same interest in validating the Jewish religion as the absolutely true one, while at the same time the ideas themselves (which had called forth allegory as the artificial mediator between the speculative and the historical) still reigned over people's intellects—Judaism sank for precisely this reason to a level where it could only be regarded as subordinate and incomplete, a merely mediating and preparatory, form of religion.[14]

[...]

[66] Pagan religion contains an essentially speculative element, insofar as it always proceeds from the opposition between spirit and matter, from a duality of principles. For this reason, pagan religion is fundamentally philosophy of religion. In contrast to the speculative character of pagan religion, the Jewish and Christian religions have a partly ethical and partly positive character. They are ethical insofar as—putting aside the opposition between spirit and matter—they only have to do with the moral relationship between the human being and God. And they are positive insofar as their content is given by a revelation whose ultimate cause is only a free act of will on the part of the Godhead.

The revelation of the Godhead is the content and the object of every religion; but while pagan religion only permits the Godhead to reveal itself because there is no other way for the spirit to pass over into action and to unfold its inner life than through the mediation by matter, in the Jewish and Christian religion, the revelation of the Godhead only serves the purpose of proclaiming God's will to man. Revelation in the latter sense rests on a free action of the divine will, but in the former

---

[13] That is, philosophical, speculative ideas.
[14] Baur's view of Judaism has been controversially debated in recent research. While for some, he represents an early version of "racialised" scholarship, others offer a more nuanced assessment. Cf. Shawn Kelley, *Racializing Jesus: Race, Ideology, and the Formation of Modern Biblical Scholarship* (London: Routledge, 2002); Peter C. Hodgson, "F. C. Baur's Interpretation of Christianity's Relationship to Judaism," in *Is There a Judeo-Christian Tradition: A European Perspective*, ed. Emmanuel Nathan and Anya Topolski (Berlin: de Gruyter, 2016), 31–51.

sense, it takes place as the result of a necessity, which can only be conceived of as a natural necessity and which also imparts to pagan religion, as far as it is philosophy of religion, the character of a philosophy of nature. Ethical religions operate within the opposition of guilt and punishment, sin and grace, without feeling compelled to move beyond this opposition. [67] But the more this opposition is positioned in [the framework of] the higher and more general opposition between the concepts of God and world, of spirit and matter, and the more one opposition is mediated by the other, the more definitively the ethical is subordinated to the speculative. Then the human being is no longer considered a free, self-determining creature, but merely something set within a great organism, the general context of nature—a creature dependent on and determined by this context.

This [notion] constitutes part of the common character of the Gnostic systems and of all systems analogous to them. But how easily the ethical passes over into the speculative, and what the inner link is between one and the other, is nowhere more evident than in the idea of salvation, which—as essentially Christian as it is—no less also belongs to pagan religion, for the simple reason that all religions, amidst all their differences, turn out again and again to be one in the concept of religion, and they therefore possess everything that comes with the concept of religion both in the same way and in differing ways.[15]

Wherever this unity and difference among the religions rose to consciousness, there Gnosis, too, had to have its origin. Gnosis first emerged in this way in the field of Jewish religion, and when the new [phenomenon of] Christianity appeared on the scene, it brought to consciousness the same relation of unity and difference to a greater extent and with greater determinateness. Regardless of Christianity's ethical character, it offered so many moments of such authentically speculative meaning which effortlessly aligned themselves with the speculative ideas of the pre-Christian philosophy of religion, that what was in place [in this pre-Christian religious philosophy] appeared simply to have been brought to completion and to full consciousness in Christianity. On this basis Gnosis was called into being in the [68] form in which we encounter it in gnostic systems.[16]

[...]

The Three Main Forms of Gnosis

[113] Following the exposition above, our main [114] focus now has to turn to the mutual relationships between the three forms of religion with which the Gnostic systems engaged.[17] Only by taking this main focus can we classify Gnostic systems in a way appropriate to the nature of the endeavor. Christianity was generally always regarded as the religion which was more or less identical with absolute religion. Thus, it always had to form a certain contrast with the two other religions,

---

[15] On Baur's view of redemption cf. also CLV, 1–5; see Chapter 5 in this volume.

[16] Baur adds a footnote here noting his agreement with Lorenz von Mosheim 1693–1755 on the pre-Christian origin of Gnosis over against more recent critics, notably Friedrich Lücke, "Kritik der bisherigen Untersuchungen über die Gnostiker, bis auf die neusten Forschungen darüber von Herrn Dr. Neander und Herrn Prof. Lewald," *Theologische Zeitschrift* 2 (1820): 132–71. Cf. Lorenz von Mosheim, *Versuch einer unparteiischen und gründlichen Ketzergeschichte* (Helmstedt: Weygand, 1748), 1–112.

[17] Baur's classification of Gnosis is discussed with reference to contemporaneous research in Volker Henning Drecoll, "Ferdinand Christian Baur's View of Christian Gnosis, and of the Philosophy of Religion in His Own Day," in *Ferdinand Christian Baur and the History of Early Christianity*, ed. Martin Bauspiess, Christof Landmesser, and David Lincicum (Oxford: OUP, 2017), 116–46, here: 124–7.

but the question was how sharply this contrast was conceived of, and thus whether the whole relationship Christianity had with Judaism and paganism was defined more or less dualistically. Thus we get two main forms of Gnosticism. When it comes to the relationship between Christianity on the one hand, and Judaism and paganism on the other, the one [form of Gnosticism] assumes a more approximating relationship, and the other a more repelling one.

The majority of Gnostic systems, among them the oldest ones, belong to the former main form: the systems of Basilides[18] and of Valentinus, and of the numerous disciples of Valentinus,[19] furthermore the Ophites[20] and those belonging to their sub-sects, those of Saturninus[21] and Bardesanes.[22] The fact that some of them defined the relationship of matter and the demiurge to the highest God more dualistically than others, and that some conceived of Christ more docetically than others, does not constitute an essential difference. It is, however, a modification which deserves attention and, insofar as it was rooted in the local conditions of the countries where the Gnostics emerged on the scene, it renders fitting a limited differentiation between Egyptian and Syrian Gnostics. But this difference has not the least influence on their fundamental character which we should keep in view here, since all these Gnostics concur that the pre-Christian period, [115] in the Jewish as well as the pagan spheres, is closely linked to Christianity, and that this period had initiated and prepared Christianity in manifold ways.[23]

These Gnostics generally are rooted in the same ground as Alexandrian Jewish philosophers of religion such as Philo, as well as Alexandrian church fathers such as Clement and Origen; indeed, the gnosis of these latter two can itself be considered another possible modification of the same basic form.[24] And thus we can also see here yet another confirmation of the view that the style of thinking which had predominated in Alexandria for such a long time, and which so decisively influenced Christianity itself, played the largest and most direct role in the whole phenomenon which we call Gnosis in the narrower sense.

The second main form of Gnosis has its only but all the more peculiar representative in Marcion, whose system, one has always had to admit, distinguished itself from all others in a conspicuous way.[25] But the most conspicuous peculiarity of his system must certainly be the relationship of harsh distantiation in which he set Christianity vis-à-vis Judaism. Marcion's verdict on Judaism automatically includes the same verdict on paganism, in which he was able to recognize even less

---

[18]Basileides (Latin: Basilides) (*fl.* 117–61), Gnostic teacher. Cf. Rudolph, *Gnosis*, 309–13; Jean-Daniel Dubois, "Basilides and the Basilidians," in *The Gnostic World*, ed. Garry W. Trompf et al. (London: Routledge, 2019), 156–61.

[19]Valentinus (*c.* 100–*c.* 160), the most influential Gnostic teacher. On him and his school see Rudolph, *Gnosis*, 317–25; Einar Thomassen, "Valentinus and the Valentinians," in *The Gnostic World*, ed. Trompf et al., 162–9.

[20]The Ophites seem to have been an early Gnostic group. Cf. Tuomas Rasimus, *Paradise Reconsidered in Gnostic Mythmaking: Rethinking Sethianism in Light of the Ophite Evidence* (Leiden: Brill, 2009).

[21]Satornilos (Lat. Saturninus) (*fl.* 100–20), early Gnostic teacher. Cf. Rudolph, *Gnosis*, 298.

[22]Bardaisan (Latin: Bardesanes) († *c.* 222). Syrian writer. Cf. Rudolph, *Gnosis*, 327–9. A fuller, more recent account in: Ilaria Ramelli, *Bardaisan of Edessa: A Reassessment of the Evidence and New Interpretation* (Piscataway, NJ: Gorgias Press, 2009).

[23]A classification system based on geography was popular among Baur's contemporaries, especially Johann Karl Ludwig Gieseler (1792–1854) and Jacques Matter (1791–1864), but sharply rejected by Baur himself. Cf. DCG, 105–6; Drecoll, "Baur's View," 125–6.

[24]Both Clement and Origen use the term "Gnosis" and "Gnostic" for the consummate Christian. Cf. Doru Costache, "Christian Gnosis: From Clement of Alexandria to John Damascene," in *The Gnostic World*, ed. Trompf et al., 259–70.

[25]Marcion of Sinope (85–160), early Christian "heretic," now often not counted as part of Gnosticism. Cf. Judith Lieu, *Marcion and the Making of a Heretic: God and Scripture in the Second Century* (Cambridge: CUP, 2015).

commonalities with Christianity than in Judaism. The relationship, then, between Christianity and Judaism, as well as [between Christianity and] paganism, is understood here mostly from a dualist stance.

I will readily admit that, once the dualist perspective occurs as characteristically as we find it with Marcion, even if only in one single regard, it automatically has an impact on the determination of the relationship of matter and the Demiurge with the highest God, as well as the docetic opinion of the person of Christ. [116] And I will also admit that, for that reason, Marcion's Gnosis is much closer to the Syrian form of Gnosis than to the Egyptian one, in accordance, incidentally, with historical [evidence]. But if the principle by which the systems are to be classified is to be kept in view in its purity, then the main issue in Marcion's dualist perspective, the issue which can only refer to the relationship between Christianity and the other two religions, has to be distinguished very precisely from the less essential issues which only concern individual points in the system.

Based on our principle of classification, there remains for us a third possible main form of Gnosis next to the two main forms defined in the above manner. As soon as a more dualistic perspective is established [as a basis] for understanding the relationship between Christianity and the two other religions, this dualism can be allowed to encompass these two religions, the Jewish and the pagan, in the same way as Marcion has done it, but this dualism can also be restricted to one of the two religions, be it the pagan or the Jewish one. Just as Marcion grouped Judaism and paganism together in order to contrast them with Christianity in a dualist way, another Gnostic could group Judaism—just to mention it first—with Christianity in order to set them both into the same opposition with paganism.

It would indeed be surprising, considering how rich Gnosticism's productivity was, if this form, which presents itself to general consideration[26] as a possible one, had never come into existence. But according to common representations of Gnostic systems one would have to believe that there was no position representing this type. Yet this is not really so, and [this oversight] [117] has to be counted among the main absences and defects in previous accounts of Gnosticism. Only the vagueness of their whole perspective in the understanding of Gnosis in general and in the classification of its different forms could make them overlook one of its main forms almost completely, at least insofar as it was not recognized as an independent form nor assigned its due place. It is Cerinthus who belongs here, whom even Neander completely passed over in the *Genetic Development of the Most Significant Gnostic Systems*[27]; only later, in [his] *Church History* did Neander place him at the front of the list with Basilides, Valentinus, and the others in that class.[28] As will be shown later,[29] however, [Cerinthus][30] is definitely gnostic in a different sense than the others who are commonly included in the Judaizing category.

But even if there were still any doubt about Cerinthus, it is impossible to deny that the peculiar system contained in the Clementine Homilies has a distinctly Gnostic character, while it also cannot be placed in the same category with any of the other systems which are commonly named as the main forms of Gnosis. It is one of the distinguishing merits of Neander's *Genetic Development of the Most Significant Gnostic Systems*, to have once again called attention to the peculiar content of

---

[26]*Betrachtung*. See Note on Text and Translations.
[27]August Neander, *Genetische Entwickelung der vornehmsten gnostischen Systeme* (Berlin: Dümmler, 1818).
[28]August Neander, *Allgemeine Geschichte der christlichen Religion und Kirche*, vol. 1/II (Hamburg: Perthes, 1826), 671–9.
[29]DCG, 403–5.
[30]Reading "er" for "es."

these pseudo-Clementine Homilies, but he only did so in a supplement which is merely intended as a contribution to the history of the Ebionites.[31] This form of Gnosis—the Cerinthian as well as the Ebionite—has not been accorded the place it is due in the succession of developmental forms of Gnosis, neither in Neander's *Church History*, nor in any of the more recent presentations of [118] Gnostic systems.

Its distinctiveness generally consists in its identifying Judaism and Christianity as much as possible, while establishing an all the more rigorous opposition between these two [on the one hand] and paganism [on the other]. It essentially distinguishes itself thereby from the two other forms of Gnosis. Thus, the only question that presents itself here is whether the only possible remaining form, which combines Christianity with paganism and contrasts these two with Judaism, can be detected in some Gnostic system. One could think in this context of the teachings of Carpocrates and Epiphanes, who placed Pythagoras, Plato, and Aristotle (from among the pagans) in one category with Christ, and who praised all [four of] them for elevating themselves to the highest contemplation through the power of the Monad.[32] While paganism appears here as equal to Christianity, the contrast with Judaism is expressed by ascribing the highest contemplation to Jesus—which he is supposed to have reached through his especially pure and strong soul—because he had liberated himself from the restrictive laws of the Jewish God and destroyed the religion proceeding from this God.

If in this way, however, Christianity is equated with paganism and not with Judaism, and if all historic religions are so deeply reduced in the face of the one absolute Monad that with regard to the latter religious opinions become indifferent, then Gnosis is at the point where it takes leave, not only from the domain of Christian Gnosis, but altogether from Gnosis proper. After all, the concept of Christian Gnosis always entails the recognition of the specific value of Christianity. But while in this respect a certain degree of identification between Christianity and [119] Judaism is possible, reducing Christianity to one level with paganism contradicts Christianity's nature. [Moreover], if all religions taken together are declared equally indifferent, there can no longer be a contrast between one form and another, and the relationship between Gnosis and the history of religion altogether ceases to exist, insofar as it can no longer be the concern of Gnosis to arrive at the absolute concept of religion through the historical moments of its mediation. The Gnosis of a Carpocrates [for instance], which is essentially a purely subjective philosophical way of thinking, can no longer be considered a true form of Gnosis; the same is true for the Gnosis of all those whose Gnosis appears to be a mainly practically minded [form of] religious indifferentism.[33]

Thus, the main forms of Gnosis—the only ones [120] we can recognize as such—according to what we have said so far rest upon the more or less dualistic perspective on the relationship of the three forms of religion with which Gnosis concerns itself. And there are two main forms, depending on whether this dualism—or the opposition which is always on the basis of the relationship between these religions, even if they are considered different stages, since there are always two religions facing a third—recedes more [into the background] or comes more to the fore. If this dualism

---

[31]Neander, *Genetische Entwickelung*, 361–421.
[32]*Monas*: The One or the Absolute. Clement of Alexandria says of Epiphanes that he "taught the knowledge of the Monad, the source of the heresy of the Carpocratians" (*Stromata* III 5,3), English text: Clement of Alexandria, *Stromateis*, trans. John Ferguson (Washington, DC: The Catholic University of America Press, 1991), 259. Epiphanes was therefore often seen as the founder of a "monadic Gnosis."
[33]Footnote omitted, DCG, 119–20.

comes more to the fore, then its emphasis can fall on either both of the [two] religions which stand alongside Christianity, or only one of these religions. For this reason, the more dualistic main form in turn separates itself into subordinate forms.

On the whole, however, there are three essentially different forms, which we can also regard as coordinated [to one another], inasmuch as each of them represents a characteristic appreciation of a particular form of religion. The first form (in the main, the Valentinian one) wants to grant to paganism its right alongside the other two. The second one (Marcionism) is primarily concerned with Christianity. The third form (in the pseudo-Clementine Homilies) especially attends to Judaism.[34] So, it is through the character of these three religions that the characteristic element of the three main forms of Gnosis gets determined. And we have repeatedly to return to the religions which correspond to these forms in order to grasp each one for itself and in its relationship with the others. This view of the relationship between the main forms of Gnosis seems grounded in the nature of the case. But that it can also be followed through historically can only be demonstrated by a closer consideration of the individual systems.

[...]

The General Significance of Gnostic Docetism

[260] Docetism everywhere can only emerge from a perspective founded on a strict opposition between spirit and matter. Its underlying idea is always the idea of the spirit's absolute rule and superiority over matter. Only the spirit is something truly substantial and existing in itself. Matter distinguishes itself from it in the same way accident relates to substance, and the imperfect to the perfect. It does not in itself have true and real being; it is, so to speak, non-being, or that which only has the appearance of being. Or, even if matter confronts spirit as an independent being that subsists for itself, it has so little absolute value that, in this respect at least, its relation to spirit is one of utter subordination.

Matter, then, merely relates to spirit in the way the impure relates to the pure, and good to evil. If matter is only the shell and the form in which spirit must appear in order to objectivize itself in a finite world, [then] matter is practically conceived as mere accident. The spirit thickens itself, as it were, into a material world of bodies, but in this passage of the spirit into matter there has to be a specific threshold the spirit must not overstep in order to retain cognizance of its absolute essence in its purity. Even though, according to this view on the relation between spirit and matter, matter is nothing but the objectivized spirit which has become finite, still [261] the material (insofar as it is distinguished from the psychic) is the inert, dead mass which so binds the free spirit that in it, the spirit loses cognizance of itself.

If, therefore, the spirit is to retain cognizance of its absolute essence and of its absolute rule over matter, it has to repeatedly confirm this rule by breaking through the material form in which it appears, by never allowing this material form to become static and rigid, but instead soaring above it by relating to it entirely freely, by treating it as a form that is entirely transparent and malleable for the spirit. In this sense, therefore, the sensory form in which the spirit appears is a

---

[34]Footnote omitted, DCG, 120.

mere pseudo-form,[35] and the redeemer cannot appear in the sensory world in any other form than in one of that kind.

For if in Gnosticism salvation consists in the spirit once again becoming aware of its absolute rule over matter and thereby winning its freedom from it, then a redeemer in this sense can only be one in whom that awareness has never been clouded by the predominance of matter over spirit—in the same way in which, according to the commonly held view, the redeemer himself has to be free of sin in order to free others from sin. All those conquered by matter; all those for whom matter has become such a thick mass and solid body that they can no longer penetrate it with the free power of their spirit—all those are in need of salvation. For this reason, they can only have their principle of salvation in someone else, a person in whom matter has not gained such consistency and whose spirit it has not subdued.

[...]

[262] But at the same time, the redeemer cannot communicate his redeeming activity without manifesting himself in a visible way in the material, finite world, the only place where the individuals in need of redemption are. This can only happen in a form which does not have anything truly material about it, but merely exhibits the appearance of a real human body. In other words, the redeemer can only establish a connection with a real human being if that human being serves him as a mere vehicle and organ. The true redeemer hovers above him as the invisible idea, and the real human being only marks the space, so to speak, in which the redeeming activity intervenes in the visible [263] world.

The human being is only the token of the redeemer, and according to Basilides as well as Marcion, one can say that the redeemer became human only in appearance, or that he only seemed to appear in a true human body.[36] Now, if we have to locate the significance of Docetism herein—and if we thus have to identify its significance not only as an intentional and arbitrary contradiction of the factual reality of the Gospel story, but instead see that in Docetism Gnosticism's fundamental idea about the absolute freedom and independence of the spirit from matter finds expression—then we can also find herein the reason why Gnostic systems have the redemptive action begin by effectively positing an absolute beginning.

[...]

The significance of Docetism in this connection is that the principle of the [264] redemptive action gets conceived as one that posits an absolute beginning; it intervenes in the visible world and in the history of humankind in a purely supernatural manner, completely independent of the material world order and its development according to natural laws. The principle of higher spiritual life can only intervene in the nature of human beings as a supernatural principle, just as—following the common view—Christ is only free of sin because his emergence does not belong in the line of human procreation and represents an absolute starting point. But even there we cannot stop. Presentations of the Valentinian system have called attention to the way in which the redeemer only calls into awareness what already lies within pneumatic natures themselves. He merely indicates that level of development which every spiritual individual has to reach if

---

[35]*Scheingestalt*. Literally "form of [mere] appearance." Cf. Docetism from Greek *dokein*—to seem or appear.
[36]According to Basilides, it was a man called Simon of Cyrenaica who was crucified having taken on the form of Jesus: Irenaeus, *Adversus Haereses* I 24, 4. For the complicated evidence in the case of Marcion see Lieu, *Marcion*, 372–80.

spirit's absolute lordship over matter, and its freedom from it, is to come to awareness in him, and thus into reality. There is no other way to think the relationship of the redeemer to the individual spiritual natures in need of redemption, not in the other Gnostic systems, nor even in the Marcionite system.

If we add to that the fact that Docetism fundamentally has to assert that the moment the redemptive principle becomes active is an absolute beginning, [it follows that for] every single individual in which the idea of redemption has to be realized, the essence of this idea can only mean that a principle becomes active in them which relates to their previous existence, to their developmental process hitherto, as something purely supernatural, something unexplainable on that basis—even though it must, regardless of that fact, [still] be within human nature's developmental capabilities. [265] Redemption is the moment when the spirit definitively becomes free from its material bondage which had lasted up to that point; it is the moment of the awakening of higher self-awareness, of the soaring of the pneumatic principle above the psychic. But if, along these lines, redemption is merely an interior act which takes place in every individual, what reason was there to make this act dependent upon the external history and person of a redeemer who appeared at a certain point in time?

The reason lay first in the historical truth of Christianity, or in the undeniable fact that Jesus was the first individual in whom the principle of redemption actively emerged in the sense described above. But if Jesus was the first individual of this kind in a succession of human individuals who followed him, his history, albeit epoch-making, was still only the history of an ordinary human being. This line of thinking did not arrive at a true redeemer, then, until it also took an interest in receiving this first individual in the succession as the archetype of all human individuals belonging to this same concept, as the universal human being who, as it were, individualizes himself in all the others and realizes the idea of his essence in them. But if, in this way, the archetypal Christ was separated from the historical Jesus, Jesus the real human being could only have the significance which Basilides left for him.[37] Inasmuch as they only wanted to retain the pure idea of redemption, Jesus, the true human being, merely marked the historical starting point in which that idea began to be active. If, however, they wanted also to understand the abstract idea in a concrete manner, the human appearance became the visible form which reflected the personified idea of redemption.

[...]

The Relationship of Hegel's Philosophy of Religion to Historic Christianity

[p. 707] Another main point that merits our attention here is the relationship of [708] [Hegel's] philosophy of religion vis-à-vis historical Christianity. We do not have to point out [709] how intimately this philosophy of religion is joined with Christianity, how thoroughly it wants to take over the whole [710] content of Christianity; indeed, its whole task is based on not wanting to be

---

[37]Baur, while writing about historical Gnostics, clearly has in view Schleiermacher's Christology of Christ as the *Urbild* (archetype) of salvation: Friedrich Schleiermacher, *The Christian Faith* §93, trans. H. R. Mackintosh and J. S. Stewart (London: T & T Clark, 1999), 377. NB: Mackintosh/Stewart render "Urbild" with "ideal."

anything but the scientific[38] exposition of historically given Christianity. For this philosophy of religion, Christianity is the turning point in world history where the spirit, in the process of its own development, for the first time raised itself to a clear awareness of its absolute nature and made the decisive beginning to return to itself from its [self-]emptying.[39]

In this respect, then, in the assessment of the historical importance of Christianity, it completely coincides with the ancient form of Gnosis. And exactly for this reason, the relationship it adopts, as philosophy of religion, vis-à-vis historical Christianity is also on the whole the same. Just as its teaching about God is nothing but the purely scientific understanding and development of the idea of the absolute spirit, so, too, its Christology is essentially only formally different from the Christology of the ancient Gnosis. Those elements and tendencies which were already contained in the ancient Gnosis but could not yet reach a pure form in it have now been elevated to their true concept. In sum, it is therefore the same [711] separation between the historical and the ideal Christ—which ensued in Gnosis as the necessary result of this speculative understanding of Christianity—that emerges in its full breadth in Hegelian philosophy of religion.

It could, admittedly, appear that precisely its teaching on the person of Christ gives the clearest proof of how seriously this philosophy of religion takes its effort to absorb the complete content of the Christian faith and to allow nothing of its deep meaning to be lost. We here learn not merely of a humanity that is well-pleasing to God as an ideal floating in some doubtful distance, or merely of some archetypical being elevating the human to the divine, or of a God-consciousness having become the divine being. [Instead], it is here asserted with the full weight of ecclesial locutions that Christ is the God-man, that God has become human, has appeared in the flesh; that the unity of the divine and human nature, existing in itself, has been revealed to humankind in a concrete way in a specific, individual subject. Moreover, the more real and objective the idea of God is to this philosophy of religion, the less, it seems, can the full reality of its God-man be permitted to be called into doubt.

It is, however, obvious that everything depends on the sense in which the Christ [of Hegel's philosophy] is the God-man. If we consider his teaching on Christ more closely, three moments can be distinguished: the entirely external, merely historical consideration sees in Christ only an ordinary human being, a martyr of the truth, like Socrates. This first moment, in which the person of Christ is still an object of unbelief, is followed by faith as the second moment, since, for faith, Christ no longer appears as an ordinary human being but as God-man, as the one in whom [712] divine nature is revealed and in whom the divine is beheld.

---

[38]*Wissenschaftlich*. Being *Wissenschaft* (frequently "the science") was of central import for Hegel's philosophy. What he meant by it, however, is neither captured by the English "science" nor by modern German *Wissenschaft*. The term is usually employed as a conscious derivative of *Wissen* (knowledge); in fact, *Wissenschaft* and *Wissen* can be used interchangeably. In 1807, Hegel advertised the *Phenomenology of Spirit* in the following words: "This volume is the exposition of the coming to be of knowledge (*das werdende Wissen*). [...] It examines the preparation for science (*Wissenschaft*) from a standpoint through which it constitutes a new, interesting philosophy and a 'first science' (*erste Wissenschaft*) for philosophy." G. W. F. Hegel, *The Phenomenology of Spirit*, trans. Terry Pinkard (Cambridge: CUP, 2018), 468.

[39]*Entäußerung*. This important Hegelian term could also be rendered "externalization," "self-divestment," "destitution," or even "giving (oneself or one's things) away." Luther's original translation of Phil 2:7 ("he emptied himself") was "eusserte sich selbst." Later revisions of the *Lutherbibel*, and in all likelihood the revisions Hegel was familiar with, rendered it with "entäußerte sich selbst." See Nicholas Adams, *The Eclipse of Grace: Divine and Human Action in Hegel* (London: Wiley Blackwell, 2013), 39. Cf. also, Inwood, *Hegel Dictionary*, 35–7.

If we ask how the first moment is mediated to the second, how the transition from unbelief to faith takes place, we are reminded that the emergence of faith is the outpouring of the Spirit.[40] This outpouring consisted in the transformation of the immediate [sense-perception] into a spiritual determination; an understanding of the sensible as spiritual; and the connection of the human Jesus, a human, sensible phenomenon, with the consciousness of a spiritual content.

For this reason, it is in Jesus' death that this passage over into the religious [dimension] works itself out; for Christ is God-man only having overcome death, slain death, negated the negation, and thereby destroyed the finite, evil, as something alien to him, and reconciled the world with God in this way. Everything depends, above all, on understanding this death; it is the touchstone against which faith has to prove itself, which is why the spirit was unable to come before Christ had been raptured away from the flesh, and his immediate sensual presence had ceased.

In a word, Christ is God-man only by the mediation of faith. [The question of] what lies behind faith, however, as the historically given, objective reality which was the basis from which the merely external, historical view could turn into faith remains shrouded in a mystery which we ought not [attempt to] penetrate; for the question is not whether Christ in himself, according to his objective, historical appearance, was the God-man; instead, the only essential point is that he became God-man to faith.

At some point, faith came into being, and only the God-man can be the object of faith. But the following consequence presents itself immediately: if it is the essence of faith that history attains to spiritual understanding, that the immediate, human, [713] sensory appearance is transfigured into spiritual content, and that the relationship to the mere human being [Jesus] is transformed into a relationship so altered by the Spirit that the nature of God is laid open within it—if, [in other words] sensual history is merely the point of departure for faith, so that the content itself of this faith is only brought forth by the community of the faithful which comes into being simultaneously with the [individual] faith, then Christ is all that he is as God-man only in and through faith.

The God-man thus, while he is the object of faith, is not its necessary presupposition.[41] The presupposition of faith is not Christ as God-man but Christ as a mere human being, as a human, sensory appearance. The divine and the human are [at this point] still separated from one another until faith joins them as the mediating bond, and until the sensory is translated into the spiritual after Christ is ruptured away from the flesh.

[...]

[714] Now, for this reason, faith has yet to be elevated to knowledge, and that spiritual content has to be lifted out from the element of faith and into the element of thinking consciousness, where it is justified no longer by history, as something that happened and is done with, but rather by philosophy or by the concept, in which it is vindicated as the truth existing in itself and present *simpliciter*. But the truth existing in itself is the absolute spirit, God as the Triune, the human being's identity with God. Knowledge of Christ as the God-man is therefore nothing but knowledge of this truth, knowledge of the truth that only the human being in its universality, [715] the spirit as

---

[40]*Geist*. See Note on Text and Translations.
[41]According to Baur, Christ as God-man cannot be *both* the product of faith *and* its point of origin. For this reason, the historical Jesus remains theologically important if Christianity is understood as a historic faith. More generally, critical, historical study is an essential part of theology. This is the core of his dissatisfaction with both Schleiermacher and Hegel (expressed here via their interpretation as representatives of Gnosis).

a non-finite spirit, has a true existence or is cognizant of the unity of the divine and human nature. Thus, what is human appearance in the first moment and divine-human appearance in the second is the pure idea, the spirit itself, in the third; and everything that refers to the appearance and to the life of Christ has its truth only in this: that in it, the essence and the life of the spirit itself is presenting itself.

What the spirit is and what it does, however, are no history.[42] So, even though for faith, the appearance of the God-man, God's Incarnation, his birth in the flesh, may be a historical fact, from the standpoint of speculative thought, God's Incarnation is not a single, historical fact that happened once, but rather an eternal determination of God's essence, by which God only becomes human (in every single human being) insofar as he is human from eternity. The same finitude and the same sorrowful abasement to which Christ subjected himself as God-man are always borne by God insofar as he is also human. The reconciliation accomplished by Christ is not a deed that happened in time; rather, God reconciles himself with himself eternally, and the resurrection and elevation of Christ are nothing but the spirit's eternal return to itself and to its truth. Christ as a human being, as God-man, is the human being in its universality—not as a single individual but as the universal individual.

Just as the move from the first moment to the second, or the passage over into the religious [dimension], worked itself out in death, inasmuch as the death of Christ sublated Christ's human condition, [so that] only in death, as the negation of negation, Christ emerged as the God-man for faith, so too is a similar relationship at work between the second and third moments. For faith, Christ [716] even as God-man is still a specific historical and personal phenomenon; only in speculative thought, Christ's human condition is utterly sublated and Christ, thus sublated, is only the universal human being, that is, the finite spirit's identity with the absolute spirit. Can all that is human and personal in Christ's appearance—even all that is symbolic and archetypical—be shed more rigorously and definitively? The idea in [all] its spiritual purity tears itself away from any worldly, sensory shell, and all facts of history to which faith still clings appear only as opaque reflections of the spirit's eternal process,[43] which even from the highest vantage point is only a game of distinction-making which never gets serious.

But if we descend from these heights of speculation, which leave far below even the Docetism of the gnostic worldview, and return to that sphere where distinctions [once more] get their due and the spirit, impelled by the inner negativity of the idea, brings to completion the untiring labor of world history, note well what great significance this philosophy of religion still leaves over for the historical appearance of Christ! The truth that exists in itself, the unity of divine and human nature, is bound to come to consciousness for humankind. Only in this consciousness does the spirit return to itself from its [self-]emptying and finitization.

---

[42]These words are an unmarked quotation from Hegel's *Lectures on the Philosophy of Religion*. G. W. F. Hegel, *Vorlesungen über die Philosophie der Religion*, ed. Walter Jaeschke. 3 vols. in 4 (Hamburg: Meiner, 1983–5), 3: 163. English text: G. W. F. Hegel, *Lectures on the Philosophy of Religion*, ed. Peter C. Hodgson, trans. R. F. Brown, P. C. Hodgson, and J. M. Stewart, 3 vols. (Oxford: Oxford University Press, 2007), 3: 232. From the critical edition it appears that these words were only part of Hegel's second lecture course, held in 1824. A few pages earlier (DCG, 696), Baur had offered the quotation in full.

[43]Baur here adds the following note: "The facts of the history of Christ contain a symbolic meaning referring to the essence of the spirit, as with the Gnostics. See [DCG], p. 140 above."

But this great turning point in world history lies in the appearance of Christ alone. Only when faith understood him as the God-man [717] could human beings become aware of that truth that exists in itself, because everything that is to become a certitude for human beings has to take the form of immediate sensory intuition for them, the form of external existence; it has to be revealed to them in object-like fashion. Even on this view, Christ still retains a dignity and a meaning which no other person can share with him, and Christianity is by no means merely one more among the stages which lead to the absolute standpoint. Rather, Christianity is the absolute stage itself, since the absolute stage is determined just as much by the content, where religion is identical to philosophy, as it is by the form which distinguishes religion from philosophy.

The Hegelian philosophy of religion considers Christ as God-man only in his relationship with faith, without declaring itself more definitively on what faith's objective connection was with the actual appearance of Christ, a connection which faith had as its presupposition. But how could faith in him as the God-man have developed without him also in some way objectively being what faith took him to be? The necessary presupposition is inevitably that the truth which exists in itself, the union of divine and human nature, first became concrete truth in Christ; in him it became knowledge conscious of itself and was proclaimed and taught as truth by him. That is what constitutes the special pre-eminence of Christ.

But if here one were to ask the question[44] (which immediately presents itself) of how Christ knew the truth, [718] whether he knew it in the only adequate form of the immanent concept, or in the untrue form of representational thinking, then in view of the indisputable fact that the teachings and the statements of Christ in the New Testament documents are presented to us in a form which is essentially different from the standpoint of speculative knowledge, one is indeed compelled to negate the former assumption and to affirm the latter. Thereby one would also be compelled to admit the consequence that this philosophy of religion, at least in view of the form of knowledge at issue, places the philosopher who has knowledge about God above the historical Christ, even if only in this one respect.

At the same time, it is not clear why this most vulnerable and truly deadly spot in the [Hegelian] system should reveal itself for the first time only at this point. After all, the difference only applies to the form of knowledge while the content always remains the same, since according to the principles of this philosophy of religion, faith and speculative knowledge—or religion and philosophy—are supposed to be different according to form but identical according to content. [719] Above all, then, the [latter] claim would have to be contested [with the aim of] showing that faith is not only absorbed by speculation according to its form but simultaneously also according to its content.[45]

But how is this proof to be executed, since the system so emphatically asserts that what constitutes the content of Christ's teaching as the God-man—the union of divine and human nature—is the

---

[44]Footnote omitted, DCG, 717–18.

[45]This question stood at the center of the debate about Hegel's interpretation of religion. Cf. Hegel, *Philosophy of Religion*, 1: 385–413. The view, here rejected by Baur, that the *content* of religion could not be preserved in its philosophical "sublation" became the hallmark of the Hegelian left in the latter half of the 1830s. In 1830 already, Ludwig Feuerbach wrote this satirical epigram against Marheineke: "Can you parry this thrust, sophist? The form is itself essence; thus you abolish the content of faith/if you abolish the representation that is its proper form." Ludwig Feuerbach, *Gesammelte Werke*, ed. Werner Schuffenhauer, vol. 1: *Frühe Schriften, Kritiken und Rezensionen* (East-Berlin: Akademie Verlag, 1963), 461. English text: Ludwig Feuerbach, *Thoughts on Death and Immortality, from the Papers of a Thinker, along with an Appendix of Theological-Satirical Epigrams, edited by one of his friends*, trans. James A. Massey (Berkeley: University of California Press, 1980), 213.

truth that exists in itself? In that case, the difference [between faith and speculative philosophy] lies only in the form after all, and can only be found in this: that faith regards the union of human nature with the divine as a truth which is revealed only historically, and which is dependent on the historical appearance of Christ; speculation, however, regards it as the truth which exists in itself, which was given by the essence of the spirit itself, and which, although it came to consciousness through the mediation of history, nonetheless in no way coincides in content with its historical appearance, nor with the form which it has in this appearance.

What reason, then, could the Hegelian philosophy of religion have to place the truth which exists in itself on the same level with a form which, from its perspective, can only be regarded as a form demanded by the needs of sense-certainty?[46] And if (with good reasons) faith is for this philosophy a transformation of the sensual given into the spiritual, why should it stop halfway and not continue this process of transformation until everything that can be distinguished from content as mere form is eliminated by the pure content of the idea, and form and content finally merge into one another? While on the one hand, then, it is claimed that in faith itself content and form are already two essentially distinguished elements, it is maintained on the other hand [720] that knowledge, since it distinguishes the content of faith from its form, possesses this content in a different form than faith does, and precisely for that reason absorbs the content itself.

Thus, in order to prevent this absorption from taking place, no distinction between content and form may be assumed in faith itself; form and content are indivisibly connected. The truth of the content simply cannot exist in any other form than in the original one, i.e., the one which is external and historically given, with which faith has immediately received its content as well. Any elevation above this form immediately posits a split between form and content; the archetypal Christ is placed above the historical one, and the split, once begun, moves through its process until, finally, the pure content is also the pure form in the bare idea.

For this reason, the main question we are dealing with is always just the following: whether the opposition between faith and knowledge is absolute or relative. If the opposition is absolute, then all truth falls to faith alone, since it is the first to have truth as its content. There is, in that case, no knowledge distinct from faith, and for the same reason no philosophy of religion either, since philosophy of religion, because of its nature as the philosophy *about* religion, takes up the content of faith in a form otherwise than faith does. But if that opposition is relative, then accordingly, the difference between the form and the content is recognized as well, and thus the philosophy of religion cannot be denied the right to carry through this distinction and opposition all the way to its uttermost end. This complete development is provided by Hegel's philosophy of religion, which brings us back to the claim above that the separation of the historical and the ideal Christ, which philosophy of religion has made its task from its [721] very beginning onward, comes to perfection in [Hegel's philosophy].

The ideal Christ of Hegelian religious philosophy is himself no longer the archetypal figure of Schleiermacher's *Glaubenslehre*, but rather the pure idea, the unity of the finite and absolute spirit as the truth which exists in itself. But while the person of the God-man (in the sense in which faith takes him as historical truth) diverges into two completely opposed extremes—the single individual

---

[46]*Sinnliche Gewissheit*. Cf. Inwood, *Hegel Dictionary*, 154–5: "In Hegel the words [*gewiss* and *Gewissheit*] usually have a subjective sense, and he constantly stresses that certainty does not guarantee *truth* in either the usual or Hegel's sense: *sensory* truth is contrasted with the truth apprehended by *perception*."

on the one hand, whose human condition is utterly sublated, and the pure ideality of truth on the other hand—it is precisely in this way that the most room is won, in the wide space in between, for the truly historical Christ. If the God-man in himself is the unity of the divine and the human—humanity united with God—then the historical Christ is humanity uniting itself with God in all its members, together making up the living body of Christ, realizing the concept of religion, and striving from earth up to heaven. It is in humanity, Christ's community continually growing and continually receiving into itself the fullness of the spirit, that Christ, the God-man, ever present in history's living truth and actuality, celebrates the eternal victory of life over death, the eternal feast of his resurrection and ascension. This philosophy of religion thus does not lack for a thoroughly concrete concept of the historical Christ.

CHAPTER THREE

On the Idea of a Philosophy of Religion

FROM: BDR, 368–73
TRANSLATION: BEATA AND MATTHEW VALE

Following his publication of *Die christliche Gnosis* in 1835, Baur had to defend his work against a variety of critics. The following extract is taken from a lengthy journal article Baur published in the Hegelian *Zeitschrift für speculative Theologie*, edited by Bruno Bauer. Its main purpose was to respond to some early reviews of Baur's book. Among them was a piece by the obscure theologian and pastor, Friedrich Rudolf Hasse, published earlier in the same journal. Hasse's review was written from a Hegelian point of view and raised the following concern. If, according to Baur, Gnosis is philosophy of religion, what does that mean for the relationship of philosophy and theology? In *Die christliche Gnosis* Baur called Gnosticism the Christian philosophy of religion but at the same time sought to distinguish Gnosis from philosophy by observing that speculative ideas are only found there in connection with the historic religions, paganism, Judaism, and Christianity.[1]

This may seem a quibble but touches on a problem at the center of Baur's theological work. How can the historical and philosophical dimensions be brought together in theology? From his earliest career, Baur had acknowledged that history without philosophy remained to him "dead and dumb," but he was also conscious that his ideal was threatened by one-sidedly speculative approaches to philosophy as much as it was shunned by positivist historians. Hasse's review therefore touched a nerve and forced Baur to define more clearly than elsewhere his understanding of the philosophy of religion and explain its relationship to speculative theology and the history of dogma. The latter is of particular interest given that Baur at the time was intensely engaged in this area publishing monographs on the doctrine of reconciliation (*Die christliche Lehre von der Versöhnung*, 1838) and on history of the Trinitarian and Christological dogmas (*Die christliche Lehre von der Dreieinigkeit und der Menschwerdung Chisti*, 1841–3) before bringing out, in 1847, his *History of Christian Dogma* (*Lehrbuch der christlichen Dogmengeschichte*). The relatively small article, therefore, shows Baur's attempt to clarify the conceptual relationship between some of his major fields of research.

ON THE CONCEPT OF THE PHILOSOPHY OF RELIGION

[368] The term philosophy of religion can be taken in three different meanings. In its previously accepted sense, philosophy of religion was understood to signify all that was otherwise counted as

---

[1] Cf., e.g., DCG, 19.

part of so-called natural religion, or natural theology: the development of the concept of religion and of those doctrines that were commonly differentiated from the positive content of Christianity as knowable by reason, such as doctrines about God, freedom, and immortality. This kind of philosophy of religion wishes to have nothing to do with the concrete content of positive religions; rather, it seeks to adhere to that which every revealed religion seems to have as its necessary presupposition, the general and abstract which, while as such comprising its own self-contained domain, receives its determinate meaning and content only from the addition of revelation. Wolff's well-known *Theologia Naturalis* was the first philosophy of religion of this kind believing it possible to draw a determinate dividing line between the natural and the supernatural, between the rational and the supra-rational.[2] Even today, all those who differentiate between reason and revelation in the same manner and understand by revelation only what is absolutely supernatural and supra-rational cannot determine the concept of the philosophy of religion in any other way.

But since this rigid, absolute opposition can no longer be maintained in its original sense, the very elimination of the dividing line which strictly separated the two areas of rationality and revelation had to lead to the expansion of the concept of philosophy of religion. There then seems to be no reason why the concept of the philosophy of religion [369] should not also include whatever must by reason be recognized as belonging to the essential content of revealed religion. Consequently, the history of the philosophy of religion would also have to extend itself to include the whole series of efforts by which reason or philosophy from the earliest times on sought to arrive at a clear articulation of the teachings of the Christian faith.

Since there can hardly be a notable movement in the history of Christian theology that is not based on viewpoints and presuppositions ultimately rooted in a specific philosophical stance, it is easy to see what a large field the history of the philosophy of religion comprises. The whole history of Christian theology inasmuch as it concerns the development of Christian dogma; by far the largest part of the so-called History of Dogma would be the main subject of this history of the philosophy of religion.

As narrowly delimited as the philosophy of religion would be in the first sense [mentioned above], as broadly extended would it be in this latter sense. But it is precisely this that has to be seen as [the consequence of] an inappropriate, overly vague determination of the concept, a determination from which the concept retreats to its natural boundaries of its own accord. Just as surely as our habits of speech already, and not without good reason, distinguish Christian religion from Christian dogma, with equal certainty is there every good reason to delimit the domain of philosophy of religion more narrowly, and accordingly assign to Christian philosophy of religion only the Christian religion as its object, just as Christian theology in the strict sense can only have Christian dogma for its object. But as soon as one speaks of the "Christian religion," one adopts, by using this name and concept, a viewpoint from which the Christian religion appears on a par with the other religions which Christianity has as its presuppositions, and subordinated to the same general [370] concept under which they, too, belong.

What, then, is the Christian philosophy of religion in its most proximate and most immediate concept other than the reflection on the relationship between Christianity and the two religions preceding it, paganism and Judaism? [What is its task other than] the determination of this

---

[2]Christian Wolff (1679–1754), *Theologia naturalis scientifica pertractata* 2 vols. (Frankfurt: Renger'sche Buchhandlung, 1736–7).

relationship on the basis of the concept of religion? This concept individualizes itself in the positive, historically given religions, thereby dividing itself into the moments it initially contained within itself, in order to come to its full realization.[3] The concept of religion itself, the determination of its essence, is the real object of the philosophy of religion in general, but next to this general task, Christian philosophy of religion is especially concerned with the relation between the Christian religion and the concept of religion itself. This relation, at the same time, cannot be separated from the analogous one between the other two religions and their common concept. A relationship is thereby posited between the idea and its appearance, a relationship of the concept to its moments, through which the entire domain thus circumscribed receives its determinate boundaries.

It is the concept of religion that cleaves itself, that moves out of its being-in-itself,[4] in order through this movement to return to itself. However, the contradiction articulated by Mr. Hasse[5] intervenes at this point:

> There must also be an immanent knowledge of Christianity, i.e. one which knows Christianity from the perspective of the inmost point of its own interior, without having mediated itself through reflection on other forms of religion. Now, this is precisely what is understood as theology in a higher sense of the word. And so there follows on the one hand, from the absoluteness (autarchy) of its object, the independence of theology; on the other hand, however, there follows also the necessity that philosophy of religion only truly [371] perfects itself as theology. For if the idea of religion, the real, concrete idea, is the principle of philosophy of religion, and if this idea only reveals itself completely in Christianity, then ultimately its consideration of previous religions already takes Christianity as its point of departure, and thus the defense of this presupposition, the demonstration of the principle, i.e. theological gnosis, has to be the ultimate and the highest towards which philosophy of religion strives.[6]

Immanent knowledge of Christianity in this sense, I believe, must be denied. If Christianity is to be known from the perspective of the inmost point of its own interior, it can only be known as the absolute religion; however, Christianity will not be known as the absolute religion based on itself [alone], but only based on the idea of religion. If Christianity, as the absolute religion, is the real, concrete idea of religion itself, [then] what I have to know most of all is what the idea of religion is in itself in order to be able to know as identical with the idea itself that [thing] in which the idea of religion has become real and concrete. But the idea of religion itself cannot in its absoluteness come to consciousness without consciousness of the moments by which the absolute idea mediates itself to itself. Now, if these moments are the positive, historical religion with which Christianity itself,

---

[3]Baur here uses Hegelian terminology. The "moments" of the concept (*Begriff*) are originally contained in it "in themselves" (*an sich*) but have to be divided into separate phenomena in order to lead to the concept's full realization. Cf. M. Inwood, *Hegel Dictionary* (Oxford: Blackwell, 1992), 58–61; 133–6. See also Note on Text and Translations under "concept" and "in itself/for itself."

[4]*Ansichsein*. See Note on Text and Translations.

[5]Friedrich Rudolf Hasse (1808–62), historical and philosophical theologian, influenced by Hegel and Philipp Marheineke. Cf. W. Krafft, "Hasse, Friedrich Rudolf," *Allgemeine Deutsche Biographie* 10 (1879): 754–5. Online: https://www.deutsche-biographie.de/pnd101740824.html#adbcontent. Accessed on August 19, 2021.

[6]Friedrich Rudolf Hasse, "Review of F. C. Baur, Die christliche Gnosis oder die christliche Religions-Philosophie in ihrer geschichtichen Entwicklung," *Zeitschrift für speculative Theologie* 1, no. 1 (1836): 209–44, here: 212–13.

according to its historical appearance, is on a par, then it will always be through reflection on these forms of religion that one becomes aware of Christianity as the absolute religion.

If we could not compare Christianity to paganism and Judaism, then even if the absolute value of Christianity were the same, then at the very least our consciousness of this value would not be the same as it now is, inasmuch as this consciousness is mediated through a comparison of the relative value of the other two religions with the absolute value of Christianity. We cannot therefore rightly go on speaking of the independence of [372] theology in this sense; theology remains dependent on the philosophy of religion.

But as far as the relationship between the philosophy of religion and theology is concerned, one can indeed admit the necessity that philosophy of religion truly perfects itself as theology, without admitting as its consequence the essential identity of both, as Hasse presupposes when he claims that the history of theology is an integrating part of the philosophy of religion. Even speculative theology is philosophy, insofar as it proceeds philosophically; only its actual object is not the Christian religion, but Christian dogma. Christian dogma, however, distinguishes itself from the Christian religion in that it takes the same object, which in the concept of religion is grasped from the general perspective of the unity of the whole, and divides it as much as possible, considering it according to the diversity and interrelation of the individual parts. Speculative theology has for its necessary presupposition the results of the philosophy of religion; its subsequent task, however, is to develop the concept of Christianity as the concept of the absolute religion, as obtained by the philosophy of religion, across all dogmas, which together constitute the content of the Christian dogma.

Philosophy of religion and speculative theology are thus most intimately intertwined, and it is difficult to draw a definite border line between the two, but why should they not be allowed to be distinguished from one another on the basis of their concepts, in the same manner as the general can generally be differentiated from the specific, and the establishment of a principle from its particular development? But this differentiation is of very special importance for history for the categorization of the historical material.[7]

Every period in Christian theology has its own principle, determined by the degree to which the idea of Christianity in its entirety [*im Ganzen*], the concept of the absolute which is supposed to be recognized in Christianity, is more or less purely grasped. The more Christianity is identified with paganism and Judaism, the more its absolute character recedes; the more it is counterposed in its peculiar difference against both paganism and Judaism, however, the more its absolute character comes to the fore. This principle, however, which determines our conception of Christianity in its entirety, does not usually emerge directly, but only indirectly through the influence it exerts upon theological disputes and movements. For this reason, it is one of the most important tasks of the historian to reduce all significant phenomena to the principle underlying them and to demonstrate by the course of their development to what degree the absolute concept of Christianity has been realized in them or not. In this sense, the particular history of Christian dogma also has a very close relationship indeed with the philosophy of religion, but how much would the history of the latter have to lose sight of its actual task if it were to follow in their entire progression all theological disputes and negotiations which might offer something of significance to it? There must, then, be

---

[7] Throughout his career, Baur was concerned with the problem of periodization of Christian history. Cf. EkG, e.g., 249–63; ECH, 242–53. See Chapter 10 in this volume.

a point where the domain belonging to the history of philosophy of religion separates itself from the domain belonging to the history of dogma, and it can be proper only to the latter to pursue the particulars, whereas the former comes to halt at the general and reserves for itself all that stands in closer connection with the principle that determines the entire character of a period.

PART TWO

History of Dogma

CHAPTER FOUR

Introduction to the History of Dogma

FROM: LD, 1–19
TRANSLATION: ROBERT F. BROWN AND PETER C. HODGSON,
IN: HCD, 47–60

Footnotes from the original edition are prefaced by [Baur]; Hodgson's footnotes are prefaced by [PCH]. All other footnotes are by the editors.

Baur lectured repeatedly on the history of dogma, and in this *Lehrbuch* or "textbook" of Christian dogma, he reflects on the nature and tasks of the history of dogma, and offers a distillation of his lectures in an overview of doctrinal development and change. The most notable feature of Baur's approach is his dialectical periodization of the history of dogma. Employing the historical dialectics he had learned from Schelling and Hegel, Baur approached history as the self-mediation of the spirit, and so saw the history of dogma as a process in which the vibrant unity and diversity of the unfolding intellect or spirit were on full display.

This selection presents the first sections of the introduction, in which Baur offers an account of the disciplinary location of the history of dogma—akin to church history and dogmatics, though it revels in flux where the latter wishes for fixity—and sketches the aim of the history of dogma as offering an account of that process of mediation. Dogma proceeds in history by means of the mediation of antitheses. Even the large-scale periodization of the history of dogma is subject to such antitheses and their mediation, and here Baur proposes a threefold division into periods:

> The period of the *ancient church* is the period of Christian religious consciousness itself producing dogma, and in dogma objectifying itself and knowing itself to be immediately one with dogma—in other words, the substantiality of dogma. The period of the *Middle Ages* and of *scholasticism* is the period of a consciousness withdrawing from the objectivity of dogma into its own subjectivity, and confronting dogma in the interest of intellectual reflection. The period since the *Reformation* is the period of a free self-consciousness dissociating itself from dogma and in principle opposing dogma, yet also producing it anew from itself, more deeply and inwardly.

The rest of Baur's book follows that typology, subdividing it further into smaller periodizations marked by antithesis and resolution.[1]

---

[1] For more detail, see the excellent, full introduction by Peter Hodgson in HCD, 1–37.

HISTORY OF CHRISTIAN DOGMA

§ 1 The Task of the Introduction

[1] <47> The introduction to the history of Christian dogma must above all develop and establish the *concept* of the history of dogma. Its task, therefore, is in the first place to identify the position that the history of dogma, as part of Christian theology, assumes in the organon of theological disciplines; then in the second place to determine both the object with which it must be occupied and the method according to which it should be treated. If its horizon is further widened, the question cannot be avoided as to how the history of Christian dogma, as part of the general history of development of the human spirit, relates to the history of philosophy that is kindred to it. Finally the introduction has the task of indicating more precisely at what level of scientific development the history of dogma as scientific discipline (*Wissenschaft*) has arrived in the most recent times. This can be achieved only by means of a retrospective study of its origins and of the various forms through which it has since passed, as well as by means of a critique of the most important treatments of the history of dogma as a whole or in significant individual parts. The concept of the history of dogma consists in all these elements together, as also does the intellectual interest in it.

§ 2 The Relationship of the History of Dogma to Church History and to Dogmatics

The history of Christian dogma is an integral part of the organon of theological disciplines, and it assumes [2] in the latter a position of great importance to the <48> extent that significance is attached to its object as the substantial foundation on which Christianity rests in its entire temporal appearance. The theological disciplines to which it is most closely related in respect to its object are church history and dogmatics.

If one understands by *church history* the history of the development of Christianity in general, to the extent that it can be portrayed in its temporal appearance as such only in the form of the church, then the *history of dogma* can relate to church history only as a part to the whole, as was of course historically the case when it was first uncoupled from church history and configured as a special theological discipline. But insofar as the concept of the church can also be taken in a narrower sense, such that "church" signifies what concerns the members of the Christian community in their external shared existence as bound together in the unity of a social whole, one can divide church history in the broader sense into two special areas. The first of these, church history in the narrower sense, would encompass Christianity as oriented to the external world and political life; while the second, history of dogma, would be concerned with its inner world of thought. Thus considered, history of dogma would not simply be set to one side: instead a certain precedence could be claimed for it insofar as the inner is the presupposition of the outer, and the latter can be conceived only from the former. In any event, even when it is regarded only as a part of church history, history of dogma is constituted independently in its special arena in such a way that it can be considered only as a self-enclosed theological discipline and can be treated scientifically only from this point of view.

While history of dogma as *history* is most closely bound up with church history, as the history of *dogmas* it stands in the closest relationship with *dogmatics*. The object is the same; only the form in which it appears is different. Dogmatics is merely the flow of the history of dogma coming to rest from its movement. Dogmatics strives [3] to bring to a standstill what in the history of dogma is always only changing and varying—delivering it, as it were, from the stream in which it is always moving to the shore of firm ground, but struggling in vain against the pressure of the waves. The history of dogma shows itself here in its overwhelming power. It is the fate of dogmatics to devolve repeatedly into the history of dogma. Schleiermacher's definition of dogmatics[2] shows how dogmatics itself can hardly disavow an awareness of the relationship in which it stands to the history of dogma.

§ 3 The Object of the History of Dogma

<49> The word *dogma* in the linguistic usage of antiquity referred to philosophical teachings, to ordinances and commandments; and in the New Testament to prescriptions of the Mosaic law; thus it signified in general what is absolutely valid and utterly binding.[3] In this sense it was [4] not unusual on the part of the earlier church theologians to call Christianity, as divinely given truth, simply "dogma" or "the divine dogma," and to speak of its dogmas. So long as there were only dogmas and not yet dogmatics, one distinguished between dogmas as the theoretical aspect and actions as the practical aspect.[4] If *kērygma* was distinguished from *dogma*,[5] the latter was said to be related to the former as the outer to the inner, but the distinction had no further significance for the linguistic usage of the word *dogma*.

Accordingly, dogmas are the doctrines or propositions in which the absolute content of Christian truth is expressed in a determinate form. We speak of a history of *dogmas* (*Dogmen*), not simply

---

[2][Baur] Friedrich Schleiermacher, *Der christliche Glaube*, 2nd edn. (Berlin: Reimer, 1830), 1: 125 (§ 19): "Dogmatic theology is the science that systematizes the doctrine prevalent in a Christian church *at a given time*." [*The Christian Faith*, ed. H. R. Mackintosh and J. S. Stewart (London: T&T Clark, 1999), 88.] Schleiermacher remarks (p. 126) that this has only rarely been expressly acknowledged, but it is self-evident from the fact that the great number of dogmatic works following one upon another can for the most part be explained only in this way.

[3][Baur] *Dogma* means literally only "opinion" or "belief." But, as the belief in an exactly formulated expression of what is to be regarded as valid and binding on another, the word designates in the strict sense what is utterly valid. Only in this way can we grasp the general concept that lies at the basis of the various meanings of the word, as when it is used of the *decreta* of philosophy (Cicero, *Quaestiones academicae* [= *Academica*], 4.9 [Ed. sic! but in reality 2.9]; Seneca, *Epistulae* [*morales ad Lucullium*], 95 [Ed. sic! but in reality 94]), and, in the New Testament itself, of the laws of Moses (Eph 2:15, Col 2:14), the decisions of the apostles (Acts 16:4), and the decrees of the emperor (Acts 17:7). It is also to be taken in this sense when Marcus Aurelius writes, *tauta soi arkeitō, aei dogmata estō*, "may these be sufficient for you, may they always be *dogmata*" (*Meditations*, 2.3). Thus what dogma is, it must remain: it has absolute validity. This validity is also expressed quite naturally in the form in which the validity of dogma is articulated, and the concept of a specific form is altogether very much part of the word. Regarding the content of the Christian faith, *dogma* is not therefore Christian teaching in its original and still indeterminate sense as *logos tou theou*, word of God, but rather already in a specific wording or formulation, in respect to which the undeniably human aspect of the form must be distinguished from the divine content subsisting in itself. That dogmas are quite simply dogmas, despite all claims to authority, the unavoidable conclusion that was not entirely foreign to even the ancient church theologians. *To tou dogmatos onoma tēs anthrōpinēs echetai boulēs te kai gnōmēs*, "the word 'dogma' means the council and judgment of men," remarked Marcellus of Ancyra according to Eusebius, *Contra Marcellum*, 1.4[.15–16], in opposition to the appeal to the dogmas of the fathers. There existed also a *dogmatikē technē*, a skill, of physicians; and the opinions of philosophers and decrees of the Senate were called dogmas.

[4][Baur] Cf. Cyril of Jerusalem, *Catecheses* [*ad illuminandos*], 4.2. In addition to *dogma* and the *akribeia tōn dogmatōn*, the accuracy of dogmas, reference is also made to the *ethikon meros*, the part from habit, and *ēthikē didaskalia*, moral teaching, as in Gregory of Nyssa, *Epistula* 6 [Ed. = *Epistula* 24.2], and Socrates, *Historia ecclesiastica*, 2.44[.4]. The separating out of the ethical belongs to the concept of dogma from the beginning.

[5][Baur] Cf. Basil of Caesarea, *Liber de spiritu sancto*, 27[.66].

of Christian dogma in general; and we mean thereby to say that the history of dogma, as indicated by its concept, is concerned with the content of Christian doctrine explicated as completely as possible. Insofar as possible at a specific time, the whole content of dogma must <50> be laid out in all its details in the consciousness of the historian of dogma. Only then is it possible to go back to the beginnings from which dogma has developed in its diverse shapes.

It of course belongs to the concept of our discipline that, as a history of dogmas, it is concerned with dogma in all its distinctions and with all its possible differences of opinion. This [5] already implies that the object of the history of dogma can be dogma in the full range of its course over time, that is, in all the particular forms it has assumed from the earliest to the most recent times. Had one sought to fix a point prior to the final moment of its development into the present—for example, had one sought to stop with the completion of the confessional and doctrinal systems—this would just be an arbitrary point because in history itself there is only a continuous process, one that does not come to a conclusion in any system. Since our discipline ought to bind together and mediate past and present to the fullest extent, it can see its limits set only as the two opposing points between which it moves—the points where the historical movement either has not yet started at all or has not yet gone any further. On one of these sides only a fluid distinction is found between the history of dogma and dogmatics, since it can only regard present-day dogmatics as the result of what precedes it, as a new moment of an ongoing movement. Likewise on the other side it cannot delimit itself so firmly from biblical theology, so-called, in such a way that its domain must begin only where the domain of biblical theology ends. Even if it must accept as the unshakable ground of all historical movement the substantial content of Christian consciousness that is connected to and identical with the person of Jesus, at the same time the original Christian teaching itself is only given to it through the mediation of the New Testament authors—in whose portrayal may already be perceived the kernel of differences that become so pronounced in subsequent developments. Thus, even on the soil of biblical theology, the history of dogma must at least stand freely, going as far back as it can find differences. The demarcation of a special field of biblical theology only means that one seeks to reserve a free scope for the special investigations that the originating period, contained in the canonical writings, requires. Thus, just as on the one side the history of dogma flows into dogmatics and loses itself in the latter, so also on the other side it has its starting point [6] in New Testament theology: it finds its element in the entire multitude of phenomena that lie in this wide field (insofar as they are concerned with dogma); it is the element that mediates these two extreme points with each other.[6]

---

[6][Baur] August Neander's statement in his history of Christian dogma is very strange: that history of dogma finds one of its two boundaries in the portrayal of the present condition of the church, a portrayal that would be the task of statistics (*Die christliche Dogmengeschichte*, ed. J. L. Jacobi, vol. 1 [Berlin: Wiegandt und Grieben, 1857], 8).

Regarding the relationship of history of dogma to New Testament theology, under no circumstances can the teaching of Jesus be assigned to the content of history of dogma: his teaching cannot be conflated with the concept of dogma, precisely defined. The teaching of Jesus is the object of the history of dogma only in the form of its historical development. In this respect, consider what a historian of dogma such as J. K. L. Gieseler offers as the teaching of Jesus: it must be regarded as the first link in the history dogma (*Dogmengeschichte*, ed. E. R. Redepenning [Bonn: A. Marcus, 1855], 12, 29–30). The more one attempts to grasp the teaching of Jesus in an abstract and fundamental way, and the more barren and empty the whole picture of the teaching of Jesus thereby becomes, all the more is it evident that this teaching is not the first link in the history of dogma—that it, like dogma, must have a more specific form of historical development. Thus the teaching of Jesus is not dogma as such but instead is what the history of dogma just presupposes—the universal and essential form of Christian consciousness, which lies at the basis of and presides over the whole development of dogma—and which can be taken up into dogma only in the form in which it has obtained its more specific formulation in the field of New Testament theology. [Ed.: Baur makes the same point at greater length in his *Lectures on New Testament Theology*, ed. Peter C. Hodgson, trans. Robert F. Brown (Oxford: Oxford University Press, 2016), 94–148].

<51> The object of the history of dogma is dogma as it enters into distinctions, increasingly splitting and subdividing itself, taking on determinate form in individual dogmas, and modifying itself in turn in diverse ways. It is already evident from this specification of its object that one should attend not merely to the multiplicity of its distinguishable elements but also to its self-contained unity found in the concept of dogma. In the same circumstance in which dogma proceeds outwardly and, in order to explicate just its own content, seems to want to separate into an endless multiplicity of determinations, it also has in turn an internal drive to hold itself together in a unity, to concentrate itself in a secure point. Dogmas in general arise in such a way that, out of the original and as yet undivided one [substantial] dogma, [7] now this and now that characteristic form is highlighted with a particular significance, seeking in the unity of the whole to shape itself as much as possible into a dogma of its own; and thus gradually one dogma follows upon another. So, with every dogmatic specification of this sort, the more powerful is its drive to an organic configuration, all the more so is there a striving to constitute itself as the substantial midpoint of a unified whole that ought to subordinate all other dogmas to itself. In this fashion a system of dogmas is shaped for the first time. For, in the sequence of individual dogmatic specifications that are attaining to the particularity of their being-for-self, each of them must establish its own validity and become as it were the ruling power of a particular period until another claims the same right for itself. As a consequence a more balanced but always newly precarious and changing relationship of equally entitled elements is established.

Here we see the further consideration in regard to the object of the history of dogma that this history deals with dogmas not merely in their individuality and separateness but also as interrelated with one another. In other words, it is concerned with the form in which, depending on where the dogmatic center of gravity of an age is located, dogmas are to be seen as the expression of the collective consciousness of an age, shaping themselves in it into a more or less comprehensive whole. If dogmas as such are the object of the history of dogma, its principal object is everything in them that more deeply affects <52> an age and works most vigorously and broadly to achieve in it a common consciousness. The important position held in this regard for the history of dogma by the deliberations and pronouncements of councils and the doctrines and systems of church theologians, which for a long time were the decisive authority, is self-evident.

For the history of dogma is concerned with the multiplicity of dogmas as well as the unity of dogma, although these two elements together—as distinction in unity and unity in distinction—constitute the organic character of dogma. The systematic form of dogma results from the scientific definition of this organic character, and from this everything follows that makes up the content of the history of dogma [8] and connects the latter with the history of dogmatics.[7]

---

[7][Baur] This is the corrective to those vague statements by which the history of dogma is customarily connected to the history of dogmatics in a purely external and arbitrary fashion (compare, for example, the textbooks of Münscher and Baumgarten-Crusius [Ed.: discussed in § 6 of Baur's full work, not included here. See Wilhelm Münscher, *Handbuch der christlichen Dogmengeschichte*, 4 vols. (Marburg: In der neuen akademischen Buchhandlung, 1797–1809); Ludwig Baumgarten-Crusius, *Lehrbuch der christlichen Dogmengeschichte*, 2 vols. (Jena: Im Verlag der Crökerschen Buchhandlung, 1832)].

§ 4 The Method of the History of Dogma

Of course one cannot speak about the object of the history of dogma without dogma already being viewed as something self-moving, shaping itself in this way or that, becoming determinate in a multiplicity of forms.[8] The method that the history of dogma must pursue is drawn from this relationship of dogma to itself. It is a question not merely of *what* it portrays but also of *how* it should portray it. Answering this question depends above all on what the history of dogma is as a science,[9] and what conception is formed of it as a whole.

It has long been agreed that the content of the history of dogma is not to be seen merely as a contingent aggregate, for in this case to assume order, connection, and unity would be a completely wasted effort. Everyone concedes that a certain lawfulness prevails in the phenomena, that the unity is to be attributed not merely to the free choice of individual subjects acting in this history, but at least equally to higher causes transcending the individual. One speaks in this sense of principles, directions, and oppositions. But this does not lead to the understanding that everything that is customarily regarded as the source of the development and alteration of dogmas—such as the nature of the human spirit in general, the external conditions in which Christians find themselves, <53> the various necessities of an age, the resources one utilizes—finally is attributable to a way of picturing things in which one would have to see, in the history of dogma, only the constantly changing play of chance and free choice. What is defective in this method, or in this lack of method, is that [9] one always remains outside of dogma, does not know how to penetrate into its interiority, its concept, from which alone the various manifestations that it produces are to be conceived.

It is dogma itself that in its various specifications sets out its content and positions the content over against itself, splitting itself up internally, so that the concept, which is its substantial being itself, may be released into the distinction of its moments and then drawn back into its unity. A choice must be made: if the changes portrayed by the history of dogma are not simply a contingent and arbitrary fluctuation, then this history can only be viewed as an intellectual or spiritual process in which the essential nature of spirit itself is revealed, for dogma itself is essentially intellectual or spiritual in nature. Thus the method of the history of dogma can only be the objective nature of the subject matter itself. One is able to enter into and follow the process of development taken by dogma in its immanent movement only because there is nothing merely contingent and arbitrary here: one moment is always to be conceived in turn as the necessary presupposition of another, and everything together is to be understood as the unity of dogma's concept. Thus it is dogma itself that is understood to be *with* itself in this process, relating itself to itself in the process, in order to come to consciousness of itself by positing its content outside itself and becoming objective to itself in it.

One can say equally well, however, that the whole course of the history of dogma is the continuing process of consciousness as it thinks about dogma; and every significant alteration that occurs in the history of dogma is only another stance that the subject's consciousness assumes toward the objectivity of dogma. The basis for the fact that both of these points [the objectivity of dogma and the subjectivity of consciousness] can be asserted and are equally valid is that on both sides there is the same essential nature of spirit, an essential nature that inherently undergoes this process. On

---

[8][PCH] On Baur's viewing of dogma in this work as an active agent in history, a moving power, see the "Editorial Introduction" to HCD, 20.

[9]*Wissenschaft*. See Note on Text and Translations.

the one side it is dogma that proceeds forth from itself, becomes objective to itself, in order to open itself up for subjective consciousness and first come to its true existence in it. On the other side it is subjective consciousness itself that takes dogma into itself [10] and seeks to know itself as one with it. This is possible only on the assumption that dogma and the consciousness juxtaposing itself to it relate to each other as the objective and subjective sides of the same self-identical spirit.

On both sides the entire movement of dogma runs its course as the endless labor of the spirit that struggles with itself and strives for the freedom of its self-consciousness in the absolute content of dogma. Every new configuration of dogma is both a new moment through which dogma, in the immanent movement of its concept, determines itself, and a new effort on the part of <54> thinking consciousness to become more certain of the truth, to master more deeply and thoroughly the content of dogma. But since the content of dogma in this or that moment is scarcely exhausted in such a way that this movement comes to rest, every new stage of development in the relationship of consciousness to its object is always once again inadequate. For this very reason, the once-initiated labor of spirit can never rest: it has within itself its driving principle; the concept must move through all its moments; and the consciousness of the subject can know itself freely and be at one with itself only where content and form, object and subject, coalesce into unity. All of this rests on the assumption that dogma in itself is not foreign to the essential nature of spirit, that dogma is only spirit become objective to itself, mediating itself with itself in this antithesis of objective and subjective.

The various moments of this process, like the process as a whole, can be conceived only in terms of the essential nature of spirit. As the process of thinking spirit, it can, in accord with its nature, develop only in a series of essentially distinguished moments. All thinking is mediation of spirit with itself: what spirit is in itself it ought also to be for consciousness. On the one hand, spirit becomes objective to itself in thinking, it distinguishes itself from itself, [11] goes into distinction from itself, posits an other that is distinct from and over against itself. But on the other hand, which is equally essential, it also becomes one with itself again in this other, it draws itself back into itself from this distinction, comes together with itself. For it can be free and self-conscious spirit only in the unity of these two sides, the objective and the subjective. This double activity of spirit, this going out from and returning into self—in other words, this distinction in unity and unity in distinction—is the principle of movement by which all moments of spiritual activity are determined. Thus in the developmental course of dogma as well, the relationship of spirit to itself varies depending on which of the two sides predominates in this double-sided, mutually penetrating activity—spirit proceeding more out of itself or spirit returning more into itself—and depending on whether, in its striving to mediate what is objectively given with itself subjectively, spirit delves into itself more deeply or less deeply, in order to find its satisfaction only in that wherewith it can know itself to be truly one in the innermost ground of its nature.

If we survey the history of dogma from this point of view, we encounter in *the first centuries* a dogmatic productivity from which it is evident how the entire striving of spirit proceeds to construct itself in the form of dogma, to objectify itself in dogma, to create for itself on the basis of dogma a new world of representations that are to have for it the same truth as dogma itself, whose determinations they are. Filled and permeated by the absolute content of dogma, spirit finds its satisfaction solely in articulating for the common consciousness what dogma is in itself, exhausting its content as far as possible. What matters at this point is not so much how the individual specifications of dogma are united with thinking consciousness, but rather that in terms of their material <55> content they are available to faith and function as universally accepted statements of faith. Even though the claims of thinking consciousness cannot go unacknowledged at this time, they nonetheless take a back seat to the pressure of faith in an age living in the effusiveness and substantiality of dogma. Spirit felt satisfied with this configuration of dogma for faith: in dogma spirit had the absolute content of its consciousness in a form that it found sufficient; but at the same time dogma became for it a more and more constraining and binding [12] objective power. Faith rests on the traditional authority of the church, and the more completely faith is fixed in the teaching of the church, all the less are individuals free to stand in a different relationship to dogma than the church wants them to. While the spirit of the age may be content with this arrangement and accustom itself to the obedience of faith, sooner or later a reaction could not have failed to appear, as soon as the awareness of this condition of dependence dawned more clearly. The striving to do away with the externality of faith and to bring it closer to thinking consciousness must have awakened.

This awakening was accomplished by *scholasticism*, which set as its great task that of mediating faith and knowledge: it attempted the very rationalization of dogma. This was a quite significant progression in the development of dogma. Spirit sought to subject dogma to an internal dialectic, to become clear about how far it could take dogma into its thinking by means of its categories of the understanding (*Verstandeskategorien*), and could make itself master of dogma's content. Yet however great the effort, it resulted in the direct opposite: instead of freeing spirit from the exteriority of the dogmas of faith, as it intended, scholasticism ended with an equally great lack of freedom. The authority of the church and of church dogma bore down all the more heavily on spirit because, through the best efforts of scholasticism, the only conviction that could be obtained was that of the impossibility of a mediation between faith and knowledge. In the nature of the case, scholasticism could not arrive at any other result: so long as the truth of church dogma was the absolute presupposition, one with which thinking remained burdened, spirit could on this account attain no overarching power over dogma or extricate itself from the relativity (*Relativität*) of the antithesis. The task itself, however, one scholasticism was never able to solve, not only cannot be surrendered but, in consequence of scholasticism's outcome, calls attention to itself all the more urgently so that a solution might be sought along another path. If scholasticism's limitation and one-sidedness consisted in its always presupposing the truth of what first of all ought to be demonstrated, and in its approaching dogma only with its own abstract intellectual interests (*Verstandes-Interesse*), by whose procedures [13] it tried to make itself inwardly one with dogma, then, put succinctly, there had to come a time for a decisive break with dogma.

This rift came about through the *Reformation*. The church, which hitherto had been one, split into the antithesis between Catholicism and Protestantism; and the latter obtained its name from the fact that the believing consciousness <56> more so than the thinking consciousness of the subject had fallen into an incurable schism from church dogma and could still know itself as one with dogma only to the extent that everything clothed in the bare form of church authority and tradition had been excised from dogma as its false shape. Protestantism rested on the principle of subjective freedom and the autonomy of self-consciousness, and it could have arisen only from the subject asserting its absolute right vis-à-vis the dogma of the church. But Protestantism once again assumed an incomplete and finite form of consciousness in two respects: it encountered, in its opposition to Catholicism, a barrier that it was unable to transcend in the consciousness of the age; and it attained to the awareness of its own principle only along the path of [a strictly] religious interest. Therefore what gained currency as freedom bore within itself in turn the character of subjective caprice, one subject standing over against another with the same religious rights, although the unity of a common consciousness threatened increasingly to dissolve into the contingency of individual consciousness. With the absence of a firm principle, deeply grounded in its own universality and necessity, the freedom that was thought to have been obtained inevitably turned about into an unfreedom and bondage. From this fact the relativity of the antithesis in which Protestantism and Catholicism confronted each other can be seen clearly enough. Protestantism too constantly faced in its dogma the constraints of an authority that the freedom of its self-consciousness could not penetrate.

The further course of the same process of which Protestantism itself in its original form was a specific moment can thus only consist in the following: that in place of the religious interest that was the mainspring of the Reformation there appeared instead the interest of [14] thinking reason—the element in which the Protestant principle might be liberated from the particularity, limitation, and one-sidedness with which it had been burdened from the beginning, and be elevated to the form of an absolute principle. If there is something in the developmental history of dogma beginning with the Reformation that, as a new element, constitutes an epoch, it can only be the new relationship that theology and philosophy assumed toward each other in consequence of the impetus taken by philosophy. Truth can indeed only be one: nothing can be true in philosophy that in the final analysis is not also true in theology, and vice versa.

From this survey of the major moments in the developmental course of dogma, its major periods become self-evident. In reality, in light of the great significance of the Reformation, only two major periods might be identified: the one portraying the consciousness that mediates itself with dogma in its unity with dogma, the other this consciousness in its rupture from and reconciliation with dogma. But since the absolute significance of the Reformation is also in turn merely relative, and since scholasticism has an essentially different character from the patristic period (although it stands on the same ground <57> of faith), the whole may be divided into three major periods. The period of the *ancient church* is the period of Christian religious consciousness itself producing dogma, and in dogma objectifying itself and knowing itself to be immediately one with dogma—in other words, the substantiality of dogma. The period of the *Middle Ages* and of *scholasticism* is the period of a consciousness withdrawing from the objectivity of dogma into its own subjectivity, and confronting dogma in the interest of intellectual reflection (*Verstandesreflexion*). The period since the *Reformation* is the period of a free self-consciousness dissociating itself from dogma and in principle opposing dogma, yet also producing it anew from itself, more deeply and inwardly. Each of these three main periods may, in looking back upon the course of their development, be further divided into two particular parts. The first main period in its first half culminates in the Council of Nicaea in the year 325, the first significant point at which the development of dogma achieves a specific form; in the second half, during the fourth and fifth centuries, the range of the ancient church in its creative activity extends as far as it can. In the second main period, [15] the first centuries of the Middle Ages form a transition to a new configuration of dogma and the preliminary stage of scholasticism, whose rise and fall provides the content of what follows. The third major period portrays the principle of the Reformation, first in its distinctive character as well as its still one-sided self-limitation, and then, since the beginning of the eighteenth century, also in its striving for an increasingly free and more universal development.

Since within each of these six periods the historical material of dogma can be organized only in accord with the systematic connection of dogmas, the systematic method is linked most appropriately with the chronological in the divisions into periods. Yet each of these methods by itself is able to treat the historical development of dogma only very one-sidedly and inadequately. Also the distinction customary in recent times between a universal and a particular history of dogma—a distinction that rests on a faulty definition of the concepts of the universal and the particular—can only lead to an unmethodical treatment of the whole. The general remarks, which preface the history of each period as an introduction, can only consist in establishing the general point of view under which each period belongs, and in determining the position that it assumes as this particular moment of the universal historical process. To be linked with these remarks is the statement of the most general data ancillary to the historical thematization.[10]

§ 5 The Relationship of the History of Dogma to the History of Philosophy

[16]<58> The history of dogma stands in a very close connection to the history of philosophy. It cannot be otherwise considering the relationship of philosophy to religion and theology. The history of philosophy, however, is not merely a so-called auxiliary discipline to the history of dogma, which one needs because a correct understanding of the development of the truths of faith is not possible without taking the influence of philosophical schools into account; rather, the two disciplines stand in such an essentially internal relationship to each other that they both can be conceived of as just elements of one and the same spiritual process. The history of dogma, like the history of philosophy, is also the history of human thought about and investigation into what is inherently existent and true [*das an sich Seiende und Wahre*], the absolute—but with the distinction that in the history of dogma thought is active wholly in the form of Christian dogma. But this form itself is so far from being something accidental that it can be explained only from its self-grounded necessity in the essential nature of spirit, just as, ultimately, even all philosophical thinking only exists in this form. In this regard the same relationship exists between the history of dogma and the history of philosophy as exists between church history and world history.

Just as there is a period in church history when world history itself becomes church history, so that there is nothing world-historical that church history does not draw into its own sphere and determine by its principle, so also is it the case with Christian dogma. It draws all thought into itself, captures it wholly under its own form, so that finally there is no intellectual movement independent of church dogma, [17] all thinking takes place within the faith of the church, and the history of dogma is thus to a very large extent only the portrayal of free thought consolidated

---

[10][Baur] In the identification of periods the historians of dogma deviate in part quite widely from one another since they do not always keep in view the truly salient points of development and pay too little attention to the distinction between history of dogma and church history. How can one designate Origen as representing a new epoch and period, in the way that Hagenbach and Neander do, when he is still only part of the rapid movement of that time of transition to the Council of Nicaea? Or how can one allow the second period to run from the Council of Nicaea to the beginning of the iconoclastic controversy [eighth century], as Gieseler does, and the third period to run from the latter to the Reformation, without even briefly recalling—in addition to the iconoclastic controversy, which is relatively unimportant for dogma—the great significance of scholasticism for dogma? Even less, moreover, have the historians of dogma hitherto made it their business to comprehend the whole developmental process of dogma from the point of view of an inwardly connected spiritual process, progressing from one moment to the next. It makes little sense, for example, to designate one period as apologetic and another as dogmatic-polemical, or one as stagnant and another as critical. See § 6 [not included here] for further discussion of these matters. [Ed.: For Neander and Gieseler, see the previous notes. See also Karl Rudolf Hagenbach, *Lehrbuch der Dogmengeschichte*, 2 vols. (Leipzig: Weidmann 1840–1; 4th rev. ed. 1857); ET *A Text-Book of the History of Doctrines*, trans. C. W. Buch, rev. Henry B. Smith (New York: Sheldon & Co., 1861–2)].

within the faith of the church and extinguished in it. Christian dogma could obtain this significance only in virtue of the fact that it is the dogma of Christianity as the absolute religion and revelation. But Christianity itself was able to become the absolute religion only <59> because it raised to universality the particular forms of the existence of spirit in the pre-Christian age, in paganism and Judaism, Greek philosophy and Jewish religion. The age in which Christianity appeared is characterized above all as one in which the impulse of spirit, everywhere evident, breaks through, and divests itself of, everything limited, national, and particular—an impulse to enter into a freer and broader sphere and to obtain its true self-consciousness in the universal that discloses itself in this sphere and alone counts as what is true and essential.

Whereas Greek philosophy, aware of its own subjectivity, broke down internally, the Alexandrian philosophy of religion emerged from this striving as a new form of spiritual life in which the Jewish national consciousness transcended its ancient limits and opened itself up to the inspired ideas of Greek philosophy, ideas that became reconfigured in Jewish religion as philosophy of religion.[11] But with all this striving to fill the old forms with a new spiritual content, which was supposed to be accomplished especially by means of allegory—an artificial tool albeit one begotten from the exigency of spirit—people could not get beyond the narrowness of positive, traditional Judaism. The combined result, in which all these efforts, so far-flung and so profound, spreading out so widely and penetrating so deeply, came to completion, was the fulfillment of a time that was prepared for, and ripe for, the appearance of Christianity. From the collapse of external life, from the denial of everything national and individual, from the whole ungodly, unethical, and lawless world that prevailed at the time of the appearance of Christianity, spirit increasingly drew back within itself. It did so by means of this inwardization and deepening within itself, in which it renounced everything simply false and finite inherent in its own [18] subjectivity, for the sake of becoming receptive to a new revelation of divinity—a revelation whose determinate principle, forming a new world view, could only be the pure objectivity of the absolute idea of God and the unconditional surrender of the humanly finite to the divine that this idea of God called for.

This is the reason why Christianity appeared in the world not as philosophy but only as religion. Yet, in the form of religion, of revelation, of an immediately self-positing absolute God-idea, it appeared as something utterly given to which subjective consciousness was able to be related only by believing. Thus Christian dogma has its starting point in faith, and it is itself faith in the mode of representation (*Vorstellung*).[12] All thinking connected with dogma, no matter how freely it might otherwise be exercised, has its final determining principle only in faith. This is the great difference between the history of philosophy <60> and the history of Christian dogma. Thinking takes a wholly different shape in the history of Christian dogma: it is a thinking that exercises itself only in the form of faith and whose entire orientation is one of deepening itself ever more in the content of faith, of objectifying itself in faith until this content is exhausted as far as possible and the free, fluid motion of thinking itself has, as it were, turned into a stable system of strictly self-enclosed dogmas defined on the basis of an external authority, into a thinking become external and transcendent to itself.

---

[11] Baur has in view here Aristobolus and particularly Philo of Alexandria.

[12] [PCH] On faith and representation, and the distinction between representation and thought (or concept, *Vorstellung* and *Begriff*), see G. W. F. Hegel, *Lectures on the Philosophy of Religion*, ed. Peter C. Hodgson, trans. R. F. Brown, P. C. Hodgson, and J. M. Stewart, 3 vols. (Oxford: Oxford University Press, 2007), 1: 385–413.

Just as it is based on the nature of spirit itself that the history of philosophy at a specific point passes over into the history of the philosophy of religion and of theology, or into the history of Christian dogma, and in this way the free thinking of philosophy becomes a thinking that is bound to faith, exercising itself only within faith, and developing itself in faith, it is thus no less based on the nature of spirit that philosophical thinking should once again free itself from this bondage. It makes this transition of its own accord, in order to pull itself out of this objectivity that it sees as an alien and transcendent world set over against it, and it withdraws into itself. It rids itself of the dogma of the external shape, in which spirit has deprived itself of its own self, in order that dogma be led back to its inner ground residing in the nature of spirit. [19] This is the process that has indeed taken place in regard to Christian dogma, and here we emphasize in particular just the relation of this process to the history of philosophy. Just as the history of philosophy eventually lost itself, and was submerged, in the history of dogma, so that there was no longer any thinking independent of dogma, now thinking once again wrested itself free of dogma, turned to its own elements, to clear proof, so that its surrender to faith was said to have been only a transient form of consciousness. Following upon the Reformation and the general revolution [in thought], the consciousness of the time had right away become freer and more deeply self-penetrating, and philosophy rediscovered itself and built its own arena of operation. Once again there was a history of philosophy taking its starting point from itself and producing its content from itself. And soon enough philosophy and theology had to come into the closest contact with one another.

CHAPTER FIVE

On the Doctrine of Reconciliation in Its Historical Development

FROM: CVL, 1–20
TRANSLATION: BEATA AND MATTHEW VALE

Baur published *Die christliche Lehre von der Versöhnung* in 1838. The book shows him at the height of his intellectual and creative powers covering an immense amount of material in over 750 pages, controlled by a clear theological and philosophical vision.

Baur starts from the notion, developed in detail in *Christian Gnosis* (1835), that the reconciliation of God and world, the infinite and the finite, is at the heart of the history of religions. Had *Gnosis* been an attempt to show that Christianity was the absolute religion by virtue of the Incarnation, which brings together God and world in a human person, *Doctrine of Reconciliation* seeks to demonstrate how this newly found idea developed throughout Christian history. Baur thus moves from the history of religions to the history of dogma, but this does not, for him, involve a change of methodology. The rules that governed the emergence of Christianity from earlier religions continue to apply to its own, later history.

Baur's fundamental intuition is that the Christian doctrine of reconciliation involves two aspects: *objectively*, God must be reconciled with humanity; *subjectively*, human beings must gain an awareness of this new reality. The objective side is explained through interpretations of Christ's sacrificial death, whereas the subjective side focuses on faith and religious transformation in the individual. According to Baur, both sides are ultimately needed to express the full truth of Christianity, but such an understanding was only accomplished as the result of a historical process whose previous phases one-sidedly emphasized the objective and the subjective side.

On this basis, Baur was able to integrate debates on the atonement from the Patristic era to his own time into a straightforward, historical schema. A first period, which lasted until the Reformation, saw the predominance of the objective side; in a second one, from the Reformation to the Enlightenment, the subjective side moved to the fore, while a third one, beginning with Kant, increasingly succeeded in bringing the two together.

Baur made no apology in *Versöhnungslehre* for his use of Hegelian concepts. The history of dogma is not just a succession of human attempts at grappling with a difficult problem; it is the history of the spirit itself which moves through stages before coming to its own fulfillment. That said, during Baur's work on the book, Hegel's philosophy became increasingly controversial. Baur was implicated in these debates if only on account of his close relationship with David Friedrich Strauss. *Versöhnungslehre* contains a passionate defence of Hegelian theology in general and Strauss' Christology in particular.

Baur's *Versöhnungslehre* was arguably the first attempt to write a full history of the atonement and has remained a point of reference for later writers although many have sharply diverged from Baur's interpretation of that history.

The following extract is Baur's Introduction to the book.

THE DOCTRINE OF RECONCILIATION IN ITS HISTORICAL DEVELOPMENT FROM THE EARLIEST TIME TO THE MOST RECENT ONE

Introduction

[1] The doctrine of humanity's reconciliation with God, or of God's reconciliation with humanity, is at the center of every religion. The general task of religion receives in the concept of reconciliation its deepest and most inward meaning. If the object of religion in general, according to its general concept, is the relationship between God and the human being, then this relationship also appears to be a double one: on the one hand, as humanity's difference from God, and on the other hand, as humanity's unity with God. The relationship between these two sides provides religion with the movement by which it separates into its moments and by which it mediates itself to itself.

Now, if this mediation, by which the concept of religion realizes itself, consists in interpreting the separation of humanity from God as one which is sublated[1] and neutralized in the unity with God, then the concept of reconciliation describes the point where one moment passes over into the other one: the doctrine of reconciliation is supposed to prove and create a clear awareness of the possibility of passing from separation from God into being one with God.

From this it is already clear that everything that differentiates the various religions from each other as essentially distinct [2] primary forms of religion, and everything that establishes them in a specific relationship with one another, must become apparent especially in their teaching on reconciliation.[2] Christianity differs from paganism and Judaism in the following way: it is only in Christianity that humanity's relationship with God in its double aspect becomes the opposition between sin and grace, where the mediation of this opposition constitutes the essence of redemption. In the same way, it is only in Christianity that the concept of reconciliation has its truly real meaning.

The unity between the divine and the human, which has only come to be revealed in Christianity in the person of the God-man, also implies the concepts of redemption and reconciliation: the same concept which in the other two religions is only expressed as an indefinite desire and as a veiled intuition, and insofar as it has risen to the level of consciousness, only presents itself in a very imperfect form, has its perfection and reality only in Christianity, in the redemption and reconciliation instituted by Christ as the God-man. The deeper discord of human beings with themselves and with the Godhead, the separation of the finite from the absolute spirit, intervenes in human consciousness—a discord which religion must bring to human consciousness and cannot leave entirely unheeded in any of its various forms—the more the idea of reconciliation acquires

---

[1] *Aufgehoben.* See Note on Text and Translations.
[2] Here, the connection with *Christian Gnosis*, published three years earlier, comes into view. See DCG, 67 [Chapter 2 in this volume].

its true meaning, and the more deeply its reality must be established: the reality which is the unity of the human with the divine on which the reconciliation between the human being and God is founded.

In paganism, or in those forms of archaic religion where the human being still entirely stands in the immediacy of nature, the idea of reconciliation, too, is still entirely present in the form of an immediacy which does not yet allow the concept of reconciliation to find its [true] place, because wherever an opposition has not yet emerged in all its pointedness, there is no mediation [3] or reconciliation either. From the purely objective perspective of this form of religion, a perspective which mediates and conceals God-consciousness through the consciousness of nature, the essence of reconciliation can only consist in an individual's union[3] with the life of nature, in the dissolution of subjective, personal feeling into objective, universal nature-feeling, in the devotion of one's entire being to the all-encompassing One, in whom the limiting consciousness of finitude is sublated. This basic, universal feeling differs in the varied forms of archaic religion, depending on their character, but the highest reality in which human beings reconcile themselves and know themselves elevated above the finite and toward the absolute is only ever their unity with nature and with physical being and life in general.

When religious consciousness elevates itself to a faith in mythical gods who break away from the ground of natural life and exhibit the character of human personality, a further step takes place by which the idea of reconciliation is able to approach human consciousness. The unity of the divine and the human, however, inasmuch as it is exhibited in the contemplation of these mythical creatures, is merely a representation of representational and pictorial unity, as implied by the concept of the mythical itself. For this reason, it still remains entirely external to man and has not yet become a concrete reality of life and an inner truth of consciousness.

In Jewish religion, religious consciousness elevates itself above nature, and the human being stands as a free, personal creature *vis-à-vis* the free, personal God who stands above nature, but [otherwise] nature-consciousness is [simply] replaced by the consciousness of nation and state, whose essential form is the law. The law, revealed by God and given to his people as the necessary norm of the theocratic [4] relationship, is therefore also mediator of the relationship between human beings and God by which the union of God and humanity is conditioned. This law, therefore, determines both the individual will and the collective consciousness of the civic association which constitutes God's community. To the extent that the individual, as a true member of the theocratic state, sees themselves included in its pleasing unity and transferred into the sphere in which alone the immediate being of God (which as such is hidden) reveals itself in the form of the divine will, they also know themselves as united with God and reconciled with him. There can, however, be no true ontological unity[4] between human beings and God while the law is the mediator between God and humanity.[5] Thus far, the nature of the law, which confronts human beings in its abstractness as the absolutely commanding norm, automatically ensures that human beings, conscious of their constantly renewed guilt, are more separated from God than they are united with him. Judaism was fairly suitable in awakening in human beings the need for reconciliation by raising to awareness the importance of the law as applicable not only to the external but also the internal, moral life. Yet it

---

[3]*Einswerdung*. Literally: becoming one.
[4]*Wesenseinheit*.
[5]Cf. Gal. 3:20.

appeared as all the more impotent truly to fulfill the need it had thus aroused. Whatever may be able to overcome the still existing, abstract opposition between God and humanity, is in Judaism only a presentiment pointing to the future, leading beyond the sphere of Judaism.

Therefore, the legalistic nature of Judaism implies its essential destiny, [namely,] to preach to itself its own end [5] in the spirit of prophecy. This is the side of Judaism in which it is primarily connected with Christianity. How little it is otherwise able to elevate itself above the outwardness of the pagan concept of reconciliation, however, is evident from the idea of sacrifice which both have in common and which is even developed into a more determined form in Judaism. The idea of reconciliation based on human guilt-consciousness and the idea of a personal God, then, does not properly come to consciousness in paganism; in Judaism, on the other hand, it does not go beyond the consciousness of its need. It is only in Christianity that this idea comes to its true reality as the fulfillment of a need increased to its highest point. Everything that elevates Christianity to the standpoint of the absolute religion, in opposition to paganism and Judaism, at the same time has the closest relation to the idea of reconciliation. As Christianity is, therefore, the religion of redemption in and through the actualized idea of the unity of divine and human in the person of the God-man, so it is also the religion of absolute reconciliation. In what way has it objectively carried out the only true, eternal reconciliation, however, and how it has subjectively realized it in every individual? This is the new task of the spirit which has received into its subjective consciousness the absolute content of Christianity and mediates it for this [historic religion].

The two concepts of redemption and reconciliation are commonly distinguished by referring the concept of redemption primarily to the concept of sin, the concept of reconciliation to the concept of guilt. Thus, Schleiermacher defines [6] the relation of the two terms in the following manner: "the redeemer assumes [believers] into the power of his God-consciousness by means of his redemptive activity," that is, his sinlessness and perfection. By means "of his reconciling activity," [he assumes them] "into the fellowship of his unclouded blessedness."[6]

Since the concept of punishment is also part of the concept of guilt insofar as guilt can only be eliminated by punishment, this differentiation [of the concept of guilt] can easily give rise to the opinion that the concept of reconciliation applies accordingly to what is external (i.e., to the elimination of the relationship of punishment which applies to the external circumstances of the human being), while the concept of redemption applies to what is interior (i.e., to the interior liberation of the human being from the power and rule of sin). But this determination of the difference between punishment and guilt only considers the human perspective, and the relationship between the two concepts is in fact the reverse. Even though human beings are liberated from the power and the rule of sin and transferred from the state of sinfulness into the state of sinlessness and perfection, where sin only clings to them as a disappearing reality, it does not immediately follow that they are also relieved from the guilt of the sin which once held sway over him.

Thus, seen from this perspective, the relationship between sin and guilt is the relationship between that which disappears and that which remains, which only gives rise to the question of how human beings, having emerged from the state of sin, could also be conscious of their liberation from the guilt of sin. Since the elimination of the guilt of sin can only be conceived of as a divine act, the grounds for its possibility can only be established in the idea of God. So, while at first

---

[6]Baur paraphrases here from §§ 100 and 101 of Schleiermacher's *Glaubenslehre*. Cf. Friedrich Schleiermacher, *The Christian Faith*, trans. H. R. Mackintosh/J. S. Stewart (London: T & T Clark, 1999), 425, 431.

the concept of redemption only addresses what is actually the case, [i.e.,] the arrangement made by God in sending the redeemer, by which such a spiritual change is to be effected in the human being, [7] by virtue of which human beings pass from the state of sin into the state of grace, the concept of reconciliation addresses the metaphysical question, one which, so to speak, establishes the reality of redemption itself in the first place: how can the possibility of the elimination of guilt, which by its nature is bound up with sin, be understood based on the idea of God? Thus, in reality, reconciliation is the interior [part] and redemption, the external [part], is its necessary prerequisite.

Human beings can only consider themselves redeemed insofar as they also know themselves to be reconciled with God: the power and the rule of sin with all its consequences is only eliminated for them if they are also permitted to know that the guilt of sin, even in relation to their earlier life, preceding their entrance into the grace of redemption, has been lifted from them. Since reconciliation and redemption are only special moments in the unity of the divine and the human, depicted in the person of the God-man, the relationship between these two concepts, developed here, must also be discernible in the person of the God-man. This is expressed in the peculiar meaning which Christ's death has acquired in Christians' general consciousness, insofar as it is recognized as the objective fact which precedes the acceptance of the individual into the community instituted by the redeemer, by which human beings as such are reconciled with God.

If Christ is redeemer by his entire appearance and efficaciousness, he is reconciler by his death. In the letters of Paul the Apostle, Jesus' death is understood in its pure objectivity as that which comes first, as something which is simply a given, which faith must have as its prerequisite [8] if it is supposed to be able to develop its full, interior power in the individual. The fact that this is the case in the letters of Paul the Apostle must be regarded as the first communication of the religious consciousness about the different moments which need to be differentiated here and as the specification of the concept of reconciliation in its difference from the concept of redemption. If the individual is to obtain a truly blissful consciousness of divine grace, reconciliation as such needs to have been accomplished as the elimination of the collective guilt which burdens everyone.

But not even Paul the Apostle gives us a developed theory on how this connection must be conceived and in what sense the death of the redeemer is the mediating element by which the reconciliation of human beings with God is accomplished. In every passage where the Apostle speaks about the meaning of Jesus' death, either only the general fact is expressed that we have been reconciled with God through him, or this fact is addressed from a perspective that does not permit [us] to understand precisely the inner, mediating connection between the external fact of his death and the divine act. Let us take, for example, the passage in 2 Corinthians 5:14-15, which is indisputably one of the most important ones in the series of passages in which the Apostle speaks of Jesus' death: "If one died for all, therefore all died. And he died for all, that those who live should no longer live for themselves but for him who died for them and was raised again." Herein lies undoubtedly the concept of vicarious death. His death is the death of all, but only in the following way: that which presents itself as a unity and principle in Christ is realized in all others. But how many mediating ideas are still missing here for a developed theory of [vicarious] representation![7]

Thus, here too, New Testament doctrine is presented to us in great, objective unity, as a simple expression of religious consciousness which, while still lacking determination in every regard, excludes any subjective one-sidedness. It had to be the task of the developing dogma to allow the

---

[7] *Stellvertretung.*

directions contained in this unity to emerge in the variety of their moments and to bring them to consciousness in order to elevate all that was in itself still [9] undetermined to its determined dogmatic concept and expression.

When we develop the concept of reconciliation, we can already conceive of different directions which could emerge from it and come to historical existence. This concept encompasses three moments, each of which accentuates itself in its peculiar way. As a divine act, reconciliation can be understood as a process which takes place in the essence of God himself, by which God mediates himself to himself in order to realize the concept of his essence. Considered from this purely objective perspective, humanity's reconciliation with God takes place not only for their own, but also for the sake of God himself; human beings are reconciled with God when God reconciles himself with himself, when he accepts human beings back into unity with him from being at variance with him, as a moment in his own life process. This entirely objective perspective is contrasted by an entirely subjective one, where human beings perform the reconciliation with God exclusively within their own self-consciousness and know themselves to be reconciled with God as soon as they believe to have removed from within themselves the obstacle which opposes their reconciliation with God. Just as in the former perspective reconciliation is an entirely divine act, it is a purely human one in this latter perspective: the reality of reconciliation, guaranteed by human self-consciousness, becomes a subjective certainty to human beings and thereby also has divine reality for them.

Between these two moments, each of which records an equally one-sided concept, falls the third moment, which primarily emphasizes the concept of mediation in the concept of reconciliation, and which places the whole meaning of the act of reconciliation into a historical fact. This fact in its external historical objectivity is considered the necessary prerequisite for the act of reconciliation that takes place between God and humanity. [10] Even though in those first two perspectives the relationship between Jesus' death and the act of reconciliation is not to be misunderstood either, his death as an external fact still has a subordinate meaning *vis-à-vis* the interior truth of the concept of reconciliation. It is only from this third point of view that a higher, independent meaning can be given to Jesus' death.

In what sense his death, seen from this perspective, should be considered the necessary prerequisite for the reconciliation between humanity and God is in turn a question which can be answered in various ways. If Jesus' death is at all to be considered the condition without which human beings cannot be granted the certainty of their reconciliation with God, it is more a merely external relationship of the same kind as the one that took place in the sacrifices in pre-Christian religions, insofar as by these means human beings were supposed to procure the consciousness of their reconciliation with God. Jesus' death as a reconciliatory death is a sacrificial death by being linked to the act of reconciliation between human beings and God, just as it had been the case with the sacrifices of pre-Christian religions. The higher value of his sacrificial death compared to the sacrifices of ancient times lies exclusively in the moral meaning bestowed upon it by the person of the redeemer. Thus it is really only a moral connection which confers upon Jesus' death its characteristic relationship with the concept of reconciliation. The moral attitude effected by Jesus' death transfers a person into the kind of moral disposition that renders them capable of being forgiven their sins. That however does not yet clarify how the guilt which by its very nature is attached to sin can itself be eliminated, unless one either refers to God's absolute will or establishes an inner relationship between Jesus' death, which already in itself, according to its inner value, infinitely surpasses all other sacrifices, and the elimination of the guilt of sin [11] due to the absolute value of the person of the God-man who gives himself away as a sacrifice.

This sheds light on the way in which the concept of reconciliation in itself already contains different moments from which the developing dogma was able to take different directions, and such clarification is the sole purpose of the present exposition. Each of these directions contains the seed of a theory that can modify itself in different ways, and each of these theories must itself come into manifold collisions with the other theories departing from other points. The manner in which these different directions, which in themselves are all possible, have historically realized themselves and the various forms they passed through is the object of the following investigation. It shall follow the concept of reconciliation in the domain of Christian dogma through its historical existence.

This already describes its main task to continually bear in mind the relationship between the concept and its different forms of appearance. If the course taken by the Christian dogma in its historical development can be taken to be anything other than mere chance and arbitrariness, then above all the inner necessity must be shown here, too, which impelled the concept of dogma to go forth from itself in order to realize itself in its true essence through the different forms of its development. Thus, everything depends on perceiving in the various forms which dogma takes according to history not merely individual attempts at forming dogma, lined up in an arbitrary order. Rather, they must be understood based on their inner relationship with one another as moments of a movement in which one form is always conditioned by the other, and all forms taken together have their unity in the totality of the concept.

[12] The spirit in its whole temporal development progresses from objectivity to subjectivity, and from subjectivity to objectivity in order to elevate itself from the immanence of natural existence to true spiritual freedom through the various moments by which it mediates itself to itself. In the same way, the history of Christian dogma in general and of every individual dogma in particular divides itself into different periods, depending on whether the moment of objectivity or the moment of subjectivity predominates, or whether both of them are united in the higher unity of the concept and interpenetrate one another. When the divine spirit, which is revealed in humanity, has elevated itself to a new form of its historical existence, the specific content included in the concept of religion in this new form must first of all encounter the consciousness of man like an [external] object. [At this stage,] the entire religious consciousness of the human being is determined by the immediacy of objective, historical givenness. The spirit's whole tendency, then, is directed toward inscribing itself ever more deeply into the objectivity of the dogma. [This occurs] through the development of dogma as a historical fact in the historical context of its causes and effects, until it is finally reduced to the single point, from which it can be grasped as an objective, historical fact grounded in the absolute essence of God and emerging out of his essence with absolute necessity.[8] This general course of dogmatic development is nowhere more evident than in the doctrine of reconciliation, whose first period reached a determined point of its development in Anselm's theory of satisfaction in which it concluded itself into a perfect unity. All elements taken over from paganism and Judaism

---

[8]The Hegelian approach to history, on which Baur here draws, aims to overcome the distinction between the history of events and their interpretation. Consequently, when Baur here writes of the role of spirit (*Geist*) in the history of dogma, he is concurrently thinking of an increasingly fuller understanding of this development and the objective completion of it. Dogma, thus understood, reaches its perfection when it is fully and perfectly conceptualized, but this includes an understanding of its historical emergence as a necessary process.

into the Christian dogma influencing its formation—as it naturally had to happen in the first period of its development [13]—only served the purpose of guiding the emerging theory toward the goal it had to pursue by virtue alone of its original tendency.

Since this whole period was about interpreting reconciliation only in its external, historical objectivity and its absolute necessity, the fundamental concept, which was the basis for the development of this first theory, could only be the concept of justice, whose two moments, guilt and punishment, laid bare the content of dogma in the historical context, which made it possible to think its inner truth. Although the second period continued to develop the concept of satisfaction and to interpret it based on the different aspects offering themselves to dialectical reflection, doubts emerged at that point regarding its objective reality. The dogma of satisfaction, with all its consequences, faced subjective consciousness with overwhelming power; one [only] escaped it on the one hand by appealing, as it were, on the basis of absolute justice to divine omnipotence standing radically above all the divine attributes, and, on the other hand, by contrasting (at least in the divine essence itself) absolute necessity with God's absolute subjective freedom. It was in this way that the moment of subjectivity first entered the history of this dogma, but only the Reformation was able to let it come into its own.

The transition from the standpoint of objectivity to the standpoint of subjectivity expresses itself simply in the following manner. On the objective side, represented in the dogma of satisfaction, it is only God who reconciles himself with the human being. From the subjective point of view, it is the other way around. Now, the very process of reconciliation [14] is to be carried out only in the human being that is to be reconciled with God. At the same time, the moment of objectivity continues to face off against the moment of subjectivity in the same, external authority; in fact, the former even seeks to extend further the rigidity of its consequence.

For this reason, the whole period is generally a time of conflict between several theories repelling each other to a greater or lesser extent. In this conflict, which extended over a lengthy period of time, the moment of subjectivity increasingly and decidedly gained the upper hand, and the consciousness of the time more and more divested itself of the ancient ecclesial doctrine of satisfaction. As subjectivity came more and more into its own, however, its whole one-sidedness also made itself felt. Consequently, the subjective spirit was compelled to recognize the necessity of doing away with its subjective arbitrariness, bringing to its own consciousness what is universal and objective as this alone provides subjectivity with a fixed point of stability.

This happened first in Kant's philosophy which in its idea of practical reason as an absolute law-giver enunciated a new reversal of the spirit. Three subsequent moments, each closely connected with the other, constitute the same number of epochs in the progress of the dogma [of reconciliation] during the final phase of its development: the moral consciousness of Kant's philosophy; the Christian consciousness of Schleiermacher's *Christian Faith*; and the self-consciousness of the absolute spirit toward which Hegel's philosophy of religion advanced.

Thus, the latest standpoint which the dogma has assumed in its historical development is once again the standpoint of objectivity, but this objectivity is very different from the one from which the whole movement of the dogma took its beginning. It is the ideal objectivity, mediated through subjectivity. Its essence includes its objectivization in the outwardness of historical existence and its entrance into the finitude of subjective [15] consciousness, but also its return from its objectivization and finitization into itself, its infinity, and absolute truth.

From this standpoint alone, the various forms through which the dogma moves in its historical development appear as the essential and mutually conditioning moments into which the concept in its immanent movement splits itself to mediate itself through them with itself and establish the absolute truth of its objective content in the form of subjective consciousness as absolute certainty. All the forms which the dogma received in the various periods of its history, therefore, have their relative truth. Absolute truth, however, can only be claimed for that form to which all the earlier ones are subordinated inasmuch as they are moments necessary [for its emergence], whereas this form itself is not a mere moment but rather [the reality] in which the free concept, liberated from all finite limitations, unites itself with itself.

Based on these determinations, the history of the dogma [of reconciliation] automatically divides itself into three main periods:

1. The period from the earliest time to the Reformation, the period of predominant objectivity in the emerging theory of satisfaction. The figure of Anselm of Canterbury splits this period into two parts. The first part really only contains the preparation and the transition to the theory of satisfaction; the second presents the theory of satisfaction in its perfection, but also the opposition against it which arose directly alongside it.

2. The period from the Reformation to Kant's philosophy, the period of increasingly predominant subjectivity. It is also divided into two parts of rather unequal duration. In the first part, which lasted from the Reformation until the middle of the eighteenth century, [16] the two moments of objectivity and subjectivity confront each other on the same footing in the various theories that came into conflict with each other [during this time]. After the middle of the eighteenth century, however, there began a time of increasingly predominant, one-sided subjectivity.

3. The period from Kant's philosophy up to the most recent times, the period of subjectivity turning itself back toward objectivity. The three moments named above divide this period, of short extent but very rich in content, into three parts.

A dogma which stands in such close relation to the essence and character of Christianity as the teaching on reconciliation was always regarded as an essential basic teaching of Christianity. But if we survey the entire temporal progression of Christianity, we can also see a notable difference between the two outermost boundaries of Christianity in this respect. The development of dogma begins at a very extrinsic and unessential point, which was subsequently no longer recorded as a special moment in Christian consciousness; even though the development of dogma then moves closer to the real center of Christianity, nonetheless, what is essential about reconciliation is merely placed in a single, specific fact; but finally, the concept of reconciliation is defined in such a way that it coincides with the concept of Christianity and the God-man. The concept of reconciliation is truly and entirely adequately expressed only in this essential equation with the absolute content of Christianity itself. In this process of reducing the exterior to the interior, the individual to the universal, the spirit's effort shows itself throughout all the changing ages and forms: its effort to seize for itself the objective content of dogma and to penetrate it in its entire compass with the power of self-consciousness.

[17] Even though a critical history of Christian dogma is generally a task yet to be completed, it is nevertheless disconcerting that a Christian doctrine as essential [as the doctrine of reconciliation] has so rarely been the subject of special investigation. In terms of richness, it is in no way inferior to the historical development of any other doctrine, and it permits us to track the development of Christian dogma more clearly and more determinedly than most other dogmas do. The reason may to some degree be that there has never been an ecclesial disagreement which would have especially

directed attention to this doctrine and to the opposing views connected with it. At any rate, the works of predecessors on the history of this teaching are partly exceedingly unimportant and partly confined to a relatively short period of time, such as the scholarly writings of Cotta[9] and Ziegler.[10] The writing of Bähr does not go beyond the period of the first three centuries.[11]

The spirit of their treatment, however, which largely consists in extraneous sequences of pertinent passages and their philological explanations, is evidenced by Ziegler's repeated complaint about the Church Fathers' excessive curiosity (who [, he says,] have robbed the pure Christian doctrine of reconciliation [18] of its innocence and entangled it in a series of audacious hypotheses and ideas unworthy of the Godhead[12]) and by the reassurance which Bähr repeatedly finds in every church father of the first three centuries [by noting] that he supposedly did not yet know about the *satisfactio vicaria*,[13] either.[14]

Always the same unmanly timidity in the face of everything threatening to rob the faith of its immediacy, expressing itself at so many turns! As if it were a great misfortune to address the difference between the different moments, which are the necessary determinations of the concept, and to enter into the oppositions of which the spirit must become aware sooner or later if it is not to be cut off from the living movement toward its inner truth and spiritual freedom—a scenario, however, which the spirit has all the power within itself to overcome. What the general treatments of the history of dogma have to offer is on the whole equally irrelevant. In this regard, the well-known work of Denys Petau does not even have the value of a rich collection of material,[15] and the more recent textbooks on the history of dogma by Augusti,[16] [19] Münscher,[17]

---

[9]Johann Friedrich Cotta (1701–79), Lutheran theologian. Cf. Christian Palmer, "Cotta, Johann Friedrich," *Allgemeine Deutsche Biographie* 4 (1876): 526–7. Online: https://www.deutsche-biographie.de/pnd116689676.html#adbcontent. Accessed on August 19, 2021. Baur's reference is to Cotta's "Dissertatio quarta, historiam doctrinae de redemptione ecclesiae, sanguine Jesu Christi facta, exhibens," in Johann Gerhard, *Loci Theologici*, ed. J. F. Cotta, vol. 4 (Tübingen: Cotta, 1765), 105–32.

[10]Werner Karl Ludwig Ziegler (1763–1809), Lutheran theologian. Cf. Heinrich Klenz, "Ziegler, Werner Karl Ludwig," *Allgemeine Deutsche Biographie* 45 (1900): 190–2. Online https://www.deutsche-biographie.de/pnd116988134.html#adbcontent. Accessed on August 19, 2021. Baur's reference is to Ziegler's "Historia dogmatis de redemptione," Göttingen 1791, in *Commentationes Theologicae*, ed. Johann Kaspar Velthusen et al., vol. 5 (Leipzig: Barth, 1798), 227–99.

[11]Karl Wilhelm Christian Felix Bähr (1801–74), Reformed theologian. Cf. Hermann Erbacher, "Bähr, Karl," *Neue Deutsche Biographie* 1 (1953): 520. Online: https://www.deutsche-biographie.de/pnd11937515X.html#ndbcontent. Baur's reference is to Bähr's *Die Lehre der Kirche vom Tode Jesu in den ersten drei Jahrhunderten* (Sulzbach: Seidel'sche Buchhandlung, 1832).

[12]Footnote omitted.

[13]Bähr's concern for this idea was evident even from the subtitle of his study. The Church's teaching on the death of Jesus in the first three centuries was "presented with specific reference to the doctrine of vicarious satisfaction."

[14]Footnote omitted.

[15]Denis Pétau (Dionysius Petavius) (1583–1652), Jesuit theologian. Cf. Michael Hofmann, *Theologie, Dogma und Dogmenentwicklung im theologischen Werk Denis Petaus* (Bern: Peter Lang, 1976). Baur's reference is to Pétau's *Opus de theologicis dogmatibus. De incarnatione* XII, 6, 1, in vol. 4.2 (Paris: Cramoisy, 1650), 171.

[16]Johann Christian Wilhelm Augusti (1772–1841), Lutheran theologian and orientalist. Cf. Friedrich Nitzsch, "Augusti, Johann Christian Wilhelm," *Allgemeine Deutsche Biographie* 1 (1875): 685–6. Online: https://www.deutsche-biographie.de/pnd116381086.html#adbcontent. Accessed on August 19, 2021. Baur's reference is to Augusti's *Lehrbuch der christlichen Dogmengeschichte*, 4th ed. (Leipzig: Dyk'sche Buchhandlung, 1835), 360–8.

[17]Wilhelm Münscher (1766–1814), Reformed church historian. Cf. Heinrich Holtzmann, "Münscher, Wilhelm," *Allgemeine Deutsche Biographie* 23 (1886): 22. Online: https://www.deutsche-biographie.de/pnd124728030.html#adbcontent. Accessed on August 19, 2021. Baur's reference is to Münscher's *Lehrbuch der christlichen Dogmengeschichte*, 3rd ed., ed. Daniel von Coelln, 2 vols. (Kassel: Krieger, 1832–4). In a lengthy note, Baur claims it "goes without saying" that his dismissive judgment would not apply to Münscher's full *Handbuch der christlichen Dogmengeschichte*, 3 vols. (Marburg: Neue akademische Buchhandlung, 1797–1802).

Lentz,[18] et al. display their superficiality and their triviality regarding the present doctrine at least as much [20] as they do elsewhere or even to a higher degree. Despite the many excellent notes and comments it contains even [on the doctrine of reconciliation] the learned work of Baumgarten-Crusius, too, in the extremely limited space it devotes to such a comprehensive doctrine, lingers partly in generalities, partly gets stuck in individual details without providing a clear and vivid conception of the main moments in the process of the development of this dogma in its entirety.[19] For this reason, there is still a broad and abundant field of research here for every historian aware of the task of our time.

---

[18] Carl Georg Heinrich Lentz (1798–1867), Lutheran preacher. Baur's reference is to his *Geschichte der christlichen Dogmen in pragmatischer Entwickelung*, 2 vols. (Helmstedt: Fleckeisensche Buchhandlung, 1834–5), esp. vol. 2, 58–65.

[19] Ludwig Friedrich Otto Baumgarten-Crusius (1788–1843), Lutheran theologian and philosopher. Cf. Ernst Henke, "Baumgarten-Crusius, Ludwig Friedrich Otto," *Allgemeine Deutsche Biographie* 2 (1875): 162–4. Online: https://www.deutsche-biographie.de/pnd116091568.html#adbcontent. Accessed on August 19, 2021. Baur's reference is to Baumgarten-Crusius, *Lehrbuch der christlichen Dogmengeschichte*, 2 vols. (Jena: Crökersche Buchhandlung, 1832), esp. 2:1152–71. In a note, Baur further adds a reference to August Neander's *Geschichte der christlichen Religion und Kirche*, vol. I/3 (Hamburg: Perthes, 1827), 1065–70 [NB: This seems to be a mistake as Neander discusses soteriology in the next section, on pp. 1070–75]. For a full bibliography, Baur refers to Christian Daniel Beck, *Commentarii historici decretorum religionis Christianae et formulae Lutheriae* (Leipzig: Dyck'sche Buchhandlung, 1801), 518 [*sic*, but rather, 521–55].

CHAPTER SIX

On the History of Trinitarian and Christological Doctrine

FROM: LDM 1:III–XXIV; 868–78
TRANSLATION: BEATA AND MATTHEW VALE

Baur published *The Christian Doctrine of God's Triune Being and the Incarnation of Jesus Christ* in three volumes between 1841 and 1843. Running to a total of over 3,000 pages, this is easily Baur's longest single work. By all accounts, it is an *opus magnum*. The first volume takes the reader to the Council of Chalcedon (451); the second covers the time until the Reformation with a special emphasis on the scholastic period. The final volume offers a full discussion of the modern period ending in Baur's own present.

Dreieinigkeit evidently continues the trajectory begun with *Christian Gnosis* and the *Doctrine of Reconciliation*. Having concluded in the former of those works that Christianity is the absolute religion because it reconciles spirit and nature, the infinite and the finite, in the person of the God-man, Baur then turned to the history of dogma in the *Versöhnungslehre* to show how the doctrine of atonement developed throughout the history of Christianity. The *Doctrine of God's Triune Being* continues this line of enquiry, as Baur emphasizes at its outset. Inasmuch as the reconciliation of God and world stands at the center of the Christian religion, its two main dogmas must be seen as the essential intellectual outgrowth of this principle. Two generations before Baur, it had been conventional among enlightened theologians to dismiss Trinity and Chalcedonian Christology as extraneous speculations; Baur's insistence on their centrality for Christianity impressively shows the radical theological transformation of the age of which Baur himself was fully conscious.

Baur was also conscious of the special role philosophers such as F. W. J. Schelling and G. W. F. Hegel had played for this change. He found there a deeper insight which decisively shaped his work: the separation of theology and philosophy since the seventeenth century was in itself of theological significance. Consequently, the third volume of *Dreieinigkeit* contains a full presentation of modern philosophy from Descartes to Kant and Hegel as one important strand without which the most recent developments could not be understood.

Doctrine of God's Triune Being is stunning in its learning. Moreover, Baur's knowledge of texts is fully matched by the ingenuity of his interpretation. And yet, it lacks the coherence of *Christian Gnosis* and the *Doctrine of Reconciliation*. Baur here does not come up with a single idea encompassing the entire developmental process. His chronological divisions seem at times dictated more by pragmatic considerations than a single, overarching narrative. Perhaps for that reason, the present work has not seen the same influence as some of Baur's other works.

The following selection offers Baur's Preface in which he defends his philosophical approach and an extract from his masterful interpretation of Augustine which brings the first volume to its conclusion.

THE CHRISTIAN DOCTRINE OF GOD'S TRIUNE BEING AND THE INCARNATION OF JESUS CHRIST

[iii]

Preface

In this volume, I follow up on my *History of the Doctrine of Reconciliation*, published in 1838,[1] with a treatment of another part of Christian dogmatic history, the dogmas of the Trinity and the Incarnation, which I thought best to treat together for reasons based in the nature of the matter itself. It is the historian of dogma's task to take individual dogmas as much as possible out of the isolated position where they have been placed by the separating and fragmenting view taken by previous theology, and to interpret them within the unity of dogma. Thus, it is really the doctrine of God and of God's relationship with the world and with humanity, as it is determined by the doctrine of the God-man, that I here for the first time make the object of a coherent, historical development. For this reason, I will not only treat these church dogmas from the speculative perspective from which the idea of God must be understood, but I will also establish a closer relationship than is common between the history of dogma and the history of philosophy in later times, where philosophy and theology separate more from one another.

[iv] I will presume that my theological position on the interpretation of Christian dogmatic history is already known [to the reader] from my writing on the doctrine of reconciliation. The latter work, however, now also imposes on me the necessity to justify my position.

The more it is my aim to give to the so-called history of dogma a deeper, scientific meaning and to understand history as what it is supposed to be for the thinking spirit, the less I can be disconcerted that my investigations in historical theology have become subject to the same opposition to which more recent, scientific theology in general has been exposed. If only this opposition would make itself heard in a more thorough and dignified manner! But when I recall the various judgments that have been passed on my earlier work, inasmuch as I have had the opportunity to learn about them, I am not sure what the true object of my apology should be. From a material standpoint, I have not been convicted of having written anything misguided or erroneous; my care in researching and utilizing sources has been acknowledged, and praise has not been withheld even from my interpretation and treatment of the historical material in general. Yet there is one thing that none of my critics can accept. After all the praise about my writings, one aspect always places the decisive weight on the side of censure and even compels some to write about me with [v] deep pains of regret: this is the fact that I am a Hegelian.[2] In these words, the whole verdict on my writings has been pronounced right away, and now it is only left for me to look at myself and consider for myself the entire, weighty content of this final judgment.

---

[1] CLV.
[2] By the early 1840s, German political and (mainstream) intellectual life had decisively turned against Hegel who was seen as the facilitator of religious and political radicalism. In Prussia, the accession of Frederick Wilhelm IV in 1840—and the appointment of Friedrich Eichhorn to the position of Minister of Culture—was accompanied by an anti-Hegelian campaign culminating in the invitation of F. W. J. Schelling to lecture in Berlin, in order to eradicate "the dragon seed of Hegelian pantheism." Cf. Gustav Leopold Plitt (ed.), *Aus Schellings Leben in Briefen. Dritter Band 1821–1854* (Leipzig: Hirzel, 1870), 35–7.

Given my own difficulty of accounting for this state of affairs, I can only thank Professor Rettberg for explaining himself in more detail on my supposed Hegelianism.³ If I remember correctly, he was the first to present an assessment of my book.⁴

Professor Rettberg finds that the main deficiency in my position, which is based in Hegelian philosophy, is that I assign to the concept⁵ the role of developing itself and mediating itself with itself. According to Professor Rettberg, speculation in the Hegelian school does not consist in the investigating [vi] thinker's examination, analysis, [and] development of the concept; instead, the concept is expected to develop itself as soon as it has received the impulse to do so. My work, he says, is the application of this method to history.

Already at this point, I must ask my reviewer if he has entirely overlooked the contradiction in which he ties himself up right away in the first sentences. The essence of Hegelian speculation is supposed to consist not in the thinker's development of the concept, but in the concept's development of itself; and yet, he immediately ascribes precisely this concern of the self-developing concept to me. Am I the concept? And if Mr. Rettberg is so fair as to not take me for the concept, will he not allow me to be considered as an investigating thinker who develops the concept? In what, then, does the difference between my purportedly Hegelian method and that other one consist? How wrong and incorrect his understanding of everything is right from the beginning!

After such a beginning, Mr. Rettberg progresses to the accusation that the potency of the concept, which I introduce into the history of dogmas and which can only be based in Hegelian philosophy, offends Protestantism's most essential demands. According to Mr. Rettberg, not only are the teachers of the Church, whose work brought about the development of dogmas, in danger of being robbed of their significance as intelligent, independent individuals, debased to the level of mere vehicles by which the process of the self-propelling [vii] concept realizes itself, but we are left with the more difficult question: What should be the position of this newly conceived potency of the concept with its absolute necessity in relation to the ecclesiastical authority which has to be attributed to the dogmas? What Protestant position in the assessment of dogmas would ignore the normative authority of Scripture, and instead accord to the concept such absolute independence that it would not be in need of [Scriptural] support?

Here, too, one can see immediately how insufficiently Mr. Rettberg is informed about the true state of the matter. What does he understand the normative authority of Scripture to be? Only if this authority is absolute in a strict sense would he be right, because only in that case would the whole content of dogma constitute such an inseparable unity with the teaching contained in Scripture that any movement of the concept would be excluded. But in that case, nothing would be left but plain dependence on the letter of Scripture. Whether or not this is Mr. Rettberg's opinion, in any case he will not be able to deny that an absolute authority of Scripture in this sense—the sense in which the oldest Protestant theologians claimed it in the most obvious contradiction to the Protestant principle, the free right to Scriptural research—has long been broken down at so many points that it can no longer be seen as a generally accepted doctrine.

---

³Friedrich Wilhelm Rettberg (1805–49), Lutheran theologian and church historian. Cf. Julius August Wagenmann, "Rettberg, Friedrich Wilhelm," *Allgemeine Deutsche Biographie* 28 (1889): 273–4. Online: https://www.deutsche-biographie.de/pnd116449837.html#adbcontent. Accessed on August 19, 2021. Rettberg's review of CLV appeared in *Göttingische gelehrte Anzeigen* 1839, no. 178–80: 1769–90.
⁴Footnote omitted.
⁵*Begriff*. See Note on Text and Translations.

But if [viii] normative authority is not absolute, if it is not the absolute concept itself, then it is reduced to a mere moment of the concept, and the form of dogma which is conditioned by the presupposition of Scripture's absolute authority is itself only one of the various forms which must be referred to and subordinated to the unity of the concept. This variety of forms is a fact of history and for this reason, Mr. Rettberg's objection merely returns us to the question of why, irrespective of Scripture's normative authority, there are so many forms of dogma that do not recognize Scripture's normative authority as absolute. Mr. Rettberg will surely not want to blame *this* fact on me and my method.[6]

The lever, Mr. Rettberg goes on to say, that I use to introduce the self-development of the concept is the opposition between the subjective and the objective. This opposition is supposed to provide in broad outline the net (what a comparison!) into which the individual phenomena are to be inscribed.

That the Middle Ages up to the Reformation should be the time of immediate objectivity, he continues, is in some respects accurate, but it is also too general and unspecific.[7] However, he says, [the period's] established character does become sharply apparent at one point in this period—Anselm's theory of satisfaction. But, he asks, is this feature sufficient to affix it to the entire period? What a violent move, he says, to include almost an entire millennium [ix] in a classification that is entirely alien to it, and whose character only emerges by the genius of one thinker after the period has run its course! But how was Mr. Rettberg able to completely overlook the fact that Anselm's theory is similar to the preceding one, which I prove throughout the entire development?

Had he not already completely misunderstood the expression, "immediate objectivity" (insofar as he does not seem to suspect that this objectivity is a merely a representational one), it would have been impossible for him to miss that reconciliation, both on Anselm's theory and on the previous one, is just the same exterior, historical course of events arranged by God, and that it is still in itself the same act, proceeding from and returning to God, regardless of whether the devil is ascribed a more or less substantial prerogative in it. The fact that the devil's position becomes different is only necessary progress, but the theory itself remains entirely the same, as can be seen from the fact that the process constantly moves around the same basic idea—the idea of justice.[8]

Thus, it is only our critic's inability to think his way into the issue, and to differentiate between the different moments of it, that lets him see nothing but a violent move here. Mr. Rettberg provides equal proof for his unpracticed hand at dealing with philosophical concepts, or else his lack of philosophical education, in everything he says about Pelagianism, my omission of which he believes

---

[6]From Baur's engagement with Möhler, it is clear that he saw the traditional Lutheran version of the scripture principle as problematic and its reinterpretation in Schleiermacher and others, an important Protestant contribution toward a rapprochement with Catholicism. GKP, 429–32 (and the note on 432–4). Cf. Chapter 13 in this volume.

[7]For Baur's characterization of the first period of the history of the doctrine of reconciliation as "objective," cf. CLV, 12–13 (see Chapter 5 in this volume).

[8]Rettberg had, quite reasonably, objected that the so-called "ransom theory" characteristic of the Patristic period was fundamentally different from Anselm's theory of satisfaction: "Baur Review," 1777–8. Rettberg did not, however, suggest how this development should be understood instead. The transition from the Patristic to the medieval view has remained a problem of historical theology. The most celebrated twentieth-century attempt to offer an alternative account is Gustaf Aulén's *Christus Victor: An Historical Study of the Three Main Types of Atonement*, trans. A. G. Hebert (Eugene, OR: Wipf and Stock, 2003). According to Aulén, the Patristic view, reasserted by Luther, is the "classical" one, as opposed to the "Latin" (Anselm's) and the "subjective" (Abelard's) theories. It is, however, fair to say that Aulén's theory is far from being the consensus view today.

is the greatest mistake in my treatment [x] of my topic; or rather, it was my intentionally ignoring Pelagianism (what a suspicion!) which alone made this treatment possible. It is precisely what I call the subjective interpretation of reconciliation, Mr. Rettberg says, and which I only attribute to the second period since the Reformation—namely, that human beings complete their reconciliation with God in their own consciousness—which is definitively an issue in Pelagianism in all its forms.[9]

According to Rettberg, only my complete silence about Pelagianism would have allowed me to present the objectivity of that era as so absolute. Insofar as Pelagianizing elements are present anywhere, he says, the character of subjectivity can also be assumed; and insofar as the medieval Catholic Church pursued that Pelagian tendency, it completely forsook objectivity in connection with this dogma. What else could monasticism be, he asks, than an attempt to effect reconciliation with God on the basis of subjectivity? Do not asceticism and chastisement amount to the same? The thirteenth century, precisely the high point of the Middle Ages, where according to my theory full objectivity should have reigned, gives rise to the penance of flagellation, which must truly be considered subjectivity in its most complete form in this domain.[10]

Moreover, what is to be said about good works, about the treasury of superabundant merits as the basis for the Catholic theory of indulgences?[11] Mr. Rettberg claims that it is incomprehensible how I could have overlooked these decisive parts of medieval dogmatics—or how I would have dared remain silent about them, given they immediately [xi] confound my entire theory. The whole passage is extremely remarkable. Mr. Rettberg is once again so certain of his claims that he repeatedly accuses me of having malevolently concealed parts [of history] for which I had no use—a presupposition, which, if it were true, would mean that mine was a very sad case, even apart from my Hegelianism!

According to Mr. Rettberg's opinion, flagellation at the high point of the Middle Ages is the most complete instance of subjectivity and for this reason also the most perfect opposite to Anselm's theory of satisfaction! If only Mr. Rettberg had thought of the well-known song of flagellators, *Stabat mater dolorosa*, and of verses such as *Crucifixi fige plagas/Cordi meo valide,/ Nati tui vulnerati, Tam dignati pro me pati,/Poenas mecum divide—Fac me plagis vulnerari/Cruce hac inebriari*, and so forth[12]—they would have shown him the connection between flagellation and the dogma of satisfaction in all its starkness.

But of course, even just seeing such a connection requires more experience in philosophical thought than Mr. Rettberg seems to possess. He thinks everything is subjective that takes place in the human being, and all that is subjective in a certain respect must be absolute subjectivity itself. And so, for him the flagellator, oppressed before God's wrath and submitting to the *flagella Dei*, is entirely [xii] on one and the same level of most complete subjectivity as the speculative thinker who recognizes only in the spirit's self-consciousness the power to make what has happened *un*happen.

---

[9] Rettberg, "Baur Review," 1779.
[10] Ibid.
[11] The theory of the treasury of merits was developed in medieval theology to account for the Church's power to issue indulgences. Christ and the saints had amassed more good works than were needed for their own salvation. This "treasury" was administered by the Church which, on this basis, could offer remission from temporal punishment to its members. Cf. Robert W. Shaffern, "The Medieval Theology of Indulgences," in *Promissory Notes on the Treasury of Merits: Indulgences in Late Medieval Europe*, ed. Robert N. Swanson (Leiden: Brill, 2006), 11–36.
[12] *Stabat mater dolorosa*. A thirteenth-century hymn about Mary's suffering with the crucified Jesus. Baur cites select lines from across the poem: "[Holy mother] inscribe firmly the wounds of the crucified into my heart; share with me the sorrows of your wounded child who so worthily suffered for me—make me wounded by his wounds, drunk by his cross …"

Can there be a more superficial interpretation? It is true that penance by flagellation is that part of satisfaction, effected by the God-man, which is performed on the subject. But what thinking person can overlook the fact that the necessary requirement for flagellation is the dogma of satisfaction and that, for this reason, the subject's position *vis-à-vis* the objective idea of God, as expressed in the notion of justice on which the dogma of satisfaction is based, is entirely the same as well? Is the person, who is bleeding from the scourge's strikes, bowing down before God's wrath in subservient fear, the free, self-confident subject—or rather the opposite of that?

The situation is no different with everything else Mr. Rettberg references. How extrinsic is the entire Catholic process of reconciliation, which places the reconciling power in the treasury of superabundant merits! Have the subjects not, in this respect too, completely relinquished their self-consciousness? And have they not given it to a purely extrinsic objectivity, with which they have a merely passive relationship? The process of reconciliation takes its course outside of the subject, and subjects are as little truly present or active as subjects, as they are for the actual satisfaction.

As Mr. Rettberg primarily places the essence of Pelagianism [xiii] in phenomena such as the ones mentioned, in this alone the entire testimony for which he invokes Pelagianism against me is refuted. For this reason, I cannot see how I could have made myself culpable by inadvertently or purposely failing to consider Pelagianism. But if Mr. Rettberg wants to continue claiming the relationship between Pelagianism and Augustinianism against me, it might already suffice as an answer to him that it was the doctrine of reconciliation I made the object of my investigation, not the doctrine of the relationship between grace and freedom.

For my esteemed reviewer, however, this is not yet sufficient, since for him Pelagianism and subjectivity have become identical concepts to such a degree that he also uses the same Pelagianism, by which he challenged my understanding of the older dogma, as a reason for a new, no less severe accusation. He contends that I have allowed myself to be led to the greatest misrepresentation of the Reformation principle in order merely to develop my hypothesis of the subjectivity of the Reformation.[13] If, [he urges,] the only reason for salvation lies in God's grace, as the Reformers so decidedly claim is the case; if by the doctrine of original sin the subject is also denied any part in the work of reconciliation; if everything comes down to the complete negation of subjective merit—then one would have to doubt one's wits [xiv] if after all that the Reformation was still saddled with a tendency for the subjective.

The only grounds, [Rettberg concedes,] that could seemingly still be appealed to would be the principle of justifying faith, which demands reconciliation as something taking place in the realm of the subject. [As understood by the Reformers], however, faith is, in fact, the most complete divestment of subjectivity; it is the most complete renunciation of one's own activity and joyful devotion to an alien objectivity. If one adds to this the fact that faith is only considered an effect of the Holy Spirit within us, the entire foundation has become strictly objective here too.

The supposed subjectivity could only be justified inasmuch as the principles of the Reformation might be accused of a Pelagianizing element which in the Lutheran Church would amount to that minimum of self-activity by which human beings are granted independent acceptance of the salvation they have been offered.[14] This, however, is such a subordinate point compared to the

---

[13] Rettberg, "Baur Review," 1780–2.
[14] Ibid., 1786.

entire doctrine of original sin, that, [according to Rettberg], any breakthrough of subjectivity could there be found only by a complete banishment of the Reformers' [broader] tendencies.

The claims of a school of thought, which on these grounds would seek to demonstrate in the Reformation a subjective tendency, could only be explained by their complete disregard for historical facts as such. It is all the more lamentable, he goes on, that my otherwise no doubt very diligent sense of historical interpretation on this point has yielded to [xv] presuppositions which on closer examination prove completely untenable. The concept of the subjective is, for Mr. Rettberg, far too general and indeterminate, too much a "wax nose,"[15] to be [the principle] to which the Reformation's main features could be traced back.

Even the formal Reformation principle of the sole authority of Scripture has its place only in Luther's first enthusiasm for his reclaimed evangelical freedom;[16] it was afterwards just as decisively rejected once again. (What a completely erroneous claim, and what a contradiction to the objection against me above, about the normative authority of Scripture![17]) Objectivity, [according to Rettberg,] coincides with the Anselmian and ecclesial view about dogma, whereas subjectivity is supposed to coincide with the Pelagian deviation from it. And thus, for Rettberg, the whole phantom of the self-propelling concept itself is utterly destroyed—instead, at all developmental stages of the church the objective stood everywhere alongside the subjective, as two potencies which continually accompany, and struggle against, one another.[18]

This opposition, he says, was already just as clearly developed in the fifth century between Augustine and Pelagius as it was in the sixteenth century between the Protestant[19] and the Socinian theory, or in the eighteenth century between those who followed the teaching of the Church and [those who adhered to] rationalism. Mr. Rettberg wishes to grant me the fact that, of those two directions in the interpretation of dogma, one or the other was at various times more foregrounded, and that an eternal law of the human spirit is discernible in this. [xvi] But he will do so only with the explicit provision that at that time, the other side had also made its claims as well. For this reason, the progress of the self-mediating concept understood in such a way that a form of dogma once overcome could not re-emerge is one of those forced historical moves which can never be supported by the hard facts of unbiased historical interpretation.

Thus, according to Mr. Rettberg, we have arrived at the significant result that the objective and the subjective have always existed as certainly as Augustinianism and Pelagianism are opposites which are present throughout the ages. And now the opponent's incisiveness has easily succeeded in dismantling my entire theory and historical construction, but only in the eyes of those who stand with him at the same summit of philosophical speculation.

---

[15]*Wachsnase.* A mutable and accommodating thing (or person).
[16]"Formal Reformation principle." In debates about the "essence" of Protestantism in nineteenth-century Germany, it was common to speak of two principles of Protestantism distinguishing faith as the "formal" principle from "Scripture" as the material one. It is unclear why Baur here refers to Scripture as the "formal" principle. A full (rather critical) account of this tradition in Albrecht Ritschl, "Über die beiden Principien des Protestantismus (1876)," in *Gesammelte Aufsätze*, ed. Otto Ritschl (Freiburg: J. C. B. Mohr, 1893), 234–47.
[17]Rettberg ("Baur Review," 1783–4) had, however, only claimed that the Scripture principle as understood by Baur, i.e., as an expression of "subjectivity," was limited to Luther's early period and later revoked as its "dangers" became clear in the radical Reformation.
[18]Ibid., 1787–8.
[19]*Evangelisch.* Here as elsewhere, Baur identifies Protestantism with its magisterial mainstream.

How little must a Protestant theologian have thought about the essence of the Reformation; how little must he have grasped its principle, if his thought has not progressed beyond the impoverished notion that the Reformation is nothing but the renewal of the same opposition between Augustinianism and Pelagianism which had already developed in all its sharpness in the fifth century? Can there be a sadder or more vacuous understanding of historical development than that which does not see anything in even the [xvii] greatest phenomena, generally agreed to be epochal, but the return of old, forgotten opposites? A view which cannot discern in history as a whole anything but eternal monotony, in which all the spirit's thoughts collapse into empty nothingness?

Whatever Mr. Rettberg's objections may be, it still remains the case that the power of that objectivity which imparted to the Middle Ages and to the entire ancient age its unique character was only broken by the Reformation, and in such a way that the subject obtained a completely different meaning from the one it had had before—that it was only by the principle of the Reformation that it became a free, self-confident subject. This free subjectivity, however, which has come into its own through the Reformation, does not consist in Pelagianism, where Mr. Rettberg locates its principle. Instead, it was only by the complete divestment of all Pelagianism that the subject was able to arrive at the true freedom of self-consciousness.

The Pelagian freedom of the *liberum arbitrium* is, after all, only bad freedom without content which relinquishes the subject to the power of objectivity and the extrinsic character of works. I will gladly accept it if one says about faith—not in the common, shallow sense of faith, but rather (it goes without saying) in its truly Protestant meaning—that it is the minimum of Pelagian self-activity; indeed, even (I would go on to say) that it is the complete negation of this self-activity.[20] But how does [xviii] Mr. Rettberg intend to explain the fact that all parties which originated as a result of the Reformation in their systems of doctrine[21] consider faith as the essential form without which nothing that is received into the subject can have a truly Christian meaning for it?[22] *This* is the immediate, living participation of the subject in everything that is to be *for* it, the infinite power of self-consciousness. This pivot from objectivity into subjectivity, moreover, does not lose any of its intrinsic significance by the fact that the principle which called it forth did not immediately penetrate it in all its purity; that free subjectivity (as history shows and the nature of the matter requires) remained as yet in many ways restrained and inhibited; and that the principle itself first had to go through its own process of mediation.

What, then, I must ask after all this, is my purported Hegelianism? Professor Rettberg clearly believes that, as a result of this accusation, he can declare my historical investigations mere mistakes and acts of violence, whose results he can consign to the dustbin in their entirety. Is it not the most obvious injustice he has done to me, and do I not have the full right to say that, what he calls Hegelianism, is nothing but the exact opposite of all that he has displayed in the assessment of my work: the scientific consideration of an issue as opposed to a quite unscientific method, which bespeaks a complete lack of philosophical thought? One can call the speculative method [xix]

---

[20]Baur had argued against Möhler in GKP that the deepest doctrinal opposition between Protestantism and Catholicism lay in the semi-Pelagian character of the latter which the Reformation decisively rejected. Baur depended for this argument on Schleiermacher's defense of predestination. Cf. Friedrich Schleiermacher, *On the Doctrine of Election*, trans. Iain G. Nicol and Allen G. Jorgenson (Louisville, KY: John Knox Press, 2012).
[21]*Lehrbegriff*. See Note on Text and Translation.
[22]Here Baur seems to imply the idea of faith as the "formal" principle of Protestantism, as one would expect.

Hegelianism, or whatever else one would like to, but the essence of speculation is and always will be the rational examination of the object with which one is engaged; the position of consciousness *vis-à-vis* this object which makes it appear as it truly is; and the endeavor to place oneself into the objective progression of the issue itself in order to follow it in all its moments through which it moves.

Thus, what is historically given is to be understood not merely extrinsically, according to this or the other relationship in which the subject engages with it, but according to its intrinsic, essential context. The only presupposition here is that history is not just a mere random aggregation, but a coherent whole.[23] Where there is coherence, there is also reason, and whatever exists through reason must also exist for reason for the rational consideration of the spirit. Without speculation, all historical research, no matter what name it may boast, is a mere tarrying on the surface and [limited to] the exterior of the issue. The more important and comprehensive the object is with which [historians] preoccupy themselves, and the more immediately it relates to rational thought, the more decisive is it that [scholars] do not only reproduce in themselves what individual people thought and did, but reflect in themselves the eternal thought of the eternal spirit, whose work history is.

One must not think that in such a consideration of what is universal, individual persons [xx] would miss out. There is still a wide field that is left to them, in which they can rove around with their subjective concerns and motives—still enough of the finite and limited, the random and the arbitrary that resists all rational consideration. But what would the singular and individual be without the universal and absolute, to which in its essence it belongs? How indifferent it is to us whether one individual was called Athanasius, another Arius, Nestorius, or Cyril? All historical persons are mere names to us unless everything each of them has thought, done, and made the task of their lives and endeavors is a thought based in the essence of spirit itself—a moment of the ongoing process, in which the spirit struggles with itself in order to overcome all opposites which time and again place new limitations on its self-consciousness. If we removed from history this universal spiritual and intellectual coherence, which alone transforms what happened into thought, how empty and impoverished of any higher concern, how spiritless does that leave all its content?

I strive to investigate this coherence and to understand from this perspective Christian dogma in its course of progression. For this reason, I can certainly only be grateful to everyone who counsels me with instructive suggestions on this matter seeking to show me the right path wherever I miss it. But to condemn my endeavor in general, to cast suspicion on it with false accusations, and to disparage [xxi] my investigations in the manner in which it has been done here, I can only declare a presumption which does not befit a man like Professor Rettberg, who would do well to use my insights for himself as the first step in philosophizing.

It offends my respect for Professor Rettberg, which I have already attested publicly, to be forced to express all this against him, when it is in no way exclusively directed against him but rather to an entire group of opponents. Mr. Rettberg has revealed in all too naïve a fashion his interior thoughts. Many others, who are no more understanding of philosophical matters and would indubitably embarrass themselves even more [than Mr. Rettberg], approach the matter more prudently and skillfully by not allowing themselves to be drawn into expositions of this kind. It is indeed [today]

---

[23] Cf. SuM, v–vi (see Chapter 1 in this volume). In defending his alleged "Hegelianism" in 1841, Baur describes his position in words starkly reminiscent of his earliest major publication written long before he had encountered Hegel's philosophy.

hardly necessary to clarify one's understanding of Hegelianism and enter into a more specific contestation of it. Once the accusation itself has been made, the main issue at stake, the purpose of such a suspicion, can be accomplished far more simply and securely. Hegelianism, after all, is the name that summarizes everything fearful: everything containing any danger—brought about by the progress of science and of rational thought in theology—for the stability of ecclesial faith, and the success of the hierarchical tendencies in an age so fussily and zealously gathering from all sides the building blocks for its visible church [xxii] as if there were no invisible church at all—as if this invisible church alone were not the truth of the visible one.

The enemies of science have always practiced the ritual of repeating the same old, trivial accusations against every philosopher and speculative theologian who injures their petty concerns with the new revival he imparts to intellectual life, until they can transfer these same accusations to a new name. In this way, people have already for some time now reconciled themselves with Schelling and Schleiermacher—though only after finding much fault and scandal in these heroes of German science during their lifetime—only to make Hegel's name all the more exclusively the object of all their attacks against philosophy and speculative theology these days.

By making things personal, they can accomplish their actual goal more easily and more reliably. They *appear* to raise their voice not against science itself, but rather only against an individual philosopher, who can only be absolutely wrong when faced with the established requirement from which they proceed. [They *seem* to oppose] only an idol of their time, who introduced the worst idol worship, the idolatry of the concept, which places the human spirit on the throne of the eternal God, whereas, of course, one must never balk at placing flesh and blood on this throne![24] [They seem to object] only against an extreme.

Doing so has two advantages [for the enemies of science]. [First,] it relieves them of the effort [xxiii] to immerse themselves more seriously into a system such as Hegel's in order to familiarize themselves more closely with the issue they would like to dismiss. [Second,] they can hide behind the shining shield of a defender of the sacred cause of the Christian faith their own lack of scientific significance, their own intellectual bondage, everything they do against intellectual and academic freedom as whose open opponent, of course, they would never want to be seen. They can practice the work of their visible church all the more merrily and be all the more unafraid to pay homage, according to their innermost sympathies, to the hierarchical spirit of the times, who offers to his servants a reward incomparable to that science can provide. This spirit at present threatens to gain more and more ground in German science and in the theology of the Protestant Church. When even men who should be altogether protected from such deception by the holy consecration of science are unable to withstand the demonic inspirations of this spirit of the age, then this is an all the more telling sign of the times in which we are now living.

In this state of things, it must appear to be a very unrewarding business to bother about investigations which once again furnish the proof that the absolute viewpoint in which the visible church thinks it can close itself off and reject all claims to scientific thought cannot be found in any age of the Christian church. [xxiv] The history of Christian dogma itself, the more deeply one penetrates into it, increasingly appears as its own internal critique, which continually pushes along, again and again posing new tasks to the thinking consciousness, whose solution can only be the result of a struggle. Nevertheless, there will never be a shortage of those who, unconcerned about

---

[24]Baur's dig against contemporaneous clericalism.

their opponents' hostilities, accept as their calling the continued walk along the narrow path that is known only to the few.

[p. 868]

THE MOMENTS OF THE INTELLECTUAL PROCESS IN AUGUSTINE'S TRINITARIAN DOCTRINE[25]

If we look back on Augustine's whole way of interpreting and treating ecclesial Trinitarian doctrine laid out here, we can see beyond any doubt that great honor is due to Augustine for this significant work.[26] After Athanasius, there is no other Church Father who was equally epoch-making in the speculative development of this doctrine.[27] Athanasius' significance in the history of this doctrine consists in the fact that he rose up from among the early ideas on subordination, which run alongside and cross one another in various ways, to form the great thought, that the Son could only be of the same nature as the Father, i.e., he is an absolute totality according to his speculative concept, just as the Father is. In the same way, it was Augustine who first expressed the no less profound idea that this absolute relationship between the Father and the Son could only be founded in the essence of the thinking spirit,[28] and that insofar it can be grasped at all, it can only be grasped as a relationship of the thinking spirit with itself.[29]

Proceeding from the essence of the thinking spirit, Augustine seeks [869] to elevate himself to the idea of the triune God.[30] For this reason, he takes his position in thinking consciousness itself, and all his attempts to explain the incomprehensible essence of the absolute God, closed off to the finite spirit, take the form of essential categories of intellection. Augustine repeatedly feels compelled to remind us that the Trinitarian relationship in God, as it had to appear to him in the form of church doctrine, is completely transcendent for representational consciousness. To the same degree, on the other hand, he cannot avoid the assumption, so profoundly established in

---

[25] Section headings are adapted from Baur's analytical table of contents.
[26] For Baur's interpretation of Augustine and the *De trinitate* in particular cf. Roland Kany, *Augustins Trinitätsdenken: Bilanz, Kritik und Weiterführung der modernen Forschung zu "De trinitate"* (Tübingen: Mohr Siebeck, 2007), 311–14; Johannes Zachhuber, "Baur, Ferdinand Christian," in *The Oxford Guide to the Historical Reception of Augustine*, ed. Karla Pollmann and Willemien Otten (Oxford: Oxford University Press, 2013). Online version (2014). Accessed on August 17, 2021: https://www.oxfordreference.com/view/10.1093/acref/9780199299164.001.0001/acref-9780199299164-e-167?rskey=ljLWfK&result=60.
[27] For Baur's treatment of Athanasius, cf. LDM 1:395–440.
[28] *Geist*. Translating this German term is notoriously difficult (see Note on Text and Translations). Yet the problem is exacerbated here and in the following as Baur draws on the ambiguity of the German noun in his exploration of Augustine's analogies between the Trinity and the human mind. While throughout the *Reader*, we mostly use "spirit," in what follows, we sometimes also use "mind" or indeed "spirit and mind."
[29] In other words, Baur sees in Augustine's Trinitarian speculation an anticipation of the idealist philosophy of spirit in his own time. It is remarkable that this parallel, which is rather obvious, does not always seem to have been noted by the protagonists of this movement. Philipp Marheineke was the main exception to this rule. See George Pattison, "Hegelian Augustinianism: Philipp Marheineke," in *The Oxford Guide to the Historical Reception of Augustine*, ed. Karla Pollmann and Willemien Otten (Oxford: OUP, 2013). Online version (2014). Accessed on August 17, 2021: https://www.oxfordreference.com/view/10.1093/acref/9780199299164.001.0001/acref-9780199299164-e-360#.
[30] Baur's interpretation of Augustine's argument is largely based on Book XV which, according to him, is "the most important of them all" (LDM 1:858, n. 30). Cf. Kany, *Trinitätsdenken*, 314.

the nature of the human mind, that, if a key exists to unlock the inscrutable mystery, it can only be found in the intellectual nature of spirit itself.

The spirit of subjective consciousness, which is finite in the first place, but which at the same time is also infinite in its finitude, is for Augustine the mirror of the eternal, absolute God determining himself as the Trinity of Father, Son, and Spirit. For this reason, the entire striving of the spirit of subjective consciousness is directed at perceiving the reflexes of the absolute archetype as they appear in this mirror in order to bring them into the unity of the logical, determined concept.

The spirit in its substantial being is intellection; thus far, the essential moments, in which it completes its immanent thought process, must be just as many moments in the Trinitarian idea of God. Those moments are, as Augustine determines them, *memoria, intelligentia,* and *voluntas* or *caritas*.[31] For this reason, the question remains what the real concept of these three moments is, insofar as the intellectual nature of spirit portrays itself through them, and how in thought they are one, but also differentiated from each other.

Augustine first understands *memoria* to be, as on the word's usual meaning, memory, or remembering; and one can only remember what is already interiorly at hand.[32] [870] Accordingly, *memoria* is for him abstract, pure thought which is the basis of conscious thought preceding all its concrete determinations; *memoria* is thought in itself, the as-yet undivided, undifferentiated unity of being and thought.

While *memoria* is the first moment in this sense, *intelligentia* as the second moment can only be particular, concrete, conscious thought. Abstract thought, existing in itself, determines itself as concrete thought, but this concrete thought must, as much as possible, be conceived without any concrete determination of content. As absolute thought, it can only have itself as its content, but is just for this reason, different from the first moment [i.e., *memoria*], thought existing in itself, because it thinks itself and thus already carries difference within itself. It is the thought that thinks itself, returns to itself, and thereby reflects itself—thought which differentiates itself from itself absolute self-consciousness.[33] As Augustine calls it, it is the word produced by thinking out of the self-enclosed depths of thinking, a word which, however, is only the word as such, without any concrete determinacy.[34]

The Father, therefore, relates [871] to the Son as abstract, pure thought relates to the uttered, or realized thought. Augustine's fundamental idea, then, is that spirit, insofar as it thinks, enters

---

[31]Augustine, *De trinitate* X 11, 17–18; XV 21, 40–1. Cf. Lydia Schumacher, *Divine Illumination: The History and Future of Augustine's Theory of Knowledge* (Oxford: Wiley Blackwell, 2011), 43–8, 53–6.

[32]Augustine, *De trinitate* XV 21, 40: "I have assigned to memory everything we know, even if we were not thinking of it. (*memoriae tribuens omne quod scimus etiamsi non inde cogitemus*.)"

[33]Baur's interpretation is arguably idiosyncratic inasmuch as Augustine's language is suggestive of the relationship of latency to its actualization rather than the self-differentiation of abstract thought. Yet cf. Kany, *Trinitätsdenken*, 313, n. 1324 for the following *nota bene*: "[Baur] does not claim simply to render what Augustine said and what he meant. Rather, Baur seeks to demonstrate from his (not from Augustine's) presuppositions, and in his (not Augustine's) categories, what progress spirit has made in history and what plausible consequences it failed to draw."

[34]Augustine here adds a note citing *De trinitate* XV 21, 40 in full. Interspersed with the Latin text, he offers snippets of his own interpretation. In what follows these interspersed comments are given in English together with the immediate Latin context. "memoriae tribuens omne quod scimus etiamsi non inde cogitemus, intellegentiae uero proprio modo quandam cogitationis informationem (There thus is not-yet-formed thinking, thinking in itself, antecedent to formed thinking, the *informatio cogitationis*). Cogitando enim quod uerum inuenerimus, hoc maxime intellegere dicimur et hoc quidem in memoria rursus relinquimus (Every determined, concrete thinking thus has as its presupposition [another] knowledge, [another] thinking and is recollection of what has been interiorly thought)."

into a relationship with itself. It can only make the content of its thought what it finds in itself that is, itself, thought existing as itself [*das an sich seiende Denken*] which is its own essence. The step from the first moment to the second consists precisely in this: that a difference is posited, that spirit distinguishes itself from itself as subject and object; that it is one as *memoria*, another as *intelligentia*.

Just as positing this difference is an essential moment in the thinking process, however, so also is the following: spirit, by distinguishing itself from itself, does not disintegrate, but in this distinction is at once one with itself. Differently put, spirit only determines itself in difference from itself in order to sublate the difference, in order to become conscious of its identity with itself through the posited difference as well as through its abolition. [872]

In This Way, Spirit Unities Itself with Itself

If each individual moment is to be both a totality in itself and an essential member of the entire thought process, then the third moment can only have this meaning: if the second moment is difference, the third must be the unity in that difference. Augustine has recognized this correctly when he located the third moment in the will or in love.[35] If the second moment is determined thought—self-consciousness or self-knowledge dividing itself into the distinction of object and subject—then an essential part of this process must be the subject's knowledge of itself as one with its object.

Self-knowledge would not be knowledge of the self if those knowing themselves did not unite themselves with themselves, if they did not grasp themselves in their unity with themselves by directing their will to themselves—if they did not love themselves with a love sublating all distinction of subject and object, a love returning to itself, and uniting itself with itself.

In this way only, the process of the thinking spirit becomes the totality of all its moments, the self-determination of spirit which encloses itself in itself and returns to itself, or the self-movement of the idea mediated to itself by itself, by which the self-positing spirit becomes spirit in spirit.[36] The unity of these [873] three moments, in which the spirit operates its spiritual, i.e., intellectual, nature, is thus the most adequate image [874] of the Trinitarian relationship to be postulated in God's essence: the image of the absolute God who is as different from himself as he is identical with himself. If God can only be thought as spirit, then he must be subject as well as object, one and the same as subject and object, the unified God identical with himself.

---

[35] Augustine, *De trinitate* XV 21, 41: "But I have shown nothing in this enigma respecting the Holy Spirit such as might appear like him, except our own will, or love, or affection (*De spiritu autem sancto nihil in hoc aenigmate quod ei simile uideretur ostendi nisi uoluntatem nostram, uel amorem seu dilectionem*)."

[36] Baur here adds a note containing the full, Latin text of *De trinitate* XV 21, 41 followed by his own assessment: "*Memoria* thus includes *intelligentia* and *dilectio*. When we think we already encounter *intelligentia* and *dilectio*; hence, they must be in *memoria*. *Intelligentia* itself is thus only *reminisci*, a return to oneself, remembering. *Dilectio*, which is the unity of the two moments, is also thinking and knowledge because it is impossible to love something that we do not know. Love itself is nothing but knowing, coming to be aware of the identity of another with ourselves. The only thing missing in Augustine's argument is only this: that Augustine does not emphasise more sharply that spirit, in these moments of its thinking activity, of *memoria*, *intelligentia*, and *dilectio*, can only refer to itself, that it can make only itself the content of these activities. Yet he nevertheless presupposes the [latter insight] since he obviously considers these moments the universal forms of the spirit's activity abstracting from any empirical content of self-consciousness. (He says, e.g., of *memoria* [in 23, 43] that it is 'that memory which beasts have not—*viz*. the memory by which things intelligible are so contained as that they have not entered that memory through the bodily senses.') But what can spirit as the pure form of thinking have as its content if not itself, inasmuch as even pure thought cannot be without a content."

The Final Limitation in Augustine's Speculation

But why is [this unity of the three moments in the human mind] nevertheless a mere image? What is the inhibiting and separating factor that still prevents us from knowing the intellectual nature of spirit, as it reveals itself in these moments, as the innermost life and essence of the triune God itself? Our whole judgment on Augustinian Trinitarian doctrine's speculative content must emerge in the answer to this question. Augustine's own answer to this question is this. Even though I have *memoria, intelligentia*, and *dilectio* within me, I am not myself this *memoria, intelligentia,* and *dilectio*. They are determinations which one and the same person can articulate *vis-à-vis* themselves, but they are not this person themselves.

In the absolute simplicity of the divine nature, however, Father, Son, and Spirit are three persons, so that each of those three moments is itself a person. In other words, the Trinity is not in God, but it rather is God himself. Thus, there is still an entirely essential difference between the Trinity itself and the image of the Trinity. The human mind or spirit, as its essential nature is posited in thought, can be no more than a mere image of the divine Trinity precisely for this reason. [875] The reason is that, were the difference between image and reality to fall away, the human mind or spirit would itself have to be the intellection determined by those three moments, just as much as God does not merely have the Trinity in himself as a determination of his essence, but is himself this very Trinity.[37] [876]

Augustine's speculative line of thought is thus met with a double obstacle. First, we do not even know whether the substantial essence of the human being can legitimately be identified with their rational nature, given that, in fact, their real self is different from their nature. It follows immediately from this that any doubts concerning the authentic essence of the human being make only more inadequate any inference from the essence of the human being to the essence of God.

Thus, the question arises whether one may legitimately even draw those analogies on which Augustine builds his speculative trinitarian doctrine. It is however clear that, according to the

---

[37]Baur here adds a note containing the Latin text of the final section of *De trinitate* XV, 22, 42 and the following comment of his own: "In this way, Augustine fittingly describes the point from which proceed two essentially divergent opinions. Whereas one of them identifies humanity's essential being with the universal (i.e. the principle of universality, thought), the other opposes the former with the notion of a personality which, while containing the universal within itself, can never be identical with it. [According to the latter view], the truly substantial being and life is precisely the specific and individual, which can never be absorbed into the universal. From this, the further view follows that overall truth is not to be found in the universal, in thought or concept, but only in what is given, in the concrete reality of the individual. What matters is thus not speculation but experience. Once this view is applied to the idea of God, it results in the claim that God ought to be conceived primarily as personal being without concern for the problem of how the idea of personality can be brought into agreement with the idea of the universal as which the being of God must be thought. Thus, the idea of a personal God moves into opposition to the idea of the Trinity as contained in the moments of the intellectual process. One might think here, e.g., of the *Christian Philosophy of Religion* by H[einrich] Steffens [*Christliche Religionsphilosophie*, 2 vols. (Breslau: Max und Komp., 1839)] with its tendency to save the proper nature of existence, personality, and love against the universality of thought, i.e. Hegel's philosophy. This whole, thus widely ranging opposition of viewpoints is implied in Augustine's simple as well as fitting comment identifying his further goal in speculating about the Trinity: 'Those three are not one human being but *of* one human being; [but] in that supreme Trinity those three are not of one God, but one God. And those are three persons, not one (*non haec tria unus homo sed unius hominis sunt, in ipsa summa trinitate unius dei sunt illa tria, sed unus deus est et tres sunt illae, non una persona*)'." The last sentence is a slightly adapted citation from *De trinitate* XV 23, 43. We have here a typical example for Baur's tendency to draw immediate parallels between his historical sources and contemporaneous debates. In Augustine, Baur finds prefigured the controversy in his own time about the relationship between the Hegelian philosophy of universal being and the metaphysics of the person advanced by the so-called speculative theists including Immanuel Hermann Fichte (1796–1879) and Christian Hermann Weisse (1801–66) as well as the late Schelling. Cf. for the context: Jan Olof Bengtsson, *The Worldview of Personalism: Origins and Early Development* (Oxford: OUP, 2006).

course taken by Augustine, one obstacle is eliminated as soon as the other falls. If, therefore, it were first of all certain that the substantial essence of the human being is their rational, thinking nature, and [877] that this nature cannot be determined in its substantial activity by any moments other than the three mentioned above (as they form a necessary unity in their relation with each other), then, just as certainly as we are given in these moments the innermost essence of the human being, their personal self, as certainly too would the substantial being of God necessarily reveal itself to us in these moments.

In the image, we would at the same time have the reality, since now nothing else can be thought which would stand as an inhibition between image and reality. The image would become reality, and humanity's relationship with God would not be the relationship between image and reality, but rather the relation of mind to mind, spirit to spirit. Even if humanity could only be considered the finite spirit and God alone the infinite, absolute spirit, it would still be certain, first and foremost, that the substantial being of the spirit is one and the same in the human being as well as in God, and that it is the very same spirit which here elevates itself as the finite to the infinite, while there it lowers itself as the infinite into finite human consciousness.

How close Augustine was to this highest point in speculative contemplation, when he established the proposition that no other nature comes between the human mind as the image of God and God himself![38] Thus, the human mind has the most immediate relationship with God, not mediated by anything, and there is no one above them besides God alone. And yet, how far Augustine then distances himself from this standpoint when, disregarding his own insight, he claims at the same time that the human spirit, even *qua* image of God, is of a different nature than God.[39] Thus, ultimately, what is lacking and one-sided in [878] Augustinian Trinitarian doctrine can only be this: as much as it seems that the whole course of his considerations is inevitably leading him to the final conclusion of identifying the substantial essence of the human being with their rational, thinking nature, declaring resolutely that human being, as their true, authentic self, is mind or spirit, he ultimately did not dare to draw this conclusion. Even though to him it is clear that human beings, if they are the image of God, can only be so in their distinguishing characteristic (in their thinking rationality),[40] as soon as it comes to holding on to this pronouncement in its full truth, the real moment of the human being's personality now appears to him to be located in something else of which he cannot give a more exact account. He thus loses his way on the path of his speculative considerations and stops halfway.

The most immediate reason for this was, of course, that he did not know how *speculatively* to determine those very moments in which the spirit's substantial being seemed to him to consist, that is, to determine them as the essential moments of the spirit mediating itself to itself; instead, he considered them merely empirically and psychologically.[41]

---

[38]Cf. LDM 1:868 and Augustine, *De trinitate* XI 5, 8: "No doubt every thing in the creatures which is in any way like God, is not also to be called his image; but that alone than which he himself alone is higher. For that only is in all points copied from him, between which and himself no nature is interposed (*Non sane omne quod in creaturis aliquo modo simile est deo etiam eius imago dicenda est, sed illa sola qua superior ipse solus est. Ea quippe de illo prorsus exprimitur inter quam et ipsum nulla interiecta natura est*)."
[39]Footnote omitted citing the beginning of *De trinitate* XIV 8, 11.
[40]Footnote omitted citing *De trinitate* XV 1, 1.
[41]Footnote omitted in which Baur offers further illustrations of his main point about Augustine's achievement and limitations through an analysis of *De civitate dei* XI 24.

PART THREE

New Testament Criticism

CHAPTER SEVEN

Prolegomena to New Testament Studies

FROM ENT, 478–83
TRANSLATION: BEATA AND MATTHEW VALE

In 1850, after Baur's major works on Paul and the Gospels had been published, he wrote a book-length article surveying the history and conception of New Testament Introduction. By "introduction" (*Einleitung*), Baur had in mind the traditional questions one should answer as a prolegomenon to interpreting a text: author, date, addressees, sources, integrity, circumstances of origin, purpose, and so forth. If the genre of texts known as Introductions to the New Testament today might be characterized by their predictability, not so in the nineteenth century, when a debate raged in German-speaking circles in the middle decades of the century. Scholars such as F. Lücke, H. Hupfeld, A. G. Rudelbach, F. Delitzsch, and H. J. Holtzmann argued about the scope, method, fundamental "concept," and place of biblical introduction in the larger theological encyclopedia. Central among these questions was a concern that still animates scholars of early Christianity today: what role does or should the canon play in these discussions? Although Baur never wrote an Introduction to the New Testament, much of his work impinged on introductory questions, and he developed strong convictions about the purpose of the "science," as he terms it, of New Testament introduction.

This long essay is divided into three parts. The first section, whose final pages are translated here, concerns the concept and task of scientific introduction. The second, longest part of the essay, offers an extended critical review of the historical development of New Testament introduction since especially the Reformation, before proceeding, in the third and final section, to consider the organization and coherence of New Testament introduction. After criticizing the approaches of W. M. L. de Wette and H. Hupfeld for definitions of New Testament introduction that Baur found too capacious, and criticizing Friedrich Schleiermacher for merely remaining at the level of external details about the text, Baur sets forth his own idea of introduction as "criticism of the canon."[1]

In this selection, Baur defines Introduction to the Old and New Testaments as "the theological science which examines the emergence and the original arrangement and character of the scriptures belonging to the canon." He stresses the necessity of doubt as a sort of acidic solution to test the genuineness of traditions about authorship and circumstances of origin, and defends the propriety of criticism's negative judgments as a necessary step in establishing what may positively be claimed about the origins of the canon.

---

[1] For further detail, see David Lincicum, "Ferdinand Christian Baur and the Theological Task of New Testament Introduction," in *Ferdinand Christian Baur and the History of Early Christianity*, ed. Martin Bauspiess, Christof Landmesser, and David Lincicum; trans. Peter C. Hodgson and Robert F. Brown (Oxford: Oxford University Press, 2017), 83–95.

INTRODUCTION TO THE NEW TESTAMENT AS THEOLOGICAL SCIENCE

[478]

Thus it is only through the concept of criticism that scientific introduction[2] becomes what it is essentially. If its object is supposed to be more than mere accidental, arbitrary, purely empirical knowledge, but instead make up an intrinsically necessary task for theological knowing, then its task can only be specified as a critical one. But the fact that this scientific introduction can relate to its object only critically is determined by the make-up of that object. The concept of scientific introduction is more exactly defined by reflecting on its object, by more precisely understanding the type and the constitution of the thing it is preoccupied with, and what about that thing is the real object of critique. The canonical scriptures are the subject matter of this science, but not the way they are in themselves, but rather together with all those ideas and prerequisites which render them canonical. As canonical scriptures they are writings associated with the concept of a certain dogmatic authority. From the perspective of dogma, they are considered divinely revealed scriptures, the documentary expression and quintessence of divinely revealed truth which is to be the determinative norm for a person's whole theoretical and practical conduct.

Now, the real object of critique is exactly this dogmatic element, the principle of their canonical authority. Thus, scientific introduction has to investigate whether these scriptures are indeed what they are supposed to be according to the dogmatic idea one has about them. And since the first presupposition under whose auspices this can take place at all is the presupposition that they were really composed by the authors they are ascribed to, then the first task of criticism is to answer the following question: What right do they have to call themselves apostolic scriptures? Just as dogmatism is counterpoised against criticism in philosophy,[3] so in theology, critique is the counterpart to dogma. Dogma is simply asserting what dogma articulates, while critique asks for the grounds of this claim by reflecting on the object's relationship to consciousness, and by insisting on becoming cognizant of everything by which the object's relation to the subject's consciousness is mediated. If the subject can know itself to be immediately one with the object distinguished from it, then this is faith as the immediate certitude of what has been given to the subject as the object of its knowledge. [479] But to the degree the subject can no longer know itself to be one with its object, a faithful consciousness passes over into a critical one, and doubt is the active principle by which the passage from the one form of consciousness into the other is mediated. There is no faith which does not also contain some seed of doubt.

So if one asks whether the situation with the canonical scriptures is indeed the same as the dogmatic presupposition of the Church, which attributes to these scriptures the highest divine authority, this question and the doubt which it includes are the awakening of critical consciousness

---

[2]*Einleitungs-Wissenschaft*, that is, the critical task of settling introductory questions about writings, such as author, date, or circumstances of origin, in a rigorous and reasoned historical fashion.

[3]Compare Immanuel Kant, "Preface to the Second Edition," in *Critique of Pure Reason*, ed. and trans. Paul Guyer and Allen W. Wood (Cambridge: Cambridge University Press, 1998), 119: "Criticism is not opposed to the dogmatic procedure of reason in its pure cognition as science (for science must always be dogmatic, i.e., it must prove its conclusions strictly *a priori* from secure principles); rather, it is opposed only to dogmatism, i.e., to the presumption of getting on solely with pure cognition from (philosophical) concepts according to principles, which reason has been using for a long time without first inquiring in what way and by what right it has obtained them. Dogmatism is therefore the dogmatic procedure of pure reason, without an antecedent critique of its own capacity."

and the beginning of critique. And this question has to arise at some point, since it is in the nature of consciousness to differentiate itself from the objects which make up its content, to break away from them and return into itself, and to come to know itself as the power [standing] above them, precisely by placing them over-against itself as something separate from itself. If ever once doubt has penetrated into consciousness in this way—even through the smallest crack—in order to place itself between consciousness and its object, and in order to create conflict within consciousness in its relationship with the object, there is no power in this world that could prevent the rupture thus created from becoming an ever greater chasm. One piece after another is detached from the subject's immediate identity with its object; doubt interferes more and more deeply and more powerfully; first one thing and then before long another is called into question, and there is no knowing what the final result of this ongoing critical process might be. That consciousness which has come to be at odds with its object thus puts its object on trial again and again, and cannot rest until it has completely subdued the object and has placed itself above it as the knowing power. Two sides of this trial need to be differentiated. Due to the nature of the matter, the beginning of the critique can only be the subject's break with its object (with the content of its consciousness). Something has to interpose itself between the object and the subject, as a result of which the subject grows uncertain of its faith in the object, and the conviction is more and more imposed on the subject that with this object things are not as the subject had presumed up till then, in its uninhibited faith. [480]

This is the negative side of critique, which must always precede the positive side. Doubt is the essence of criticism. A criticism which does not doubt and does not allow doubt to come into its own, a critique which, even if it has doubts, reassures itself by assuming that these doubts surely cannot be significant and will be resolved on their own, is no critique at all. Critique must above all be truly and totally serious about doubt. It must not allow anything to be hidden or withheld from itself. It must not be too soft and forbearing. It must firmly and resolutely consider all things. Critique must not be deterred by any consequences, whatever they might be; doubt can only be thoroughly disproved and lifted when it has been given its fullest due. But of course, whether doubt is ever disproved or lifted is a completely different question; in no way, however, can critique be reproached if it remains merely negative critique. It has recently become very common to call critique—inasmuch as it often has only a negative result—destructive, and so to cast doubt on it.[4] But in doing so, great injustice is done to critique; for why should critique not be permitted to deconstruct, if truth can only be found by showing above all how untrue and wrong, how untenable and null a thing is which has hitherto been held as true and irrevocable? If by calling critique destructive, people mean to say that it often destroys what in itself should not be destroyed, and that it takes such pleasure in destroying and tearing down that it even lays hands on what is holy and divine, then it is just as arbitrary to falsely attribute to critique a corrupt motive and interest as it is simply to presuppose that the scriptures, whose origin and character critique is supposed to examine in the first place, are to be regarded as holy and divine. In all this, after all, one must not forget that no matter how much one might regret the destructive element in a critique, nothing can be destroyed that is not in itself destructible, and that what it always comes down to is *why* something is destroyed.[5]

It is, of course, true that critique far more often destroys and tears down than it builds. But that is partly because of the nature of the thing—that in so many cases it is far easier to show how

---

[4]Baur is probably thinking of the popular reaction to Strauss' *Life of Jesus*.
[5]See also Chapter 14 in this volume.

things are *not* than to show how things *are*—and partly because people overlook the positive result critique brings, over and beyond the negative result. [481] Of course, if the nonsensical (but not unheard-of) demand were made of critique that it should rebuild what it has destroyed, it will never be able to do what is being asked of it; whatever it has once dismantled with good reason cannot be rebuilt, at least not in the same way. But wherever it is confident in its negative course, it will seldom be able to confine itself to these negative aspects without at the same time revealing the data for a positive result. The positive is joined together with the negative in such a way that it cannot be separated from it. After all, a negative critique can only strive toward allowing its subject matter to appear once more in its pure objectivity by clearing away all that has attached itself to the original and gradually given it an altogether different form. Thus, even though a critique may be left with ever so narrow a strip of ground remaining after it has accomplished its destructive work, through continued efforts (and insofar as it knows how to use what little is left at its disposal), it will still not lack the means to build its own addition on this ground, and to raise, in place of the old building crumbling in on itself, a new one better corresponding to the truth of the matter.

The current state of New Testament criticism, which will be the subject of our first discussion here, is proof of this. Critical research has long enough done no more than establish the conviction that the canon was constituted very differently from the way presupposed by the traditional dogmatic notion.[6] New Testament criticism, by contrast, has by now entered a developmental stage where it endeavors, with increasing resolve, to obtain a positive conception of the canon's development, to demonstrate more precisely how circumstances and interests worked together to call these scriptures into existence in the first place, and to give them the significance they have acquired as this specific class of those writings making up the canon.

The more firmly New Testament criticism is aware of its task, the more it will strive to obtain as definitive a result as possible on the origin of these scriptures; the question of that origin, however, poses itself under a double aspect. [482] It is not enough to know whether or not the scriptures under discussion were indeed compiled by the authors they are attributed to. In order to examine their origins even more deeply, one has to ask further how the author arrived at writing such a piece of scripture, whereby not only the external circumstances under which he wrote must be considered, but even more importantly the motives determining him interiorly. The more significant and rich in content a piece of scripture is, the more depends on penetrating into its inner center and grasping the fundamental idea on the basis of which the author proceeded and which determined his presentation with the goal of obtaining the specific end which he is concerned about. The fact that this [task]—which is intimately linked with the concept of "introduction"—is also a very important part of New Testament criticism's task is obvious, no matter how insufficient the typical introductory texts still are on precisely this issue.

This procedure of going back to the consciousness on the basis of which the writer wrote—a procedure already called for by Schleiermacher[7]—can also be included in the question of canonical texts' origins, since the origin of a text has only really been researched when it is known not only

---

[6] Cf., for example, the critical work of Johann Salomo Semler, *Abhandlung von freier Untersuchung des Kanon*, 4 vols. (Halle: Carl Hermann Hemmerde, 1771–5), on whom see Friederike Nüssel, "Semler, Johann Salomo," *Religion Past and Present*. Consulted online on August 13, 2021. http://dx.doi.org.proxy.library.nd.edu/10.1163/1877-5888_rpp_SIM_124819.

[7] See, e.g., Schleiermacher, *Hermeneutics: The Handwritten Manuscripts*, ed. Heinz Kimmerle, trans. Jack Forstman and James Duke (Atlanta: Scholars, 1986). This whole paragraph echoes Schleiermacher's conception of the psychological aspect of the hermeneutical task.

who wrote it, but how the text itself arose in the spirit of its author. If, from this perspective, the task of New Testament criticism is always the same question about the origin of canonical scripture, then this question itself comes to have an all the more crucial meaning. The concept of New Testament criticism only achieves its highest degree of understanding when there is a demand that it place itself in the writer's innermost conception and from there reproduce his literary product in the same manner in which it emerged; this is done by way of the most precise analysis possible of the entire content of [the writer's] thought. All questions preoccupying New Testament criticism must of themselves be subordinated to this highest task. If the inquiry into the [text's] external origin or into its author thus comes to a halt with a negative result, which is often the case due to the nature of the endeavor, nothing can hinder the critical gaze—sharpened with each new attempt—from approaching as closely as possible the inner, ideal, spiritual origin of the scriptures in question. [483] And the more criticism has succeeded at grasping its object in this way, the more certainly it is thereby given the possibility of also identifying the historical location in which to place it, at least in a general sense.

If we summarize the results of this exposition so far, we can define introduction to the scriptures of the Old and New Testament as the theological science which examines the emergence and the original arrangement and character of the scriptures belonging to the canon, and which provides a picture[8] that is as well defined and as objectively substantiated as possible. Seen in this way, introduction is, in a nutshell, critique of the canon. And the traditional name, "introduction," is not as unsuitable as it seems to some, either. If an introduction to a text provides above all an orientation to the reader on the most salient aspects in order to understand the text at hand from an appropriate perspective, and if an introduction is to put the reader in a position where they can arrive at a clear understanding of specific elements, based on the idea of the whole, then the following must be true: the concept of what is important in this context is very relative, and one cannot hold it against scientific introduction that it held as the most important and essential in its underdeveloped state something that now seems very inessential and unimportant from the perspective of the current state of science. Despite all this, it goes without saying that from this perspective, scientific introduction can only consider important or essential what relates to the origin and original character of canonical texts. If, in addition to that, this science is also described as a historical discipline, according to the attribute commonly attached to it nowadays, there is even less reason to doubt its independent scientific significance.

---

[8]*Vorstellung*, a term that Hegel thematizes as involving "three main phases, recollection, imagination and memory" (see Michael Inwood, *A Hegel Dictionary* [Oxford: Blackwell, 1992], 257–9).

CHAPTER EIGHT

Critical Investigations of the Canonical Gospels

FROM: *KUKE* (EXCERPTS)
TRANSLATION: BEATA AND MATTHEW VALE

All footnotes by the editors except those marked as [Tr.], which are by the translators.

Baur's *Critical Investigations of the Canonical Gospels* offers a summary of his research on the Gospels and their individual "tendencies," at greatest length for John and Luke, but also for Mark and Matthew (a separate monograph on Mark followed in 1851[1]), incorporating several long articles published in the preceding years. Despite the importance of Baur's work, this book has never been translated, and so relatively long selections are offered here in order to give the reader a sense of Baur's argumentative style and basic conclusions.[2]

The present selection contains excerpts from the introduction and from the sections on the Gospels of John and Matthew. In the introductory selections, Baur articulates his appreciation for but also his differences with his one-time student David Friedrich Strauss,[3] and offers a sketch of the task of criticism: to understand the Gospels in their historical circumstances, in order to grasp each text's own theological tendency. The second excerpt, on the Gospel of John, demonstrates Baur undertaking precisely that task of locating the fourth Gospel in the context of its time, arguing that it presupposes but goes beyond both synoptic and Pauline ideas, and articulates the highest principle of Christian consciousness in identifying Jesus with the *Logos* who is both with God and God himself. Baur questioned traditional assumptions about the authorship and character of the Fourth Gospel, and so posed the "Johannine question" to posterity.

At a time when New Testament scholarship had begun to argue for Markan priority (and for early versions of the two-source hypothesis), Baur defended the traditional assumption of Matthew as the earliest Gospel, adhering to the so-called Griesbach hypothesis of synoptic relations. In this he was almost certainly wrong, but his careful historical sifting of the Gospel of Matthew still repays careful reading; even if one might disagree with Baur about the "unbiased" character of the work, the selection enables one to grasp how Matthew fits into his schema for grasping the historical development of early Christianity. As an early, Jewish-Christian Gospel, Matthew shows

---

[1] See Ferdinand Christian Baur, *Das Marcusevangelium nach seinem Ursprung und Charakter. Nebst einem Anhang über das Evangelium Marcions* (Tübingen: L. F. Fues, 1851).

[2] For broader orientation, see Martin Bauspiess, "The Essence of Early Christianity: On Ferdinand Christian Baur's View of the Synoptic Gospels," and J. Frey, "Ferdinand Christian Baur and the Interpretation of John," in *Ferdinand Christian Baur and the History of Early Christianity*, ed. M. Bauspiess, C. Landmesser and D. Lincicum; trans. P. C. Hodgson and R. F. Brown (Oxford: Oxford University Press, 2017), 177–205 and 206–35 respectively.

[3] See U. Köpf, "Ferdinand Christian Baur and David Friedrich Strauss," in *Ferdinand Christian Baur and the History of Early Christianity*, ed. M. Bauspiess, C. Landmesser, and D. Lincicum; trans. P. C. Hodgson and R. Brown (Oxford: Oxford University Press, 2017), 3–44.

the roots of the Christian proclamation in Judaism, but also prepares the way for its own sublation in Pauline Christianity. But again, what is most interesting here is not the concrete set of results Baur achieves, but rather his critical attempt to fix the Gospels in their historical situation and then to read them as reflections of and evidence for a larger superstructure: the total view of the development of early Christianity and its theology.

CRITICAL INVESTIGATIONS IN THE CANONICAL GOSPELS

[1]

Introduction: The History of Gospel Criticism and the Position of Current Research

The relationship between the four canonical Gospels as historical[4] depictions of Jesus' life is so peculiar that nothing compares to it in all secular or Christian literature. According to their essential content, all four describe the course of those few years of Jesus' public life with such a great degree of agreement that one might believe at least the writers of the first three wrote in agreement with one another. But then again, they write with considerable differences, as if each of these writers had quite purposely wanted to differentiate himself from the others. Depending on whether one of them is more or less drawn to one or another, the common relationship of kinship that runs through the entire content of these Gospel narratives is modified in different ways, and we encounter all kinds of possible variations of this relationship, ranging between the two extremes which can be differentiated here: from being continuously identical and in literal agreement, on the one hand, to contradictions which are truly apparent to the eye, on the other.

Now, how should we solve the problem of this mysterious phenomenon presented to us? This question has had to be posed since the most ancient times, ever since the four Gospels could be compared with one another in the order which they have in the canon, and since people became conscious of their relationship with one another. The answer to this question was very different, based partly on the difference between the positions which were inherently possible, partly on the theological character of the times in which this question was handled. It already made an essential difference whether one proceeded from unity toward difference, or from difference to unity, and thus whether one wanted to explain the differences based on the unity, or the unity based on the difference.

[2] But what could cause one to preferentially or exclusively take one or the other possible positions if not the entire character of the consciousness of the age each time [the question was addressed]? Thus, it is the nature of this issue that the general course of development of theological consciousness is reflected in the whole line of different attempts made at solving that problem. The main answers given to that question are as different as the main periods of this theological consciousness. In general, the course of the issue here, too, could only be that the theological consciousness that dealt with the phenomenon at hand as its given object gradually purified and

---

[4][Tr.] Baur's *geschichtlich* and *historisch* are often synonymous. When there is a difference, *historisch* tends to evoke the meaning of "what 'actually' happened" (as opposed to the way it is related by the gospel texts), and *geschichtlich* tends to evoke Baur's philosophy of "the historical" as that which is mediated by consciousness in its developmental epochs.

freed itself from the dogmatic and other subjective presuppositions which more or less stood in the way of the cause and obstructed or blurred it. This consciousness learned to place itself in the midst of the objectivity of historical circumstances which this phenomenon itself [i.e., the literary relationship of the Gospels] belongs to in such a way that it was able to grasp it as one that had sprung from these very circumstances. If we survey the different main attempts made at solving this question from this perspective and name them in a brief and general manner, we can differentiate between (1) a dogmatic, (2) an abstractly critical, (3) a negatively critical or dialectical, and (4) a historical understanding of the relationship of the four Gospels in question.[5]

[....]

THE HISTORICAL VIEW

[71] Here, we return to the question mentioned above, where we broke off with our evaluation of Strauss' work.[6] Because further attempts since then at determining the Gospels' relationship have not led to a decisive step forward, the awareness of the necessity of progress can only develop on the basis of Straussian criticism. The error in Strauss' work is that it makes the Gospel account the object of its critique without first having come to a more solid result in the criticism of the writings. But this error was natural, not just because of the position of criticism at the time; it was also a necessary moment for the mediation of the further development of criticism. [72] It was natural, after prolonged fruitless efforts in preoccupation with the texts, to turn away from the texts and to their content, the matter itself, since critique of the texts could only be essentially related to the account (*Geschichte*) contained in them. As impossible as it is to separate historical critique[7] from critique of the texts, it is as certain that at the same time, a free and unbiased critique of the texts is not possible unless one has dealt with their content in such a way that their critical

---

[5]Baur thus proposes to treat the interrelationship of the Gospels, including both what modern scholars refer to as the synoptic problem and the Johannine question. He argues that the evaluation of the literary problems involved cannot be undertaken apart from a consideration of the theological stance of the interpreter, and goes on to discuss at length (in sections omitted from this selection) the ways in which theological perspectives have clouded or informed such literary critical judgments. He classifies some of these attempts as "dogmatic" (Augustine, Gerson, A. Osiander, M. Chemniz, J. A. Bengel, Storr), others as "abstractly critical" (J. G. Eichhorn, Hug, Gieseler, Schleiermacher, de Wette, Credner), and a third group as "negatively critical or dialectical" (D. F. Strauss, Neander, Ebrard, Wieseler, Weisse, Bruno Bauer, Wilke)—all of whom Baur criticizes. In the fourth section, given here, Baur presents his own "historical" view.
[6]I.e., KUKE 40–71.
[7][Tr.]: Baur's *Kritik der Geschichte* is suggestive of multiple English meanings, both because of the ambiguity of the word *Geschichte*, and because of Baur's philosophical understanding of what "the historical" (*das Geschichtliche*) is. *Geschichte* may mean both "history" (with all the vagueness and philosophical problems attached to that English word) and "narrative." *Die evangelische Geschichte*, then, is ambiguously "the Gospel history" (what "historically" happened, however the meaning of "historical" is specified) and "the Gospel account" (the story told by the canonical Gospels). As Baur will say just below, however, what is "historical" (*alles Geschichtliche*), what is the object of historical knowledge (*historisches Wissen*), is for him not a third-person objectivity, or a brute fact separate from consciousness. The historical, Baur says, is what has been mediated by consciousness, what has attained its expression through the mediation of the consciousness of an author or past era. So in Baur's notion of "historical critique" (*die Kritik der Geschichte*), there can be no notion of the "real" Gospel history as a brute objectivity essentially apart from the subjective "Gospel account;" nor can there be the notion of an irrevocable separation of "what 'really' happened" from "what the evangelists understood," and mediated to us by their conscious activity.

examination is dulled as little as possible by the interference of a false, subjective interest. There is no true, objective critique without relating to the result more or less indifferently and removing from oneself all subjective relationships with the object of criticism as much as possible.

Despite all objections that the situation of the entire Gospel account's historical credibility is very different from what it had been customary to assume, such free criticism, so devoid of presuppositions as Strauss' is, and the view it is increasingly communicating to the general consciousness of the age, also necessarily had the effect on scriptural criticism that people learned to consider scripture from a more unbiased perspective, free from dogmatic presuppositions.[8] This, however, made the necessity of a return from historical critique to criticism of the writings even more evident. Even though the path Strauss embarked on may be natural and in a sense necessary, it is undeniable that by the very nature of the issue it is impossible to arrive at reliable results in a historical critique as long as criticism of the writings is still so unresolved and uncertain.

The position one should take on Strauss' criticism, in order to get over the negativity of its result (as much as that is at all possible), can only be a criticism of the texts that are the sources of the Gospel account.[9] The degree to which that criticism is justified or not in all the essential points will have to be demonstrated in subsequent Gospel criticism. Strauss' criticism declares the content of the Gospel account to be essentially mythical. But in order to know whether it is making use of its mythical view of the Gospel account too broadly, one must before all else ask whether the content believed to be mythical had developed as unconsciously and unintentionally for the evangelists themselves as one must assume it to be the case for the mythical view. All that is mythical is ahistorical, but not all that is ahistorical is mythical; much that appears to be mythical has only obtained its ideal form, which is similar to *mythos*, as the narrating writer's free production. [73] This is an important point, which must be claimed against the mythical view carried out by Strauss, and it already indicates to us the general position in which we must situate the Gospel account in contrast to him.

Since for us generally all that is historical first passes through the narrating writer's medium, so too, in the criticism of the Gospel account the first question is not what the objective reality of this or the other narrative is, but rather how the narrated material relates to the narrating writer's consciousness, by whose mediation it [has become] an object of historical knowledge[10] for us. That is the position historical criticism must occupy; only from there, by determining the boundary between the historical and the ahistorical—"this most difficult question in the realm of criticism"[11]—can it hope to at least come to a more well-founded view. The negativity of the results of Strauss' critique emerges, after all, as mentioned before, not so much from the content

---

[8] By suggesting that Strauss has a "presuppositionless" criticism, Baur does not intend to say that Strauss is a *tabula rasa* free of any commitments, but rather he was free from the prevailing dogmatic presuppositions of the time.

[9] Here Baur repeats his charge that Strauss' results are "negative" in the sense of merely destructive; see Köpf, "Ferdinand Christian Baur and David Friedrich Strauss," and Chapter 14 in this volume.

[10] *Historisches Wissen*.

[11] Baur mentions this earlier in the book, KUKE 44. Compare Strauss, *The Life of Jesus Critically Examined*, trans. Maryann Evans [= George Eliot], ed. Peter C. Hodgson (Philadelphia: Fortress, 1972), 90: "That is to say, what is the precise boundary line between the historical and the unhistorical?—the most difficult question in the whole province of criticism." Strauss himself points to Origen (p. 43), *Against Celsus* 1.42: "an attempt to substantiate almost any story as historical fact, even if it is true, and to produce complete certainty about it, is one of the most difficult tasks and in some cases is impossible" (trans. Chadwick).

of the Gospel account that is immediately declared mythical, but rather from the uncertainty about everything else that is created in connection with an account suffused with mythical elements.

Even though this question still ultimately remains to be answered, it presents itself from a different perspective as soon as one seeks to understand as much as possible the question of whether the writer himself intended to present himself as a historical reporter in one part of his historical work or another. If it becomes clear upon closer examination that he himself did not narrate in a strictly historical manner, and that he has a special interest in understanding the object of his narrative from a specific perspective, what a profound limitation that fact alone imposes on the question about the boundary between the historical and ahistorical! But in order to be in a more plausible position to judge every single case of this kind, one has to first know what a writer wanted and what his purpose was, what interest motivated his historical depiction, what tendency he pursued in it, and what character his portrayal obtained by it. And how else could this question be answered than by examining as accurately as possible the historical circumstances of the writer's work? Every writer belongs to the period in which he writes and the more the object of his depiction stirs his age and interferes with its spiritual life, calling forth through the writer varying contrasts between opinions, interest, and parties, the more confidently one can assume that everyone who undertakes a historical depiction of this kind carries the markings of his times in himself, and the motives for his depiction can be found in the circumstances of his age.

[74] Why should this [fact], which no one can deny in general, not be applicable to our canonical Gospels? The fact that they present themselves as historical depictions of Jesus' life by no means precludes the assumption that their authors were led by certain motives and interests in their portrayals; indeed, it is not possible to think of them in any other way than as literary products of the time in which their authors lived. Thus, the first question a criticism of these Gospels must ask can only be: what did each author want and what was his goal? It is only with this question that we arrive on the solid ground of historical truth. All those questions whose interpretation has been the occasion for great and futile exertions—whether each of the four evangelists wrote chronologically and following upon one another, how their narratives that partly agree and partly differ relate to one another, whether Mark used Matthew and Luke, or Matthew and Luke used Mark, how the Synoptics relate to John and the other way round—are nothing but vague and aimless talk, a random seizing upon this issue and then another without getting closer to the issue itself and being able to enter into it more deeply—a purely abstract way of considering an object which cannot be grasped concretely enough.

Thus, let us at last rid ourselves of all these questions, which never get beyond the generality of abstract categories and theories, never exhaust the subject but merely touch upon it superficially, which do not bring it closer to consciousness but only move it further away! Let us dare to ask each of these authors about his individuality and his literary peculiarity and to look at them with the utmost rigor to see if they are indeed just simple and plain reporters of the Gospel account, whether here and there one can glimpse something in them, too, that allows us to look deeper into his soul and the interests and motives animating him. If one succeeded at listening in on even just one of the evangelists' secrets of his Gospel conception, criticism would have a solid point from which it could gain further ground.

[75] Now, once it is deemed necessary to keep to what is concrete, individual, and peculiar in order for criticism to occupy a new position that is different from previous ones, which Gospel could be better suited for this than the one that has always occupied one of the more peculiar

positions in all the possible combinations made so far, and which has proven most recalcitrant to all critical attempts? It is well known that even Strauss' critique was led astray in its attempts at John's Gospel. Nothing is more telling about the state of criticism at the time than Strauss' admission in the preface to the third edition of his *Life of Jesus*: the changes presented in this new edition, he says, more or less all have to do with the fact that a new study of the fourth Gospel based on de Wette's commentary and Neander's *Life of Jesus Christ* has caused him in turn to doubt his earlier uncertainties about the authenticity and credibility of this gospel.[12] Not that he was persuaded about its authenticity, he says; rather, he is no longer convinced of its inauthenticity, either. Among the features of authenticity and inauthenticity, which contradict and disrupt one another in such a unique way, as well as the proximity and distance from the truth in this extraordinary Gospel, he says he had emphasized with one-sided, polemical zeal only the neglected, disadvantageous side in the first version of his work, as it seemed to him; he says, in the meantime, though, the other side's validity had gradually also become apparent to him. It is just that he cannot bring himself, he says, to readily sacrifice contradictory observations to it the way almost all contemporary theologians do, with the exception of de Wette.

Is it possible to express oneself in a more inconsistent and uncertain way on one of the main questions in New Testament criticism? But this statement was made only to take back this doubt about his doubt yet again in the next edition of the *Life of Jesus*.[13] What could be the outcome of a criticism in such disagreement with itself other than a completely negative result? Thus, if a position exists that goes beyond this negative criticism and opposes it, then its greatest certainty must consist exactly in what is most uncertain in the negative one.

All that a Gospel can exhibit in terms of specificity, individuality, purely subjective [elements], and its own spiritual tendency of ideality which is spread over it all, and all that so essentially differentiates its whole way of understanding Christianity from the way the other Gospels understand it, gives it such a unique character and such a determinate tendency that if anywhere, it is here that it must be possible to deduce its origins from such data. [76] But if we have evidence in even just one of the Gospels that a Gospel is not just a simple historical *relatio* [a narration, that is, of events], but that it can also be motivated writing, writing with a tendency (*Tendenzschrift*),[14] then that is generally the perspective from which criticism must consider the Gospels. This, in turn, gives rise to the following principle: the more a certain cause (*Tendenz*) is expressed in a historical portrayal of this kind, the less this portrayal can be what it has usually been held to be, i.e., an authentic, historical report.

---

[12] For the changes in Strauss' subsequent editions, see Hodgson's "Editor's Introduction," in Strauss, *Life of Jesus Critically Examined*, xxii–xlvii, and Strauss' own prefaces, li–lviii. W. M. L. de Wette, *Kurzgefasstes exegetisches Handbuch zum Neuen Testament*. I.3. *Kurze Erklärung des Evangeliums und der Briefe Johannis* (Leipzig: S. Hirzel, 1837); August Neander, *Das Leben Jesu Christi in seinem geschichtlichen Zusammenhange und seiner geschichtlichen Entwickelung* (Hamburg: Perthes, 1837). de Wette (1780–1849) was a theologian and biblical scholar who held positions in Heidelberg (1807–10), Berlin (1810–19), and Basel (1822–49). Neander (1789–1850) was an eminent church historian who held a chair in Berlin from 1813.

[13] Note Strauss' remark in the preface to the fourth edition: the third edition "contained too much of compliance. The intermingling voices of opponents, critics, and fellow laborers, to which I held it a duty attentively to listen, had confused the idea of the work in my mind; in the diligent comparison of divergent opinions I had lost sight of the subject itself" (trans. Peter C. Hodgson in the introduction to Strauss' *Life of Jesus*, lviii).

[14] By a *Tendenz*, Baur thinks of a set of theological or ideological convictions that motivate the writer's presentation of Jesus and other elements of the story. The mapping of early Christianity in terms of the competing "tendencies" on display in the extant texts is the project Baur undertakes most fully in his CCK/CCC.

"Tendency writing," however, can only be called such insofar as it is a product of its time. The kind of criticism which considers such writing from this perspective and which can see in this perspective alone a new moment in critical consciousness justly calls itself historical, because it makes its essential task to immerse itself in the whole combination of circumstances in the times from which these texts have emerged. But if it does not want to proceed from an arbitrary presupposition, it must not limit the radius of these circumstances to the time of these texts' assumed apostolic origin. Rather, it must extend its circle as far beyond the texts' historical existence as the data at hand permit. The more uninhibitedly and conscientiously, the more precisely and thoroughly such criticism investigates all that can shed light on the origin of our Gospels in everything within this widened radius of given historical circumstances, the less it will want for a result which attains to the degree of probability at all possible in such matters.

[...]

The Gospel of John's Relationship to the Consciousness of the Time

[311] By moving on to this next point in our historical-critical investigation, we can immediately connect this investigation to the question we discussed last.[15] As has been shown, in Jesus' Johannine discourses the idea of the high and absolute significance which is expressed in the idea of the *Logos* and which our Gospel gives to the person of Jesus becomes apparent with the whole energy of a consciousness filled with it. It is precisely this significance given to Jesus that most clearly describes the Gospel's position in the development of the Christian consciousness in the most ancient times.

In the texts of the canonical New Testament (taken as a whole and not including mediating transitions), three types of Christian teaching can be distinguished, three main forms of Christian-religious consciousness, which also make up three developmental stages.[16] The synoptic Gospels and the New Testament texts which belong with them form the first type. In these we see the side of Christianity where it is still closest and most connected to Judaism and where it is only just about to develop out of Judaism and to break away from it with its own, independent meaning. Christianity has its absolute meaning only in its being the spiritualized law which has been generalized with the new covenant of the forgiveness of sins, which Jesus as the Messiah, or as the Son of God in a higher messianic sense, institutes by his death. The second form is represented by the Pauline Epistles in the opposition of the Law and the Gospel and in the higher meaning which Christ, who has been transported beyond the synoptic concept of the Messiah or the Son of God, has as the object of faith in the Pauline sense or as Lord of the community. [312] Moving beyond even the doctrinal conception of the smaller Pauline Epistles, the Johannine Gospel rises even above this form, by equating Jesus, as the subject of the Gospel narrative, in an absolute way with the *Logos*, who from eternity is with God and God himself.

In the Pauline position we get the next criterion for the Johannine position. The relationship between the two positions can rightly be identified in the following way: what in Paul is the mediation of opposites in humanity's relationship with God, which only comes about through struggle and conflict, is in John the peace of the unity elevated above opposites, and what in Paul is

---

[15]That is, on the speech of Jesus in John (KUKE, 280–310).
[16]This broad movement also marks the more detailed presentation in CCK/CCC.

still a human-divine relationship when we consider the person of Christ is in John an entirely divine one. The greatest opposition which the Pauline doctrinal concept addresses is between the Law, on the one hand—which is developed from the theocratic history of the Jewish nation or of the old covenant—or sin, which has come to its full power by the mediation of the Law,[17] and God's mercy, on the other hand, who forgives and suspends sin in the Gospel, or, insofar as the seat of sin is the flesh, the anthropological opposition between the flesh and the spirit.[18]

Placed in the midst of this opposition, in faith a person must first gain the consciousness of forgiveness and grace in the suffering Christ as the object of their faith, who died for the world and who himself became the sin and the curse of the Law.[19] In this faith, a person is already justified before God and has become one with Christ by completing in themselves the same process of overcoming sin: eliminating its power and liberating themselves from the law which makes up the essence of Christ's reconciliatory death. The highest meaning of the person of Christ himself is this meaning which he represents for the faith, or being the Son of God who has died for the sin of the world, and has reconciled the world with God in his death, which is immediately connected to the fact that he is the one who has died as well as the resurrected one, the one elevated to the right hand of the Father, and the ruler of the community of the faithful who rules with the power of God. Even in his divine power and dignity he is essentially human, he is the second, or heavenly man *vis-à-vis* the first, worldly man,[20] or, just as the principle of the sin which has been eliminated by his death is actually the σὰρξ [flesh] in its opposition to the πνεῦμα [spirit], he is the pneumatic man, who in his difference from the fleshly, worldly man has in himself the πνεῦμα ζωοποιοῦν [life-giving Spirit][21] or the πνεῦμα ἁγιωσύνης [spirit of holiness].[22]

[313] If we compare the Pauline doctrinal conception in this context with those two fundamental concepts in the synoptic perspective—the fulfillment of the law in the Gospel and the forgiveness of sins, which is added to the law—it is easy to see that the Pauline doctrinal conception is merely the mediating development between these two concepts which stand beside one another as yet unmediated. As soon as the forgiveness of sins and the liberation from the power of the Law according to its more precise moments had been conceived, it could only be understood as a process of reconciliation which takes place in Jesus' death. The higher the conception of Jesus' death was and the work of reconciliation accomplished in it, to the same degree the meaning of the person of Christ had to become more elevated. However, as long as one only ascends on this path to the divine power and dignity of Christ, which goes upward from below, and thus as long as one can ultimately only consider the divine in him as an accident of his substantial, human nature which has only been added—beyond this we are not justified to go at least in the undoubtedly authentic letters of the apostle—the Christian consciousness has not yet reached its absolute point.

Despite all the elevation of its concept, the Pauline Christ is after all the human Jesus, elevated to divine dignity; Christ is essentially human, even if at the same time he is also called heavenly (1 Cor 15:47), and for this reason, the task is still left to oppose the path which ascends from the finite to the absolute, by which contemplation moves upwards from below and what is substantial

---

[17] For example, 1 Cor 15:56; Rom 7:7-13.
[18] Gal 5:17; Rom 8:5-17.
[19] Gal 3:10-14.
[20] Cf. 1 Cor 15:47-49.
[21] 1 Cor 15:45: "Thus it is written, 'The first man, Adam, became a living being'; the last Adam became a life-giving spirit."
[22] Cf. Rom 1:4.

of Christ's person is not what is human but what is in itself divine, the *Logos* which is identical to God's absolute essence. What is primary and essential about Christianity is not that process which is determined by the power of sin and of the Law, which runs through such firm opposites, and which is fulfilled objectively in the reconciling death and subjectively in faith in its reconciling power. Rather, the essence of Christianity is the revelation of God's glory in the only begotten Son of the Father, the fullness of his grace and truth, in which all that is incomplete, finite, negative in the Law given by Moses is suspended in an absolute way, opened up in him, the one who was made flesh. The appearance of the only begotten Son is itself the absolute realization of salvation, the immediate communication of the divine nature to humanity.

[314] The *Logos*, which as the principle of life and light has entered into the opposition between light and darkness, draws to himself as its own kin all those who in faith become children of God,[23] and this becoming one with him in faith, which as such is also an action (ποιεῖν ἀλήθειαν [doing the truth], 3:21), encompasses in itself all that can only be understood as an opposition from a Pauline perspective, all that must first be mediated through a line of different moments. In a nutshell, what from Paul's anthropological perspective is the opposition between flesh and spirit, sin and grace, which engrosses the individual's subjective consciousness, is from John's metaphysical perspective the objective opposition of the two principles which encompass the physical and the ethical world, the light and the darkness, and the process of the *Logos*, which glorifies itself in the struggle against the unbelief of the world and which returns in this glorification to absolute identity with itself.[24]

No matter what one's opinion on the objective relationship between these different positions may be, it is certain that the developed consciousness of the Johannine position could only have had the Pauline one as its prerequisite. It was only from the Pauline position that one could move forward to the Johannine one, but not the other way round, returning from the Johannine to the Pauline, and for this reason, the Johannine Gospel can only belong to a period which had already progressed beyond the Pauline form of Christianity.[25] That is precisely what the relationship indicates in which Christianity appears *vis-à-vis* Judaism and paganism in our Gospel. Based on the main passage which applies here, 4:22,[26] even though Judaism has the absolute advantage over paganism that its worship of God is a knowing worship, i.e., directed toward the true object of religious consciousness, pagan worship, which is represented by the Samaritan religion in the passage mentioned here, is erroneous and unknowing in relation to its object. If, as it is said in 17:3, knowing the only true God is eternal life, only Jewish religion carries this absolute truth in it. That is why it is only from among the Jews that messianic salvation can come (4:22), the Messiah, who is to be the savior of the world (4:42). Thus, a continuous prophecy and indication of the one who is to be sent as the savior of the world by the one true God is connected with the knowledge of the true God in the scriptures of the Old Testament. [315] Moses already wrote about the Messiah (5:46),[27] and in the same way the messianic period is mentioned in the writings of the prophets

---

[23] John 1:1-13.
[24] Footnote omitted.
[25] Baur dates John infamously late, well into the latter half of the second century; see Frey, "Ferdinand Christian Baur and the Interpretation of John," 217–20.
[26] "You worship what you do not know; we worship what we know, for salvation is from the Jews."
[27] "If you believed Moses, you would believe me, for he wrote about me."

(6:45).[28] Abraham even saw the day of the Messiah (8:56)[29] with great joy, and Isaiah prophesied about him in contemplating his glory (12:41).[30]

Old Testament religion proves itself as the true one also by the fact that the most important moments in the Gospel account merely fulfilled what was in part explicitly announced and in part typologically portrayed in the Old Testament (2:17, 3:14, 6:32, 7:38, 12:14f., 38f., 19:28, 36, 37). Even though Old Testament Judaism is thus most closely related to Christianity, paganism also has a certain part in the *Logos*, which from the beginning shines in the darkness. For the light which came into the world already before the incarnation of the *Logos* illumines all human beings (1:9), and when the evangelist (12:52)[31] stresses with special emphasis that Jesus was not to die merely for the Jewish nation but also in order to unite the scattered children of God into a whole, he was also presupposing [the existence of] these scattered children of God in the pagan world. The greater the Jews' unbelief was, and the less for this reason it was possible to accomplish the goal of Jesus' ministry with them, the more its purpose had to be fulfilled in the pagan world, i.e., a greater receptiveness for God's word and for faith in Jesus had to exist in comparison with the Jews, just as the evangelist indeed distinguishes the pagans in this way from the Jews in several passages (see chapter 4:12, 30).[32]

The same permission and enablement of pagans to participate in Messianic salvation is a long-decided issue for the evangelist, a question which is no longer, as it is in the Apostle Paul's letters, the object of debate and of spirited negotiations which hold the interest of the age captive, but which has already been solved in reality by the existence of a Christian community consisting of pagans and Jews, which has assumed the unity of a whole. The evangelist repeatedly emphasizes this unity of a Christian community that consists of different elements and he regards it mainly as the effect which only Christ's death was able to have (11:51, 13:24):[33] as simply a public sign which draws everyone's gaze to itself (3:14-15),[34] or as the necessary condition under which Christ's earthly existence, like the germ which has sprung up from the seed he sowed, was able to become the foundation of a community which grows to acquire greatness (12:24). This seems to indicate that he already saw before himself this unity realized. [316] The evangelist would not be able to see in this in such a definitive way the immediate consequence of Jesus's death (as 10:15 is also immediately connected with the τιθέναι τὴν ψυχὴν ὑπὲρ τῶν προβάτων [laying down his life for the sheep] that he brings about ἄλλα πρόβατα, ἅ οὐκ ἔστιν ἐκ τῆς αὐλῆς ταῦτης [other sheep that are not of this fold], so that there would be a flock) if it had not already truly had this effect at the time when he was writing his Gospel.[35] Thus, the evangelist only saw the purpose of Jesus'

[28]"It is written in the prophets, 'And they shall all be taught by God.' Everyone who has heard and learned from the Father comes to me."

[29]"Your ancestor Abraham rejoiced that he would see my day; he saw it and was glad."

[30]"Isaiah said this because he saw his glory and spoke about him."

[31]Baur writes 12:52, but seems to intend 11:52: "and not for the nation only, but to gather into one the dispersed children of God."

[32]4:12: "Are you greater than our ancestor Jacob, who gave us the well, and with his sons and his flocks drank from it?" 4:30: "They left the city and were on their way to him."

[33]11:52: "and not for the nation only, but to gather into one the dispersed children of God." Baur writes 13:24, but 12:24 seems to make more sense: "Very truly, I tell you, unless a grain of wheat falls into the earth and dies, it remains just a single grain; but if it dies, it bears much fruit."

[34]"And just as Moses lifted up the serpent in the wilderness, so must the Son of Man be lifted up, that whoever believes in him may have eternal life."

[35]Footnote omitted.

apparition and ministry fulfilled in the unity of the Christian community composed of pagans and Jews equally, and the more negatively the Jewish people in their lack of faith comported themselves toward the pagans—the narration of which is the main theme of the Gospel—the more significant was the part he had to ascribe to the pagans in the fulfillment of Jesus' purpose.

This entirely free position occupied by the evangelist in relation to Judaism is a particularly characteristic property of his and it is the mark of a time in which Christianity had already moved beyond those oppositions of the first age in the course of its development. Judaism is already in the distant past; all that is positive about it, the Sabbath and circumcision (7:21),[36] has become perfectly indifferent for the position represented by the evangelist. Significantly, he even speaks of the Mosaic Law as something that only concerns the Jews, and which only they can call their own (8:17, 10:34).[37] Just as the apostle Paul, even though the evangelist does not want to misunderstand either the higher, inner meaning of the Old Testament, nor the claim which the Jews have first to Messianic salvation (they are, after all, the ἴδιοι [his own], to which the *Logos* εἰς τὰ ἴδια ἦλθε [came into his own]; 1:11), but he is equally certain that given the Jews' unbelief as it had by then become an established historical fact, the pagans have factually entered into the same right of ownership. Thus, we have here a completely Pauline view of Judaism's and paganism's relationship with Christianity, but here it no longer appears to us as a view which has yet to validate itself by struggle and opposition; rather, it has factually already realized itself in its objective reality by the existence of the Christian community consisting of Jews and pagans. [317] By then, Christianity has already placed itself in its absolute meaning above Judaism and paganism. In Jesus' words (4:21), the hour has already come when the Father is no longer worshipped either on Mount Gerizim, or in Jerusalem; rather, the true worshippers of God are those only who will worship him in spirit and in truth. In these words, the evangelist expressed his own consciousness of his age. It had already become historically true for him that both Judaism and paganism can only have the same negative relationship with Christianity as the only true, absolute religion, but that exactly for this reason, pagans and Jews also have the same equal part in messianic salvation, realized in the Christian community, in order to form in this unity of the whole the one flock under the one shepherd.[38]

It has justifiably been pointed out[39] how peculiar it is that the established name for Jesus' enemies in John's Gospel, no matter the various classes to which they belong, is οἱ Ἰουδαῖοι [the Jews]. This is characteristic of the evangelist's relationship with Judaism. It has been pointed out that this expression is by no means uniformly used, and thus does not carry the meaning of a limit or specificity. We have passages where this expression can only seem to describe the Sanhedrin, then again ones where it alternates with οἱ Φαρισαῖοι [the Pharisees], while the evangelist otherwise differentiates between them and the ἄρχοντες [leaders], and then again passages where it can only mean the inhabitants of the capital, while the evangelist in turn knows to separate these from the ἄρχοντες [leaders]. Finally, there are also passages where οἱ Ἰουδαῖοι [the Jews] even alternates with ὁ ὄχλος [the crowd], to which they are otherwise opposed. For all Jesus' opponents, it has been noted, wherever they may occur, wherever they may counter him in fact or in a dispute, this

---

[36]Here read 7:22: "Moses gave you circumcision (it is, of course, not from Moses, but from the patriarchs), and you circumcise a man on the Sabbath."
[37]8:17: "In your law it is written that the testimony of two witnesses is valid." 10:34: "Jesus answered, 'Is it not written in your law, "I said, you are gods"'?"
[38]See also Baur's argument in Chapter 11 in this volume.
[39]Footnote omitted.

expression had been chosen. In Jerusalem, just as much as in Galilee, in the temple as well as on the banks of the Sea of Galilee, it is οἱ Ἰουδαῖοι [the Jews] that Jesus had to contend with. It is said that he is one and they are the second moral person introduced as speaking and acting.

In the Synoptics, however, it is said that this expression for Jesus' enemies does not occur at all since they always describe them specifically and separately, and it is only in John that all manners of possible enemies are summarized under the one name of οἱ Ἰουδαῖοι [the Jews].[40] [318] The assumption has justifiably been that this phenomenon could only be explained by the Gospel's peculiarity as a whole, by its plan and purpose. The same is true for explaining these enemies' characteristic feature which corresponds to this name and according to which all individual properties of the Ἰουδαῖοι [Jews] and all individual motives of their opposition to Jesus coalesce in the one trait that they do not believe in him and that unbelief is thus their basic character. It has been held that the peculiarity of John's Gospel lies in its reliance on this contrast to obtain its purpose of presenting the revelation of the incarnated *Logos*' glory. However, from this immediately the consequence was drawn that the term οἱ Ἰουδαῖοι [the Jews] for all Jesus' opponents fluctuates and is used very generally, which in connection with the universalist tendency of depicting the Jewish people as a whole as unbelievers seems to point toward the later pagan Christian position from which the Gospel was written.

An eyewitness, a Palestinian, who was familiar with the nation's interior circumstances at the time of Jesus' life, and who was even the high priest's acquaintance, could not have expressed himself in such unspecific terms, they say. It has also been noted that this expression for the Jewish elders or for other individual Jewish parties does not occur anywhere else, either. Instead, this term is always indicative of the later times which are far from the original vision and would thus be a sign for this Gospel's inauthenticity.[41] Undoubtedly, the whole peculiarity of the Gospel is concentrated in the name Ἰουδαῖοι [Jews]. What follows initially from this name is no more than what this peculiarity connotes in itself, namely, that the Gospel's author, whoever he may be, understood the Gospel story, which is the object of his presentation, not from a purely historical but from a higher religious or dogmatic perspective. Since he had the great opposition between Judaism and Christianity before him as a historical fact which was already complete, he transferred this opposition onto the Gospel story. For this reason, the same enemies of Jesus that the Synoptics, who lived in the historical view of those circumstances, call by their specific historical names,[42] Pharisees, scribes, etc., he generally called Jews, so that by this name he could trace back to its first beginnings and causes the opposition as it had subsequently developed, and in order to consider the whole relationship between Judaism and Christianity from the general perspective that is a result of a higher worldview.

[319] However, the fact that he saw the historical circumstances of his age from this perspective, and that—irrespective of the very significant Jewish-Christian element in the Christian community—Judaism's complete break with Christianity appeared to him as a determined fact, this was only possible from the position of an author who had not only absorbed the Pauline view on Judaism's relationship with Christianity, but who had also further developed it himself with a

---

[40] The problem Baur is addressing here has come to the fore again in recent scholarship, beginning particularly in the article by Steve Mason, "Jews, Judaeans, Judaizing, Judaism: Problems of Categorization in Ancient History," *JSJ* 38 (2007): 457–512, with much subsequent discussion.
[41] Footnote omitted.
[42] [Tr.] Historical—historical: Baur uses first "historisch," then "geschichtlich." See note above.

free, independent spirit, and from there had penetrated into the full consciousness of Christianity's absolute idea. For him, Christ is the son of David to such a minor degree (ἐκ σπέρματος Δαβὶδ [from the seed of David], Rom 1:3) that he even seems to consider his birth at Bethlehem a Jewish fictional account (7:42).[43] In John's Gospel, the place of Jewish genealogy is taken over by the general humanity of the *Logos*' σὰρξ γίνεσθαι [becoming flesh; 1:14]. It is only the scene of the entrance into Jerusalem which he allows to take place in the same way as the other Synoptics present it, as far as the Messianic element of this scene is concerned. But this scene, too, is only supposed to be another moment in the Jews' testimony against themselves in their unbelief. After the immediately preceding miracle of Lazarus' resurrection, which he so closely connects to the entrance into Jerusalem as well as to the catastrophe taking place now in general, the Jews could not resist the impression of Jesus' divine dignity, so that they offered up to him this messianic homage of their own accord. However, the fact that they still did not recognize him as the Messiah can only be seen as new proof of the overwhelming, ineradicable power of their unbelief. According to the evangelist, what Jesus does and allows here to happen that is messianic is in reality only a certain kind of accommodation from Jesus' side in order to cut off the Jews' pretext for their unbelief, according to which they would not have been able to believe in him due to Jesus' lack of Jewish messianic criteria.[44]

But the evangelist's understanding of Jesus' death proves that from his perspective, all that is Jewish has so little enduring, immanent, and inner meaning that he looks back on the entire Old Testament merely as on a period in religious history which has come to fulfillment but precisely for that reason has also expired and has disappeared as far as Christian consciousness is concerned.[45] [320] On the question of the relationship between Judaism, paganism, and Christianity, John had very determinedly positioned himself on a side which one could not occupy without agreeing to the principles first applied by the Apostle Paul.

In light of this, and considering what a great authority the Apostle Peter was in the Jewish-Christian part of the Christian communities of the most ancient times,[46] one will hardly find it unexpected in John that he did not entirely neglect to address this moment in the historical circumstances of his times, either. If we could consider chapter 21 original, the evangelist would have done so in a very particular way. For as unclear as it is what one should understand in v. 22f. by the remaining of the disciple until the coming of the Lord, one can clearly understand this much: the martyr's renown which distinguishes the Apostle Peter should be seen in comparison with another merit, which distinguishes the Apostle John. If it was the Lord's explicit will that John should remain until he would come, John was thereby relieved of any claim one could have made on him regarding a martyr's death, and he could not be placed below even those apostles whose names, like Peter's, shone with the brightest brilliance of martyrdom. If in the end he only remained

---

[43]"Has not the scripture said that the Messiah is descended from David and comes from Bethlehem, the village where David lived?"

[44]Footnote omitted.

[45]Footnote omitted.

[46]See already Baur's essay, "Die Christuspartei in der korinthischen Gemeinde, der Gegensatz des petrinischen und paulinischen Christentums in der ältesten Kirche, der Apostel Petrus in Rom," *Tübinger Zeitschrift für Theologie* 4 (1831): 61–206. Reprint in *Ausgewählte Werke in Einzelausgaben*, ed. Klaus Scholder, vol. 1: *Historisch-kritische Untersuchungen zum Neuen Testament*, with an introduction by Ernst Käsemann (Stuttgart and Bad Cannstatt: Frommann-Holzboog, 1963). ET: *The Christ Party in the Corinthian Community*, ed. D. Lincicum; trans. W. Coppins, C. Heilig, L. Ogden, and D. Lincicum, Early Christianity and Its Literature (Atlanta: Society of Biblical Literature, 2021).

as the disciple who outlived all other apostles and who was eventually the only one left to wait for the Lord, then that was the unique distinction destined for him, one which placed him all the higher the less he was able to share it with another. [321] He was the disciple who, as the one waiting for the Lord's future, was not to die; the correction provided in v. 23 regarding the legend about the apostle John rejects the οὐκ ἀποθνήσκειν [not to die] as too positive an interpretation of the Lord's words, but it also does not want to have anything to do with a true ἀποθνήσκειν [dying]. It does not say that he truly passed away or that he was also destined to die. So, this way he still remains the disciple about whose death no one has anything to say, no one dares say anything about, and in whose name, just as in whose Gospel, death in life has been eliminated.

It is indisputable that this is supposed to be the advantage which distinguishes the Apostle John even compared to the Apostle Peter. Only those who wanted to concede at least as much authority to the Apostle John as to the Apostle Peter, who was the highest authority in the Jewish Christian party, could have had an interest in distinguishing him in this way.[47] But since chapter 21 must be considered merely a later addition, even though we can see in this parallel between John and Peter the concerns of John's party, which based itself on the Johannine Gospel, that does not appear to bear any relation to the Gospel itself. [322] It is, however, most curious that in the last chapter the same tendency that can already hardly be mistaken in several passages of the Gospel itself is expressed more determinedly.

Strauss[48] first called attention to the fact that the presentation of the relationship between Peter and John in the Fourth Gospel betrays a certain purpose and that in several of its features it shows itself peculiarly eager to place John at the side of Peter, or even to place him before Peter. Just as the Fourth Gospel already singles out John by the established name of ὁ μαθητὴς, ὅν ἠγάπα [the disciple whom he loved], or ἐφίλει ὁ Ἰησοῦς [(whom) Jesus loved] before everyone else, who is doubtless the only one who comes to mind at the thought of this name. This is done in a way that is unknown to the Synoptics, among whom Peter maintains the indisputable primacy. Thus, this intimate relationship between the favorite disciple and Jesus automatically brought about situations where even Peter needed John's mediation, as he could only have learned through John who Jesus had meant by name (13:24) in his words about the imminent betrayal.[49] Peter's necessary acknowledgment of his less close relationship with Jesus is thus very unambiguous. According to the fourth Gospel alone, it is John who as γνωστὸς τῷ ἀρχιερεῖ [known to the chief priest] procures entrance for Peter to the high priestly palace at Jesus' interrogation (18:15-16).[50] Even though this is only an external advantage, as Strauss notes, and without any reference to a closer relationship with Jesus, it is immediately connected with the fact that the Synoptics in general ascribe the eagerness to follow his imprisoned master to Peter, and not to John, too.

[323] This is where another factor needs to be mentioned, also observed by Strauss, whereby the fourth Gospel places John under Jesus' cross while in the Synoptics none of the disciples appear, and it lets John enter a relationship with the Mother of God which the Synoptics do not report at all (19:26-27).[51] Such a distinction could only be the result of John's intimate

---

[47]Footnote omitted.
[48]Footnote omitted.
[49]"Simon Peter therefore motioned to him to ask Jesus of whom he was speaking."
[50]"Simon Peter and another disciple followed Jesus. Since that disciple was known to the high priest, he went with Jesus into the courtyard of the high priest, but Peter was standing outside at the gate. So the other disciple, who was known to the high priest, went out, spoke to the woman who guarded the gate, and brought Peter in."
[51]"When Jesus saw his mother and the disciple whom he loved standing beside her, he said to his mother, 'Woman, here is your son.' Then he said to the disciple, 'Here is your mother.' And from that hour the disciple took her into his own home."

relationship with Jesus, but even irrespective of this relationship, the two disciples are noticeably placed next to one another wherever possible, or at the very least, John is not allowed to take second place to Peter. The Gospel author pursues this rivalry most conspicuously in the narration of 20:2f., where to each apostle something is attributed that is to balance them out with each other.[52] Both disciples go to the tomb together and at first, they keep pace with one another.[53] But John then runs ahead, more quickly than Peter, and comes to the tomb first, where he, bending down into the tomb, sees the linens—without, however, going inside. Peter, by contrast, even though he comes after John, goes into the tomb and looks at the shrouds more closely, whereby he also perceives that the head shroud is not with the other burial cloths but it has been placed in a special place as if on purpose. It is only then that the other disciple who first arrived at the tomb walks into it; thus, he only does something that Peter has already done before, but the text says only about him—and not about Peter—that as a consequence of this seeing he believed, just as the disciples' faith still depended on seeing and was not a knowing faith in general at that time.[54] It is a similar case with 21:3-8, but here it is Peter, true to his general character, who is the quicker one, and who immediately, when he hears that the Lord is close by, throws himself into the sea, and hurries toward him.[55] But it is John who recognizes the Lord first and who tells Peter that it is him. Strauss observes that Peter's virtues, such as the epithet honoring him, which Jesus gives him (1:43),[56] and his faithful confession (6:68-69)[57] are not concealed in the fourth Gospel, just as the Synoptics do not omit to mention his weaknesses and Jesus' rebukes.

Nevertheless, if one summarizes everything about this special relationship between the two disciples, the following must also be included: some things [sayings and actions] are ascribed to Peter, which, even though he is otherwise the head of the disciples, do not make him appear in exactly the best light. It is only John, however, the author of the fourth Gospel, who knows anything about these instances, while there is no mention about them in the Synoptics. [324] How

---

[52]20:1-9: "Early on the first day of the week, while it was still dark, Mary Magdalene came to the tomb and saw that the stone had been removed from the tomb. So she ran and went to Simon Peter and the other disciple, the one whom Jesus loved, and said to them, 'They have taken the Lord out of the tomb, and we do not know where they have laid him.' Then Peter and the other disciple set out and went toward the tomb. The two were running together, but the other disciple outran Peter and reached the tomb first. He bent down to look in and saw the linen wrappings lying there, but he did not go in. Then Simon Peter came, following him, and went into the tomb. He saw the linen wrappings lying there, and the cloth that had been on Jesus' head, not lying with the linen wrappings but rolled up in a place by itself. Then the other disciple, who reached the tomb first, also went in, and he saw and believed; for as yet they did not understand the scripture, that he must rise from the dead."
[53]Footnote omitted.
[54]Footnote omitted.
[55]21:3-8: "Simon Peter said to them, 'I am going fishing.' They said to him, 'We will go with you.' They went out and got into the boat, but that night they caught nothing. Just after daybreak, Jesus stood on the beach; but the disciples did not know that it was Jesus. Jesus said to them, 'Children, you have no fish, have you?' They answered him, 'No.' He said to them, 'Cast the net to the right side of the boat, and you will find some.' So they cast it, and now they were not able to haul it in because there were so many fish. That disciple whom Jesus loved said to Peter, 'It is the Lord!' When Simon Peter heard that it was the Lord, he put on some clothes, for he was naked, and jumped into the sea. But the other disciples came in the boat, dragging the net full of fish, for they were not far from the land, only about a hundred yards off."
[56]Read 1:42: "He brought Simon to Jesus, who looked at him and said, 'You are Simon son of John. You are to be called Cephas' (which is translated Peter)."
[57]"Simon Peter answered him, 'Lord, to whom can we go? You have the words of eternal life. We have come to believe and know that you are the Holy One of God.'"

conspicuous is it that even though all evangelists agree that at Jesus' arrest one of his followers drew his sword and cut off the ear of the high priest's servant, it is only the fourth evangelist who records it as Peter's act, disapproved of by Jesus? And this incident is not only narrated in 18:10-11[58] but the evangelist returns to it on occasion of Peter's three denials, which he narrates with great precision, in order to use them as a motive. This motive, as Strauss rightly observes, sounds so artificial and contrived in its context that one can only see one purpose in it: to firmly weave into the narrative the correlation between Peter and that swipe with the sword (18:26-27).[59] Even though Peter's refusal (13:8)[60] to let his feet be washed by Jesus provides a beautiful witness of his devotion to Jesus, it also shows no great ability to correctly understand the deeper meaning of Jesus' act. It could not have been in his interest, either, that in 21:15-19 his threefold denial is brought back by Jesus' doubting question, which is also repeated three times, in a manner so painful to Peter.[61]

If we wanted to merely see corrections and emendations of the Synoptic narration in all these instances, our Gospel would have to reflect this attitude to the Synoptics in general. But how improbable is it that all these features from the Synoptic tradition about Peter and John should have been completely lost?[62] Should the favorite disciple's special relationship with Jesus have really been so insignificant to the Synoptics that they did not even hint at it? And still, how can one doubt it when John as the writer of the Gospel gives witness about it himself? But do we not have to ask ourselves even more if John really is the author or not? Whichever may be the case, the deliberate treatment of these two disciples' relationship in John's Gospel remains the same, and the reason for it can only be found in the historical circumstances at the time of the Gospel's emergence and in the Apostle Peter's great authority in such a large part of the Christian community.

[325] For what must we understand the real purpose of the Johannine Gospel to be, whoever its author is? Its purpose can only be to bring about the recognition of the particular form of Christian consciousness which is distinctive of the Johannine Gospel. But how else could this have taken place than in opposition to the dominant directions, the already-existing forms of Christian consciousness, the Pauline and the Petrine one in general? It had to be the necessary tendency of a Gospel, in which the principle of Christian consciousness in its absolute meaning asserts itself so determinedly, to place itself above these two. What is the favorite disciple reclining on the Lord's breast, the confidant of his innermost thoughts, compared to whom even Peter is still distant from the Lord? Is he not precisely the carrier of the form of Christian consciousness expressed in his

---

[58] 18:10-11: "Then Simon Peter, who had a sword, drew it, struck the high priest's slave, and cut off his right ear. The slave's name was Malchus. Jesus said to Peter, 'Put your sword back into its sheath. Am I not to drink the cup that the Father has given me?'"

[59] "One of the slaves of the high priest, a relative of the man whose ear Peter had cut off, asked, 'Did I not see you in the garden with him?' Again Peter denied it, and at that moment the cock crowed."

[60] "Peter said to him, 'You will never wash my feet.' Jesus answered, 'Unless I wash you, you have no share with me.'"

[61] 21:15-19: "When they had finished breakfast, Jesus said to Simon Peter, 'Simon son of John, do you love me more than these?' He said to him, 'Yes, Lord; you know that I love you.' Jesus said to him, 'Feed my lambs.' A second time he said to him, 'Simon son of John, do you love me?' He said to him, 'Yes, Lord; you know that I love you.' Jesus said to him, 'Tend my sheep.' He said to him the third time, 'Simon son of John, do you love me?' Peter felt hurt because he said to him the third time, 'Do you love me?' And he said to him, 'Lord, you know everything; you know that I love you.' Jesus said to him, 'Feed my sheep. Very truly, I tell you, when you were younger, you used to fasten your own belt and to go wherever you wished. But when you grow old, you will stretch out your hands, and someone else will fasten a belt around you and take you where you do not wish to go.' (He said this to indicate the kind of death by which he would glorify God). After this he said to him, 'Follow me.'"

[62] Footnote omitted.

Gospel, of the absolute idea of Christianity as it is adequately determined and expressed in the Johannine teaching on the person of Christ? How can one be surprised, therefore, that the great import with which the Johannine form of Christian consciousness feels itself called to interfere with the historical circumstances of the time is also recognizable in Peter and John's position *vis-à-vis* each other in John's Gospel?

Since Peter is the representative of the twelve apostles, his relationship with the apostles is already discernible by the position which the evangelist accords himself in relation to Peter. This deserves to be considered more closely to further illuminate what we have noted above. Even though there is no evidence of a hostile, polemical relationship of the kind we will find in Luke here,[63] the evangelist portrays the apostles' entire level of knowledge and of spiritual ability during Jesus' whole life as so low and incomplete that it infinitely deviates from his position as he looks back on this early period. Relevant passages should be mentioned here, in which the evangelist himself explicitly notes that the disciples at first did not understand the real meaning of Jesus' words and actions at all, but did so only later, [326] after his death and resurrection. See 2:23.[64] The disciples remembered his words in verse 19[65] only after his resurrection, they understood only then what he had wanted to say, and they believed the scripture and Jesus' words. In the same way, the disciples at first did not understand (12:16) the messianic reference of the events at Jesus' entrance into Jerusalem.[66] They only did so after his glorification, τότε ἐμνήσθησαν [then they remembered], as it says so here too, ὅτι ταῦτα ἦν ἐπ'αὐτῷ γεγραμμένα, καὶ ταῦτα ἐποίησαν αὐτῷ [that these things had been written of him and had been done to him]. How many of the numerous misunderstandings of Jesus' words, of the clumsy questions posed to him, are due to the disciples! See 4:31-34, 5:5f., 11:8-10, 16.[67] Especially Jesus' last words to the disciples contain much evidence of how little they were still able to grasp his meaning, and the evangelist even seems to be out to rather vividly demonstrate their spiritual inability. How clueless is Thomas' question (14:5),[68] how incomprehensible the demand made by Philipp (v. 8),[69] how humbling for the disciples in general is Jesus' response: τοσοῦτον χρόνον μεθ'ὑμῶν εἰμι, καὶ οὐκ ἔγνωκάς με, Φίλιππε; ([have I been with you all this time, Philip, and you still do not know me?] v. 9)! See 14:22, 16:17, 29.[70]

---

[63]See KUKE, 522–31.

[64]Read 2:22: "After he was raised from the dead, his disciples remembered that he had said this; and they believed the scripture and the word that Jesus had spoken."

[65]"Destroy this temple, and in three days I will raise it up."

[66]"His disciples did not understand these things at first; but when Jesus was glorified, then they remembered that these things had been written of him and had been done to him."

[67]4:31-34: "Meanwhile the disciples were urging him, 'Rabbi, eat something.' But he said to them, 'I have food to eat that you do not know about.' So the disciples said to one another, 'Surely no one has brought him something to eat?' Jesus said to them, 'My food is to do the will of him who sent me and to complete his work.'" Baur writes 5:5f., but presumably has 6:5-14 in mind, which begins, "When he looked up and saw a large crowd coming toward him, Jesus said to Philip, 'Where are we to buy bread for these people to eat?' He said this to test him, for he himself knew what he was going to do ... " 11:8-10, 16: "The disciples said to him, 'Rabbi, the Jews were just now trying to stone you, and are you going there again?' Jesus answered, 'Are there not twelve hours of daylight? Those who walk during the day do not stumble, because they see the light of this world. But those who walk at night stumble, because the light is not in them ....' Thomas, who was called the Twin, said to his fellow disciples, 'Let us also go, that we may die with him.'"

[68]"Thomas said to him, 'Lord, we do not know where you are going. How can we know the way?'"

[69]"Philip said to him, 'Lord, show us the Father, and we will be satisfied.'"

[70]14:22: "Judas (not Iscariot) said to him, 'Lord, how is it that you will reveal yourself to us, and not to the world?'" 16:17: "Then some of his disciples said to one another, 'What does he mean by saying to us, "A little while, and you will no longer see me, and again a little while, and you will see me"; and "Because I am going to the Father"?'" 16:29: "His disciples said, 'Yes, now you are speaking plainly, not in any figure of speech!'"

The disciples had to be in such an incomplete state in their spiritual life mainly because they had not yet received the Spirit, and because the Spirit was only able to come after Jesus' glorification (7:39).[71] For this reason, the tendency in all the farewell discourses is to point toward a moment in time where the Spirit which is imparted to the disciples will have elevated them to a completely different level of knowledge and of spiritual consciousness. But the greater the difference between that earlier and this later period, the more all that elevates the Christian consciousness to this higher perspective belongs to a period beyond Jesus' earthly life, and the more the evangelist is distanced from the Judaic view which sought to tie a person's ability to hold the office of apostle to Jesus' earthly life and to the disciples' physical closeness to the still immediately present Lord.[72]

Judaism follows the personal; it follows particular individuals as carriers of the whole, the apostles, and among these, preferentially the Apostle Peter. That quiet irony about the Apostle Peter emerges from the contrast with this view in our evangelist. For him, the spirit as the general principle of Christian consciousness and life is placed above the personal in the apostles, too. The greater the fullness of the spiritual life that has already developed from the principle which became effective in the Christian community only after Jesus passed on, the more the apostles recede into the background, for the spirit should be received by the faithful generally (7:39). For this reason, it is already apparent in the farewell discourse that the concept of the apostles passes over into the broader concept of the disciples (insofar as most of what is contained in this farewell discourse equally applies to the former as well as to the latter). [327] In this regard, it can also be pointed out that the solemn name of Ἀπόστολοι [Apostles] is never mentioned in this Gospel, and the twelve are only mentioned where something is connected to their name that cannot make a very good impression of them. Thus, Jesus asks the Twelve (6:67) if they, too, wanted to leave him, and as laudable as Peter's confession is, it is precisely the evangelist who notes that one of the twelve was Judas, the traitor.[73] Thomas is also mentioned as εἷς ἐκ τῶν δώδεκα [one of the twelve] in the scene which is so characteristic of his lack of faith (20:24).[74] If we take all this together, we can only see in the evangelist a writer who is already more distant from that oldest circle in Judaism.

[...]

The Gospel of Matthew's Historical Character

[600] If we survey this portrayal of the Gospel account in its entire context which is presented here, it is certainly impossible to misunderstand that everything develops in a very natural order, and there is no sufficient reason for the objection that the historical course of events of the matter itself could in reality have been different, at least in its most essential moments. The historical progression has nothing improbable about it on the whole. There is no lack of true progress in the development, its individual moments are appropriately motivated, and the catastrophe eventually

---

[71] "Now he said this about the Spirit, which believers in him were to receive; for as yet there was no Spirit, because Jesus was not yet glorified."
[72] Cf. Acts 1:21-22.
[73] I.e., 6:70-71.
[74] "But Thomas (who was called the Twin), one of the twelve, was not with them when Jesus came."

takes place in such a way that it could hardly have happened any differently after all the previous events. The evangelist himself emphasizes at certain main points the progress of the historical development and the moment of a new main part in his Gospel account. [601] This is especially the case in 19:1,[75] where he himself very decidedly marks the meaning of the epoch-making new period in Jesus' life and ministry which begins there, by letting Jesus pass over from Galilee to Judea and by letting him work there just as uninterruptedly as his ministry had been up to that point when it only covered Galilee.

If the Gospel is to assert its historical character, it must before all else be established that Matthew only has Jesus appear in Galilee and then only at the end of his life in Judea. If one did not want to recognize this as historically valid, one could only say the following against it: just as Matthew in general followed a specific conceptual order, in the same way, he divided Jesus' Galilean and Judean ministry into two large parts without precisely separating the events belonging to the one or the other according to chronological order, and without thus precluding the possibility that Jesus had also previously been in Judea many times. But why would one entertain this assumption when surely nothing is in itself more natural than to presuppose that Jesus' life and ministry, the way it developed historically, were divided into a Galilean and a Judean part? What kind of arbitrariness would one have to presume in the evangelist's historical treatment if the assumption was that even though in 19:1 he had emphasized Jesus' passing over from Galilee to Judea as a significant, epoch-making step, the evangelist had only done so fully aware of the combination which was his own making? It is entirely natural that the decisive step in 19:1 loses its historical significance to the same degree to which Jesus' messianic ministry had previously already been Galilean and Judean. We have already shown above that an objection to the portrayal provided in 19:1 cannot be based on 23:37-39.[76] It is essential to the historical portrayal in the Gospel of Matthew in general to consider Galilee as the real setting of Jesus' messianic ministry and to only have him go to Jerusalem for the catastrophe of his death. This is also evident in the consistency of this portrayal all the way to the end of the Gospel, which is achieved when Jesus immediately after his resurrection gives his brothers the instruction to go to Galilee, where he then appears to the eleven disciples for the first time (28:10 and 16).[77]

[602] Thus there is no cause, unless one wanted to deny the Gospel's historical character, to doubt its portrayal in this regard. Both in this and in the way in which Jesus' conflict with the Pharisees and the heads of the Jewish nation develops more and more and takes on an increasingly serious and hostile character—especially from 21:23[78] onwards—the portrayal of events follows a very natural, historical progression. Even though many elements may appear to be ahistorical when examined in isolation, they cannot be contradicted in those moments which shape the course of the development as a whole.

---

[75]"When Jesus had finished saying these things, he left Galilee and went to the region of Judea beyond the Jordan."
[76]See KUKE, 599–600. Matt 23:37-39: "'Jerusalem, Jerusalem, the city that kills the prophets and stones those who are sent to it! How often have I desired to gather your children together as a hen gathers her brood under her wings, and you were not willing! See, your house is left to you, desolate. For I tell you, you will not see me again until you say, 'Blessed is the one who comes in the name of the Lord'.'"
[77]28:10: "Then Jesus said to them, 'Do not be afraid; go and tell my brothers to go to Galilee; there they will see me.'" 28:16: "Now the eleven disciples went to Galilee, to the mountain to which Jesus had directed them."
[78]"When he entered the temple, the chief priests and the elders of the people came to him as he was teaching, and said, 'By what authority are you doing these things, and who gave you this authority?'"

The guarantee that the Gospel is safe from objections which appear to be justified by the deviating portrayal of events in the other Gospels provides the basis for recognizing the historical character of the Gospel in the first place, which in turn emerges from examining the Gospel itself. Such a guarantee is only possible based on the position of our examination. Of course, it is inevitable that the historical credibility of Matthew should repeatedly be questioned as long as one considers the Johannine portrayal to run parallel to Matthew's, as long as one at least grants that Luke, wherever he concurs with Matthew's Gospel, has the advantage of having arranged some discourses and events in the Gospel account historically more accurately, and as long as even Mark's Gospel counts as an independent, historical authority when compared to Matthew's. All those questions cannot come up again for us in the position we assume here. Once it has been proven, as is the purpose of this investigation, that the other Gospels are not only based on the Gospel of Matthew, but that their portrayal, which deviates from Matthew's, was also determined by a motive beyond historical interest, then Matthew's Gospel is moved beyond the parallel relationship with the other Gospels in such a way that its historical credibility cannot very easily be contested at least from this perspective.

Thus, what can be argued against it can only be taken from the Gospel itself. In this respect, the question justifiably arises if the pragmatism peculiar to the Gospel also influenced the material aspect of its historical portrayal, and since this question, as has been shown, cannot simply be negated, it follows that the Gospel's historical character, however firmly it may generally be established, can in no way apply to every detail. [603] If one distinguishes between the Gospel's factual content and the discourses, the evangelist's peculiar way of grouping the objects of his presentation according to specific points must in many cases have rearranged the historical position of events. How can it be assumed that Jesus at one point did nothing but work wonders and healed the sick and another time he merely presented parables? Thus when one comes to a more precise understanding of the Gospel's historical character, even though it has a historical framework, which is founded on a historically given, basic understanding that encompasses the whole and which holds together increasingly firmly all that it includes in the further development of the Gospel account, within this framework itself and in its different compartments not only has some material come to be in this position only by random or purposeful grouping, but the individual stories themselves cannot even be said to be entirely historical.

Who would believe that all those miracles which Jesus is said to have worked in the first period of his public ministry simply happened the way they are narrated here, not to mention the infancy narratives as well as Jesus' baptism and temptation? The fact that the Gospel account also contains mythic elements cannot be denied unless all principles of historical-critical research on the Gospels were abandoned.[79] The concept of myth has been accorded an unwarranted scope by utilizing it even where the ahistorical content must be seen from a completely different perspective, as is the case especially with John's Gospel. Nevertheless, accounts from the Gospel of Matthew, where there is no discernible, particular interest that could have been the occasion for their creation and which instead only exhibit the general character of tradition and legend, which is formed freely, provide all the more reason for a mythical interpretation. No matter how much one might limit the Gospel's peculiar pragmatism to the merely formal elements of the writer's depiction, this pragmatism has itself already emerged from an interpretive way which makes the possibility of the development of myths all the more understandable.

---

[79] Invoking once again Strauss' *Life of Jesus*.

If it is a feature of Jesus' messianic character that it had to be possible to prove the Old Testament criteria of Messianism in him, and if he could not be acknowledged as the Messiah without his also having appeared as θεραπεύων πᾶσαν νόσον καὶ πᾶσαν μαλακίαν ἐν τῷ λαῷ ([healing every disease and every sickness among the people] 4:23, see also 8:17[80]), how can one fail to see that this understanding of his person had given a more or less mythical form to some elements of the Gospel account already at the time before there were written Gospels? [604] How can one maintain that the Gospel has a strictly historical character while also completely excluding all mythical elements when there is no shortage of passages where the mythical obviously even passes over into the apocryphal, as can be clearly seen in 27:53[81]? But all concessions which have to be made to the mythical perspective, just as all that may be a result of the evangelists' own pragmatism, can in no way question the Gospel's basic substantial, historical character. And from this the necessity emerges to separate more and more firmly and as much as possible the elements which have grown together, the historical and the ahistorical, by progressively, critically investigating its content.

What is true for the factual elements is on the whole also true for the discourses, which make up such a considerable part of the Gospel's content. And since the mythical tendency of the tradition cannot have had the same influence on the discourses based on their very nature, one is all the less authorized to cast doubt on their historical character. But not even in the discourses can the claim of their historicity be expanded to every particular element. It has already been shown in the Sermon on the Mount that the evangelist treated his historical material with the awareness of his freedom as a writer.[82] One can deduce from this that the same will have been true for other discourses. Apart from the Sermon on the Mount, there is another of Jesus' other, longer discourses, where it can be shown that it is impossible that Jesus should have spoken in the way the evangelist has him speak: it is the last, eschatological discourse in the twenty-fourth chapter. Unbiased interpreters admit that Matthew has given us Jesus' speech as a reproduction which is not free of Matthew's own additions. They also admit that he put the words in Jesus' mouth as a prophecy about the expectation of Christ's near future, shared with the apostolic age. By admitting this, much has already been granted to the evangelist's freedom as a writer, but one cannot stop there either, because Jesus could also not have spoken the way the evangelist has him speak about the destruction of Jerusalem, [605] to which, as is generally assumed, the twenty-fourth chapter refers.[83]

The Apocalypse furnishes us with the proof for this, if we consider it a genuine writing of the Apostle John, as indeed it is becoming less and less possible to deny. How could the author of the Apocalypse have ignored the destruction of Jerusalem, how would he not have been compelled to make it one of the main points of his apocalyptic depiction, if Jesus had truly already prophesied it, the way he supposedly prophesied about it according to the Gospel of Matthew? In chapter 11 of the Apocalypse, its author only foretells that Jerusalem shall be trampled on by the pagans for four and a half years,[84] but the temple as well as the inner courtyard shall be spared. The rest of the city shall not remain in the possession of pagans either, nor shall it be destroyed by them. An earthquake

---

[80]"This was to fulfill what had been spoken through the prophet Isaiah, 'He took our infirmities and bore our diseases.'"
[81]"After his resurrection they (sc. saints who had fallen asleep) came out of the tombs and entered the holy city and appeared to many."
[82]See KUKE, 583–9.
[83]See esp. 24:1-2.
[84]Rev. 11:1-2 actually mentions forty-two months (three and a half years).

shall destroy a tenth of the city; however, those who remain shall convert, and as a result, the rest of the city itself shall not be destroyed.[85] Thus, the author of the Apocalypse knows nothing about the destruction of Jerusalem; he only knows a Jerusalem which abides and is destined to be the seat of the thousand-year empire, as a clear proof that it is only the evangelist who makes the destruction of Jerusalem in this particular form, in which of course it only appears as an *oraculum post eventum* [an oracle after the event], the content of Jesus' eschatological speech. The necessary consequence to be drawn from this is that, even in Jesus' discourses, formally and substantially, a considerable part must be ascribed to the evangelist's composition, much as the historicity of these discourses is above all doubt when it comes to their substantial content.[86]

[606] Thus, we cannot assume that Matthew's Gospel is a purely historical (*rein historische*) telling of the original, real elements of the Gospel account, either. [607] It has a specific, individual, as well as authorial character. Even based on its peculiar pragmatism, it can only be called the most judaizing Gospel in contrast to the other Gospels. [608] If this rather liberal authorial [609] composition, which is also unmistakable here, can be traced back to a concern which is particularly guiding the author, that concern is the endeavor to understand the Gospel account based on the perspective of the Old Testament ideal of the Messiah and to prove by specific criteria that it was realized in the person of Jesus and that the Messiah who has appeared is identical to the one who had been prophetically beheld. So, let us ask further in which properties the judaizing character of Matthew's Gospel is mainly expressed, and how we are to evaluate this Gospel from the standpoint of historical consideration.

1. The way Matthew's Gospel declares itself on Mosaic law, its absolute meaning, and its eternal validity in the main source of 5:17 needs to be mentioned here first of all.[87] But as long as it has not been proven that the view of Mosaic law in this passage was not part of Jesus' original teaching, it cannot be considered a special mark of the Gospel's Judaic character. We do not encounter anything that is particularly Judaic with respect to retaining Mosaic law anywhere else, either. No further conclusions can be drawn from 23:3,[88] where it is said that the disciples should observe everything and do what the Pharisees and the scribes say they should observe, since the opposition which is established here between Pharisaic teaching and Pharisaic works can only be understood in the following way: much as everything that the Pharisees teach is the norm since it is an essential content of the Mosaic law, and one is to follow this norm in order to act morally, the Pharisees' own actions can only count as an example of moral action. Concerning the commandment of circumcision, specifically, there is [610] no evidence that the author of the Gospel of Matthew would still have recognized the Ebionite principle.[89] Instead,

---

[85]Rev. 11:13.
[86]Footnote omitted.
[87]"'Do not think that I have come to abolish the law or the prophets; I have come not to abolish but to fulfill.'"
[88]"Therefore do whatever they teach you and follow it; but do not do as they do, for they do not practice what they teach."
[89]That is, that circumcision is necessary for salvation. Baur seems to be referring to Epiphanius's tradition about "Ebion" (a misunderstanding of the origin of the term Ebionite), that he advocated "adherence to Judaism's Law of the Sabbath, circumcision, and all the other Jewish and Samaritan observances" (*Pan[arion]*, 30.2.2, trans. Williams; cf. also 30.17.5, and esp. 30.26.1–28.7). Baur conceives of the opponents of Paul in Galatians as Ebionite, and at points in his work, Baur can use the epithet "Ebionite" as roughly synonymous with "Jewish Christian." See the essays in F. Stanley Jones, ed., *Rediscovery of Jewish Christianity: From Toland to Baur*, History of Biblical Studies (Atlanta: Society of Biblical Literature, 2012).

in Matthew 28:19 only baptism, which has already taken the place of circumcision, is mentioned as the external form of the membership in the messianic kingdom.[90]

2. The national, Jewish particularism, mentioned by name in Jesus' words in 15:24,[91] is more conspicuous. But here, too, it depends on how these words are understood. They cannot be given too much importance even just because Jesus' way of acting in precisely this passage shows how little it is to be understood in the sense of an absolutely applicable principle. Now, since the Gospel otherwise in several passages unambiguously confesses Christianity's universalism, it cannot be accused of limited Judaism in this respect, either. The timidity with which the other Gospels, in order to avoid conceding too much to Judaism, have omitted or changed such passages is indisputably a more telling criterion of a certain tendential character than the uninhibitedness with which the author of the Gospel of Matthew has taken seemingly contradictory passages from tradition and has left them standing next to one other.

3. In the same way, the fact that Jesus in so many passages is distinctly more often described as υἱὸς Δαβὶδ ([Son of David] 9:27, 12:23, 15:22, 20:30, 31, 21:9, 15) than in the other Gospels cannot be claimed as a special criterion of his Judaism either, since in all these passages the name of the Son of David only features as a popular characterization of the Messiah in the mouths of contemporaries. It is a different matter with the first two chapters in which the author's purpose is directed toward proving Jesus to be the promised descendent from the lineage of David in the sense of the Jewish messianic concept. Even if one can still ask if these two chapters originally belonged with the real Gospel, there can be no doubt that the scene of the entrance, in which Jesus likewise appears as the Son of David, is an integrating, constituent part of the Gospel; this scene could only be counted as Judaistic if we could be certain that it had not taken place the way it is narrated here. From 22:41-45 one could deduce that to be the case.[92] If Jesus attached so little importance to the idea that the Messiah was the Son of David as seems to have been the case based on his skeptical argumentation [611] in this passage, how could he have arranged a scene which would only have been due to him as the Son of David? This scene belongs with the especially problematic events in the Gospel account because it is equally easy to explain how such a narrative could develop out of the Jewish idea of the Messiah, as it is difficult by contrast to make the claim that the events really happened the way they are narrated. But since it is impossible to make decisions about this with certainty, here too, when it comes to the evaluation of the character of our Gospel, we encounter a point beyond which we cannot go. Only if the scene were pure poetry or legend would the evangelist have provided special proof of his Judaic direction by unknowingly including the scene in his depiction of the Gospel account without taking offense at it the way the author of the original Gospel of Luke did.

---

[90]"Go therefore and make disciples of all nations, baptizing them in the name of the Father and of the Son and of the Holy Spirit."
[91]"He answered, 'I was sent only to the lost sheep of the house of Israel.'"
[92]"Now while the Pharisees were gathered together, Jesus asked them this question: 'What do you think of the Messiah? Whose son is he?' They said to him, 'The son of David.' He said to them, 'How is it then that David by the Spirit calls him Lord, saying, "The Lord said to my Lord, 'Sit at my right hand, until I put your enemies under your feet'"? If David thus calls him Lord, how can he be his son?'"

4. The preference for the Old Testament is characteristic of the Gospel, as is returning to the Old Testament for the constant use of passages derived from it. Such passages are applied everywhere and they are connected with the story in such a way that often one does not know whether the citation is there because of the story or whether the story is there because of the citation.[93] This peculiarity of the Gospel of proving the New Testament by the Old Testament, of seeing in the main facts of the Gospel account the fulfillment of Old Testament prophecies, is carried throughout the entire Gospel, but it is most conspicuous in the first two chapters. The fact that Jesus was born of Mary as a virgin, τοῦτο ὅλον γέγονε [all this took place], as it says in Matthew 1:22, ἵνα πληρωθῇ τὸ ῥηθὲν ὑπὸ τοῦ κυρίου διὰ τοῦ προφήτου [to fulfill what had been spoken by the Lord through the prophet], see [Isa] 7:14[94]; his birth in Bethlehem occurred according to the prophecy in Micah 5:2, see Matthew 2:6.[95] He had to flee to Egypt and remain there, ἵνα πληρωθῇ τὸ ῥηθὲν ([in order that what was spoken might be fulfilled], Hosea 11:1; see Matthew 2:15).[96] The words of the prophet Jeremiah (31:15) were fulfilled in the murder of the infants, see Matthew 2:18[97]; and when Joseph took his dwelling after his return from Egypt with the child Jesus in Nazareth, it, too, happened because the prophet had said, ὅτι Ναζωραῖος κληθήσεται [that he will be called a Nazorean], 2:23. It is conspicuous how far-fetched and how labored this latter reference is. Just as the reference is only made here in order to prove with an Old Testament passage the events to which it is supposed to refer, so the opposite is true in 2:13-15, apparently. The flight to [612] Egypt is as ahistorical as anything, and this story is only created in order to apply to it the Old Testament reference already available in the Messianic passage. It is an entirely different case when in 3:3 the appearance of the Baptist is proven messianically, see [Isa] 40:3.[98] Instead we encounter once again the same pragmatism, which delights in itself by dragging in Old Testament types and prophecies, in 4:14,[99] in using the passage Isa 9:1 for Jesus' effectiveness in the areas of Galilee mentioned in 4:14.[100] Thus, Jesus cannot do

---

[93]This reads like an early anticipation of the later debates about whether the passion narratives are "prophecy historicized" or "history prophesied."

[94]"Therefore the Lord himself will give you a sign. Look, the virgin shall be with child and bear a son, and you shall name him Emmanouel" (Isa 7:14 LXX, NETS translation).

[95]Micah 5:2 LXX: "And you, O Bethlehem, house of Ephratha, are very few in number to be among the thousands of Judah; one from you shall come forth for me to become a ruler in Israel, and his goings forth are from old, from days of yore" (NETS, modified); Matt 2:6: "And you, Bethlehem, in the land of Judah, are by no means least among the rulers of Judah; for from you shall come a ruler who is to shepherd my people Israel."

[96]Hosea 11:1 LXX: "For Israel was an infant, and I loved him, and out of Egypt I recalled his children." Matt 2:15: "This was to fulfill what had been spoken by the Lord through the prophet, 'Out of Egypt I have called my son.'"

[97]Jer 31:15 (=38:15 LXX): "A voice of lamentation and weeping and mourning was heard in Rama; Rachel did not want to stop weeping for her sons, because they are not." Matt 2:18: "A voice was heard in Ramah, wailing and loud lamentation, Rachel weeping for her children; she refused to be consoled, because they are no more."

[98]Isa 40:3 LXX: "A voice of one crying out in the wilderness: 'Prepare the way of the Lord; make straight the paths of our God'" (NETS). Matt 3:3: "The voice of one crying out in the wilderness: 'Prepare the way of the Lord, make his paths straight.'"

[99]Read 4:15.

[100]Isa 9:1–2 LXX: "O country of Zaboulon, the land of Nephthalim, and the rest who inhabit the seashore and beyond the Jordan, Galilee of the nations, the parts of Judea. O you people who walk in darkness, see a great light! O you who live in the country and in the shadow of death, light will shine on you!" Matt 4:15-16: "Land of Zebulun, land of Naphtali, on the road by the sea, across the Jordan, Galilee of the Gentiles—the people who sat in darkness have seen a great light, and for those who sat in the region and shadow of death light has dawned."

anything and nothing can take place having to do with him without it being possible to justify its messianic relationship and meaning based on Old Testament passages. The evangelist has hardly narrated the first healings of the sick and the casting out of demons, when he reminds us in 8:17 of the passage which has thereby been fulfilled (Isaiah 53:4).[101] In 12:18-21, Isaiah 42:1, in which the soundless working of the servant of God is described, is straightaway applied even to Jesus' rejoinder to those he has healed that they should not make him known as the Messiah.[102] In the latter two passages, at least Old Testament criteria for the Messiah are included of the kind which become the leading points in the portrayal of the Gospel account in their more general, typical meaning. And Jesus' parabolic way of teaching the evangelist relates in 13:14f and 35 to the passages from Isaiah 6:9 and Psalm 78:2.[103] The Pharisees are called hypocrites in 15:8 in accordance with the passage from Isaiah 29:13.[104] In the scene of the entrance into Jerusalem it is only the prophecy of the prophet Zechariah 9:9 which is fulfilled, and in the same context Jesus' messianic dignity is also proven by Ps. 8:3.[105] Several Old Testament citations of this kind can also be found in the account of the passion,

---

[101]Isa 53:4 LXX: "This one bears our sins and suffers pain for us, and we accounted him to be in trouble and calamity and ill-treatment." Matt 8:17: "This was to fulfill what had been spoken through the prophet Isaiah, 'He took our infirmities and bore our diseases.'"

[102]Isa 42:1-4 LXX: "Iakob is my servant; I will lay hold of him; Israel is my chosen; my soul has accepted him; I have put my spirit upon him; he will bring forth judgment to the nations. He will not cry out or send forth his voice, nor will his voice be heard outside; a bruised reed he will not break, and a smoking wick he will not quench, but he will bring forth judgment for truth. He will blaze up and not be overwhelmed until he has established judgment on the earth, and nations will hope in his name" (NETS). Matt 12:18-21: "Here is my servant, whom I have chosen, my beloved, with whom my soul is well pleased. I will put my Spirit upon him, and he will proclaim justice to the Gentiles. He will not wrangle or cry aloud, nor will anyone hear his voice in the streets. He will not break a bruised reed or quench a smoldering wick until he brings justice to victory. And in his name the Gentiles will hope."

[103]Matt 13:14-15: "With them indeed is fulfilled the prophecy of Isaiah that says: 'You will indeed listen, but never understand, and you will indeed look, but never perceive. For this people's heart has grown dull, and their ears are hard of hearing, and they have shut their eyes; so that they might not look with their eyes, and listen with their ears, and understand with their heart and turn—and I would heal them.'" Matt 13:35: "This was to fulfill what had been spoken through the prophet: 'I will open my mouth to speak in parables; I will proclaim what has been hidden from the foundation of the world.'" Isa 6:9-10 LXX: "And he said, 'Go and say to this people: "You will listen by listening, but you will not understand, and looking you will look, but you will not perceive." For this people's heart has grown fat, and with their ears they have heard heavily, and they have shut their eyes so that they might not see with their eyes and hear with their ears and understand with their heart and turn—and I would heal them'" (NETS). Ps 78:2 (=77:2 LXX): "I will open my mouth in a parable; I will utter problems from of old" (NETS).

[104]Matt 15:7-9: "You hypocrites! Isaiah prophesied rightly about you when he said, 'This people honors me with their lips, but their hearts are far from me; in vain do they worship me, teaching human precepts as doctrines.'" Isa 29:13 LXX: "The Lord said: These people draw near me; they honor me with their lips, while their heart is far from me, and in vain do they worship me, teaching human precepts and teachings" (NETS).

[105]Matt 21:4-5: "This took place to fulfill what had been spoken through the prophet, saying, 'Tell the daughter of Zion Look, your king is coming to you, humble, and mounted on a donkey, and on a colt, the foal of a donkey.'" Matt 21:15-16: "But when the chief priests and the scribes saw the amazing things that he did, and heard the children crying out in the temple, 'Hosanna to the Son of David,' they became angry and said to him, 'Do you hear what these are saying?' Jesus said to them, 'Yes; have you never read, "Out of the mouths of infants and nursing babies you have prepared praise for yourself"?'" Zech 9:9: "Rejoice greatly, O daughter Sion! Proclaim, O daughter Ierousalem! Behold, your king comes to you, just and salvific is he, meek and riding on a beast of burden and a young foal" (NETS). Ps 8:3: "Out of mouths of infants and nurslings you furnished praise for yourself, for the sake of your enemies, to put down enemy and avenger" (NETS).

Matt 26:31 based on Zech 13:7,[106] Matt 27:9 based on Jer 32:6 and Zech 11:12,[107] and Matthew 27:35 based on Ps 22:15.[108]

From all the features collected here, the fact indisputably emerges that the author of the Gospel of Matthew occupies the position of an Old Testament point of view far more than any of the other evangelists do. Even if for this reason one is justified to call the character of his Gospel judaizing, at the same time one has to acknowledge that it does not display the same kind of tendencies that are part of the other Gospels' peculiarities. It cannot be claimed that the Gospel's judaizing direction could have had the kind of influence which would have determined its entire layout and composition and which would have altered its historical depiction. If the Gospel [of Matthew] is compared to the other Gospels, the elements which the others do not have based on their specific tendency should far more be considered a characteristic differentiating feature than the elements the Gospel of Matthew does have. And based on the nature of the matter one cannot expect anything but that the oldest of the canonical Gospels, the one which developed out of a Hebrew Gospel, should have the most Old Testament passages and that it should present that side of Christianity in particular which is still interwoven with Judaism.

[613] This is the point where the question of the principal character of Matthew's Gospel becomes inseparable from the question of Christianity's original character, and the final question which criticism sees itself pushed toward can only be the following: Is Christianity's national specificity, which it necessarily retained by the very nature of its immanent roots in Judaism, the particular difference which sets the Gospel of Matthew apart from the other Gospels? Nothing is more significant for answering this question than Jesus' words in the Sermon on the Mount: he had not come in order to abolish the Law but in order to fulfill it [5:17]. The meaning of these words is the same for evaluating the historical character of our oldest Gospel as well as for the question of Christianity's original character. Thus, these words may only be interpreted in a way that allows one to recognize that they express both: the elements which Christianity still retains and which are identical to Judaism and the elements which are the principle of further, independent development and which carry Christianity beyond Judaism. In this way, both are contained in and equally characteristic of Matthew's Gospel: on the one hand, the Jewish national element, which is indisputably part of Christianity, and on the other hand, the pure givenness of this national element, i.e., the fact that this element is not random, purposeful, arbitrary, merely individual as it is contained in those words and in their context, but rather it is merely the necessary

---

[106]Matt 26:31: "Then Jesus said to them, 'You will all become deserters because of me this night; for it is written, "I will strike the shepherd, and the sheep of the flock will be scattered".'" Zech 13:7: "'Awake, O sword, against my shepherds and against my fellow citizen,' says the Lord Almighty. 'Smite the shepherds, and remove the sheep, and I will bring my hand against the shepherds.'"

[107]Matt 27:9: "Then was fulfilled what had been spoken through the prophet Jeremiah, 'And they took the thirty pieces of silver, the price of the one on whom a price had been set, on whom some of the people of Israel had set a price.'" Baur writes Jer 32:6, but presumably has in mind 32:7-8: "Hanamel son of your uncle Shallum is going to come to you and say, 'Buy my field that is at Anathoth, for the right of redemption by purchase is yours.' Then my cousin Hanamel came to me in the court of the guard, in accordance with the word of the Lord, and said to me, 'Buy my field that is at Anathoth in the land of Benjamin, for the right of possession and redemption is yours; buy it for yourself.' Then I knew that this was the word of the Lord." Zech 11:12: "And I will say to them, 'If it is good in your sight, give me my wages, or refuse.' And they set my wages at thirty pieces of silver" (NETS).

[108]Matt 27:35: "And when they had crucified him, they divided his clothes among themselves by casting lots." Ps 22:15 [read: 22:18]: "They divided my clothes among themselves, and for my clothing they cast lots" (NETS).

national determination which Christianity itself had to have just as every [other] specific, historical phenomenon does.

The perfect fulfillment of the Law is just as equally the abolition of Old Testament Law as well as the maintaining of it in the idea of the truly perfect δικαιοσύνη [righteousness], which encompasses in itself both the objectiveness of the perfected fulfillment of the Law and the subjective possibility of the Law in a person's pure, unconditional devotion to God, the Father in the specific sense in which the Sermon on the Mount interprets God's fatherly relationship with humanity as the content which essentially fulfills Jesus' consciousness.[109] [614] Based on this idea of the perfected fulfillment of the Law, Christianity's origin can be understood the way it must be understood based on its very nature, as an immanent development out of Judaism, which, however, as such carries in itself the principle of a form of religious consciousness that goes beyond Judaism and is specifically different from it. This indisputably gives Matthew's Gospel the imprint of a historically faithful portrayal of early Christianity. In the same regard, it is equally characteristic of Matthew's Gospel that the person of Jesus retreats into the background to allow the universality of the cause, the principle expressed in the perfected fulfillment of the Law, to come forward.

Much as the entire positioning and peculiarity of the Sermon on the Mount is to provide the core of Jesus' messianic significance, it does not emphasize the person of Jesus as the center anywhere. In this respect, the Gospel of Matthew even more represents a very determined opposite to the latest one of our canonical Gospels, the Johannine Gospel, than even the Gospel of Luke does. In the Johannine Gospel, the whole content of Christian consciousness coincides with the absolute meaning of the person of Christ. Only the well-known passage of Matthew 11:27 is different in this respect.[110] But precisely with regard to this passage one must admit that it basically stands alone and that it bears a unique imprint that is not very adequate to the other content of the Gospel. But however one might interpret this passage, why should not the original Gospel of Matthew have already had a starting point for a form of Christology which, if it had not already been established in the original essence of Christianity itself, would surely not have been able to develop such independent significance, neither in the Apostle Paul, nor in the Johannine Gospel? Thus, from considering this passage, too, the [615] general assessment begs to be made that the seemingly disparate elements of Matthew's Gospel in their relation to Christianity's original idea are only an even stronger proof for its truly historical fundamental character.[111]

[616–18 omitted][112]

[619] As far as the writer's position as eyewitness is concerned, enough reasons against it can of course be found in the Gospel. But what right does one have to carry the question about the Gospel of Matthew this far, since the historical reports about it do not authorize us to immediately trace it back to an apostolic origin? After all, the tradition, according to which it was written by the apostle Matthew, is only based on its connection with the Gospel of the Hebrews. Examining its content only confirms the historically obtained result, according to which it contains elements which might

---

[109]Footnote omitted. Cf. LNT, 105-15.
[110]Matt 11:27: "All things have been handed over to me by my Father; and no one knows the Son except the Father, and no one knows the Father except the Son and anyone to whom the Son chooses to reveal him."
[111]Footnote omitted.
[112]In these pages Baur skirmishes with contemporary exegetes about whether the Gospel of Matthew could have been written by an eyewitness.

originate from an apostle but in the form in which it is before us, as a whole it is impossible for it to be of apostolic origin. It contains way too much that is obviously ahistorical, traditional, and mythical to be classified as simply apostolic. But even if it is definitely not the case that the Gospel is of apostolic origin and that its writer is an eyewitness in the sense in which it is commonly claimed, nothing would be more wrong than claiming that the Gospel's historical credibility would have to be abandoned as well. Its credibility can be established with all the more certainty, the more readily one renounces any historical presuppositions.

The main point is to consider the historical credibility of the Gospel from the correct perspective. It is clear that with the unmethodical process, which can justly be called the art of new criticism, one can never be in a position to arrive at an established result. As long as one always proceeds from holding Matthew up against Luke, and then Luke against Matthew, the Synoptics against John, and John against the synoptics, one can never know who will eventually be proven right, and it is a continuous warfare against all with no end in sight. For one should eventually also arrive at the insight that just as the affair of Gospel criticism stands, it is merely arbitrary and prejudiced to make John's eyewitness the last instance and to erect it as the highest axiom. If the situation of John's eyewitness was the way it is still commonly claimed even now, then of course the entire argument about all this would be very easy to decide. One could not doubt for a moment that in all cases where there is a smaller or a greater difference between John and the Synoptics, one has to choose the apostolic eyewitness' side. [620] But here, the well-known, logical canon applies: *qui nimium probat, nihil probat* [one who proves too much, proves nothing]. Those who always apply John's eyewitness as the last and highest authority still do not dare to draw from it the consequence which they actually should, namely that compared to it the historical authority of the other evangelists basically must become entirely meaningless. Their accounts only merit to be believed insofar as they agree with the Johannine account and are confirmed by it. But by not wanting to go this far after all, by repeatedly re-thinking the idea of simply abandoning their credibility, and for this reason seeking to balance their portrayal with the Johannine Gospel as much as possible, and by even occasionally agreeing that the synoptics are right in contrast to John, one admits that it is not possible after all to put such unconditional faith into that axiom of John's eyewitness. This way, however, one merely turns around in those old circles from which there is no escape as long as one can find a leading aspect and a specific canon for judging this relationship. Since the special investigation of the Gospels yields proof that several of them are not purely historical, but that in their historical portrayal they follow certain tendencies, as a standard for judging their relationship and for the degree to which only the canon is a valid measure of their historical value, the Gospel which is least proven to have a particular tendential character has the greatest claim to historical credibility.

Only with the help of this canon does Gospel criticism obtain a methodical attitude and the possibility of attaining a certain result. This is the path we followed from the Johannine Gospel to Matthew, in order to arrive at the latter with the conviction that in it, we have the most unbiased and thus also most credible portrayal of the Gospel account. But since even the Gospel of Matthew is not entirely free from a particular interest and from certain tendential relationships, one cannot speak of absolute credibility, either, which goes without saying anyway. Thus, everything in general is relative here, but that is exactly what everything depends on: to communicate this relativity and the degrees of it as precisely as possible. Even though, based on this, the Gospel of Matthew is relatively [621] the most original and most credible of our canonical Gospels, we must not forget that in order to arrive at its present form, it has already passed through a medium which we are no longer in a position to penetrate. This Gospel, too, is already a secondary account, whose relationship with the objective state of facts can only approximately be determined.

CHAPTER NINE

Paul, the Apostle of Jesus Christ: His Life and Works

FROM: PAJC 1.275–79, 2.133–45
TRANSLATION: ROBERT F. BROWN, IN: PAJC(E), 161–63; 338–46

Footnotes from the original edition are prefaced [Baur]; Hodgson's footnotes are prefaced [PCH]. All other footnotes are by the editors

Perhaps no book of Baur's is as famous—or infamous, depending on the perspective—as his treatment of the Apostle Paul's life, letters, and influence, first published in 1845. According to Eduard Zeller, Baur's son-in-law who edited the posthumous second edition, it was Baur's favorite of his own books.[1] Drawing on and synthesizing his investigations from the preceding fifteen years, Baur performed a critical sifting of the literary heritage of Acts and the Pauline letters, reducing the number of indisputable Paulines to four—the so-called *Hauptbriefe* of Romans, 1 and 2 Corinthians, and Galatians—and cast Paul as an apostle of universalism in opposition to all marks of Jewish particularity. There are few today who would follow Baur on all fronts,[2] but in this book he posed fundamental questions to New Testament scholarship that are still being negotiated today.[3]

Two excerpts are presented here. The first offers Baur's summary of his influential judgment on the sources for Paul's life and thought: Acts must be discounted, and the Pauline letters should be divided into three classes, taking up and transforming categories first used by Eusebius: undisputed, disputed, and spurious. The second, longer excerpt offers Baur's idealist interpretation of Paul's theology. He argues, problematically and erroneously in retrospect, that Paul finds Christianity to be the religion of absolute freedom, the religion of the Spirit, in which everything finite and particular is overcome—most notably, in which Judaism itself is overcome and surpassed through the work of the messiah. Baur's interpretation is in certain ways a refraction of Lutheran tradition through the lens of the German idealist tradition, one that privileges the consciousness of the infinite Spirit, and so the individual's freedom and sense of superiority to the finite world.

---

[1] Eduard Zeller calls it Baur's *Lieblingswerk* in "Ferdinand Christian Baur," in his *Vorträge und Abhandlungen geschichtlichen Inhalts* (Leipzig: Fues's Verlag [L. W. Reisland], 1865), 366.
[2] Though note that Daniel Boyarin suggests, in his own provocative book on Paul, that "the reading of Paul which I undertake here seems to be closest in spirit (and often in detail) to the work of Ferdinand Christian Baur." See his *A Radical Jew: Paul and the Politics of Identity* (Berkeley: University of California Press, 1994), 11.
[3] For a fuller account of Baur's interpretation of Paul, see Christof Landmesser, "Ferdinand Christian Baur as Interpreter of Paul: History, the Absolute, and Freedom," in *Ferdinand Christian Baur and the History of Early Christianity*, ed. Martin Bauspiess, Christof Landmesser, and David Lincicum, trans. Robert F. Brown and Peter C. Hodgson (Oxford: Oxford University Press, 2017), 116–46.

PAUL THE APOSTLE OF JESUS CHRIST

Introduction to Part Two

[275] <161> The preceding investigation demonstrates that we would form a very false picture of the person of the Apostle Paul if we had to draw on the Acts of the Apostles as our only source.[4] The epistles of the Apostle in fact provide the only authentic information about the history of his apostolic activity and where he stood as a man of his time. These epistles give voice to a great and original spirit; they are the truest and liveliest reflection of it. The more deeply we enter into the study of the epistles, the life to which they bear immediate witness becomes all the richer and more distinctive.

Yet the same doppelgänger, that false counterpart who completely supplants the true apostle in the Book of Acts, also appears in the epistles. For the thirteen Pauline epistles that Christian antiquity unanimously acknowledged as such, and handed down as epistles written by the Apostle, cannot all make an equal claim to authenticity. Recent criticism overwhelmingly suspects that some of them are not authentically by Paul, and this view is becoming more widely accepted.[5] Given the present state of criticism of the Pauline epistles, it may well be time, by summing up the results of these previous investigations, to firm up the critical verdict about them by employing a classification [276] similar to that used by Eusebius, in his classical passage on the canon.[6] Eusebius rendered his verdict on the various writings claiming to be admitted to the New Testament canon, based on the historical evidence he had. For us, the Pauline epistles fall into the two classes of "homologoumena" and "antilegomena."[7]

Only the four major epistles, those superior to the others in every respect, can count as homologoumena. They are: the Epistle to the Galatians, the two Epistles to the Corinthians, and the Epistle to the Romans. There has never been even the slightest suspicion that these are inauthentic. They so incontestably manifest the character of Pauline originality that there is no conceivable ground for critical doubts about them.

<162> All the rest of the epistles commonly ascribed to the Apostle belong to the class of antilegomena. This does not mean positively asserting that they are inauthentic. (For Eusebius, the antilegomena are simply writings whose authenticity has been, or may be, called into question.) Yet objections may be raised about the authenticity of each of these lesser Pauline epistles when they are compared with the four major epistles. Their whole nature is so essentially different from the first four epistles that, even if they are considered to be by Paul, they can only form a second class of his epistles, ones composed for the most part only at a later point in his apostolic career.

---

[4] Baur is referring to Part One of the book, which is a sustained subjection of Acts to historical scrutiny.

[5] These suspicions were first aired in F. D. E. Schleiermacher, *Über den sogenannten ersten Brief des Paulos an den Timotheos. Ein kritisches Sendschreibung an J.C. Gass* (Berlin: Realschulbuchhandlung, 1807) and were then taken up in subsequent Introductions to the New Testament by J. G. Eichhorn and W. M. L. de Wette, and then prosecuted more fully by Baur himself in his PAP.

[6] [PCH] Eusebius, *Ecclesiastical History*, 3.25.

[7] [PCH] That is, works that are accepted as genuine, and those that are regarded as dubious or doubtful (written by someone other than the presumptive author). The Greek terms ὁμολογουμένα and ἀντιλεγόμενα mean respectively, confessed or acknowledged, and spoken against or contradicted. It should be noted that Eusebius himself, in drawing this distinction between genuine and dubious writings, does not suggest that any of the Pauline epistles are not genuinely by Paul.

Eusebius himself further divides his antilegomena into two groups, one of which he calls the *notha*[8] because they are not just questionable, for he thinks it extremely likely that they are inauthentic. These deutero-Pauline epistles include ones critical [277] judgment is increasingly inclined to regard as inauthentic. In my opinion and that of other critics, the so-called Pastoral Epistles are Pauline antilegomena and are to be placed in this subdivision of *notha*. Thus we have three classes of Pauline epistles [authentic, questionable, and surely inauthentic], a classification that can also appeal to an ancient authority.

The Marcionite canon, whose Ἀπόστολος is the most ancient collection of Pauline epistles known to us, contains only ten epistles of the Apostle, the three Pastoral Epistles being excluded. For the canon of Marcion, then, the Pastoral Epistles are a class unto themselves, and this may be why they are omitted from it. If they were missing from it because they did not yet exist, as *notha* they could not afterwards have been accepted in a collection that was supposed to contain only genuine Pauline epistles. If they did exist then but were unknown to Marcion [as being Pauline writings], which is scarcely credible if they had long been current as genuine Pauline epistles, this changes nothing since they were not included because Marcion did not know them as Pauline writings. But if, as known writings, they were excluded from the canon, they were omitted because the compiler of the canon regarded them as not being Pauline. Even if they were not known to date from a later period, the decision to exclude them was because they hardly had a genuinely Pauline character and could not pass muster as Pauline writings. In any event, when considered in light of the Marcionite canon, these epistles must be viewed as comprising the last class of epistles customarily ascribed to the Apostle Paul.

Aside from them, we find two classes of epistles included in the Marcionite canon that agree with our classification, namely, a series of Pauline epistles of the first order, and another of the second order. According to Epiphanius,[9] the canon of Marcion arranged the Pauline epistles in the following order: Galatians, 1 and 2 Corinthians, Romans, 1 and 2 Thessalonians, Ephesians [278] (which Marcion calls the "Epistle to the Laodiceans"), Colossians, Philemon, and Philippians. In this arrangement of the Pauline epistles, what usually catches people's attention is just the listing of Galatians <163> first, because of the importance it must have had in the teachings of so decided an anti-Judaizing Paulinist as Marcion. But then the rest of the epistles had to have been arranged in terms of how important they were for the teachings of Marcion, and we fail to understand why the two Epistles to the Corinthians should precede Romans, and still less why the remainder should follow precisely in the order they do. If, to the contrary, the sequence follows the supposed order of their composition, then the two Epistles to the Thessalonians present an obstacle because they ought not to come just after Romans but ahead of all the others, as they were the first to be written. Yet we must recognize a certain deference to their temporal order in placing Thessalonians immediately after the four principal epistles. In light of all these factors, we can only explain the Marcionite canon by assuming that it consists of two separate collections. The first collection is composed of four epistles, Galatians, 1 and 2 Corinthians, and Romans, and it is arranged in chronological order. The second collection can also have been arranged just chronologically, since on any other basis it would be hard to comprehend why it begins with 1 and 2 Thessalonians, and why Philippians follows Philemon.

---

[8][PCH] The Greek term νόθος means illegitimate or spurious.
[9][Baur] [Epiphanius], *Pan[arion]*. 42.9.

Whatever may be the origin of these two collections, it remains a remarkable feature of this canon that in it we find all these lesser Pauline epistles placed in a second series, and that in many respects they differ so much from the principal epistles as to raise critical doubts about them to varying degrees. So it forces us to assume that, if there are otherwise serious objections to their authenticity, it is quite natural to suppose that the secondary [279] position of this group of epistles can be due to their having first appeared as deutero-Pauline writings after the collection of genuine Pauline epistles was already set. Since they posed as Pauline epistles, they were linked to the original and authentic epistles of the Apostle; but the manner in which they are attached to the original epistles betrays their later origin. It is just as natural that, as later epistles, they should stand apart from the original ones, although still held to be Pauline, as it is natural that the Pastoral Epistles, which were opposed to the Marcionite teaching, should be entirely absent from that canon. Marcion is an epochal figure in the history of Pauline Christianity. To him Paulinism was the only pure and unalloyed Christianity. On this issue he has far more importance than people usually grant to a heretic. He provides important, critical information for modern criticism of the Pauline epistles.[10]

[...]

The Principle of Christian Consciousness

[133] <338> To understand the principle of Christian consciousness in its full depth and distinctiveness, as seen from the Apostle Paul's standpoint, we can simply begin by sticking as much as possible to what is notable about his conversion. Paul not merely switched from Judaism to Christianity and from one form of religious consciousness to another; he also changed the direction of his life to its exact opposite. The fact that he made this move just as decisively as he did swiftly and unexpectedly shows what power and significance Christianity had for him. The same person who, only a short time before this, had been persecuting Christianity in the most hateful way, now came at once to believe in the one whose followers he had sought to destroy. By believing in him, Paul had become an entirely different person. What else can this be but a victory that Christianity owed simply to the inner power of its truth? Of all those who have ever been converted to faith in Christ, there is no one in whom the Christian principle has asserted itself so clearly and directly, in its absolute superiority, by cutting through all that stands opposed to it, as it has in the Apostle Paul.

What sets the manifestation of the Christian principle apart in Paul's case is above all the fact that it makes itself known in its absolute power and significance, and establishes its absoluteness, by overcoming an antithesis that must first be overcome if it is to be active as the higher, overarching principle.[11] [134] Newly aware of a standpoint he had made his own with all his strength and energy, the Apostle now sees things from the absoluteness of his Christian perspective. Thus for him Christianity itself is the absolute power of spiritual life, at work through the greatest antitheses and overcoming them. What he experienced as his internal spiritual process in the process of his

---

[10][Baur] The reasons adduced against the origin and character of the lesser epistles, as opposed to the first four epistles, will not in all likelihood be diminished by further unbiased critical research, but rather strengthened by it. Thus the simplest and most natural way of proceeding at this point is to divide the epistles attributed to the Apostle in the canon into authentic and inauthentic, Pauline and pseudo-Pauline epistles, and to arrange the latter in their probable chronological order.

[11][Ed.] The logic here is basically Hegelian. See Michael Inwood, "Absolute," in his *A Hegel Dictionary* (Oxford: Blackwell, 1992), 28: "Usually, the item characterized as absolute comes at the end of a series of items: absolute spirit comes after, and is in some sense higher than, subjective and objective spirits."

conversion is just the blossoming within Paul himself of the self-explicating Christian principle. But the absoluteness of the Christian principle consists simply in its being essentially identical with the person of Christ. So for Paul Christianity's absolute significance resides wholly in the person of Christ. Hence in the person of Christ Paul also became aware of the Christian principle for what it essentially is. He attests to <339> this in speaking of his conversion: "But when God, who had set me apart before I was born and called me through his grace, was pleased to reveal his Son to me ... " (Gal 1:15-16). That is, through an inner act of Paul's consciousness the person of Jesus was disclosed as being what he essentially is, the Son of God—this Jesus Paul had been so hostile toward that he not only did not acknowledge Jesus as the messiah, but could just see him as a false messiah completely at odds with the idea of the messiah.

The expression "Son of God"[12] signifies the essential change in Paul's conception of the messiah following his conversion. So we must take a closer look at it if we are to correctly understand its significance. We have already noted that the entire difference at that time, between Jews who believed in Jesus and those who did not, basically lay in the fact that the believers held Jesus of Nazareth to be the messiah who has actually appeared, notwithstanding the fact that everything about him, and especially his ultimate fate, so greatly contradicted all that the ordinary notions of the messiah expected from the appearing of the real messiah, the one the Old Testament promises and prophecies supposedly foretold. Belief in Jesus' resurrection put an end [135] to that contradiction. The most essential factor in the Apostle's conviction as to Jesus' messianic status was likewise his belief in Jesus as the resurrected one (1 Cor 15:8).[13] However, for Paul the distinctive inner process by which belief in Jesus as the messiah was established in him initially rested far more on the concept of the Son of God, now recognized as a concept fulfilled in Jesus, than was the case for the other apostles. For these others, their belief in the resurrection counteracted the offensiveness of Jesus' death, but actually just meant that they could hope for the resurrected one to come a second time so that, by doing so, he will have accomplished what his first coming left unfulfilled (on which, see Acts 3:19-21). To the contrary, the Apostle Paul could not entertain the element of Jesus' death, considered for its own sake, without that producing an upheaval in his messianic consciousness, one having the greatest significance for his entire understanding of Christianity. Whereas the other disciples had consciously modified the messianic idea associated with the Jews as a people, by just linking it in another form to expecting a second coming of Jesus, in the mind of the Apostle Paul the death of Jesus was stripped of all such parochial associations. For Paul the death of Jesus dispelled all that the messiah was as a Jewish messiah. By his death Jesus himself had ceased being the messiah for Judaism, had withdrawn from any exclusive ties to the Jewish people, and had entered into a freer, more universal, purely spiritual sphere in which the absolute significance heretofore claimed for Judaism all at once was ended.

<340> The Apostle speaks about this complete upheaval in his messianic consciousness due to how he regards Jesus' death, in a very important passage in this context, 2 Cor 5:15-16,[14] which we have previously discussed and whose meaning fits in very well here. He says here that, since he has

---

[12][PCH] Paul, according to Baur, does not use this term in a metaphysical sense designating the divine nature or person of Christ, but rather in a familial sense, designating the relationship of children to parents. This becomes clear below where Baur speaks of Christian consciousness as "the awareness of being children of God."

[13][PCH] 1 Cor 15:8: "Last of all, to one untimely born, he appeared to me."

[14][PCH] 2 Cor 5:15-17: "He died for all, so that those who live might live no longer for themselves, but for him who died and was raised for them. From now on, therefore, we regard no one from a human point of view; even though we once knew Christ from a human point of view, we know him no longer in that way. So if anyone is in Christ, there is a new creation: everything old has passed away; see, everything has become new!"

begun to live for the Christ who died and was raised from the dead for him, as Christ was for all, he no longer knows Christ κατὰ σάρκα ("according to the flesh," or "from a human point of view"). So he is declaring [136] that, from the moment his eyes were opened to a full awareness of the meaning of Jesus' death, he has renounced all the limitations of his Jewish outlook and of the Jewish notions of the messiah. For Paul the Jewish messiah had been just a messiah of the flesh, because a messiah who had not undergone death still intrinsically had all the fleshly attributes that death, as the negation of the flesh, alone can annul. So the Apostle recognized that Christ's death purged the messianic idea of all the sensuous elements associated with it in Judaism. He saw this idea now in a higher and truly spiritual consciousness, in which Christ could first be understood as the absolute principle of the spiritual life—which is his meaning for the Apostle. The absolute significance the person of Christ has for the Apostle is the absoluteness of the Christian principle itself. With his idea of the person of Christ, the Apostle is conscious of a standpoint infinitely higher than Judaism, where Christ is removed from all that is merely relative, limited and finite in the Jewish religion, and he has been elevated to the absolute religion.

This absoluteness of the principle of Christian consciousness, as presented in the person of Christ himself, is then spelled out in more detail in the fact that, in this principle, the Apostle is conscious of spirit being essentially different from the flesh, that is, of freedom from everything to which one is related just externally, and of human beings' reconciliation with God and their oneness with God. The principle of Christian consciousness expresses its absolute character in all these relationships. In Gal 3:2-3 the Apostle straightforwardly designates Christian consciousness as "the Spirit." In addressing the Galatians who are wavering in their Christian faith, he asks: "Did you receive the Spirit by doing the works of the law or by believing what you heard [preached to you]? Are you so foolish? Having started with the Spirit, are you now ending with the flesh?" It is foolish to relapse from spiritual Christianity to fleshly, materialistic Judaism. [137] Here the Apostle wants to point out to the Galatians a direct and incontrovertible fact of their Christian consciousness. What is most directly expressed in a Christian, what is constitutive of one's Christian consciousness itself, is this: the fact that within one is the Spirit, an essential spiritual principle in which one can see that one's blessedness is not dependent on anything merely external, sensuous, material; that instead we are conscious of our immediate fellowship and oneness with God.

<341> As essentially spiritual consciousness, Christian consciousness is the awareness of being children of God, inasmuch as it is faith resting on the certainty of divine grace. For all who are moved by God's Spirit are also God's children. They do not receive a spirit of bondage, which could only make them fearful. Instead it is "a spirit of adoption" in which they cry out "Abba! Father!" For "it is that very Spirit bearing witness with our spirit that we are children of God" (Rom 8:15-16). Since "our spirit" in v. 16 is the same spirit Gal 3:2 says is received, then the Spirit of God expressing itself in us as Christian consciousness is, in doing so, identical with spirit in itself (spirit as the objective principle of Christian consciousness), such that both express this adoption by God. Therefore this is not merely a subjective expression of our subjective Christian consciousness; instead it has its objective reality and absolute certainty in the absolute Spirit of God that is existent within itself.[15] With πνεῦμα

---

[15][PCH] This mediation of subjective consciousness and objective reality is characteristic not only of Baur's interpretation of Paul but also of his own theological position, which is informed by Schleiermacher as well as Hegel. On the one hand the Christian principle is a principle of subjective consciousness, and in this respect Baur follows Schleiermacher. But whereas for Schleiermacher this principle is a "consciousness of absolute dependence," for Baur it is a consciousness of absolute freedom. This is true because for Baur, following Hegel, the "objective reality" of this consciousness is the Spirit of God, which *gives* freedom (by adopting us as children) and *is* freedom.

ἡμῶν (our spirit) συμμαρτυρεῖν (bearing witness in accord with) αὐτὸ τὸ πνεῦμα (spirit in itself), with this identity of the subjective spirit with spirit in itself, we therefore have the highest expression for the absolute truth of what Christian consciousness declares to be its immediate content.[16]

[138] The spirit, as the principle of Christian consciousness, leads back to spirit in itself and is identified with it. So the Apostle adopts the same absolute standpoint in 1 Cor 2:9-12, where he expresses his Christian consciousness in these words: "'What no eye has seen, nor ear heard, nor the human heart conceived, what God has prepared for <342> those who love him'[17]—these things God has revealed to us through the Spirit; for the Spirit searches everything; even the depths of God. For what human being knows what is truly human except the human spirit that is within? So also no one comprehends what is truly God's except the Spirit of God. Now we have received not the spirit of the world, but the Spirit that is from God, so that we may understand the gifts bestowed on us by God." Therefore Christian consciousness is an essentially spiritual consciousness, and what expresses itself in it, as the principle of it, is spirit. For the divine element that constitutes the contents of Christian consciousness can only be something known by spirit. That is because spirit alone is what searches everything. Inasmuch as all searching and knowing as such has the divine, the absolute, as its content, this searching and knowing can only occur in the element of the spirit.[18]

This spirit knowing the divine is [139] the spirit from God but not merely the spirit imparted by God. Instead, as the spirit of Christian consciousness it is also identical with the Spirit of God itself—the same Spirit that in God is the principle of the divine self-consciousness in the same way as the spirit in human beings is the principle of human self-consciousness. Thus in the oneness of this spirit, human beings' knowing the contents of their Christian consciousness is God's knowing

---

[16][Baur] Gal 4:6 completely parallels Rom 8:14-16. [PCH. Gal 4:6: "And because you are children, God has sent the Spirit of his Son into our hearts, crying, 'Abba! Father!'" Rom 8:14-16: "For all who are led by the Spirit of God are children of God. For you did not receive a spirit of slavery to fall back into fear, but you have received a spirit of adoption. When we cry, 'Abba! Father!' it is that very Spirit bearing witness with our spirit that we are children of God ...."] When Galatians reads: "Because (as ὅτι must be understood) you are children, God has ..., " with the sending of the Spirit therefore of course presupposing it being the Spirit of the Son (υἱὸς εἶναι), this is simply explained as the principle of Christian consciousness, based on the relation of faith to the Spirit. One of course becomes a child of God via faith. However, this is in principle still an abstract relationship that must have the concrete content that, in the living reality of consciousness, it must first receive through the spirit that is none other than the principle of Christian consciousness itself. The Apostle intentionally has "when the fullness of time had come, God sent his Son" of Gal 4:4 correspond to "God has sent the Spirit of his Son" of 4:6. The former sending is objective, as an objective historical fact, whereas the latter is subjective. The sending of the Son first becomes an inner experience, an empirical fact of consciousness, through the Spirit, which first makes objective Christianity something subjective. The Apostle designates this subjective element by adding "into our hearts" in v. 6. Because, in its subjectivity, this is simply the subjectivizing of that objective sending, he quite fittingly calls the Spirit here "the Spirit of his Son." Christian consciousness, whose principle is the Spirit, is imparted by Christ himself, is Christ himself becoming inward.

[17][PCH] The NRSV suggests that this quotation "may come from the *Apocalypse of Elijah* (thus the third-century CE exegete Origen), cited here as scripture." The wording of 1 Cor 2:9 in part suggests Isa 64:4. Parenthetically in the text, after "those who love him," Baur says these are the υἱοὶ θεοῦ (children of God) referred to in Rom 8:14 and Gal 4:6.

[18][PCH] The translator faces a challenge in knowing when and when not to capitalize "spirit" (the German *Geist*, as a noun, is always capitalized, and the Greek πνεῦμα is always in lowercase). Our imperfect solution is as follows: when *Geist* or πνεῦμα refers to the human spirit or to a quality or principle that humans share with divinity (e.g., spirituality), we translate as "spirit." When *Geist* or πνεῦμα refers specifically to the Spirit of God or the Holy Spirit, we translate as "Spirit." In some cases it is not so easy to decide, as the term may ambiguously refer to both. Alternatively, we might have always either capitalized or lowercased the term. Of course when scripture is quoted, we follow the NRSV. [Ed.] See also Note on Text and Translations.

of himself. In the content of their Christian consciousness, as an essentially spiritual consciousness, Christians therefore know themselves as identical with God's Spirit, because only spirit, the Spirit of God, the Absolute Spirit, can know the divine that is the content of Christian consciousness. Christians are at this lofty, absolute standpoint with the contents of their Christian consciousness revealed to them by God. It is a truly spiritual consciousness, a relation of spirit to spirit, in which the Spirit of God, existent in itself, in becoming the principle of Christian consciousness, opens itself up for human consciousness.

As a spiritual consciousness in this sense, Christian consciousness is also an absolutely free consciousness, released from all finite limitations, opened up in the full clarity of absolute self-consciousness. As the Apostle says in 2 Cor 3:17, "Now the Lord (as the content and principle of Christian consciousness[19]) is the Spirit, and where the Spirit of the Lord is (in other words, the Lord as Spirit, as the principle of an essentially spiritual consciousness and life), there is freedom (the freedom of self-consciousness)."

<343> The Apostle elucidates this point in a passage we have cited, in a context that merits more careful consideration. At the end of ch. 2 of 2 Corinthians he speaks with elation about the effect of his teaching, about the successful results of his apostolic activity. Yet in doing so he sets aside all merely subjective considerations so as not seeming to just praise himself or wanting to take too much credit himself, when in ch. 3 he turns to the Corinthians' own self-awareness that has to be the evidence of his own successful activity, and in a sense documents it. [140] Here it is not a matter of something that is merely subjective, not of something that is just a feature of subjective consciousness. Instead this is something that is objectively real and factual. It is success that is undeniable, but the Apostle through whom it was achieved also does not, in regarding it, merely stop with himself as the person who did it. He did not accomplish it as a particular subject, by his own personal activity. He only did so inasmuch as he is a διάκονος καινῆς διαθήκης, "minister of a new covenant" (3:6). The personal aspect must be wholly subordinate to that of his office.

This now gives the Apostle the opportunity to explain, in opposition to his Judaizing adversaries, the nature of the new covenant. He declares that the vacillation, hesitation, and self-seeking they accuse him of is contrary to the nature and principle of this covenant and so cannot be characteristic of one of its ministers. The principle of this covenant is an absolute principle, so the mind of one of its ministers cannot harbor anything that would disrupt or restrict it, any limitation that would cancel out its absoluteness. With the antitheses in 3:6-16 the Apostle explains how the new religion differs from the old one, and thus shows how Christianity, as the new covenant, is the absolute religion as opposed to the old one. It is not a religion of the letter like the old covenant written on stone tablets, but the religion "of spirit; for the letter kills but the Spirit gives life" (3:6).

The glory of this διακονία τοῦ πνεύματος (ministry of the spirit) very far outshines all others. So Paul presents this point by referring to the radiance on Moses' face as a symbol of the glory also befitting the old covenant (Exod 34:29-35). Of course the old covenant had its glory, yet the old and new covenants are just as different as are the letter and the spirit, as are condemnation and justification. So the glory that the old covenant had also did not remain, because the glory of the new covenant outshines it. For how could the glory of the new one do other [141] than outshine it (2 Cor 3:10-11)? If what, being finite and vanishing, had glory, then the glory of what is enduring must be a far greater glory. The Apostle goes on to say (3:12-13) that

---

[19][PCH] Parenthetical insertions by Baur into scriptural quotations occur from time to time.

since, then, we have such a hope (that the glory of the new covenant is a glory also enduring for the future and continually developing[20]), we act from great boldness (that is, quite openly and freely[21]), not like Moses, who put a veil over his face to keep the people of Israel from <344> gazing at the end of the glory that was being set aside.

The Apostle wants to say that, since Moses concealed the radiance of his countenance by a veil, the Israelites could not be aware of how long this radiance would actually last—for it always just lasted for a certain time. This is first of all τὸ τέλος τοῦ καταργουμένου, "the end of [the glory that] was being set aside" (3:13), but the Apostle understands it at the same time as the finite character of the old covenant, with the recurring radiance of Moses' face being its symbol. The Israelites could not see beyond it, could not see the glory being set aside, and so they could not know whether or not it would continue. Thus they were unaware that the end of one covenant, which from the outset was determined to endure for just a limited time, had now come, and that the new covenant is at hand.

Mosaism is by nature the opposite of that free self-consciousness or "great boldness" (3:12). Interpreters have erroneously taken the "opposite" referred to in this passage[22] to be a *tecte* (covering), in other words a completely *fraudulenter agere* (fraudulent action) on Moses' part, as if he would have intentionally set out to deceive the Israelites by concealing the truth about this, by acting dishonestly. But that is not what this "opposite" is. Nor, as de Wette supposes, is it the fact that [142] Moses enveloped the truth in imagery.[23] We have to look at the situation from the Israelites' standpoint vis-à-vis Moses, at their being unaware that the old covenant is finite. They were limited by having no idea of its finite nature, and, as long as they remained unaware of this, that made them always just Jews. The advance from Judaism to Christianity could only happen by becoming aware that Judaism is merely a finite form. That the Jews were not conscious of this fact, and for this very reason had no inclination toward Christianity, was the κάλυμμα, the covering, the concealing veil that, as the Apostle specifically states in v. 14, overlays their consciousness as it did the face of Moses. They do not see the end. "Their minds were hardened. Indeed, to this very day, when they hear the reading of the old covenant, that same veil is still there,[24] since only in Christ is it set aside. Indeed, to this very day whenever Moses is read, a veil lies over their minds; but when one turns to the Lord, the veil is removed" (3:14-16). As soon as this happens, everything "comes from the Lord" (v. 18).

Conversion to the Lord removes the veil. But the Lord one has upon removing the veil is "the Spirit, and where the Spirit of the Lord is, there is freedom" (v. 17). Then whoever, from this standpoint, is a minister of this covenant can also have the complete freedom and clarity of

---

[20][PCH] Insertions by Baur.

[21][Baur] Παρρησία (boldness) is here in fact freedom of self-consciousness, as is only possible from a Christian standpoint. Because the principle of the Christian's self-consciousness is the freedom of spirit, nothing can remain hidden or concealed for it. Therefore all hesitation and vacillation must also be foreign to it. It is clear that the Apostle sets this freedom, as the principle of his actions, over against the accusations of his opponents.

[22][PCH] 2 Cor 3:13-16: " ... not like Moses, who put a veil over his face .... But their minds were hardened."

[23]See W. M. L. de Wette, *Kurzgefaßtes exegetisches Handbuch zum Neuen Testament. II/2. Kurze Erklärung der Briefe an die Corinther* (Leipzig: Weidmann, 1841), 177–8.

[24][Baur interpolates:] (This shows even more clearly than before that this κάλυμμα [veil or covering] is just subjective; that the reason for it is not in what is read itself, in the Mosaic books of the Old Testament. Instead the reason lies only in the subjective states of those reading these scriptures or hearing them read).

self-consciousness of being far above and beyond all that is limited, veiled, and finite about the standpoint of the old covenant. But the <345> Apostle adds that all of this applies not merely to him as an apostle, as the minister of this new [143] covenant, for it holds good generally, for all of us. In Christ we all have the principle of spiritual freedom, of a self-consciousness released from all finite limitations, freed from all obscuring intermediaries. What Christ is objectively as the object of our consciousness, as the δόξα (glory) we see before us "as though reflected in a mirror," he also should be subjectively for us; that objectivity for us should become one with ourselves, in our "being transformed into the same image from one degree of glory to another," which cannot be otherwise, since this transformation "comes from the Lord" whose essential nature is "the Spirit" (3:18).[25]

Therefore the essence and principle of Christianity is designated as spirit absolutely. The sense in which it is spirit clearly follows from all these antitheses between the old and new covenants. Its essence is spirit because there is no limitation, no veil, nothing obscuring and restrictive, nothing finite and fleeting, in the consciousness of those who occupy this standpoint. It is a consciousness clear and free within itself, identical with itself. In other words, the Lord is the Spirit because, to put it succinctly, the principle of Christianity and of Christian consciousness is an absolute principle in which all else, as something merely relative and finite, naturally terminates. Those who at this standpoint, who are themselves conscious of their freedom and infinitude, know themselves as subjects in relation to everything, knowing everything ultimately with reference to themselves; they know their own selves, know that they can never be objectified by others, know that all is simply for them because they are above all of it. To awaken a Christian self-confidence in the Corinthians, one making it impossible for them to surrender to others who wish to make them mere objects of their own sectarian egoism, the Apostle says, in 1 Cor 3:21-23: "For all things are yours, whether Paul or Apollos or Cephas or the world or life or death or the present or the future—all belong to you, and you belong to Christ, and Christ belongs to God." Therefore you are the absolute subject, but only in that identity with Christ and God where the Christian has the principle of his or her own consciousness and life.

From this standpoint of absolute self-consciousness [144] the Christian's whole way of looking at the world is different from that of other people, because the Christian can consider everything simply from the perspective of the absolute idea that one begins to be conscious of in Christianity, as the Apostle shows us in 1 Cor 1:19-31 and 2:6-16. In ch. 1 he says that those who think to become wise in the things of this <346> world become fools in doing so, for the wisdom of this world is foolishness in God's eyes. The standpoint of Christian consciousness completely reverses the relationship between wisdom and foolishness. Here wisdom is actually foolishness, and foolishness actually wisdom. Thus the divine element in Christianity is very different from,

---

[25][PCH] Christ, according to Paul, is the "mirror" in which the "glory" of the Lord is "reflected" rather than being hidden by a veil, and "the Lord is the Spirit." This is a Spirit-Christology that understands Christ as a fully human being (no divine Logos comprises his personal nature), but he is one who is indwelt so fully by the Spirit that he shines with a radiance, a splendor of glory. He is essentially spirit and light, the reflected light of God, a "speculum that shines" (to use Elliot Wolfson's phrase from his *Through a Speculum That Shines: Vision and Imagination in Medieval Jewish Mysticism* [Princeton: Princeton University Press, 1994], a book about Jewish mysticism). Through faith in Christ, this reflected glory becomes our own interior principle. (This point is elaborated in chap. 8 of Baur's *Paul, the Apostle of Jesus Christ*). Paul's use of the categories of light, radiance, glory, mirror, and spirit shows how deeply Jewish his Christology really is, developed in relation to the prototype of Moses. This is a spiritual Judaism as opposed to the fleshly Judaism of which Paul is critical.

and antithetical to, the whole human way of looking at things. The two are related as finite is to infinite, what is relative to what is absolute. From the absolute standpoint for looking at it, everything not itself absolute, everything finite, however important it may be on its own terms, just appears in its finitude and emptiness; whereas of course for those who just exist in the finite realm and do not understand how to be governed by what is absolute, there is nothing absolute at all. It is an entirely inaccessible domain for such a person, completely outside his own consciousness and incomprehensible, so he can only regard talk of it as foolishness.

This is the difference between psychical and pneumatic or spiritual human beings. The psychical person does not apprehend what is spiritual or divine, what is the contents of Christian consciousness, inasmuch as it is something essentially spiritual. For him it is foolishness. It is above and beyond the scope of his consciousness, and he cannot comprehend it because it must be understood spiritually. The spiritual person has the kind of comprehension suited for understanding everything, but cannot be properly understood by someone who is not spiritual himself (see 2 Cor 2:14-15). So here we have the absolute superiority of the standpoint of Christian consciousness. Whoever occupies it has in the absolute the absolute measuring stick for everything merely relative. But whoever just stops with what is relative and finite forever remains in an [145] inadequate relation to the absolute. All of this belongs to the Apostle's own explanation of the principle of his Christian consciousness.

PART FOUR

Church History

CHAPTER TEN

On the History of Ecclesiastical Historiography

FROM: EKG, 1–6; 247–63
TRANSLATION: PETER C. HODGSON, ECH, 46–50; 241–53

Published in 1852, Baur's monograph *Die Epochen der kirchlichen Geschichtsschreibung* is an unusual writing. Baur here applies his historical approach to the writing of Church History. The plan for this publication seems to have arisen in connection with Baur's decision to make use of his extensive lecture courses and previous publications to compose a full history of the Christian Church. When Baur published the first volume, *Das Christenthum und die christliche Kirche der ersten drei Jahrhunderte*, in 1853, he referred back to the *Epochs* as an introduction to this work.[1] *Epochen* is thus Baur's Prolegomena to Church History, produced by means of an investigation of the development of the historiography of the Church. Thus far, the book seems the culmination of the historicization of theology characteristic of Baur's work in its entirety.

In preparing the volume, Baur could draw on his extensive lecture notes which he had developed since the 1820s. These notes contained a lengthy section on the major church historians through the ages; it is this account which in the main served Baur as the source of his fuller account in the *Epochen*.

In his Preface to the volume, Baur identified for the book the following three tasks: (1) consider the major church historians in their individual character; (2) arrange them into chronological and thematic groups; (3) relate them to each other in such a way as to identify "in them [...] the whole course of development."[2] The final point was most important to Baur. He aimed to show how the development of ecclesiastical historiography has its own internal logic and necessity. To this end, he divided the whole history into six main periods of which the final one, "recent historiography with its tendency to 'objective historiography,'" is by far the most extensive. Clearly, Baur's main interest was to identify the historical moment into which his own work fell, but it is all the more remarkable that he omitted any reference to his own historical publications or indeed those of his Tübingen School in its entirety. He is, however, emphatic about the main task of the time which is to bring together philosophical *ideas* and empirical research: "The Idea still hovers indefinitely and at a great distance over the manifestations to which it must be related."[3] Throughout his career, Baur saw his own vocation as addressing this persistent lack in ecclesiastical historiography.

---

[1] CCK, iv; CCC, xxiv.
[2] EkG, iv–v. English text: ECH, 43.
[3] EkG, 247. English text: ECH, 241.

The present extracts are partly taken from the book's Introduction and partly from its final section, "Conclusions and Suggestions." Notes from Baur's own text are prefaced by [Baur]; notes from Peter Hodgson's translation, by [PCH]. All other notes are the editors'.

EPOCHS OF CHURCH HISTORIOGRAPHY

[1] <46>

Introduction

The word *history* has both an objective and a subjective meaning. This double meaning sets up as an immediate unity that which critical analysis causes to split widely and indeterminably apart. History is both what has happened objectively and the subjective knowledge of what has happened. But just as not everything that has happened is a historical occurrence, so also not all knowledge of what has happened is historical knowledge. Historical knowledge first emerges when the event becomes important enough not merely to be known for the moment but also to be transmitted to the enduring knowledge of posterity.

Once interest in such a presentation of what has happened has been awakened, the question arises as to how knowledge concerning events is related to the events themselves. The more precisely this relation is concerned, the less can it simply be assumed that historical presentation is nothing but the true, adequate reflection of what objectively has happened. The difference in time that separates the historian from the object of his presentation is often considerable. And, in general, a great deal can come between the historian and his object, so that it may appear to him in a light completely other than would accord with the actuality of the subject matter. Thus, there is no historical presentation that must not first be critically tested in order to determine the relation in which its author stands to the pure objectivity of historical truth. But even if [2] all those questions concerning the credibility of the historian, his talent for historical presentation, the character of the sources he employs—everything that has to be drawn into the realm of historical criticism—can be answered as satisfactorily as possible, history itself, as the essence of what has happened, remains something so infinitely large that its contents can never be exhausted by historical knowledge, through which what has objectively taken place is also to become subjectively known.

The first requirement of a presentation corresponding to the idea of history would seem to be above all that the historian stand as close to the <47> object of his presentation as possible, in order to become acquainted with all the details that can be obtained only by immediate perception. But on the other hand, after further consideration, we are aware of the opposite: the data of history appear to us in their true light only when we consider them from a greater distance, and when the causes and effects that determine the character of a given historical realm not merely are present in their first beginnings but have already developed in a wider connection. History itself is an endless tissue of varied manifestations, interpenetrating in the most manifold of relations. The truth itself thus emerges in something like genuine objectivity only through the comparison of various possible standpoints, from each of which must be removed whatever has too subjective a character. How else could it be explained that all parts of history, especially those belonging to more or less ancient times, repeatedly become the object of historical presentation, if it were not of the nature of history itself that, from every standpoint from which we look anew back into the past, there is presented a new image, through [3] which we obtain a truer, more vital, and more significant perception of what has happened, even if only in a particular respect?

What applies to history in general applies also to the history of the Christian church. Indeed, in this more limited field, the nature of historical presentation becomes all the clearer when its task consists in setting forth the objectively given for subjective consciousness. One cannot trace an extensive period of general history, either as a whole or in one of its more significant parts, without having certain questions grow increasingly important—such as the means by which the whole series of phenomena that make up the continuity of causes and effects are joined together in unity; or how the particular is subordinated to the universal; or which Idea serves as the dynamic principle of the whole. Likewise, all this takes on a considerably higher and more definite significance as applied to the sphere within which the Christian church follows its historical course.

Here we may not simply abstract the end toward which every individual thing is striving from an indeterminate flux of manifestations. Rather, everything proceeds from a starting point in which the Idea that is to be realized through its entire temporal manifestation is clearly and definitely expressed; and once initiated, the development proceeds from one point to another in a continuity in which it should not be difficult to relate everything individual to the Idea that is the basis of the whole, or <48> to determine the relation in which one thing stands to another. Historical presentation seems to have here only the simple task of following the objectively given course, and of grasping and assembling everything so that it corresponds to the objectivity of the subject matter itself. But this is only the apparent prerogative of church historiography. The more everything in the history of the Christian church depends on the beginning from [4] which it proceeds and by which it is conditioned through the whole continuity of its development, the more everything depends on the way one understands this beginning itself, which is so significant. The historical presentation as a whole is based on this fundamental perception. Easy as it may be, once the general point of view is established, to subordinate particular details to it, and to understand those details under the unity of this perspective, nevertheless all the difficulties to be overcome by a historical presentation are concentrated in the beginning itself. From every point of historical presentation, therefore, we are constantly referred back to the beginning, in relation to which we must orient ourselves for the purposes of a general survey.

If historical presentation follows the movement of the subject matter itself, as is its task, it will repeatedly arrive in the course of its procedure at points leading in very different directions, all reaching backward and assuming varied modes of perception with reference to the whole. Thus at the outset we cannot enter the entire course that subsequently is divided in such multiple fashion without knowing beforehand with which side we are to align ourselves throughout all differences. Just as the church, which at the beginning was at unity with itself, split asunder, and divided into the great antithesis of Protestantism and Catholicism; and just as other religious parties appeared in addition to the Protestant Church, as well as views that emerged within the Protestant Church itself, deviating more or less from orthodox doctrine and claiming for themselves the same title to the Protestant principle—so also all these differences embrace equally numerous and varied points of view from which the entire development of the Christian church could be understood. Just as Protestant historiography is essentially different from Catholic, even so that of the rationalists is wholly different from that of the modern [5] supernaturalists. And as the respective theological systems of rationalism and supernaturalism have outlived their usefulness, having each evolved to a degree that oversteps the antithesis between the two, so it is impossible for the most recent historiography of the Christian <49> church, if it is not to remain attached to an obsolete standpoint, to be either rationalistic or supernaturalistic in the older, absolute sense.

The more highly developed a theological position is, the more a particular historiography tends to be conditioned by it, or rather to emerge from it. The first and most important task of every theological position can only be to investigate the nature of Christianity; but this can occur only through a return to the beginnings of Christianity and through the most precise investigation of the sources from which a knowledge of its origin must be derived. But once the basic point of view has been established in this way, the necessary consequence must be that the entire view of the course of development of the Christian church is also determined by it. If each of the various theological standpoints that have achieved a high degree of independence has disclosed and impressed itself in its own treatment of the history of the Christian church, then there can be no comprehensive work in church history whose view of history does not wholly manifest the theological vantage point of its author. Thus there are as many different views of history as there are different theological vantage points; and it is worth the trouble to consider them more closely in their relation to one another and to set them in the perspective of a historical process taking its own peculiar course. If the general task of raising the content of the objectively given into the clarity of subjective consciousness remains always the same, nevertheless the attempts at its solution [6] are very different; and it can be seen at each important juncture not only how differently the same objects can be interpreted, but also how the view concerning them always changes in accord with the general conditions determining the consciousness of the time. Taken together, all these attempts, representing the various possible points of view in particular historical presentations, form the epochs of church historiography, in whose course the Spirit working in the depths and struggling toward the solution of its task has raised itself, at first gradually, to the level on which it stands in the present mode of perception.

No matter how, in accord with the general and formal requirements that are to be made of a historical presentation, we evaluate the merits and weaknesses of individual church historians—their faithfulness and credibility, the quality of their sources, the ways and means of their presentation—the first thing we need to investigate in order to obtain a more specific and concrete picture of their individuality is their entire historical perspective, including those characteristic attitudes in which it <50> is expressed. To sketch at least the preliminary outlines in a characterization of the major church historians, from the most ancient to the most recent times, is the purpose of the following essay. It is not our task to review the entire corpus of works that make up the literature of church history,[4] but only to focus upon the main points at which church historiography has made a more specific, more deeply penetrating, and more comprehensive effort toward the completion of its task.

[...]

[247]<241>

---

[4] [Baur] Cf. Karl Friedrich Stäudlin, *Geschichte und Literatur der Kirchengeschichte*, ed. Johann Tychsen Hemsen (Hannover: Hahn'sche Hofbuchhandlung, 1827). [Ed.] Stäudlin (1761–1826), Lutheran theologian. Cf. Paul Tschackert, "Stäudlin, Carl Friedrich," *Allgemeine Deutsche Biographie* 35 (1893): 516–20. Online: https://www.deutsche-biographie.de/pnd100276318.html#adbcontent. Accessed August 19, 2021.

Conclusions and Suggestions

1 The Idea of the Church We have still to ask what is the result of our survey of all these attempts, from the most ancient up to the most recent times, to portray the history of the Christian church. The materials are available in greater abundance than ever before, since the historical data, both in content and in scope, have been investigated thoroughly and from many points of view, and have been studied critically. Furthermore, it has long since been acknowledged that the historian can be equal to his task only in so far as he transposes himself into the objective reality of the subject matter itself, free from the bias of subjective views and interests, whatever they may be, so that instead of making history a reflection of his own subjectivity, he may be simply a mirror for the perception of historical phenomena in their true and real form.

Nevertheless, there is still a lack, even in the most recent treatments of the history of the Christian church, that prevents them from achieving greater perfection. That lack, put briefly, consists in a wrong relation of the Idea to the manifestations in which its historical development is to be presented. The Idea still hovers indefinitely and at a great distance over the manifestations to which it must be related. It is not yet strong and vital enough to penetrate and vivify the historical material, as the soul animates the body, or to become, through such an organic unity, the moving principle of the entire series of manifestations in which the history of the Christian [248] church takes its course.[5] Or should there still be any doubt as <242> to whether the history of the Christian church is the [249] movement of the Idea of the church, and therefore consists of something more than a succession of changes following one another at random? If it is right to speak of an Idea of the church, then that Idea, like any other, must possess within itself the living impulse to go out from

---

[5][Baur] To put the same thing another way, a progression from the pragmatic standpoint of historiography to the universal is still lacking. Since church history at last came down from the transcendent heights of abstract dualism to the empirical soil of history, it has become pragmatic; but in essentials it has still not moved beyond the pragmatic mode of treatment. Schelling very actively distinguished and characterized the vantage points that confront each other here in his *Vorlesungen über die Methode des akademischen Studium* (Stuttgart and Tübingen: Cotta, 1803), 213 ff.; and a reminder of these brilliant ideas about history generally is all the more appropriate here since of themselves they apply especially to church history. "The opposite standpoint to the absolute," says Schelling, 216 f., "is the empirical, which in turn has two components: the pure perception and determination of what has occurred—a matter for the historical researcher, who represents only one side of the historian as such—and the combining of the empirical materials into an intellectual identity [*Verstandes-Identität*], or (since the latter cannot be found within the occurrences as such, which from an empirical perspective can only appear contingent and unharmonious) an arrangement designed by the subject in accord with a purpose, which thus far is didactic or political. This treatment of history with a quite specific, non-universal intention is, in accord with the word's ancient meaning, called pragmatic ....Modern men are inclined to regard the pragmatic spirit as the highest in history, and among themselves to assume it as though it were the highest praise .... Among the Germans, as a rule, it is with the pragmatic spirit as with Famulus in Goethe's Faust: 'What they call the spirit of the times is their own spirit, in which the times are reflected.' ... History with a pragmatic purpose of itself excludes universality and also necessarily demands a limited object. The purpose of instruction demands a correct and empirically based linking of occurrences, by which the intellect [*Verstand*] is indeed enlightened, but the reason [*Vernunft*], without another ingredient, remains unsatisfied ....It is clear that since the mere linking of occurrences according to empirical necessity can never be anything but pragmatic, and since history in its highest Idea must be independent and free of all subjective connection, the empirical standpoint could not on the whole be its highest representation ....For the first time, then, history is completed for the reason when the empirical causes, while satisfying the intellect, becomes the tools and means of manifestation for a higher necessity. In such a portrayal history cannot fail to be the result of the greatest and most astonishing drama, such as can only have been composed in an infinite Spirit." And where should it have lacked this result least than in the field of church history?

itself and to become actualized in a series of manifestations that can only be regarded as various aspects of the relation that exists generally between the Idea and its manifestation.

But it is not even necessary to take the standpoint of the Idea. Even the most fleeting glimpse into the history of the church can show how significant and radical a turning point the Reformation is, and how church history after it takes a wholly different course from what went before. The church is so deeply involved in the antithesis between Protestantism and Catholicism that we cannot but believe its history to have been guided in that direction, as though intentionally, from the beginning. <243> This is at least the Protestant view of history. The high significance of the Reformation for the entire conception of the history of the Christian church is shown by the fact that concerning it the historical views of Catholicism and Protestantism stand in an irreconcilable antithesis. The Catholic is unable to imagine how, from within the bosom of the Catholic Church, an opposition could arise which the church with all its might [250] cannot suppress and reassimilate to itself, and on this account he is likewise unable to connect the Reformation and Protestantism with a view of history whose foundation is the unchanging church in the unity of its principle of an unbroken tradition. Conversely, the Protestant sees in the same phenomenon so epoch-making a transition from an obsolete form of the consciousness of the church to one newly emerging that for him the whole historical process of the church remains an unsolved riddle, if he cannot regard it as a continuous development, progressing from moment to moment, and if he cannot understand the Reformation itself as simply one of the moments in whose interaction the course of development of the church consists.

If we ask what is epoch-making about this point of transition, then the difference between pre- and post-Reformation periods of the church can only be described as a difference in the relation between the Idea and its manifestation. Is it not then self-evident that during the entire epoch of the church up to the Reformation, the Idea of the church as a whole tended to enter into the reality of the world of manifestations and to merge with it in an inseparable unity, whereas since the Reformation the development of the church strives just as much to retract the Idea from the reality of the visible church and to separate Idea and manifestation to the full extent of their distinction?[6] Everything that constitutes the distinction between Catholic and Protestant conceptions of the church lies <244> on the boundary between the two great epochs into which the history of the church is divided.

If this of itself suggests a consideration that takes into account only the most general elements, then the further question surely arises as to what content the Idea of the church intends to transpose from itself and to realize in the visible church, or, since it can realize nothing other than itself, [251] what it is essentially. The church is the real form in which Christianity is made manifest. If

---

[6][PCH] On the basis of this statement Karl Hase, in his *Die Tübinger Schule: Ein Sendschreiben an Herrn Dr. Ferdinand Christian von Baur* (Leipzig: Breitkopf und Härtel, 1855), charged Baur with arguing that for Protestantism the Idea soars far above the opaque positivity of the historical church and that for it the only authentic church is the ideal or invisible one. Baur replied that Hase had overlooked the adverb "just as much" (*ebensosehr*), which, he said, binds these two statements together equally, "so that Protestantism, in the same proportion that it seeks to introduce the Idea into the reality, must also withdraw it, and so that it does this indeed as Catholicism does, but not one-sidedly, rather only so that in the relation of Idea and reality these two sides, which belong together, may be well distinguished and set in the right relation to each other– the unity of Idea and reality and the incongruence of both." *An Herrn Dr. Karl Hase: Beantwortung des Sendschreibens "Die Tübinger Schule"* (Tübingen: Fues, 1855), 83–4. This further clarification of a statement that Hase justifiably found obscure is important for a precise understanding of Baur's position.

we inquire about the Idea of the church, we inquire, therefore, about Christianity itself. Difficult as the response to this question seems to be, it becomes obvious, as soon as we proceed with it, that Christianity can be essentially nothing other than that which the Christian consciousness of all times, in whatever form it may have occurred, has perceived in the person of Christ: the unity and union of God and man.[7] However else we may conceive the essence of Christianity—as everything it is intended to be for man in its various aspects, such as the revelation of Absolute Truth, the establishment of redemption, reconciliation, blessing—it has its absolute conception and expression in the unity and union of God and man, as that unity is perceived in the person of Christ, and in this perception becomes a fact of Christian consciousness. The substantial content of the historical development of the Christian church is therefore nothing other than this unity. All things can aim at realizing this unity for the Christian consciousness in the various forms in which it can be grasped only in such fashion that they are themselves but forms of this absolute content. Are not the major components in the historical development of the church themselves really to be placed under this guiding point of view? The two major forms in which the Idea of the church realizes itself are dogma and polity. In both, the development of the church proceeded to realize the Idea of that unity in such fashion that Christian consciousness could find in it the adequate expression of its Idea.

In the area of dogma, this happened above all through the doctrine of the Person of Christ, which, together with all the doctrines belonging to it (the Logos, the Trinity, the two natures of Christ and their relation), was the object of so much theological and ecclesiastical activity during the first centuries. Nothing is seen more clearly [252] from all the controversies <245> and proceedings connected with that doctrine than the great impulse, which dominated the entire age, to objectify its innermost Christian religious consciousness in the Christological dogmas. The endeavor to develop dogma in its various aspects from the focal point of Christology and according to the analogy of the basic conception given in it is the essential content of the church history of the first six centuries, in which the dogmatic system of the church obtained all those essential determinations that since then have remained unchanged. In no other period did dogma have so predominant an influence as in the first, which brought it forth and fixed it for the total consciousness of the church. A portrayal of the first major period that does not permit its dogmatic character fully to appear can therefore only give a very unfaithful picture. It would merely adopt for itself without justification the now customary separation of the history of dogma from church history; the setting apart of the dogmatic for special treatment must not be intended in such a way that it thereby ceases to be an integral component of church history. The more closely dogma is joined to dogma, and the more uniform the characteristics with which all dogmas are developed together into a system, the less it can be misunderstood that the church in this whole period of its theological activity only follows an inner tendency of its nature. It has in itself the irresistible impulse to bring the unity and union of God and man, which is the absolute content of its consciousness, to firm conception and expression in all the dogmas of the Christian faith, and to set it forth in this definite form.

---

[7][PCH] "Die Einheit Gottes und des Menschen." *Einheit* carries the meaning of both "unity" and "union" in English. It suggests a unity achieved by union, rather than a sheer identity on the one hand, or an outward combination of factors on the other. *Einheit* will be translated by either "unity" or "union," or by the hendiadys "unity and union," depending on the context.

2 The Church before the Reformation Just as the first period is that of the development of dogma, so the second, which embraces the whole of the Middle Ages up to the Reformation, is above all that of the history of the hierarchy, or [253] more specifically of the Papacy. This is the same movement of the Idea of the church that, once it has arrived at a particular stage of the church's historical development in the area of dogma, moves in the same direction to another area. The formation of the hierarchy goes hand in hand with that of dogma. Dogma is first given some specific form by the bishops, but the bishops themselves exist only for the sake of dogma. They are the preservers, witnesses, and interpreters of dogma, the representatives of the church, whose total consciousness, illuminated by the Holy Spirit, is <246> the highest source and authority for dogma. Through their decision it obtains the form in which it is universally and unconditionally valid as holy, untouchable truth.

Just as the bishops are the main pillars of the hierarchical system, so the Papacy is simply the acme of the same, to which it mounts step by step. The Pope is the absolute bishop; and the Idea of the church realizing itself in the form of the hierarchy already possesses in the earliest foundation of the bishopric a predisposition toward everything it attains through its complete realization in the Papacy. The bishop, as the head of his congregation, already represents Christ, and is related to a single congregation in the same way that Christ, as its universal head, is related to the church as a whole. Similarly, the Pope in absolute fashion is the representative of Christ, the deputy of God and Christ. The same unity and union of God and man, which in Christology, as the epitome of the dogmatic system of the church, is the absolute content of religious consciousness brought to specific conception, has in the Papacy the absolute form in which the realized Idea of the church is perceived. Everyone who has faithfully accepted the dogma of the church, and who faithfully and willingly subordinates himself to the Pope as the representative of God and Christ, is aware of the beatifying union with God through this mediation. All the humanity of the Catholic Church is joined in absolute union with God through dogma and Papacy. [254] The idea of the church, as it sought to realize itself from the earliest development of the church, is realized in the Papacy as the acme of the hierarchical system. The Catholic Church in its visible manifestation is the wholly adequate and concrete representation of the Idea of the church. God and man have become one in the two major forms in which this unity finds specific, concrete expression.

If the whole historical development of the church up to the Reformation, so considered, is divided into two periods, in which the Idea of the church has objectified itself in the two major forms of dogma and of hierarchy, then it automatically follows that the transition from the first period to the second can be located at the time when the still incomplete hierarchy takes the decisive step toward its fulfillment in the Papacy. That happened at the same time as the great transition from the ancient world to the Middle Ages. At this boundary between periods stands Gregory the Great, like an ecclesiastical Janus, since on the one hand, looking backward, he brings to an end the succession of church fathers, while on the other he initiates the succession of the medieval Popes, <247> whose prototype is already clearly to be seen in him. Therefore, to make Charlemagne the beginning or terminus of a period is to assume an extra-ecclesiastical standpoint alien to the subject matter.[8] The iconoclastic controversy also becomes secondary; and since in any event Gregory VII heralds himself as epoch-making, there is no reason to fix upon Innocent III in particular as

---

[8][Ed.] This was Hase's view: Karl von Hase, *Kirchengeschichte: Lehrbuch zunächst für akademische Vorlesungen*, 3rd edn. (Leipzig: Breitkopf und Härtel, 1837), §12, p. 5.

the culmination of the Papacy. The entire age with which we are here concerned can in a general way be conceived only as the period of absolute power for the church, which spared no effort to become in outer manifestation what it was implicitly in Idea. As though the Idea could have reality only to the degree that it actualized itself in definite forms of outer, sensible [255] existence, it is intent only on taking form in the world of manifestation with all its power, and on expanding and establishing itself there to its full extent. The further the church progresses in its development, the more unconditionally must everything be subordinated to it. There is no existence independent of it; and if there is still something beyond its power to reach and suppress absolutely, then this has its basis only in the impossibility of the matter itself.

Implicitly, in the nature of the case, the Idea and its outer manifestation cannot be unified in such fashion that they are related only as two mutually superimposed quantities. But this was unable to hinder the church from asserting itself as the absolute power of the age. From it everything proceeded; it was, for that age, the absolutely determinative form of consciousness. Even scholasticism, attempting to encompass dogma with intellectual categories, followed, in the service of the church, the same systematizing tendency of the age, which had been organized by the hierarchy into a well-articulated system. We can therefore understand all manifestations characteristic of that age only in so far as we are able to transpose ourselves into the consciousness of the time as it was filled by the Idea of the church and of ecclesiastical religion. This form of consciousness was to remain dominant until it brought about its own destruction. But this it had to do, as surely as there was no intrinsic possibility that the visible church could be the adequate representation of the Idea of the church and of Christianity.

3 The Church after the Reformation The Reformation is the great transition point, after which the Idea of the church seems only to exhibit a tendency to unravel the fabric it has <247> woven. Whereas hitherto, the development of the church has only moved forward in a straight line, now it seems with one stroke to reverse the trend, to turn backward and in upon itself. The spirit now animating the church is one of opposition and protest, antithesis, negation of what is. [256] Since on all sides negation confronts the previous affirmation, its wish seems to be to move only backward—not, surely, so as to arrive at an absolute nullity but rather all the more strongly to affirm the true and enduring by a new absorption in itself, in the absolute content of the Idea, and in the denial of what is acknowledged as untrue and void. No one can deny that the moving forces of the Reformation, its causes and its effects, lie far beyond the controversy over Luther's theses and their immediate consequences, even though in many accounts the epoch-making character of the Reformation period still seems to depend solely on the person of Luther—who loses none of his significance if we regard him as the particular vital point at which various converging rays ignite into a blazing flame.

But if we bring together the various factors under consideration, where else can their unity of principle be more correctly recognized than in the concept of the church? That the perception of the church has become essentially different as a consequence of the Reformation is already shown by the distinction that since then has become customary, between a visible and an invisible church. The meaning of this distinction becomes clear if we bear in mind that, although before[9] the Reformation Christian religious consciousness in general found no offence in perceiving the

---

[9][PCH] Reading *vor* rather than *von*, as printed in the text.

true church in the visible church, or in regarding the visible church as the manifestation adequate to the Idea of the church, since then it has become increasingly evident that this awareness of unity between the church and its idea has been badly and irreparably shattered. The Idea of the church is torn away from its manifestation as the visible church; it is in itself the driving and moving principle of progression away from one form of consciousness, in which as an untrue existence it can no longer remain, to another form, in which it is freely related to the manifestation in the same proportion that it stands above it. [257]

The period in which the intent of the church was to set forth the absolute content of its Idea in visible manifestation, and to regard the Idea as absolutely one with its manifestation, is the period of the absolutism of the church. Of necessity, that absolutism conflicted with twin interests, the recognition of which was forced by the inner necessity of the matter <249> itself upon the consciousness of mankind in its progressive development–the interests of the individual and of the state. Where the church rules with absolute power, the focal point of the individual's existence and consciousness is to be found only in the unity of the whole into which he is incorporated, in the objective reality of the church, and in everything that makes the church the essential mediator of his salvation, external and contingent though it may be. The externalization of that which possesses its truth only in an interior relation with the subject—since it exists for the subject, and the subject possesses himself in it and is directly aware through it of his salvation and his unity with God—sooner or later makes inevitable a turning point at which the subject draws back into himself from this externalizing of his religious consciousness, becoming aware that he himself is the absolute subject for everything that makes up the essential content of his religious consciousness. Protestantism is the principle of subjective freedom, of the freedom of faith and conscience, of the autonomy of the subject in opposition to the heteronomy of the Catholic conception of the church.

Just as only in Protestantism can the subject come to the right of his individuality, his free self-existence, the true consciousness of himself, so it is with the state. The absolutism of the church had removed from the state in advance the ground on which it could have arrived at an independent existence. Only when the church finally withdraws from this domain, with the acknowledgment [258] that it is not in a condition to realize its Idea in the world of outer manifestations so as to be the power permeating and dominating everything, can the state claim for itself the area released by the church and assert its absolute right against the church. Where the church cannot or may not rule, the state appears with its full authority. Thus for the state, also, the claim to autonomy—an existence independent of the absolute power of the church—is established for the first time by Protestantism, or by the principle of subjective freedom that comes to its outer recognition only in Protestantism.

Even after the bond of unity between the Idea of the church and its outer manifestation, as established in the Catholicism of the Middle Ages, was dissolved by Protestantism, the church could not cease to aspire toward the realization of its Idea. Two factors now stand as the absolute condition under which alone the church can be recognized in manifestation as the Idea of the church, corresponding to Christian religious consciousness: the freedom of the subject and the autonomy of the state. No matter how the Idea of the church may otherwise be realized, as long as <250> these two factors do not remain an absolute right, the existence of the church will become as false and self-destructive as before. In these two equally essential principles Protestantism has broken permanently with the Papacy, denying it every right to exist in the Protestant domain because of a certainty that the unity and union of God and man, which is the absolute content of Christianity and of the church as the form of its manifestation, cannot be recognized in a form of the church such as is represented by the Papacy. Accordingly, from the standpoint of the Protestant principle, man can know himself to be one with God and therefore certain of his salvation only when he is aware also of being free in himself, [259] and sees himself placed in the state in the sphere of an existence free from the absolutism of the church.

However, in regard to the past, justification for Catholicism and the Papacy is by no means hereby denied; rather, for the first time it is now truly recognized, since only by means of it could the Idea of the church progress to a new form of realization, and Christian consciousness to a higher level of development. From a higher level one can understand for the first time the true significance of a subordinate level, because it now appears for the first time for what it really is— not the whole and complete truth, but only a momentary aspect of the same, through which the Idea in the course of its development must first pass, or a form of consciousness that must first be fully lived in order to be able to move on with the awareness of having the maturity for a higher level.[10] Therefore, <251> even though Protestantism [260] may have demonstrated clearly and convincingly to the Papacy and Catholicism the whole body of conclusions, false in principle, on which they erected their bold edifice, they nevertheless retain their full historical right, but only for the past. Protestantism itself must remain an unsolved riddle if it were to imagine another way of becoming what it has become than that by which its self-consciousness was mediated to it through the Papacy and Catholicism.

The opposition raised by Protestantism against Catholicism above all concerned the Papacy as the form in which absolutism must evoke well-justified opposition. But once the bond that brought the Idea of the church into union with its visible manifestation had been severed in only one of the two major forms, the same incongruity between Idea and manifestation necessarily became evident in the other as well. Dogma could likewise no longer serve as an adequate expression for religious consciousness of the Idea that should have been the absolute content of dogma. And just as the realization of the Idea of the church in Catholicism progressed from dogma to hierarchy and its completion in the Papacy, so the dissolution of the unity that Catholicism perceived in the visible church proceeded from the denial of the Papacy to the denial of dogma. What was denied in dogma concerned first of all only the elimination of elements introduced into dogma by the hierarchy and the principle of tradition on which it rested. [261] But once ignited, the process of dissolution had here as well to pursue its further course, and it did so in the same fashion as with the Papacy.

---

[10][Baur] What is to be said here cannot be elucidated more simply and strikingly than by the words with which Hegel in the *Philosophie der Geschichte* (*Werke*, IX [Berlin, 1837], 398) concludes his treatment of the period of the Crusades. "At the grave of Christ the same answer is given to the Christians as to the disciples who sought his body there: 'Why do you seek the living among the dead? He is not here; he is risen.' The principle of your religion you have to seek not in the sensible, in the grave among the dead, but in the living Spirit in yourselves. We have seen the tremendous Idea of the union of the finite and the infinite made spiritless; the infinite is sought in a wholly isolated external thing. Christendom found the empty grave but not the union of the worldly and the eternal, and therefore lost the Holy Land. To all practical purposes, it is disappointed .... This, however, was the ultimate result of the Crusades. Here begins the period of self-reliance, of independence; at the Holy Sepulcher the West has taken leave of the East forever and grasped its principle of subjective, infinite freedom." [PCH. Cf. *The Philosophy of History*, trans. J. Sibree (New York: Dover, 1956), 393.] This is equally true of the whole medieval period of the church. The Spirit that became conscious of the true Idea of the church through the Reformation took leave forever of the Papacy and the papal church, with a conviction that grew to certainty during the entire previous course of the same, but also only in this sense, that from now on it was no longer to seek the true essence of Christianity in this visible existence of the church.

It is generally agreed that in the period from the Reformation to the present should be divided into two parts. But what should be the point of division? The Peace of Westphalia, from which Hase dates the most recent period, has merely too political a significance, since it did not bring about an essential change either in the inner nature of Protestantism or in its position with respect to Catholicism.[11] Unquestionably, the epochal point can be located only in the general revolution of dogmatic consciousness during the course of the eighteenth century. Here for the first time Protestantism accomplished the same analytical criticism of dogma—which had remained unchanged since the ancient church—that it had already brought against the Papacy in the time of the Reformation.[12] It was the same process of dissolving a unity whose elements could no longer be unified in the consciousness of the age. Just as the Papacy was overthrown when in the person of the Pope the person of Christ himself, the God-man, the representative of God and Christ, the infallible head of <252> the church, could no longer be recognized, but only a weak and fallible human being; even so, faith in the authority of dogma disappeared completely once the consciousness of the age was no longer prepared to accept a form of dogma in which the person of Christ was to be perceived as the totally adequate and exclusive unity of the divine and the human. The reshaping of the ancient ecclesiastical system came about largely because all those ideas, principles, and teachings by which Socinianism first criticized and polemicized against the doctrine of the person of Christ[13] also gained entrance and acceptance in the Protestant church,[14] and were carried out to a far greater degree and with more rigorous consistency of principle. [262] In opposition to the Papacy the intention of Protestantism was to allow what man is in himself, as a self-constituted individual, as a free, self-conscious subject, to come into its own, and to set him free for himself from the complex of the hierarchical system in which he was entangled by the sacrifice of his independence and personality. Similarly, in the realm of dogma the major task concerning the doctrine of the person of Christ was to posit the true humanity of Christ in place of a transcendent supernaturalism in which the human was only a disappearing moment of the divine, and to grasp his entire manifestation as much as possible from the natural historical continuity in which it belongs. It was now regarded as a first principle that if the unity and union of God and man, which is the absolute content of Christianity, were to be perceived in the person of Christ, this could occur only under the assumption that his humanity remained in its full integrity and was regarded as the essential, substantial foundation of what he is as a whole.

Thereafter, the whole conception of Christianity followed a course corresponding to this basic perception. The humanization, rationalization, subjectivization, interiorization, and spiritualization of Christianity was, in different forms and directions, the watchword of the time. Just as it was believed that the Papacy had not been transcended as long as it was not analyzed into the basic elements out of which it came, so likewise there was no specific terminus in the criticism and analysis

---

[11][Ed.] Karl August von Hase (1800–90), Lutheran theologian. Baur's reference is to Hase's *Kirchengeschichte*, §12, p. 6.

[12][Ed.] Baur here anticipates the distinction between Old and New Protestantism forcefully argued for in the early twentieth century by Ernst Troeltsch. For a full discussion of the ensuing controversy taking cognizance also of Baur's earlier contribution, cf. Heinrich Hoffmann, "Literatur zum Neuprotestantismus," *Zeitschrift für Theologie und Kirche* 32 (N. F. 5) (1924): 382–406.

[13][Ed.] Socinianism: Followers of Fausto Sozzini (1539–1604). On their Christology cf. Mark W. Elliott, "Christology in the Seventeenth Century," in *The Oxford Handbook of Christology*, ed. Francesca Aran Murphy (Oxford: OUP, 2015), 297–314, here: 298–300.

[14][Ed.] Protestant Church. From the context it is clear that Baur means specifically the Protestantism flowing from the magisterial Reformation.

of dogma. Everything that at one time or another had been dogmatically defined must be sharply and precisely scrutinized to see whether it was not already a moment of the process in which the Idea of the church objectified itself in order to enter into union with its visible manifestation. Here even the canonical writings could not set any firm [263] limits. Historical criticism would have labored in vain in the investigation of Christianity's historical origin had it not at least established that within this first historical <253> sphere Christianity was already involved in a process of development so closely connected with the history of the first centuries that the view of the process of the development of Christianity held by the most recent criticism could not but differ essentially and at many points from previous views.

On the whole, can history have a greater task than the ever deeper investigation of the historical continuity linking all phenomena that lie before it as given objects? Thus its natural endeavor is to penetrate with all the means at its disposal into that which still confronts it as a solid, closed mass—as much by investigation of particulars as by subordination of particulars to a guiding higher point of view, from which alone they first obtain their firm position in the whole—in order to melt and dissolve this mass and to draw it into the general flux of historical becoming, a flux in which, in the endless concatenation of causes and effects, one event is always the presupposition of another, in which all together are mutually supported and maintained; and what alone must remain forever incomprehensible is that which could in advance make the claim to stand in the midst of history outside of all historical continuity.

CHAPTER ELEVEN

Christianity in Its First Three Centuries

FROM: CCK, 1–41
TRANSLATION: ROBERT F. BOWN AND PETER C. HODGSON, CCC, 3–37

Baur's *Christianity and the Christian Church of the First Three Centuries* might be the book that most fully brings together Baur's variegated interests: critical study of the New Testament, historiographical reflection on the nature of history, and philosophical reflection on the meaning of that history understood as the self-mediation of the spirit. If many of Baur's exegetical results can be paralleled in prior scholarship, what is unique is his quest for what he calls the "total view" (*Totalanschauung*) of the development of early Christianity. In this book, Baur offers a lucid account of that total conception, beginning with the long excerpt presented here, comprising the first section of the book.

Here Baur begins by arguing that Christianity, as the "absolute religion," arrives in history at a moment that enables it to take up and surpass the concerns of both paganism and Judaism. Although his characterization of neither paganism or Judaism is objective, nor defensible in these terms today, in Baur's view Christianity exploits both the universalism and the inward moral seriousness of the Greco-Roman philosophical tradition, and the monotheism and spiritual concerns of Judaism, but surpasses them both in its own universalist concern and spiritual-mindedness. He offers an account of Jesus as the founder of this new religion, arguing that the Gospel of Matthew (in Baur's view the earliest of the four canonical gospels) gives us the most useful insight into Jesus' life and messianic self-conception. Jesus exhorted his hearers toward inward obedience and moral transformation, and if he took on a messianic self-understanding (for which Baur finds evidence in his use of the term "Son of Man" as a self-designation, a handful of stories including Peter's confession and the transfiguration, and especially in the entry into Jerusalem), he ultimately subverts and transforms a nationalistic concept of the Messiah into a universalizing, spiritual conception. Moral seriousness is therefore the essence of participating in the Kingdom of God, as the parables attest, and not some political or eschatological expectation. The resurrection of Jesus is unavailable to historical scrutiny, but Jesus' earliest followers operated out of the conviction that he had overcome death, even if some of them still stubbornly clung to the nationalistic ideas Jesus had tried to undo.

It is a remarkable beginning to a remarkable book. Baur will go on in the remainder of the book to map out the landscape of early Christian literary production as a site marked by competing theological tendencies and conflicting missions, ultimately culminating in the production of "early Catholicism."

CHRISTIANITY AND THE CHRISTIAN CHURCH IN THE FIRST CENTURIES

Part One
The Entrance of Christianity into World History; Primitive Christianity

[1] <3>

The Universalism of the Roman Empire as a Preparation for Christianity

In no area of historical examination does everything that belongs to a specific series of historical phenomena depend so much on the starting point from which it proceeds as it does in the history of the Christian Church. Thus nowhere else does so much depend on the representation we form of that point from which the entire historical course takes its beginning.

The historian who enters upon the object of his presentation with the faith of the church is confronted at the very outset with the miracle of all miracles, the primal fact of Christianity—that the only-begotten Son of God descended to earth from the eternal throne of the Godhead and became human in the womb of the Virgin. Whoever regards this as simply and absolutely a miracle immediately steps completely outside the nexus of history. Miracle is an absolute beginning, and to the extent that such a beginning conditions everything that follows, the whole series of phenomena that belong to the field of Christianity must then bear the same miraculous character. That is because severing the historical connection at the outset makes it possible to do so again. Therefore a truly historical examination or reflection[1] very naturally is concerned to draw the miracle of the absolute beginning into the historical nexus and to resolve it, insofar as possible, into its natural elements.

People have often attempted to do this, and various objections have been brought against their attempts, but the task [2] itself remains always the same. By just asking why <4> the miracle with which the history of Christianity begins has entered into the nexus of historical events precisely at this point in world history, we have already raised a series of questions that can only be answered by means of historical examination and reflection. Therefore the first task in a history of Christianity, or of the Christian Church, can only be to orient ourselves to Christianity at the point in time when it enters into world history. So we ask whether we can recognize, on the one hand, something here that belongs to the essence of Christianity itself, and on the other hand, something here that expresses the general character of the age in which Christianity appears. Where such common points of contact emerge, they shed light on the historical origin of Christianity itself.

In doing so, early Christian apologists already found it especially significant that Christianity appeared precisely at the point in time when the Roman Empire reached the zenith of its worldly dominion. They inferred from this that, even in the eyes of the pagans, a religion could not but

---

[1][PCH] *Betrachtung* is the term Baur typically uses for critical, scientific (*wissenschaftlich*) historical method. It has both an empirical and a speculative (reflective) component, as our double translation suggests. Empirically, it investigates the wealth of historical materials and follows where they lead regardless of the historian's subjective interests. Speculatively, it knows "how to grasp historical phenomena as appearances of the idea objectifying itself within them, and how to comprehend them as moments of the idea's immanent working within history" (KGNJ, 416. CTNC, 385). This immanent working does not sever, but rather constitutes, the historical nexus (*Zusammenhang*). When the systematic meaning is not so evident, *Betrachtung* is translated as "consideration," "view," "perspective," etc.

appear auspicious whose epoch coincided with the fullest flourishing of the Roman Empire. This coincidence of Christianity with the Roman world monarchy[2] appeared to them so remarkable that they could not attribute it to chance.[3]

The true point of contact between Christianity and the Empire, however, is the universal tendency of both. It is a reflection of genuine significance for world history that, at the same point in time when the Roman Empire united all the peoples of the then-known world in a universal monarchy, the religion that subsumed[4] all religious particularism into universality began its course in the world. Thus the universalism of Christianity was comparable to the stage already attained by the power and genius of Rome with its world monarchy. [3] This was in fact the time when universal world-consciousness first made this momentous advance. As the barriers and divisions between peoples and nationalities vanished before the encroaching power of the Romans, and people became aware, through their subjection to a common head, of the unity subsuming their differences, spiritual consciousness as such was proportionately enlarged and led more and more to disregard the particular traits that separated one group from another, and to elevate itself to a universal perspective.

The general striving of the age toward an all-encompassing unity, into which everything particular and individual might be resolved, found its most imposing expression in the universalism of the Roman Empire. This universalism was the very goal toward which the course of world history had aimed for many centuries. Alexander the Great had opened to the West the portals of the East; and, by means of so <5> many newly opened routes for the lively and diverse intercourse of peoples, the Greek language and culture had spread throughout the known world. It was but the next step on the same road of world-historical development when the Roman dominion gave all these peoples a new bond of political unity in forms never seen before. This all-encompassing unity found its basis in Roman civilization and law, and operated through the vast and highly organized Roman state. Under the empire, not only was there a reduction in the former hostility among its constituent peoples; but also everything national and individual increasingly resolved itself into a universality that smoothed over their differences.

A group that from its beginnings had kept itself apart from other peoples by the distinctiveness of its national character, and that had clung to this distinctiveness in the most obstinate and persistent way, nevertheless could not remain outside this general unity, which bound peoples together not merely politically but also in a new spiritual bond. After the Jewish state had twice been destroyed,[5] [4] the Jews were forced to associate with other peoples in the wider world. When the successors of Alexander founded their own kingdoms, in those cities that became the chief centers of political and intellectual intercourse among peoples, Jews were an important part of the population. These Jews became Hellenists and assimilated the most diverse elements of Greek culture. Ultimately they were also drawn into the ever-widening net of Roman dominion. So it came about that the

---

[2][PCH] Baur uses the term "monarchy" here and several times below, although the Romans were very clear that the emperor was not a "king." The Roman Republic had replaced the earlier kings, and the Romans wanted no more of that kind of monarchy.

[3][Baur] See the fragment of the *Apology* of Melito of Sardis in Eusebius, *Ecclesiastical History*, 4.26; and Origen, *Against Celsus*, 2.30.

[4][PCH] The verb *aufheben* means both to annul and to preserve or take up. Thus particularism does not simply disappear but is "taken up into" universality. See Note on Text and Translations.

[5][PCH] Through the Assyrian and Babylonian conquests.

birthplace of Christianity on Jewish soil was already in contact with the power that was said to be its forerunner on the road to world conquest.

Thus the universalism of Christianity has its essential presupposition in the universalism of Roman world dominion. But in considering how these two world powers came into contact with each other, we must not think in customary teleological terms. We must not think that, in these external circumstances and connections, Christianity entered into the world by the special favor of divine providence—a providence that, so the supposition goes, could have selected no more appropriate a time than this for the accomplishment of its purposes. On that view the major consideration is merely the fact that so many new routes of communication facilitated the diffusion of Christianity throughout the provinces of the Roman Empire, and that the protection of the Roman legions and civil order removed many obstacles the messengers of the gospel otherwise could have faced.[6]

<6>. The bond that connects the two [5] powers is based, far more deeply and inwardly, on the general spiritual and intellectual movement of the time. The main point is that Christianity could not have been the universal form of religious consciousness that it is had the entire development of world history, up to the time when it appeared, not prepared the way for it. First came the general intellectual culture that the Greeks made the common property of the nations, then Roman rule uniting the nations, with its political institutions serving as the basis for universal civilization. Roman rule removed the limitations of national consciousness and set aside the many differences that had kept peoples separate, not merely in their outward relationships but even more so inwardly. The universalism of Christianity could never have passed over into peoples' general consciousness had not political universalism prepared the way for that to happen. Christianity is itself essentially the same form of general consciousness to which the development of humankind had already advanced at the time of Christianity's appearance.

Christianity and the Pre-Christian Religions <7> By viewing Christianity as a universal form of religious consciousness that corresponds to the spirit of the age, and for which the entire previous historical development of peoples has been preparing, we have grasped it at the point where it enters into world history. But what gives Christianity this universal form? It appears as the universal form of religious consciousness because it increasingly overcame the other religions, absorbed them, and transcended them by its universal dominion over the world. As opposed to those particular

---

[6][Baur] See Origen, *Against Celsus*, 2.30. To the objection of Celsus that the sun first displays itself by illuminating all other things, and that the Son of God ought to have presented himself in the same way, Origen answers that he in fact did so. "For 'righteousness arose in his days and abundance of peace' began with his birth; God was preparing the nations for his teaching, that they might be under one Roman emperor, so that the unfriendly attitude of the nations to one another, caused by the existence of a large number of kingdoms, might not make it more difficult for Jesus' apostles to do what he commanded them when he said, 'Go and teach all nations.' It is quite clear that Jesus was born in the reign of Augustus, the one who reduced to uniformity, so to speak, the many kingdoms on earth so that he had a single empire. It would have hindered Jesus' teaching from being spread through the whole world if there had been many kingdoms, not only for the reasons just stated, but also because men everywhere would have been compelled to do military service and to fight in defence of their own land. This used to happen before the times of Augustus and even earlier still when a war was necessary, such as that between the Peloponnesians and the Athenians, and similarly in the case of the other nations which fought one another. Accordingly, how could this teaching, which preaches peace and does not even allow men to take vengeance on their enemies, have had any success unless the international situation had everywhere been changed and a milder spirit prevailed at the advent of Jesus?" [Ed] English translation: Chadwick, 92.

forms of religion, it is the absolute religion.⁷ But what is it in Christianity that gives it its absolute character? The first answer to this question is [6] that Christianity rises above all the defects and limitations, the one-sidedness and finitude, that constitute the particularism of those other religious forms. It is not polytheistic like paganism; it does not, like Judaism, attach itself to outward rites and ordinances, or to the positive⁸ aspects of a purely traditional religion. Speaking generally, it stands above them as a more spiritual form of religious consciousness.

This, however, is saying very little and is self-evident as soon as we compare Christianity with the other two religions it encountered [paganism and Judaism]. When Christianity attained its world-historical significance, these two religions had long fallen into decay. They had become empty, inwardly dying, purely external forms that had lost their hold on the religious consciousness of their peoples. Paganism had sunk to the level of a spiritless folk religion. With all educated people, belief in the old gods had become more or less disconnected from religious consciousness. The myths in which the simpler faith of earlier times had expressed its finest religious intuitions seemed now mere fables in which there was no longer a spiritual bond joining form and content into a harmonious unity; they were merely pictorial forms for ideas that had grown up from a totally different soil. The only thing that maintained general interest in the national religion was that, as the religion of the state, it was closely intertwined with all the institutions of political life, and not easily separable from them.

Judaism, to be sure, rested on a wholly different religious foundation. For the Jews "the religion of their fathers" was never a meaningless expression, and religious <8> worship continued undiminished, with all of its elaborate ceremonies. But the fragmentation into so many sects and parties that hardly agreed on the most important issues clearly shows that here too the national religion was tending toward dissolution.

These two religions had been making way in this fashion for a new religion; and if we look at the situation from the teleological point of view, we can only regard it as a special dispensation of divine providence that Christianity came into existence at precisely the point in time when there was so great a void to be filled in the religious life of [7] the ancient world. But this point of view also fails to provide deeper insight into the inner connection of Christianity, as a new form of religious consciousness, with the preceding development of religion.

In addition to everything that constituted a more or less harsh antithesis between the pre-Christian religions and Christianity, their main point of contact has generally been taken to be how these earlier religions were negatively related to Christianity and the religious feelings and needs awakened thereby. People said that disbelief and superstition were of course two forces in the paganism and Judaism resistant to Christianity. Yet these forces also involved factors that facilitated the transition to Christianity and made souls receptive to it. There was also a disbelief sustained simply because the need to believe could not be satisfied by anything the ancient world could offer in terms of religion and philosophy. Human nature has an undeniable desire to know the supernatural and be in communion with it. So when disbelief is all-encompassing, that only intensifies the desire to believe. The same was the case to a large extent with superstition, at the root of which lay a need that looked for satisfaction and could find it only in Christianity—the

---

⁷[Ed.] See also Chapter 4 in this volume, where Baur advances the same claim about the absoluteness of Christianity.

⁸[PCH] The tension between "the positive" (historical and authoritative) and "the spiritual" (ideal and inward) is a constant theme of this volume. Both are present in every religion, but the balance between them shifts as we move from Judaism to Christianity, and within Christianity itself.

need for deliverance from a deeply felt disconnect, for reconciliation with an unknown God whom people were looking for, whether consciously or not.[9]

Here some interpreters resort to immediate religious feeling as the source of people's receptivity for Christianity. Christianity too undoubtedly has its roots, like every other religion, in this primary ground of all religious life. But to just trace Christianity back to this feeling still leaves us very much in the broad and ill-defined realm of subjective contexts. The question is not what distinctive frame of mind might dispose this or that individual to adopt [8] Christianity, or what individual circumstances might make a person more or less receptive to its content. The question rather is how Christianity, objectively considered, relates to everything constituting the religious development of the world, not merely in its negative but also in its positive aspects. The universal tendency of Christianity presupposed the universalism to which the <9> collective consciousness of the age had already expanded under the influence of the Roman world empire. If this is the case, then the overall religious and spiritual development of the world must be inwardly and objectively related to everything that constitutes not merely the universal, but also the absolute, character of Christianity.

Here, however, it is of first importance to not understand this absolute character of Christianity too narrowly and one-sidedly. Some have thought to find the absoluteness merely in the fact that Christianity welcomes, and most fully satisfies, the human longing for belief; or in its being a supernatural revelation, a universal arrangement for the reconciliation of human beings with God; or because it sets before us, in the person of its founder, one who is the Son of God and the God-man, in the sense the church uses these words. But these answers just lead us to ask what it is about these features of Christianity that makes it superior to the other religions, for the pre-Christian world believed it had more or less analogous features. Every religion claimed to be a supernatural revelation, and there were numerous procedures for reconciling human beings with God. People thought that fellowship with God was provided by beings whose functions were nearly the same as those of the Christian Son of God. What is it then that gives Christianity its peculiar and specific superiority over everything that more or less resembled it in the pre-Christian world? Christianity may be regarded under various points of view, each of which always exhibits only one of the various aspects we can distinguish in it as such. But what forms Christianity's common and all-encompassing unity?

In brief, it is the [9] spiritual character of Christianity as such. We take into account the fact that it is far freer than any other religion from everything merely external, sensible, and material. It has a deeper basis than any other in the innermost substance of human nature and in the principles of moral consciousness. It says that it knows no worship of God other than "worship in spirit and truth."[10] When we fix our attention on its spiritual character as such, the absoluteness of its essence in this broadest and most general sense, how then is Christianity linked to the pre-Christian world and the world contemporaneous with it? What features do we find in the general development of

---

[9][Baur] See August Neander, *Allgemeine Geschichte der christlichen Religion und Kirche*, 2nd edn., 4 vols. (Hamburg: Friedrich Perthes, 1842–7), 1:7ff. and 56 ff. [PCH] ET: *General History of the Christian Religion and Church*, trans. Joseph Torrey (London and Boston: Crocker and Brewster, 1849–51), 1:5 ff. and 46 ff. August Neander (1789–1850), born David Mendel, converted to Christianity under the influence of Schleiermacher, and was a popular and prolific professor of church history at the University of Berlin. Baur became increasingly critical of Neander's partisanship in later years. See his discussion of Neander in KGNJ, 223ff., 369, 380, 382, 384 [CTNC, 209ff., 339, 350, 352, 354].

[10][PCH] John 4:24: "God is spirit, and those who worship him must worship in spirit and truth."

the world that are closest and most related to it, ones that are preconditions for it in regard to its inner essence?

The two religions preceding Christianity, as we have already noted, were in such a condition of decay and dissolution that, at the time they came into contact with Christianity, no one who had become aware of their imperfection and finitude, or who had seen them as they really were, could come away without the feeling of an infinite void, a craving for satisfaction that could not be filled by anything in the entire sphere of these religions, the longing for a positive point of contact to which religious consciousness might attach itself. But what had caused such decay and dissolution in these religions and brought them to ruin? How could this have happened even before the arrival of Christianity? Some other power, a greater power than they, must have <10> come over them. It is a common and very serious mistake to suppose that periods of transition, such as occurred during the time of the appearance of Christianity, are simply times of decay and dissolution, times of a completely moribund spiritual and religious life. The forms of previously active religious life do indeed become increasingly decadent until they are completely emptied of the content that once filled them. But the reason for this is that they have become too narrow and limited for the spirit whose religious consciousness they had served to mediate. [10] When something old collapses, something new is always already there to replace it; the old could not decay if the new had not arrived, even if only as a seed, and had not been long laboring to undermine and render meaningless the previously existing structure. It may take a long time for a new form of religious and spiritual life to take shape in an outwardly evident way, but the spirit doing the shaping is nevertheless silently long at work; there is already fermentation in the depths, and the vital process moving ahead in its unbroken continuity cannot rest until it has brought forth a new creation.[11]

Greek Philosophy

<11> The decay of paganism is not to be dated from the time when Christianity appeared, and it is certainly not brought about by Christianity. It had been under way from the beginning, from the time when there was not simply a Greek religion but also a Greek philosophy. This philosophy not only offered critical reflection on the popular religious myths but also constituted for itself a world independent of the myths, in the realm of free thought. In this world, the spirit that could no longer find an adequate form for its consciousness in the myths of the popular religion was elevated to a new sphere of its own thinking and intuition.

Thus, in addition to the religious teaching of the Old Testament, Greek philosophy provides the only other spiritual point of contact between Christianity and the pre-Christian historical

---

[11][PCH] This is a very Hegelian perception, as expressed for example in Hegel's lectures on the philosophy of world history. See G. W. F. Hegel, *Lectures on the Philosophy of World History*, vol. 1, ed. Peter C. Hodgson, trans. Robert F. Brown and Peter C. Hodgson (Oxford: Oxford University Press, 2011), 107–10, 155–66 (passages on historical development, transitions, and progression). At the very end of his discussion of the Greek World, Hegel refers to the circumstances described by Polybius in which "good and practical persons must either despair or withdraw. And such circumstances, together with such personalities, call for a power to which they themselves finally succumb—a power that judges and discloses the impotence of the old way. Over against these parochial concerns, and the fixation in these finite circumstances in which all that is particular in states and personalities rigidifies itself, a destiny appears that can only negate what has gone before; it is blind, harsh, and abstract. And the Roman Empire plays the role of this fate" (425). It is under this fate that Christianity arrives in the world, introducing a new principle antithetical to the Roman principle, the principle of freedom as opposed to that of dominion and servitude (447ff.).

development of humankind. Its relation to Christianity has always been taken into account, first and foremost, when people have tried to get their bearings on Christianity's place in world history. But the negative rather than the positive aspect of this relationship has customarily been emphasized far more. Despite its apparent defects and biases, people simply give the edge to Platonism. It spiritualized religious thought; it turned away from polytheism to a secure unity of God-consciousness; it stimulated many ideas akin to Christianity, such as the idea of redemption as a deliverance from the blind force of nature that opposes the divine; in Christianity it elevated people to the standpoint of a divine life, beyond the influence of natural powers.

[11] Both Epicureanism and Stoicism[12] are regarded as much less likely candidates. It is said to be self-evident that a system of atheism and eudaemonism such as the Epicurean philosophy can have nothing whatsoever to do with Christianity. And there is the strongest possible contrast between the proud self-sufficiency of the Stoic sage and <12> the humility of the believing Christian. We cannot judge otherwise as long as we focus only on the points where the contrasts are most extreme. Our task, however, is not to focus on individual instances, but to place all the phenomena under the universal perspective of historical development. The question, therefore, is how Greek philosophy, from its principal epoch onward, has been related to Christianity.

The question appears in quite a different light when we recall the well-known parallel so often drawn between Christ and Socrates.[13] There is some truth in it, for Christianity culminates an orientation in the field of pagan religion and philosophy that began with Socrates. All the principal ensuing forms of Greek philosophy serve a mediating function for Christianity. The more closely we follow the course taken by the thinking spirit in this most important period of Greek philosophy, the more clearly we also see why Christianity entered into world history at just this point in time. If the essence of Christianity is located solely in its character as a supernatural revelation, then there is no point in considering its appearance in a broader context, and looking back to the period beginning with Socrates. But in any event Christianity has a genuinely human side; and the more sharply we bring into view its origin, the manner and means by which it introduced itself into the world and sought to gain entrance into human hearts, the more directly it appears to us in its genuinely human character. The first words it proclaims are the demand that human beings must look within themselves[14] and repent (μετάνοια). These [12] words already articulate how Christianity addresses human beings and the entire standpoint from which it understands their relationship to God. Above all it earnestly calls human beings to direct their gaze within, to turn within themselves, to plumb the depths of their own self-consciousness. In this way they are to learn what their relationship to God is, and what it ought to be, and to become aware of everything in their moral nature that awakens, in all its depth and intensity, the need for redemption. In short, it rests on everything that makes Christianity to be religion in the absolute sense—that human

---

[12][PCH] Epicureanism is a system of philosophy based on the teachings of Epicurus (c. 307 BCE), which advocated "pleasure" as the greatest good, but a pleasure that can be achieved only by living modestly, gaining knowledge of how the world works, and limiting one's desires. It originally challenged Platonism but later became the main opponent of Stoicism. Stoicism is a system of Hellenistic philosophy that flourished throughout the Greek and Roman worlds for about 600 years, so-called because its founder, Zeno (c. 308 BCE), taught under a colonnade (stoa) in Athens. It offered a system of personal ethics based on accepting what is given by life and not indulging one's desire for pleasure or fear of pain.

[13][PCH] Socrates (c. 470–399 BCE) was the teacher of Plato and Xenophon and the chief protagonist in Plato's dialogues, through which he is known to the world, since he is not known to have written anything himself.

[14]*Insichgehen.*

beings know themselves as moral subjects. If human moral consciousness had not already been fully developed in all those aspects that concern its deeper significance [as it had with Socrates], Christianity could not have appeared in human history with its own distinctive character as a genuinely moral religion.

Human beings first became moral subjects, however, when they became aware of the concept of the subject, the principle of subjectivity. This is the truly epochal significance of Socrates.[15] [He was the first to demand] that the subject look within, that <13> human beings go within themselves, that the mind or spirit withdraw from the outer world to the interior world of subjectivity, so as to apprehend what is intrinsically true and actual in the contents of conceptual thought. Likewise, in the practical arena, by referring virtue back to knowledge, we have the demand for moral self-knowledge, the intensifying of moral consciousness within itself, so as to find the norm of action in the inner self-certainty of the subject. From this point forward we find a series of developments—the epistemological theories of Plato and Aristotle concerned with the general nature of things, the ethical systems of the Stoics and Epicureans, and the later orientations of Skepticism and Eclecticism[16]—in which practical interests increasingly [13] predominated over theoretical ones, and the moral nature of human beings became the chief object of reflective thought in the same way that Christianity must understand it. The Stoics and Epicureans applied themselves most directly and earnestly to the moral task of human beings and the conditions under which it is accomplished. All those frequently discussed questions about the idea of the good, or the highest good, the relation of virtue to happiness, the value of moral action, and so on, are simply the ethical expression of the same major issue that Christianity poses to humanity from its religious point of view. Divergent as these two orientations [Stoicism and Epicureanism] were, the very opposition between the two systems served to arouse moral consciousness and to expand and shape it from all sides such that the ground was already prepared on which Christianity could accomplish its higher moral-religious task.

Given the rigor and purity of its moral principles, Stoicism may certainly seem superior to Epicureanism; but it has been rightly acknowledged[17] that the latter, which leads human beings back from the outer world into themselves, and teaches them to seek the highest happiness in the splendid humaneness of an inwardly satisfied and cultivated mind, has contributed just as much, in its more sensitive fashion, as Stoicism has in its more rigorous way, to a free and universal ethical life.[18] Both systems start from the same guiding idea of post-Aristotelian philosophy—the requirement that the subject withdraw into its pure self-consciousness in order to find its unconditioned satisfaction there. According to the one, humanity's vocation and happiness are found only in the subordination of the individual to the reason and law of the whole, which is

---

[15][Baur] See my book, *Das Christliche des Platonismus, oder Socrates und Christus* (Tübingen: L. Fues, 1837), 20ff.; and Zeller, *Die Philosophie der Griechen in ihrer geschichtlichen Entwicklung*, 2nd edn., vol. 2 (Tübingen: Fues, 1859), 78 ff. [PCH] Eduard Zeller (1814–1908) was Baur's student and son-in-law. He taught theology in Bern and Marburg before shifting to philosophy because of church opposition. Subsequently he taught philosophy in Heidelberg and Berlin, and became best known for his history of Greek philosophy, which was translated into English.

[16][PCH] Pyrrho of Elis (365–275 BCE) is generally credited with founding the school of Skepticism. Eclecticism comprises a group of Greek and Roman philosophers who selected from existing beliefs those that seemed most reasonable to them. Cicero was one of the best-known Eclectics.

[17][Baur] Zeller, *Die Philosophie der Griechen*, 1st edn., vol. 3.1 (1852), 263ff.

[18]*Sittlichkeit*.

virtue; according to the other, they are found in the independence of the individual from all that is external, in the awareness of this independence, in the undisturbed enjoyment of individual life, and in freedom from pain. Thus both strive for [14] the same goal in opposite ways, namely the freedom of <14> self-consciousness; and this led them to a position that contrasts very sharply with the fundamental religious consciousness of Christianity.

The Stoic and Epicurean sages are ideals equally foreign to Christianity. The common endeavor of both systems is to put human beings on their own and, through the infinitude of their own self-conscious thinking, to make them utterly independent of external factors; and that is opposed to Christianity's feeling of dependence.[19] But even the Stoics found it necessary to descend from the heights of their moral idealism and to acknowledge its limits by returning to practical needs. Skepticism was the next stage Greek philosophy took in its development. We see from this process that the unbounded character of consciousness ultimately led, through the contradiction of opposed and mutually annulling tendencies, to an awareness of the limitations of knowledge and to consciousness withdrawing into itself by completely abandoning knowing. The subject withdraws into itself, but it cannot remain so utterly inactive in its abstract and self-imposed subjectivity as not to resort to one form or another of what was called "the probable."[20] Thus Skepticism in its turn gave birth to Eclecticism. This mode of thought moderated the harshness and one-sidedness of the earlier schools by choosing the best ideas available and lifting individual ones out of their systematic settings. It was also well-suited for conjoining religious and practical concerns. At the time of the appearance of Christianity, Eclecticism was the most widely held way of thinking, and it had taken the form of a popular philosophy and natural theology. The writings of its chief representatives—Cicero, Seneca, Epictetus, and Marcus Aurelius[21]—contain many elements related to Christianity. Their views and doctrines not only present us with the most well-established and practical concerns, mainly drawn from all their predecessors. [15] They also already seem to place us on the soil of Christian religious and moral teaching, and we often come upon sentences whose Christian tone we find surprising.

The firm basis for Eclecticism, which required a standard for testing different opinions, is articulated by Cicero, the best known and most popular writer of the school. This basis is found in immediate consciousness, inner self-certainty, the natural instinct for truth, or innate knowledge. The seeds of morality are innate in us; nature has not merely given the human mind a moral faculty but has bestowed on it the fundamental moral conceptions as an original endowment prior to any instruction; <15> our task is simply to develop these innate conceptions. The closer an individual stands to nature, the more clearly these conceptions will be reflected in him; we learn from children what is in conformity with nature. Belief in divinity rests on a similar foundation. By virtue of the human mind's affinity with God, God-consciousness is given directly with self-consciousness. Humans need only to recollect the mind's origins in order to be led to their creator. Nature itself,

---

[19] *Abhängigkeitsgefühl*. [PCH] Baur here employs the term famously associated with Friedrich Schleiermacher's *Glaubenslehre*. See *The Christian Faith* §4, trans. H. R. Mackintosh/J. S. Stewart (London: T & T Clark, 1999), 12. Even as he transitioned to Hegel, Baur continued to incorporate important elements from Schleiermacher (and from Kant and Schelling).

[20] [PCH] This is an allusion to the teaching of Carneades (c. 214–129 BCE), a dialectician and head of the New Academy.

[21] [PCH] Marcus Tullius Cicero (106–46 BCE) was one of Rome's greatest orators and prose stylists. Lucius Annaeus Seneca (4 BCE–65 CE) was a Roman philosopher, statesman, and dramatist. Epictetus (c. 50–135 CE) was a Greek-speaking Stoic philosopher. Marcus Aurelius (120–181 CE) was a Roman emperor whose *Meditations* is a source for understanding Neo-Stoic philosophy.

therefore, teaches us of the existence of God, and the strongest proof of this truth is its universal recognition.[22] [16] In these few sentences we see clearly traced the outlines of a natural theology, which subsequently was elaborated on within Christianity itself on genuinely Christian grounds. The view that self-consciousness is at the same time God-consciousness is ultimately on the way to regarding its original knowledge as something merely given to it and, in the immediate consciousness of a higher source of knowledge transcending the finite subject, to receiving the revelation of divinity. In its longing for a higher communication of truth and an immediate revelation, Greek philosophy finally concluded its course of development in Neoplatonism.[23]

In summary, when Christianity is viewed from this angle, all these elements indicate to us how it entered into the general history of humanity at a point when preparations had been made for it in many important ways. This is the very point when the profound significance of moral consciousness had dawned on the pagan world—a time when the most spiritual and the most practically important results that Greek philosophy produced in the entire sweep of its ethical endeavors had become the essential content of the general consciousness of the age. It was a generally acknowledged truth that the human being is a moral subject with a specific moral role to play in life. Christianity is itself the key point at which the various orientations pursuing the same goal coalesced, in order to find their specific conceptuality and richest expression in Christianity. When approached from the side of paganism, this is Christianity's position in the nexus of world history. As the absolute religion, however, it likewise unites <16> the other two religions, paganism and Judaism. Let us therefore consider its relationship to Judaism in order to observe how, in this respect too, Christianity comprises everything that has attained a higher spiritual significance.

Judaism

<17> Christianity arose on Jewish soil, and it is far more closely and directly connected with Judaism. It professes to be nothing other than spiritualized Judaism; [17] its deepest roots originate in the soil of Old Testament religion. In paganism, Greek philosophy developed the content of moral consciousness to the stage at which Christianity could consolidate with it, whereas Judaism shares the same religious concerns with Christianity. The specific superiority of Judaism vis-à-vis all the religious forms of paganism is its pure and refined monotheistic concept of God, which from the earliest times was the essential foundation of Old Testament religion. In its consciousness of

---

[22][Baur] See Zeller, *Die Philosophie der Griechen*, 1st edn., vol. 3:1, 371 ff. [He says:] the natural theology that arose on the foundation of Stoicism appears in its purest form, and the one most analogous to the teachings and principles of Christianity, in the writings of Seneca. Compare my essay, "Seneca und Paulus, das Verhältniss des Stoicismus zum Christenthum nach den Schriften Seneca's," *Zeitschrift für wissenschaftliche Theologie* 1 (1858): 161–246, 441–70. A peculiar characteristic of Seneca's Stoicism is his tendency to approach the Christian religious mode of perception to the same extent that he departs from the old system of the Stoa. I have pointed this out under the following aspects: (1) God and the feeling of dependence; (2) human beings and their need for salvation; (3) the relationship of human beings to each other; (4) belief in a future life; and (5) the difference in principle between the Stoic and Christian worldviews. At the same time I have tried to show how unjustified the rash but popular conclusion is that this tendency must be ascribed to Seneca's acquaintance with Christianity as he heard it proclaimed.

[23][PCH] Neoplatonism was a philosophical tradition arising in the third century CE and lasting about 300 years. Plotinus and Proclus were among its most important thinkers. Despite a great diversity of views, most Neoplatonists saw the whole of reality as subordinate to, and dependent on, a single principle, "the One." Many Christian theologians through the ages have been influenced by Neoplatonism.

God, therefore, Christianity knows itself above all to be at one with Judaism. The God of the Old Testament is also the God of the New, and all the teaching of the Old Testament concerning the essential distinctness of God from the world, and the absolute transcendence and holiness of God's being, is also an essential part of Christian doctrine. But on the other hand the Old Testament concept of God bears such a truly national stamp that the particularism wholly connected with, and springing from, this feature placed Judaism in the most decisive contrast with Christianity. If the Old Testament God-concept was ever to be an adequate form of religious consciousness for Christianity, with its universal and absolute standpoint, this concept first had to be liberated from, and purged of, everything one-sided and deficient, that is, freed from everything just belonging to the limited perspective of Jewish theocracy, and from the anthropomorphic and anthropopathic views inherent in antiquity.

The course taken by the history of the Jewish people involved, of its own accord, various modifications in their religious views generally, and this led to a gradual broadening and spiritualizing of their religious consciousness. Yet on the other hand the fortunes of the people only led them to cling more tightly to their narrow particularism, and to their nationalistic preconceptions and legalistic tradition. A comprehensive change in their outlook first occurred when the Jews found themselves living in kingdoms founded after the death of Alexander the Great, specifically in Egypt and in a city such as Alexandria. In Alexandria, [18] Judaism was reshaped, first of all, by becoming open to the influence of new ideas, ones originally foreign and contrary to it, ideas leading it to abandon its narrow national and political isolation.[24] The Jewish <18> diaspora among foreign peoples had already produced a new hybrid group that blended Judaism with Greek practices and culture. This naturally had to become very important for their general spiritual and religious development. The Hellenism that arose in this way acquired its great world-historical significance when it generated an entirely new form of consciousness, based on the Greco-Jewish philosophy that took shape in Alexandria. In such a setting the Jews were powerfully influenced by Greek thinking, and they could hardly resist the temptation to become more closely acquainted with the ideas and teachings of Greek philosophy. Such an interest could not have arisen without transcending the standpoint of pure Judaism; and the more deeply they occupied themselves with Greek philosophy, the more they had to feel the conflict with their national religious consciousness. On the one hand they could not rid themselves of their interest in the new ideas; on the other hand, their ancestral faith asserted its ancient inalienable authority. This contradiction had to be resolved one way or another.

As is well-known, they reconciled the two by the allegorical interpretation of scripture. According to the way the Jews viewed their sacred books, nothing could be true that was not already contained in them, so scripture had to be the source of the new ideas people had adopted. All that was necessary was to find the right key for the interpretation of the Old Testament writings, and then the interpreter could draw forth from the scriptures the same ideas he himself [19] had unconsciously put into them. In this way an entirely new form of Judaism arose. People believed they were simply holding on to the old faith, whereas they had in fact substituted something entirely new for it. So the writings of the Old Testament that were said to also contain the new content became the mere form for something that far surpassed them. The distinctive character of this

---

[24][Baur] See Georgii, "Die neuesten Gegensätze in Auffassung der alexandrinischen Religionsphilosophie, insbesondere des jüdischen Alexandrinismus," *Zeitschrift für die historische Theologie* 9, nos. 3 and 4 (1839): 3, 1–98; 4, 1–98. [PCH] Ludwig Georgii (1810–96), a theology student in Tübingen, later a pastor in Württemberg.

Alexandrian Judaism consisted in its breaking through the limits of the old Jewish particularism, in setting them aside as far as this could be done without completely abandoning the standpoint of Old Testament religion. Its teachings took on a greatly modified and generally freer and more spiritual shape. New ideas were introduced that came from a worldview completely different than that of Judaism; and in particular the Old Testament concept of God was raised far above all those elements that belonged merely to the limited sphere of Jewish theocracy. The profound influence that the Alexandrian philosophy of religion—in its highest and most elaborate form as it appears in the writings of Philo[25]—later exercised on Christian theology is the clearest proof that the mode of thought on which it was based had great affinity with the spirit of Christianity. Here, however, we need merely trace the influence of Philo's writings in the sphere where they came into the closest contact <19> with Christianity on its original soil. When looked at in this way, the sects of the *Therapeutae* and the *Essenes*,[26] especially the latter, are a very noteworthy phenomenon.[27]

The Therapeutae are the link between [20] Greco-Alexandrian Judaism and the Essenes of Palestine. However, although closely related to the Egyptian Therapeutae, the Essenes are associated with the sects into which Palestinian Judaism divided. They represent the form in which the Greco-Alexandrian way of seeing things became for Palestinian Jews as well a profoundly religious view of life. This is what puts the Essenes in such a close relationship with Christianity. Of course we should hardly suppose that Christianity itself sprang from Essenism; yet it cannot be denied that the religious view of life of the Essenes is far more closely allied with the original spirit of Christianity than are all the features that marked the sectarian character of the Pharisees and Sadducees. The Essenes certainly attached great value to outward practices, but they were not caught up in the rules and traditions of Pharisaic Judaism or in the external forms of Levitical temple worship. Their religious piety had a more spiritual and inward character, and a thoroughly practical orientation. Their highest goal in life was to rise above material and sensuous things, and to make all their activity the constant practice of all that could lead them to this one end.

---

[25][PCH] Philo of Alexandria (*c.* 25 BCE–*c.* 50 CE) was a Hellenistic Jewish philosopher whose allegorical exegesis was important for Christian theologians but had no discernible influence on Rabbinic Judaism.

[26][PCH] The Therapeutae were a Jewish sect that flourished in Alexandria and other parts of the diaspora of Hellenistic Judaism. The primary source concerning them is the account *De vita contemplativa* purportedly by Philo, where they are an example of contemplative life as opposed to the active (but ascetic) life of the Essenes. The Essenes were a Jewish sect that flourished from the second century BCE through the first century CE. The Dead Sea Scrolls were discovered in what is believed by many to be an Essene library.

[27][Baur] On the Essenes, see Zeller, *Die Philosophie der Griechen*, 3.2:583. Ritschl, [Ed. "Ueber die Essener"], in the *Theologische Jahrbücher* 14 (1855): 315–56; and *Die Entstehung der altkatholischen Kirche*, 2nd edn. (Bonn: A. Marcus, 1857), 279ff., traces Essenism to an endeavor to realize the ideal of the priestly kingdom held up before the people of Israel (Exod 19:6), and to form a society of priests answering to it. Zeller opposes this view and argues ([Ed. "Ueber den Zusammenhang des Essäismus mit dem Griechenthum,"] *Theologische Jahrbücher* 15 [1856]: 401–33) for the commonly accepted view of a connection between Essenism and the Orphic-Pythagorean ascetic discipline and way of life that were so widely diffused in the ancient world and also had an influence on Judaism. The reasons he adduces are enough to refute Hilgenfeld's view that Essenism arose from apocalyptic prophecy (*Die jüdischen Apokalyptik in ihrer geschichtlichen Entwicklung* [Jena: Mauke, 1857], 245ff.); and these reasons are likely to prevail against any similarly eccentric theories in the future. [PCH] Baur is referring here to a dispute within his own school. On Zeller, see above. Albrecht Ritschl (1822–89) studied at Bonn, Halle, Heidelberg, and Tübingen, where he came under the influence of Baur. But he diverged from the Tübingen School with the 2nd edn. of *Entstehung*, and developed his own theological views, influenced by Kant, Schleiermacher, and Hermann Lotze, when he taught at Bonn and later Heidelberg. For Baur's critique of this work, see CCC, Part 2, n. 74. Adolf Hilgenfeld (1823–1907) studied at Berlin and Halle and later taught New Testament at Jena. He was a member of the Tübingen School but did not study under Baur.

The name "Essenes" indicates that they are "physicians of the soul." They sought to use all the means that seem suited to promote the soul's healthy and therapeutic life, and to keep one always open to the influences and revelations of the higher world. Their many features that remind us of the spirit of primitive Christianity include the prohibition of oaths, zealous practice of the duties of benevolence, and collective ownership of goods. One of their distinctive characteristics is their principle of voluntary <20> poverty—a view of poverty that says it is better to be poor and possess as little as possible in this world, so as to be all the richer in the goods of the world to come.[28] This [21] is the same sense of poverty that we find in Christianity when its first followers are called "blessed" because they are poor in spirit (Matt 5:3). We may reasonably assume that Essenism also had friends and followers who did not share every one of its features. It was a widespread way of thinking and view of life practiced with various modifications and different degrees of rigor. All those who embraced the general turn of religious piety from the external world to inwardness were touched to some degree by the Essene spirit. Thus it is certain that Essenism is one of the most truly spiritual points of contact between Judaism and Christianity. In addition to these affinities in the religious life as such, there is the external factor that the Essenes had their settlements in the same Jewish outlying areas inhabited by a population also including Gentiles, places where Christianity preached the blessedness of the poor. Where else could this gospel of the poor have found such receptive hearts than among those meek of the land whose piety was in so many ways the basis from which Christianity itself arose?

Thus all these various movements, starting from such different quarters, repeatedly meet at the same point; and Christianity, when it is placed in its world-historical context, appears as the natural unity of all these elements. Various and manifold as they are, they belong to one and the same process of development. This process, which moves gradually forward and increasingly eliminates everything that simply bears the marks of what is particular and subjective, can only start out from where the origins of Christianity lie. On what ground, therefore, can we regard Christianity itself as a purely supernatural phenomenon, as an absolute miracle introduced into world history without any natural agency, and thus incapable of being grasped in any historical connection, when wherever we turn we find so many points of connection and affinity linking Christianity most intimately with the entire history [22] of the development of humanity? It contains nothing that was not conditioned by a preceding series of causes and effects; nothing that had not been long prepared in different ways and brought forward to that stage of development at which it appears in Christianity; nothing that had not previously demanded recognition, in one form or another, as a result of rational thinking, as a need of the human heart, or as a requisite of moral consciousness. How then can it be surprising that what had so long been in different ways the goal of all rational striving, and had been forcing itself increasingly and with inner necessity on the developing consciousness of humanity as its most essential content, should have at last found its simplest, purest, and most natural expression in the form in which it appeared in Christianity?

---

[28][Baur] See my commentary *De Ebionitarum origine et doctrina ab Essenis rependa* (Tübingen: Hopfer de l'Orme, 1831). Note the passages I have quoted there (p. 30) from Philo, *Quod omnis probus liber* [75], ed. Mangey, 2:457, and *De vita contemplativa* [13], Mangey, 2:473; and from Josephus, *de Bello Judaico*, 2.8.3 [122–3]. See also A[ugust] F[erdinand] Dähne, *Geschichtliche Darstellung der jüdisch-alexandrinischen Religionsphilosophie* (Halle: Waisenhaus, 1834), 1:476ff. [PCH] Titus Flavius Josephus (37–c. 100 CE) was a Romano-Jewish historian, best known for his *Jewish Wars* and *Jewish Antiquities*.

Primitive Christianity and the Gospels

<21> However, the essential nature of Christianity itself involves many different aspects, ones that cannot all be placed under the same heading. The question arises, therefore, as to whether what has been said holds good for Christianity in its whole scope and extent, or only for a specific aspect of it, and whether it applies to what we must regard as its authentic kernel and substantial center. When Christianity is considered from the viewpoint set forth above, it is of course self-evident that this means sticking to all those points of connection and affinity that tie Christianity so closely and internally with the whole preceding history of human development.

But does this aspect then constitute the original and substantial essence of Christianity? Perhaps this historical setting is just a secondary factor. Is it possible to speak of the essence and contents of Christianity as such [23] without making the person of its founder the main object to be considered? Must we not recognize its distinctiveness in that everything that Christianity is, it is solely through the person of its founder? If so, is not understanding the essence and contents of Christianity in terms of its world-historical connection of little consequence? Is not its entire meaning and significance so conditioned by the person of its founder that historical examination and reflection can only start out from him?

These questions lead us to the sources of the gospel story, and to the distinction that the most recent critical investigations must draw among these scriptures.[29] The sources of the gospel story are the four gospels. The major question concerns the relationship of the Fourth Gospel to the first three. It is obvious that our way of understanding Christianity will be essentially different depending on whether we assume that the four gospels agree with each other throughout, or instead recognize that the differences between the Gospel of John and the three Synoptic Gospels amount to a contradiction that cannot be resolved in historical fashion.[30] [24] If we assume <22> that the four gospels can be harmonized, then the absolute significance that the Johannine Gospel assigns to the person of Jesus must be utterly determinative of how we understand the gospel story. From the fact of the incarnation of the eternal Logos, we must regard Christianity as a miracle in

---

[29][Baur] Compare my work, *Kritische Untersuchungen über die kanonischen Evangelien, ihr Verhältniss zu einander, ihren Charakter und Ursprung* (Tübingen: Fues, 1847); Köstlin, *Der Ursprung und die Composition der synoptischen Evangelien* (Stuttgart: Mäcken, 1853); Hilgenfeld, *Die Evangelien nach ihrer Entstehung und geschichtlichen Bedeutung* (Leipzig: Hirzel, 1854). [PCH] On Hilgenfeld, see above. Karl Reinhold Köstlin (1819–84) was one of Baur's former students, a member of the Tübingen School, and later a professor of aesthetics.

[30][Baur] The main question of concern here is not the authenticity of the Johannine Gospel. Regardless of who wrote the Gospel, whether the Apostle John or someone else, the obvious fact cannot be denied that the gospel story in the Fourth Gospel is essentially different from that in the first three gospels [Ed.: see also Chapter 8 in this volume]. Since this historical difference must either be acknowledged or denied, we have here the parting of two roads that lead in essentially different directions, and whose divergence extends to the whole conception of church history. Whoever overlooks this divergence from a dogmatic point of view will also view the entire history of the church quite differently from one who is not invested so heavily in this principle, and who regards what is historically given from a purely historical point of view. As for the question of authorship, the more the well-known critical dilemma of the Johannine authorship of the Gospel and of the Apocalypse [the Book of Revelation] is faced (as Lücke rightly does in the second edition of his *Einleitung in die Offenbarung des Johannes* [Bonn: E. Weber, 1852], 659–744), the less will any sophistry be able to prevent assigning most of this evidence to the Apocalypse, when the external testimonies for the Johannine origin of the two works are impartially weighed. [PCH] Baur's view is that the Book of Revelation could well have been written by the Apostle John, but not the Gospel of John, which arises from a different *Sitz-im-Leben* in the second century and has a distinctive worldview. Friedrich Lücke (1791–1855) was a professor of exegesis, dogmatics, and ethics in Göttingen, and a friend of Schleiermacher, to whom the latter wrote his "open letters" concerning the *Glaubenslehre*.

the strictest and most absolute sense. The human dimension vanishes into the divine, the natural into the supernatural; and, despite all the differences between the first three gospels and the Fourth Gospel, the authority of the latter must be decisive. This amounts, however, to an abandonment of the historical treatment of the gospel story, and miracle becomes so overwhelming and overriding that we completely lose any firm historical footing.[31] As a consequence, allowing the Fourth Gospel its claim to absolute miracle means downgrading the historical credibility of the other three gospels to the point where they basically no longer serve as historical sources.

The only way to escape these difficulties is to be convinced that the Johannine Gospel is related to the other three gospels in a wholly different way than has been customarily assumed. Whether we look to its differences from the Synoptics, or to its general spirit and character, how can a gospel such as John possibly be regarded also as a purely historical portrayal, simply in the sense in which the Synoptics can be called historical? So even with all their differences as to the gospel story, we take our stand [as historians] only on the side of the Synoptics. In doing so, we gain a firmer historical foundation; whereas placing John on the same level as the Synoptics can only serve to call the whole gospel story into question, owing to the arguments justifiably favoring John over the Synoptics, or vice versa.

However, here we must further circumscribe what can count as critical historical analysis. The most recent investigations into the mutual relations of the gospels show that the Synoptics cannot all be approached in just the same way. The Gospel of Mark is [25] so largely dependent on the other two that we cannot regard it as an independent source at all.[32] The Gospel of Luke is stamped by the Paulinism of its author, the key to <23> its own distinctive portrayal. So we are thrown back on the Gospel of Matthew as the relatively most genuine and trustworthy source for the gospel story.

But if we examine more closely the contents of the Gospel of Matthew, we must distinguish two different elements in it, the content of the teaching and the purely historical narrative. The early tradition about the Apostle Matthew states that he wrote down the λόγια, the sayings and discourses of Jesus, for the Hebrews and in the Hebrew language.[33] Now the main content of our Greek Gospel of Matthew, its actual substance, consists of the discourses and sayings of Jesus, as can be seen above all from the Sermon on the Mount, which is such a meaningful beginning for his public ministry. We may justly conclude from this that the author placed his emphasis from the beginning on treating Jesus' life, and what he manifested, from this point of view. This Gospel differs greatly from the Gospel of John, where the teaching serves to reveal Jesus' personal identity

---

[31][Ed.] For an analysis of Baur's view of miracles, see Stefan Alkier, "Belief in Miracles as the Gateway to Atheism: Theological-Historical Remarks about Ferdinand Christian Baur's Critique of Miracles," in *Ferdinand Christian Baur and the History of Early Christianity*, ed. M. Bauspiess, C. Landmesser, and D. Lincicum; trans. P. C. Hodgson and R. F. Brown (Oxford: Oxford University Press, 2017), 261–86.

[32][Baur] See my book, *Das Markusevangelium nach seinem Ursprung und Charakter* (Tübingen: L. F. Fues, 1851). Also my "Rückblick auf die neuesten Untersuchungen über das Markusevangelium," *Theologische Jahrbücher* 12 (1853): 54–94; and Köstlin, *Ursprung und Composition*, 310ff. [PCH] Baur endorsed the so-called Griesbach hypothesis, which accorded priority to the Gospel of Matthew, followed by Luke, and regarded Mark as dependent on both. He had many reasons for doing so, which are elaborated in his KUKE as well as in *Das Markusevangelium*. For a summary, see the chapter by Martin Bauspiess on Baur's view of the Synoptic Gospels in *Ferdinand Christian Baur and the History of Early Christianity*. Today the two-source hypothesis (Mark and Q), or the Farrer thesis, is favored over the Griesbach hypothesis, but the issue is still debated. On purely literary-critical grounds, Mark can be placed either first or last.

[33][PCH] Papias, Hegesippus, and other church fathers bear witness to this. See Eusebius, *Ecclesiastical History*, 3.39.16.

itself and its supernatural standing. What the discourses in Matthew present is the human and familiar face of Jesus, his direct appeal to the moral and religious consciousness, his simple answer to the first and most pressing question as to what one's intentions must be, and what one has to do, in order to enter the kingdom of God. This is not to say that the Gospel of Matthew fails to also ascribe full significance to the person of Jesus, or that this significance is not also perceptible in the Sermon on the Mount. But in the whole of the Sermon on the Mount the personal element remains as it were in the background; it is not the person who gives the discourse its meaning, but rather the content-laden discourse that first reveals the person in his true light. The [26] inner power of truth, directly impressed on the human heart, is Jesus' subject matter here—truth proclaimed here in its world-historical significance.

The Consciousness of Primitive Christianity and Its Principle

<24> Now what does this direct and original element, this principle of Christianity, consist in, as it is expressed in the Sermon on the Mount as well as in the parables and the whole of the teaching contained in the Gospel of Matthew? It may be summed up briefly in its main elements.

The beatitudes of the Sermon on the Mount (Matt 5:3-12) offer the deepest and most comprehensive insight into the central way of looking at things and frame of mind from which Christianity emerged. What is behind all those pronouncements—"Blessed are the poor in spirit, those who mourn, the meek, those who hunger and thirst after righteousness, the pure in heart, the peacemakers, those who are persecuted for righteousness' sake"—but a consciousness feeling most profoundly the pressure of finitude and all the contradictions of the present day, yet a religious consciousness that, in this feeling, is infinitely exalted above, and extends far beyond, all that is finite and limited. The most pregnant expression of this primitive Christian consciousness is the poverty of those poor in spirit, which rightly comes first in this recitation of all the blessings.[34]

As opposed to the customary interpretation, the poor spoken of here are not to be understood as merely those who feel inwardly poor and empty in the awareness of their spiritual needs. Outward, bodily poverty is an essential part of the conception of this poverty. We ought not overlook this aspect of it because the parallel passage in Luke (6:20) speaks not of the πτωχοὶ τῷ πνεύματι (poor in spirit) of Matthew but simply of the πτωχοί (poor); and because historically the gospel found its first adherents almost exclusively among the poor. That being so, we see that, when looked at in spiritual terms, this poverty in spirit is exactly the opposite of what it appears to be outwardly. Since these poor accept their poverty readily and voluntarily, and of their own free will choose to be none other than what they are, their poverty becomes to them a [27] sign and proof that, though outwardly poor, in themselves they are not poor. Here [on earth] they are the poor who have nothing, in order that there [in heaven] <25> they are all the more certain to be the opposite of what they are here. They are the poor who have nothing and yet possess everything. They have nothing because, being poor in physical terms, they have no worldly possessions; and what they may count as their possessions in the world to come are for them simply something in the future. In having nothing, their existence and their lives are simply the longing and desire for what they do not have; but in this longing and desire they already have in themselves everything that is the object

---

[34][Baur] See my *Kritische Untersuchungen*, 447ff. [PCH] See Matt 5:3. See also Baur's NTT, 106–8.

of such longing and desire. As having nothing, they have everything; their poverty is their riches; the kingdom of heaven is already now their most intimate possession because, as surely as they have nothing here, so surely they have everything there.

In this contrast of having and not having, of poverty and riches, of earth and heaven, of present and future, Christian consciousness attains its purest ideality; it is the ideal unity of all the antitheses that press upon temporal consciousness. It comprises all that the most elaborated dogmatic consciousness can include; and yet its entire meaning consists in its being the immediate unity of all antitheses. However diverse they sound, all the beatitudes are simply different expressions of the same original and fundamental outlook and sentiment of Christian consciousness. What they express is the pure feeling of the need for redemption, though as yet undeveloped, a feeling that contains in it itself implicitly the antithesis of sin and grace, a feeling that already has in itself the whole reality of redemption. Because all antitheses are held together here in their unity, this original consciousness is so vigorous and rich in content. It is not only the most intensive self-consciousness but also the most wide-ranging world-consciousness. We see this from the words Jesus himself uses immediately after the beatitudes (Matt 5:13-16), when he calls his disciples "the salt of the earth," which must not lose its savor if the world is not to be deprived of the sustaining power that holds it together and preserves it from decay. Jesus says: "You are the light of the world," which must not be set "under a bushel," [28] but must "shine before others so that they may see your good works," the works of those who let their light shine, and "give glory to your Father in heaven."

The beatitudes of the Sermon on the Mount describe, in an absolute manner, the innermost self-consciousness of the Christian as something that subsists in itself. Likewise, the original element of Christianity, its principle, appears in the form of the absolute moral command, both in the parts antithetical to the Pharisees and elsewhere in the Sermon on the Mount. Here Jesus insists emphatically on one having a pure heart and the right disposition, on a morality that consists not merely of the outer deed but the inner disposition; and on an earnest and moral observance of the law that can admit of no arbitrary exception or limitation, no toleration of false hypocritical pretenses, no half-heartedness and partiality. But to what extent is Christianity setting up a new principle? Jesus declared at the outset that he had come not to destroy the law and the prophets but to fulfill them (Matt 5:17). So he seems to have taken up a purely affirmative relationship to the Old Testament. One <26> could say that the only difference between the teaching of Jesus and the law or the Old Testament is quantitative, not qualitative.[35] On this view no new principle is advanced; rather the moral precepts already contained in the law are extended to include the whole of the moral sphere to which they are applicable. Jesus simply includes under the law what should never have been excluded from it. He makes explicit the extension and generalization of which it is inherently capable. This interpretation of the Sermon on the Mount is supported by the fact that Jesus always just speaks about individual commandments, so as to give them a significance corresponding to their original sense in the law, or to the moral consciousness.

The sermon never enunciates a general principle applicable in all cases. [29] Nevertheless, the individual stipulations for fulfilling the law, for what alone gives moral worth to human acts, always revert to the difference between the outer and inner aspects, between the mere deed and one's inner

---

[35][Baur] See Ritschl, *Die Entstehung der altkatholischen Kirche* (Bonn: A. Marcus, 1850), 27ff. Ritschl changed his views in the 2nd edn. (Bonn: A. Marcus, 1857), although the position characterized above retains its value as a precise formulation, as an inherently possible way of understanding this passage. [PCH] On Ritschl and this work, see above.

disposition. So we cannot but recognize in this a new principle, and one that differs essentially from the Mosaic law. What the law indeed contains, but only implicitly, now explicitly becomes the main thing and is enunciated as the principle of morality. The quantitative extension of the law becomes of itself a qualitative difference. The inner is opposed to the outer, the disposition to the deed, the spirit to the letter. This is the essential, basic principle of Christianity, and by insisting that the absolute moral value of human beings depends simply and solely on their disposition, it is an essentially new principle.

In this way the affirmative relationship Jesus adopted toward the law also includes a contrasting aspect, an antithesis to the law; and it is difficult, therefore, to understand how Jesus could say that not a letter of the law, not the least of its commandments, should be taken away (Matt 5:18). How could he say this, when the very opposite came about so soon afterwards, and the whole law was declared to be abolished? How can he have affirmed the continuing validity of all the injunctions of the law, when we think, for example, of the one injunction of circumcision?[36] It is unthinkable that Jesus himself was so little aware of the principle and spirit of his teaching; and the only choice seems either to understand his words as exclusively about the law's moral content, leaving aside the ritual law, or else as being cast in this strict Jewish form only later. Jesus' stance toward the Old Testament was as affirmative as it could be, and he did not oppose the traditions of the Pharisees, and their additions to the law, to the point of demanding an open break with them. Even when he set aside their <27> excessive scrupulosity and countered it with inherently reasonable practices as being one's inalienable and incontrovertible right, he nevertheless recognized the Pharisees as the legitimate successors of Moses. Examples of this include Jesus' action seeming to violate the Sabbath law (Matt 12:1-14), and his defense against the Pharisees' unwarranted expectations (e.g., Matt 9:14, 15:1).[37] [30] He said the Pharisees and the scribes sit in the chair of Moses, the seat of the teacher and legislator, and the people are required to follow their precepts, if not their example. Jesus does not reject out of hand even the most petty regulations Pharisaic scrupulosity devised for obedience to the law (Matt 23:1ff., 23).[38]

It is also true, however, that he declares the Pharisaic requirements to be heavy and intolerable burdens, and it could not have been his intention to allow this oppressive weight on the people to continue (Matt 23:3).[39] He also said, when speaking out against the Pharisees, "Every plant that my heavenly Father has not planted will be uprooted" (Matt 15:13). His actions were in great measure directed to this end, for he made it one of his most important tasks to challenge the Pharisaic attitude at every opportunity he had. When we think of how antithetical the two sides really were in principle, we can understand how Jesus regarded it as unnecessary to speak in generalities or to derive specific consequences from this antithesis. Instead he could leave to the further development of the spirit of his teaching everything that it involved and that must follow from the teaching itself.

---

[36][PCH] Compare what Paul says about circumcision in Rom 2:25-29, namely, that "real circumcision is a matter of the heart." Also, Gal 5:2-6.

[37][PCH] In Matt 12:1-14 the Pharisees criticize the disciples for picking grain on the Sabbath, and Jesus himself for healing on the Sabbath, to which Jesus responds that "it is lawful to do good on the Sabbath." Matt 9:14ff. is concerned with fasting, and 15:1ff. with purification rituals; in the latter case Jesus accuses the Pharisees of hypocrisy.

[38][PCH] Jesus says, "The scribes and Pharisees sit on Moses' seat; therefore do whatever they teach you and follow it; but do not do as they do, for they do not practice what they teach" (Matt 23:2-3).

[39][PCH] Jesus continues (Matt 23:4, 23). "They tie up heavy burdens, hard to bear, and lay them on the shoulders of others; but they themselves are unwilling to lift a finger to move them .... Woe to you, scribes and Pharisees, hypocrites! ... You have neglected the weightiest matters of the law: justice and mercy and faith."

That he himself was quite aware of the difference in principle, and of its necessary consequences, is evident in the saying in Matt 9:16,[40] where he not only declares that the spirit of the new teaching is incompatible with that of the old, but also intimates that, although he himself had held as far as possible to the old traditional forms, thus putting new wine into old wineskins, he had done this with the specific awareness that the new contents would soon break through the old forms.

But what all-encompassing content in the new principle breaks through the old forms? It could be nothing other than going back to the inward disposition, to everything that expresses itself as inherently existent in a person's entire consciousness, as its absolute content. Since one's disposition ought to be pure and simple, free from <28> all self-seeking, and since it alone is the root from which the good can proceed as its fruit, human consciousness as such ought to be directed to the one thing that it [31] recognizes as its absolute content. This is the fundamental idea that runs throughout the whole of the Sermon on the Mount. The sayings in it that strike us as most significant are those that forever present most directly this absolute character of Christian consciousness. As the sayings in Matt 6:19–24[41] demand, this consciousness excludes all half-heartedness and ambivalence, all detachment and diffidence. This is just the requirement in Matt 7:12,[42] to which so many have looked for a principle of Christian morality, for its foundational significance. If Christians are conscious of their absolute standpoint, they must be able to stand apart from their own ego, and to know themselves as so much one with all others that they regard everyone else as subjects equal to themselves. This is exactly what Jesus means when he says of this requirement that it is the sum and substance of the law and the prophets; that it has the same meaning as the Old Testament commandment to love your neighbor as yourself.[43] Those who love their neighbors as themselves must renounce everything egotistical, subjective, particular. Above the multiplicity of individual subjects, each of whom is the same as we are, there stands on its own the objectivity of the universal, which subsumes everything particular and subjective. This universal [principle] is the form of the action in accord with which we do unto others what we wish others would do to us. The moral good is thus what is equally right and good for all; in other words, what can be the same object of everyone's action.[44]

Here we see the distinctiveness of the Christian principle expressed once again. It looks beyond the outward, contingent, and particular, and rises to the universal, the unconditioned, to what is existent in itself; it locates human moral value solely in what intrinsically has absolute value and

---

[40][PCH] Matt 9:16-17. "No one sews a piece of unshrunk cloth on an old cloak, for the patch pulls away from the cloak, and a worse tear is made. Neither is new wine put into old wineskins; otherwise, the skins burst, and the wine is spilled, and the skins are destroyed; but new wine is put into fresh wineskins, and so both are preserved."

[41][PCH] "Do not store up for yourselves treasures on earth, where moth and rust consume, and where thieves break in and steal; but store up for yourselves treasures in heaven …. For where your treasure is, there your heart will be also. The eye is the lamp of the body. So, if your eye is healthy, your whole body will be full of light; but if your eye is unhealthy, your whole body will be full of darkness …. No one can serve two masters; for a slave will either hate the one and love the other, or be devoted to the one and despise the other. You cannot serve God and wealth."

[42][PCH] "In everything do to others as you would have them do to you; for this is the law and the prophets."

[43][PCH] Matt 22:37-9: "'You shall love the Lord your God with all your heart, and all your soul, and all your mind.' This is the greatest and first commandment. And a second is like it: 'You shall love your neighbor as yourself.' On these two commandments hang all the law and the prophets."

[44][PCH] Baur here uses a very Kantian formulation. As he says in his NTT: "This is a formal principle of action that essentially coincides with the Kantian imperative so to act that the maxim of your action can be the universal law of action." The will of God is the universal law of action, but also more than that, as Baur explains below in the discussion of righteousness and the kingdom of God.

content. This same energy of consciousness, which finds the substantial essence of the moral life solely in the innermost core of the disposition, makes itself felt in the demand to lift the individual ego up to the universal ego, to the ego or self of the whole of humanity that is identical <29> with itself in all single individuals. This requirement differs from the commandment [in Matt 7:12] only in that the commandment is its simplest practical expression.

[32] Thus the absolute content of the Christian principle finds its expression in the moral consciousness. What gives human beings their highest moral value is simply the purity of a genuinely moral disposition that rises above everything finite, particular, and purely subjective. This morality of disposition is also the definitive standard for the human being's relationship to God. What gives human beings their highest moral value also places them in an adequate relationship to God that corresponds to the idea of God. When they are viewed in terms of their relationship to God, the supreme task of the moral consciousness appears in the requirement to be perfect as God is perfect (Matt 5:48). The absolute character of the Christian principle comes to its most direct expression in this requirement. Christianity has no other standard for human perfection than the absolute standard of God's perfection. If people are perfect as God is perfect, then in this absolute perfection they stand in an adequate relationship to God, which is described by the concept of righteousness. Righteousness in this sense is the absolute condition for entering into the kingdom of God. In the context in which Jesus speaks of righteousness in the Sermon on the Mount, we can only understand righteousness as the complete fulfillment of the law—but of course only in the sense in which Jesus speaks in general terms of the continuing validity of the law. If we ask how human beings can attain this righteousness, we find it a distinctive feature of Jesus' teaching that it simply assumes the law can be fulfilled; it assumes that the will of God will be done on earth as it is in heaven, and doing so will attain the righteousness that puts human beings in an adequate relationship to God.

It appears, however, that a forgiveness of sins on God's part is an essential element by which the shortcomings in human conduct are offset and made good, as becomes clear from the Lord's Prayer, in which the forgiveness of sins is something one asks for oneself [Matt 6:12]. Therefore, one cannot be related to God as God wills unless one is also forgiven for one's omissions and sins. Since the teaching of Jesus in principle defines the moral value of human beings as based not on external deeds but only on one's disposition, his teaching can only locate the righteousness consisting in conduct adequate to the will [33] of God in the disposition—the disposition by which people completely cease to will on their own and surrender unconditionally to the will of God. This is worked out in the teaching about the kingdom of God,[45] which is found principally in the parables.

The Teaching about the Kingdom of God

<30> In the kingdom of God, where every individual is absolutely required to fulfill the will of God, what God wills becomes the common task of a specific community in which all together are to actualize within themselves the purpose established by the will of God. The more closely they

---

[45][PCH] Baur understands this "kingdom" (*basileia*) not in political terms as the territory ruled by a king but in moral terms as a spiritual fellowship of those who are righteous in the eyes of God. He interprets the teaching of Jesus generally in moral and religious rather than political or eschatological categories.

are bound together, the more fully they do so. The shared or communal element that comprises the essence of religion is also the essential aspect of the kingdom of God. The Old Testament concept of theocracy is spiritualized in the teaching of Jesus, so that everything concerning the relationship of human beings to the kingdom of God is based purely on moral conditions. The moral dimension is so exclusively the condition here that there is not yet any mention of those objective means that later were thought to enable the acceptance of people into the kingdom of God or for fellowship with God. It is simply assumed that partaking of all that God's kingdom has to offer depends solely on human beings themselves, on their own volition.

How clearly and vividly this simple truth is portrayed in the parable of the sower![46] What makes a person fit for the kingdom of God is the Word, the embodiment of all teachings and precepts a person heeds to actualize the will of God. The Word is given to human beings; they can hear and understand it, but everything depends on how they receive it. What does ordinary experience show us? That, as the scattered seed cannot grow and bear fruit unless it falls on fertile soil, so the subjective capacities of human beings to receive the Word are very diverse. A few may receive the Word in a right spirit, but it is always their own fault when the Word does not produce in people what it is intrinsically capable of producing. The reason lies simply in their lack of receptivity, and they need only will [34] to be receptive for their part. Such is the simplicity of the human relationship to God. Their entry into the kingdom of God depends only on themselves, on their own will, their own natural capability and receptivity.

For this reason, the whole relationship of human beings to the kingdom of God can only be thought of as a moral one. Hence what matters, first and foremost, is that people recognize this, and not suppose that their participation in the kingdom of God depends on anything other than what is of a purely moral nature. The first requirement made of them, therefore, is that they renounce everything on which they might <31> rely as giving them merely an outward claim to the kingdom of God—that they should simply go back into themselves and, only in themselves, in their inner nature and moral consciousness, become aware of whether they are fit for the kingdom of God. If they rid themselves of everything that would put them in a merely external relationship to the kingdom of God, and face the kingdom of God with this mindset that makes no claims and looks purely within itself, then their receptivity can all the more surely consist in their being entirely receptive to what the kingdom wants to provide for them. This is the meaning of the words in which Jesus deals with all the claims the Jews, with their prevailing notions, make about the kingdom of God. In Matthew 18:3, Jesus says: "Unless you change and become like children, you will never enter the kingdom of heaven." To become like children is to cease wanting to be something on our own, and to remain rather in that purely natural condition that just makes us aware of our dependence and need. The less we have within ourselves what we ought to have, the more clearly we long for what only the kingdom of God can give, and the more surely we come to recognize the kingdom of God as possessing the highest, the absolute, value. This truth is evident in the parable of the pearl of great value, for which the merchant sold all that he had and bought it (Matt 13:45-46). There can be no doubt that the parables dealing with the subjective stance of human beings toward the kingdom of God, and portraying the moral conditions for one's participation in it, are, together with the Sermon on the Mount, the most genuine and original materials that have come down to us from the content of Jesus' teaching.

---

[46][PCH] Matt 13:1-9; Mark 4:1-9; Luke 8:4-8.

The Person of Jesus and the Messianic Idea

[35] <32> If we view everything discussed thus far as the most original and direct content of the teaching of Jesus, we see that it contains only what is clearly focused on morality, and its aim is simply to restore our focus on our own moral and religious consciousness. People only need to become aware of what their own consciousness expresses as its highest moral goal, and thus that they can actualize this goal by their own efforts. Regarded in this fashion, Christianity in its earliest elements is a purely moral religion; its highest and most distinctive aspect is that it bears a thoroughly moral character that is rooted in the moral consciousness of human beings.

Faith in the person of Jesus does not yet emerge here as the essential condition of the new relationship to God into which people should enter through Jesus—at least not in the sense that the Gospel of John makes this faith the precondition for everything else. Other elements belong to the character and content of Christianity, and the relation they have to its most original and immediate aspect may be variously described. But there can be no question that the purely moral element from which Christianity springs constantly remains its substantial foundation. Christianity has never been dislodged from this foundation without denying its true and proper character. People have always been compelled to return to this foundation whenever they went astray in excessive dogmatism from which they drew conclusions undermining the innermost basis of moral-religious life. This original moral element, its significance in principle, has remained the same despite all changes, and, as the very foundation of Christianity's truth, can also simply be regarded as Christianity's proper substance.

And yet had Christianity been nothing more than a teaching of religion and morality such as we have described, what would it have amounted to, and what would have come of it? Although it may, as such, be the sum and substance of the purest and most immediate truths given expression in moral-religious consciousness, and may have made them accessible to the general consciousness of humankind in the simplest and most popular way, this moral Christianity still lacked the form appropriate for concretely shaping religious life. A firm center was needed around which the circle of its followers [36] could rally as a community able to gain supremacy in the world. When we consider the way in which Christianity developed, we see that its entire historical significance depends solely on the person of its founder. How soon would <33> all the true and meaningful teachings of Christianity have taken their place among the now mostly forgotten sayings of the noble humanitarians and philosophic sages of antiquity, had not its teachings become words of eternal life as spoken by its founder?

But we cannot help asking what we should see as the actual foundation of Christianity's world-historical significance with regard to the person of Jesus himself. However much we emphasize the total impact of Jesus' person, we see that he must have affected the consciousness of the age from an already existing perspective, if a world-historical development could emerge from the appearing of an individual. Here then is the place where Christianity and Judaism are so closely intertwined that Christianity can only be understood in terms of its connection with Judaism. Succinctly put, if the national idea of Judaism, the messianic idea, had not been so identified with the person of Jesus that people could find in him the fulfillment of the ancient promise of the Messiah, a Messiah coming for the salvation of his people, then faith in Jesus would never have attained such a great world-historical significance. The messianic idea first gave the spiritual content of Christianity the concrete form in which it could embark on the path of its historical development. People's consciousness of Jesus was thus able to expand into a general world-consciousness, via the route of Judaism's national consciousness.

The gospel story itself supplies us with an abundance of evidence for the great national importance the messianic expectations had at the time of Jesus, not only for individual pious souls but also for the faith of the Jewish people as a whole. The greater the discrepancy between the present condition of the Jewish people and the theocratic idea [37] basic to their entire history, the more they looked back to a past in which, at one point at least, albeit for just a short time, the theocratic ideal appeared to have been actualized.[47] But after that one time things were in fact quite different from how they ideally should have been. People expected, even more confidently, that the near or distant future would bring what the past had failed to realize. They handed down, from generation to generation, the promise given to their forefathers, and longed for its fulfillment. It is a characteristic of Judaism that, because of the continuing, ever more apparent, contradiction between idea and actuality, Judaism became principally a religion of the future with its belief in a Messiah who was still to come. Thus nothing of greater import could take place on the soil of the history of the Jewish people and the Jewish religion without being connected with the messianic idea or introduced by it. It also prescribed the course that Christianity must take. The Synoptic account of the gospel story introduces Jesus with all the miracles that were said to proclaim him to be the long-expected and now-appearing Messiah, and to be the Son of God in terms of the Jewish outlook.

From the standpoint of critical reflection we can only ask how it came to be an established fact in Jesus' consciousness that he was called to be the Messiah. Three elements in the gospel story merit special attention in this regard: the title υἱὸς τοῦ <34> ἀνθρώπου, "Son of Man," which Jesus applies to himself; the group of narratives comprising the confession of Peter, the scene of the transfiguration, and the first announcement of his approaching death; and Jesus' entry into Jerusalem. The manner in which Jesus applies the title υἱὸς τοῦ ἀνθρώπου to himself is so unusual that, however we define its meaning more precisely, we must assume he intended some reference to the messianic idea when he used it.[48] Such a reference is even clearer in the aforementioned group of narratives. If we follow the gospel story up to the point [38] where we find these narratives, which are so interrelated both externally and internally, we clearly see that Jesus' cause has reached a decisive turning point. Both he and his disciples are now expressly aware that he is the Messiah.[49] It certainly remains quite inconceivable how at that point in time this belief could still require confirmation, when the gospel story has already provided a number of such evident proofs of Jesus' messiahship. But it is of all the greater historical significance that, in a presentation such as that of the Synoptic Gospels, such information could have been convincing only in the wake of the prior established facts.

The most unambiguous demonstration of Jesus' messianic consciousness, however, is furnished by his presence in Jerusalem, even apart from the specific scene of his entry. After his extended activity

---

[47][PCH] The time of the monarchy from Saul to Solomon.

[48][Baur] It is very doubtful that this expression was applied to the messiah at the time of Jesus. The most apparent explanation is that, in contrast to the Jewish υἱὸς θεοῦ, "Son of God," and its associated images, Jesus intended to allude all the more emphatically to the genuinely human character of his appearance and vocation. [PCH] Cf. Baur, "Die Bedeutung des Ausdrucks: ὁ υἱὸς τοῦ ἀνθρώπου," *ZWT* 3 (1860): 274–92.

[49][Baur] *Theologische Jahrbücher* 12 (1853): 77 ff. [PCH] Article by Baur, "Rückblick auf die neuesten Untersuchungen über das Markusevangelium," 54–94.

in Galilee,⁵⁰ and after all his experiences of people accepting his teaching and of the opposition to it by the adversaries he met up with there, he resolved to leave Galilee and go to Judea, to appear in the capital itself at the seat of those rulers against whose prevailing system his entire activity up to now had been most decisively opposed. He can only have taken such a momentous step based on the conviction that his cause had now necessarily come to a head. People must either accept or reject [39] his teaching and his person; the whole nation must in fact declare whether it will persist in its traditional messianic belief, inherently bearing the sensuous marks of Jewish particularism, or will acknowledge the kind of Messiah he was and had shown himself to be, in his whole life and influence. The only answer <35> to this question could be the one he himself had long accepted, consciously and with complete self-assurance.

The Death and Resurrection of Jesus

<36> What seemed to be on its surface just ruin and annihilation was never turned into such a decisive victory, and breakthrough to life, as this happened in the death of Jesus. Before now there had still been the possibility that belief in the Messiah might be the bond linking Jesus with the people, that is, with the people acknowledging him to be the one supposed to come to fulfill the nation's expectation, and the contradiction between his messianic idea and the Jewish messianic faith still being amicably resolved. But his death caused a complete breach between Jesus and Judaism. A death like his made it impossible for Jews, as long as they remained Jews, to believe in him as their Messiah. To believe in him as the Messiah after such a death would have of course required eliminating from the Jews' notion of the Messiah everything inherently of a Jewish and fleshly nature. A Messiah whose death denied everything Jews expected of their messiah—a messiah who died to life in the flesh—was no longer a Χριστὸς κατὰ σάρκα, an "Anointed One according to the flesh" (2 Cor 5:16), as the Messiah of the Jewish national faith had been. Even to the most faithful adherent of Jesus' cause, what could a Messiah be who had himself fallen prey to death? Only two alternatives were possible: either with his death faith in him must be extinguished; or this faith, if it were firm and strong enough, must necessarily break through even the bonds of death and press on from death to life.

Only the miracle of the resurrection could dispel these doubts that seemingly had to cast faith itself out into the eternal night of death. What the resurrection is in itself lies outside the sphere of historical investigation. Historical reflection has to stick just to the fact that, for the faith of the disciples, the resurrection of Jesus had become the most secure and most incontestable certainty. Christianity first attained [40] the firm ground of its historical development in this faith. For history the necessary presupposition of all that follows is not so much the fact of the resurrection of Jesus itself as it is the belief in the resurrection. We may regard the resurrection as a miracle

---

⁵⁰[Baur] The duration of this activity is one of the unsettled points in the life of Jesus about which in its external outlines we know so little. The usual assumption of a teaching activity lasting three years is based only on the number of festival journeys mentioned by John, and this depends on the way the Johannine question is settled. The great weight of the tradition of the early church is that Jesus taught only one year. This one year, however, is the ἐνιαυτὸς κυρίου δεκτός of Isaiah 61:2 ["the year of the Lord's favor"], cf. Luke 4:19; and it is doubtless only a dogmatic assumption. It is not in itself probable that the public activity of Jesus extended over so short a period. Cf. Hilgenfeld, *Die clementinische Recognitionen und Homilien* (Jena: J. G. Schreiber, 1848), 160ff.; *Kritische Untersuchungen über die Evangelien Justin's* (Halle: C. A. Schwetschke und Sohn, 1850), 337; and my *Kritische Untersuchungen über die kanonischen Evangelien* (Tübingen: Fues, 1847), 363ff.

occurring objectively, or as a subjective psychological miracle. But if we assume the possibility of such a subjective miracle, no psychological analysis can penetrate the inner, mental process by which, in the consciousness of the disciples, their disbelief upon the death of Jesus became belief in his resurrection. In any case it is forever only through the consciousness of the disciples that we have any knowledge of what was, for them, the <37> object of their faith. We can say no more than that, whatever the means that produced this faith, the resurrection became a fact of their consciousness, and had for them all the reality of a historical fact.

However great the significance of this fact, and however much it had to make the disciples who believed in Jesus break decisively with Judaism, we still must ask: What would this belief in the risen one have amounted to if he had just passed from death to life and risen from earth to heaven, so as to return, after a short interval, the same as he had been before, now just as one seated on the clouds of heaven and clothed with all the power and majesty that belonged to the Son of Man, so as to realize at last what his early and violent death had left unaccomplished? The initial followers thought that the Lord's second coming, which was to be the consummation of the whole world, would occur soon after his departure from the earth.[51] So their faith in the risen one was simply a new and stronger form of the old messianic hope. The only difference between the believing disciples and their unbelieving compatriots was that, to Jesus' followers, the Messiah was one who had already come, and to the latter he was one who was still to come. Had this latter view prevailed, the Christian faith would have become the faith of a Jewish sect in which the entire future of Christianity would have been placed [41] in question. What was it then that first invested the belief in the risen one with a significance enabling the principle that had entered the world in Christianity to develop into the great and imposing network of phenomena that shaped its historical existence? What enabled it to overcome all the restrictive limits on its all-inclusive universalism?

---

[51][Baur] Cf. Matt 24:29; Acts 3:19-21.

PART FIVE

Baur in the Controversies of His Time

CHAPTER TWELVE

Baur on Baur and His School

FROM: KGNJ 394–9
TRANSLATION: ROBERT F. BROWN AND PETER C. HODGSON, CTNC 363–8

Hodgson's footnotes are prefaced by [PCH]

Baur's extensive lectures on the history of the church were gathered, initially during his lifetime and then posthumously as well, into five substantial volumes. The fifth and final of these treats "Church and Theology in the 19th Century." Here we find Baur writing about his predecessors and his contemporaries, and he includes a brief but revealing section surveying his own work and, to a limited extent, that of his School.

Baur frames the discussion in terms of the reaction to Strauss' publication of his *Life of Jesus Critically Examined*. This framing has the effect of narrowing Baur's survey to his own work on the New Testament and Christian origins, passing silently over his substantial philosophical and dogmatic-historical volumes. An over-riding aim seems to be to emphasize his own independence from Strauss, and the way in which his own research program can solve challenges to which Strauss only pointed. Baur appears alternately defensive and self-congratulatory in this retrospective evaluation of his achievements, but he is not wrong to emphasize that he produced a novel total picture of early Christianity, by critically assessing the writings' authorship and tendency, and by assigning a positive role to disagreement and antithesis as the engine that propels innovation and change.

Although Baur mentions "talented students" obliquely, he singles none of them out for special mention here, save his critical remarks about Strauss.

CHURCH AND THEOLOGY IN THE NINETEENTH CENTURY

Baur and the Tübingen School

[394] <363> Strauss' *Leben Jesu*, our main point of departure here, posed for itself the task of investigating critically and grasping historically the early history of Christianity from the life of Jesus.[1] But the results were so overwhelmingly negative that the entire early history of Christianity seems to dissolve into a series of myths and traditions. The response from the critics was as unable to contradict Strauss' views as it was to further secure the old views.

<364> So both sides faced a dilemma. If one chose to disregard the fact that through Strauss' criticism an irreparable rift had opened up in the previous representation of the gospel history, still the negativity of its results, and the unclear and indeterminate picture that it gave of the early

---

[1]David Friedrich Strauss, *Das Leben Jesu kritisch bearbeitet*, 2 vols. (Tübingen: Osiander, 1835/6). English translation: *The Life of Jesus Critically Examined*, trans. Maryann Evans [= George Eliot] 3 vols. (London: Chapman brothers, 1846). NB: The English text translates the fourth German edition.

history of Christianity were so unsatisfying that one could not come to a halt at that point. As a consequence, one could see that the task that had become central to the time, that of grasping early Christianity historically, had not yet been solved. In the nature of the case things had to move on. And since the consequences that critics such as Bruno Bauer[2] drew from Strauss' results only led to a self-annulling [395] extreme, one could only hope to approximate a solution to the problem along another path. So the question had to be raised whether the negativity of Strauss' results did not reside in a deficiency of the investigation, of its critical method; and whether one could not from a different point of view penetrate more securely into the inner aspects of the early history of Christianity and bring light to bear on its obscurity.

This is where I may mention my own efforts at research into early Christianity.[3] I started my investigations long before Strauss, and thus began from an entirely different point.[4] My engagement with the two Corinthian epistles first provided the occasion to bring more sharply into focus the relationship of the Apostle Paul to the older apostles. I became convinced that in the letters of the Apostle himself sufficient evidence is available to see that this relationship was something entirely different from what previously had been assumed—that where people supposed a thorough harmony of all the apostles is to be found, rather an opposition exists, an opposition that, from the Jewish-Christian side, went so far as to call into question the authority of the Apostle Paul. A closer investigation of the Pseudo-Clementine Homilies, a writing whose importance for the history of the earliest period I had especially noted along with Neander,[5] allowed me to see more deeply into the significance of this opposition in the post-apostolic period. It became increasingly clear to me that the opposition of the two parties, which in the apostolic and post-apostolic periods are to be distinguished much more sharply than hitherto has been the case, the Pauline party and the Petrine or Judaizing party, had a decisive influence not simply on the configuration of the sayings of Peter but also on the composition of the Book of Acts.

<365> I published the first results of my investigation in the fourth issue of the *Tübinger Zeitschrift für Theologie* of 1831, [pp. 61–206], in the essay, "Die Christuspartei in der korinthischen Gemeinde, der Gegensatz des paulinischen und petrinischen Christenthums in der ältesten Kirche, der Apostel Petrus in Rom."[6] My investigations into Gnosticism[7] led me to the Pastoral Epistles, and

---

[2] Bruno Bauer (1809–82), Hegelian philosopher and biblical critic. He originally criticized Strauss from an orthodox Hegelian point of view, but Baur here has his later, more radical position in mind, as expressed in his *Kritik der evangelischen Geschichte des Johannes* (Bremen: Schünemann, 1840); and *Kritik der evangelischen Geschichte der Synoptiker*, 3 vols. (Leipzig: Wigand, 1841–2).

[3] [PCH] Baur does not address here his own stance in relation to the Hegelian school, or the effects of that stance on his works in church history and history of dogma. He could be described as a center-left Hegelian, who on the one hand rejects the absolute identity of the idea of divine–human unity with an individual human being, but who on the other hand affirms the positive historical significance of Jesus for Christianity, and who treats the history of the church and its faith with idealist categories influenced by Hegel. He is, in Martin Wendte's terms, "a historically informed idealist of a distinctive kind" (See M. Wendte, "Ferdinand Christian Baur: A Historically Informed Idealist of a Distinctive Kind," in *Ferdinand Christian Baur and the History of Early Christianity*, ed. M. Bauspiess, C. Landmesser, and D. Lincicum; trans. P. C. Hodgson and R. F. Brown [Oxford: Oxford University Press, 2017], 67–79).

[4] The later relationship between Strauss und Baur is not free from ambiguities. Here and in what follows, Baur is clearly eager to separate himself from Strauss' work. But even some of his closest collaborators saw the *Life of Jesus* as the starting point of a novel phase in the history of the Tübingen School. Cf. U. Köpf, "Ferdinand Christian Baur and David Friedrich Strauss," in *Ferdinand Christian Baur and the History of Early Christianity*, 3–44.

[5] August Neander, *Genetische Entwickelung der vornehmsten gnostischen Systeme* (Berlin: Dümmler, 1818), 361–421.

[6] CPKG. ET: *The Christ Party in the Corinthian Community*, ed. D. Lincicum; trans. W. Coppins, C. Heilig, L. Ogden, and D. Lincicum, Early Christianity and Its Literature (Atlanta: Society of Biblical Literature, 2021).

[7] DCG; ET: CG. See Chapter 2 in this volume.

the results of the latter study published in 1835⁸ led to the conclusion that these letters could not have been composed by the Apostle Paul. [396] Rather their appearance is to be explained from the same partisan tendencies that were the moving principle of the church as it took shape in the second century. Continuing engagement with the Pauline epistles, and deeper penetration into the spirit of the Apostle and of Pauline Christianity, solidified in me the view that a very essential distinction exists between the four major letters of the Apostle and the lesser ones, and the authenticity of most if not all of the latter must become very doubtful. What I subsequently gathered together and further expounded in my book on the Apostle Paul⁹ is the result of investigations that placed me in this position totally independently of Strauss' critique.

If a period becomes more clearly known the more deeply one sees into its circumstances and its endeavors, into the antitheses operative in it, I believe I have attained a historical comprehension of a period of the most ancient history of Christianity, which hitherto has remained in principle immune from historical examination because, on the basis of a dogmatic assumption, people held that what happened [in the events recorded in the New Testament] was not at all possible in the ordinary course of events. I have shown how deeply antithesis itself penetrated into the heart of apostolic Christianity, and how the differences of a later period have their beginnings already in this first sphere. On this basis one can for the first time form a clearer and more concrete picture of the formation of the ancient church, its oppositions and conflicts and the way they were harmonized <366> into the unity of the Catholic Church.¹⁰ Ebionitism and Paulinism were the factors of the historical movement of that time.¹¹ These results had to be of particular importance for the history of the canon. Despite the resistance they encountered, I believe I am right to assert that by means of these results the old, baseless concept of the canon as a self-contained unity has been destroyed forever.

My first series of critical works referred to the Pauline epistles and the Book of Acts accompanying them. When Strauss' *Leben Jesu* appeared and evoked its notorious emotional response, I remained a passive observer. [397] The matter represented nothing new for me since I had witnessed the emergence of the work close at hand and had frequently discussed it with the author. However, I could come forward neither for nor against it because at the time I still lacked the fuller studies requisite for doing so.

Only after I had made the Gospel of John, the subject of lectures did I find myself in a position to adopt a new and independent position in regard to the Synoptic Gospels. The fundamental difference of John from the Synoptics became so compelling for me that I at once formed the view of the character and origin of this Gospel that I set forth in the *Theologische Jahrbücher* of 1844.¹² In this way I attained a new ground for criticism of the gospel history. If the Gospel of John is not a historical gospel like the others, if it itself does not intend to be genuinely historical, and if it undeniably has an idealizing tendency,¹³ then it can no longer be taken together with the Synoptics and be juxtaposed to them. Thus it is no longer possible, using the Straussian tactic and

---

⁸PAP.
⁹PAJC; ET: PAJC(E). See Chapter 9 in this volume.
¹⁰See CCK; ET: CCC. See Chapter 11 in this volume.
¹¹By "Ebionitism" Baur means basically "Jewish Christianity," which he sees as in opposition to Pauline, Gentile Christianity.
¹²"Ueber die Composition und den Charakter des johanneïschen Evangeliums," *ThJb(T)* 3 (1844) 1–191, 397–475, 615–700.
¹³*Ideelle Tendenz.*

modus operandi, for the Synoptics to win out over John, or vice versa. Thus the result is that no one any longer knows to which of them one should adhere in the gospel story. To the extent that the historical value of John sinks, that of the Synoptics correspondingly rises. We can no longer have any basis for doubting the credibility of the Synoptics for the sake of John. The disagreement between the two sides is entirely due to John. This is surely not to say that we have in the Synoptics a purely historical portrayal, but with them we nevertheless have a wholly different historical basis; and the question can only be whether, since now one of the canonical Gospels has been shown to be written with a tendency of a specific type, one or another of the Synoptic Gospels should not also be placed in the same category.

<367> This occasioned my further investigation into the Gospel of Luke in the *Theologische Jahrbücher* of 1846,[14] following which I pulled the whole together and completed it in my second major work on New Testament criticism, the *Kritische Untersuchungen* [398] *über die kanonischen Evangelien* (1847).[15] The more narrowly in this fashion the circle is drawn within which the original gospel tradition is to be sought, the more the task of criticism is simplified and illumined. The whole question is concentrated on the Gospel of Matthew. Also, because of this, the mythical approach Strauss applies with such a broad brush faces very essential constraints. If it is established that most of our canonical Gospels are to be seen as tendency writings, this raises the question as to whether, where previously it was believed necessary to take the gospel traditions as a myth, this tradition has not been modified in the interest of the author's literary tendency, or even that it is an outright fiction.

Since the tendency recognizable as the specific character of several of the Gospels can have its basis only in the distinctive circumstances of the time in which their authors have written, in the partisan stances they embody, then our stance as to gospel criticism can only be taken within the entire sphere in which such phenomena are evident to us, in the way they have to be presupposed in this case. We should not draw our historical horizons too narrowly. From this it is self-evident how important it is, not merely in the apostolic age but also in the post-apostolic age, to survey everything that can serve for more precise information about the different orientations that can be distinguished in this period. My investigations into the Gospels quite naturally are therefore linked with my earlier research into the Pauline epistles. They have their foundation and firm support in that Pauline research. On the other hand these investigations also contribute essentially to allowing the post-apostolic age to appear more clearly and vividly in its concrete shape. Our canonical Gospels are products of the post-apostolic age, with the antitheses and interests that are its moving forces.[16]

In doing this I have also permitted myself to give a brief sketch of my own activity in this area. Talented students, of whom I have been fortunate to have many, have further elaborated my views and principles, and have collaborated in their dissemination and reception. This has provided <368> an occasion to regard me as the founder of a school. The "New Tübingen [399] School" has become the customary label for the most recent critical direction.[17] I make no claims of this

---

[14] "Der Ursprung und Charakter des Lukas-Evangeliums mit Rücksicht auf die neuesten Untersuchungen," *Theologische Jahrbücher* 5 (1846): 453–615.

[15] KUKE. See excerpts in Chapter 8 in this volume.

[16] See VNT. ET: NTT.

[17] This is in contrast to both an "Old Tübingen School," consisting of late-eighteenth- and early-nineteenth-century theologians like G. C. Storr, and the "Catholic Tübingen School," which included J.-A. Moehler, Drey, and others. See U. Köpf, "Tübinger Schule," *TRE* 34: 165–71.

kind, and I am content to have contributed what I can, to the best of my ability, to the research into the most important issues that occupy the present age. My critical standpoint is the only one from which Strauss' criticism can be both revised and carried further. My criticism is more methodical than Strauss' because it goes back to the question that Strauss, above all, is said to have posed so clearly. One cannot make the life of Jesus the object of criticism as long as one is not in a position to form a definitive, critical view of the writings that are the source of our knowledge of this life, and of their relations to each other. My criticism is for this reason also more conservative than Strauss' inasmuch as it knows how, from a specific point of view, to distinguish the historical elements from the non-historical. Whatever may be the future results of investigations undertaken with such great interest, in any event I believe I may with certainty hold that no view will succeed in obtaining more general recognition vis-à-vis mine before mine can be contradicted in its entire extent and on wholly other grounds and proofs than those that have been advanced against it thus far.

CHAPTER THIRTEEN

On Protestantism and Catholicism

FROM: GKP, 367–436 (EXCERPTS)
TRANSLATION: BEATA AND MATTHEW VALE

INTRODUCTION

Baur and Johann Adam Möhler (1796–1838) were colleagues at the University of Tübingen from Baur's appointment in 1826 until 1835 when Möhler accepted a chair at the University of Munich. Möhler was the rising star in the Catholic Faculty which had only been incorporated into the University in 1817. In 1832, Möhler published his *Symbolik oder Darstellung der dogmatischen Gegensätze der Katholiken und Protestanten nach ihren öffentlichen Bekenntnisschriften* (*Symbolik or Presentation of the Dogmatic Opposition between Catholics and Protestants on the Basis of their Published Confessional Texts*), the first systematic attempt by a Roman Catholic theologian to investigate Protestant and Catholic doctrinal systems in a comparative perspective. There is little doubt that Baur was deeply impressed by Möhler's work which seemed a Catholic counterpart to similar, recent works on the Lutheran side, notably Philipp Marheineke's *Christliche Symbolik*, published in three volumes between 1810 and 1813. Baur was also aware of Möhler's nod to Schleiermacher in his *Unity in the Church* from 1825 as well as his brief study on Gnosticism (*Versuch über den Ursprung des Gnosticismus*, 1831), a topic central to Baur's own research during those years.

These broad sympathies did not prevent Baur from writing an essentially polemical response to Möhler's book. *Der Gegensatz des Katholicismus und Protestantismus nach den Principien und Hauptdogmen der beiden Lehrbegriffe* (*The Opposition of Catholicism and Protestantism according to the Principles and Main Dogmas of the Two Systems of Doctrine*) was published in 1834. Toward its end, Baur expressed his wish "that both parties might increasingly communicate with an open love of truth about their true mutual positions, unrestrained by any extraneous considerations."[1] Even Baur's most critical reader will perhaps grant him that he kept to this principle throughout the exchange.

That said, it is clear from the following extract, which is taken from Baur's concluding chapter, that he was hopeful at that point that a new chapter in the relationship of the confessions was about to begin. He willingly acknowledged that Catholic criticism directed at Protestant rationalism or supranaturalism was justified. Yet his counterparts should be willing to turn a leaf too and not measure the likes of Baur or Marheineke against the standard of the previous generation. The thought of Schelling, Schleiermacher, and Hegel, after all, was attractive to a new generation of both Protestant and Catholic theologians and could furnish a novel kind of rapprochement.

---

[1] GKP, 436.

This positive spirit, unfortunately, did not last. Möhler was hurt by Baur's pugnacious tone, and Baur was in turn deeply disappointed by Möhler's rebuttal of his critique. In the second edition of the *Gegensatz* and in another, separate writing, *Erwiderung auf Herrn Dr. Möhler's neueste Polemik* (*Reply to Dr Möhler's Latest Polemic*, 1834), Baur's stance had visibly hardened and no further communication between the two theologians ensued. Baur did, however, return to the problem of Protestant identity and the relationship between the confessions in a number of articles in the 1840s and 1850s.[2]

THE OPPOSITION OF CATHOLICISM AND PROTESTANTISM ACCORDING TO THE PRINCIPLES AND MAIN DOGMAS OF THE TWO SYSTEMS OF DOCTRINE

Part Five: The Contrast between the Two Systems in General

[p. 367] The preceding account[3] of the main doctrines in which the two systems oppose one another indisputably shows a deeply entrenched contrast, the deepest and most comprehensive one possible in the domain of Christian dogma. Two systems present themselves here that are based on essentially different principles, and for this reason they impress a completely unique character on all doctrines in which they develop and make visible their material content. In order to give further consideration to this relationship and in order to grasp it from the varying perspectives from which it can be viewed, the examination of individual aspects shall now be followed by some more general suggestions.

The Parallel between Protestantism and Gnosticism[4]

The parallel, which the author has already drawn between Protestantism and Gnosticism in his teaching on justification, provides us with a link that is not unwelcome. He claims [p. 186, 1st ed.; p. 215, 2nd ed.][5] that there is no religious phenomenon which bears more similarities to the reformers' system than Gnosticism. The main moments of this kinship, he says, are the following:

(1) Gnostic dualism emerged from such a deep feeling of human wretchedness in general and from the wretchedness of sin in particular that it found evil simply incompatible with the good God's creation and—just as the Protestant view—simply undetachable from the current form of human existence.

---

[2]Ferdinand Christian Baur, "Kritische Studien über das Wesen des Protestantismus," *Theologische Jahrbücher* 6 (1847): 506–81; "Das Princip des Protestantismus und seine geschichtliche Entwicklung, mit Rücksicht auf die neuesten Werke von Schenkel, Schweizer, Heppe und die neuesten Verhandlungen über die Unionsfrage," *ThJb(T)* 14 (1855): 1–137.
[3]The first four parts of Baur's work dealt with the following doctrines in a comparative perspective: (1) the doctrine of sin and the original state of the human being; (2) justification; (3) the sacraments; (4) the Church. In text references are from Baur's work.
[4]Section headers are adapted from Baur's table of contents.
[5]Johann Adam Möhler, *Symbolik oder Darstellung der dogmatischen Gegensätze der Katholiken und Protestanten nach ihren öffentlichen Bekenntnisschriften* (Mainz: Kupferberg, 1832; 2nd edn. 1833).

(2) However, this sentiment of sin is in itself so confused and pathological that it works on its own destruction, according to Protestants as well as Gnostics. The greater one assumes the measure of objective sinfulness to be, in which subjects find themselves entangled with no personal guilt of their own, the more the extent of subjective evil, committed by themselves, diminishes. [368] For this reason, in order to heighten the concept of evil as much as possible, the moral concept of evil was suspended by Protestants as well as by Gnostics.

(3) Just as Gnosticism demanded of its followers a consciousness that they were sons of the good God who could not be lost, Protestantism includes in its faith the unconditional hope for eternal life and along with that the teaching that from eternity some are predestined to beatitude and others for damnation, which is only another expression of the gnostic classification of human beings (pneumatics, psychics, hylics).[6]

In order to appreciate the deeper meaning of this parallel, [369] another view on the origin and the nature of Gnosticism must actually be added [here], which the author has developed in a different work.[7] According to this work, Gnosis did not emerge out of a speculative interest inspired outside of Christianity (as it is commonly assumed), but it arose very immediately and directly out of Christianity itself, namely, from a practical urge, so that it only took on a speculative direction in its [further] development. Gnosis, interpreted from a negative perspective, is the demonization of nature, and for this reason, it has to be understood as the countermovement to a phenomenon whose peculiarity lay in its deification of nature. Thus, Gnosis is a reaction not against Judaism but against paganism, where the spirit was absorbed in deified nature and perished in it. Gnosis as a Christian extreme, as Hyperchristianity, simply sought to leave nature behind completely and for this reason demonized it. The feeling of not-being-at-home[8] in this world, along with the dualism derived from it, remained unchanged in all the relationships and transformations which Gnosis underwent.[9] [370]

But even if we include the latter view [here], it is immediately clear that the truth of the alleged kinship between Gnosticism [371] and Protestantism can only be proven in a very limited sense. Protestantism, just as Gnosticism, is supposed to be a Christian extreme, a Hyperchristianity, because both are based on the same profound consciousness of evil.[10] It cannot, admittedly, be denied [372] that these two forms of Christianity share a certain link in the profound consciousness of evil expressed in them. But even if we ignore everything else that separates the two making Gnosticism in comparison with Protestantism hardly even appear like a form of Christianity, the

---

[6]A full note is here omitted in which Baur adds the point that Möhler also compared Marcion specifically with Luther (GKP, 369–70).
[7]Johann Adam Möhler, "Versuch über den Ursprung des Gnosticismus," in *Beglückwünschung seiner Hochwürden [...] D. Gottlieb Jac. Planck [...] zur Feier seiner 50-jährigen Amtsführung, am 15. Mai 1831, dargebracht von der katholisch-theologischen Fakultät Tübingen* (Tübingen: Hopfer de l'Orme, 1831), 1–30.
[8]*Unheimlichkeit*. What Möhler has in mind here, Hans Jonas will later call "Entweltlichung" (acosmism) and, as such, wield a huge influence over twentieth-century studies of Gnosticism. Cf. Hans Jonas, *The Gnostic Religion: The Message of the Alien God and the Beginnings of Christianity*, 3rd edn. (Boston, MA: Beacon Press, 2001), 51.
[9]A full note is here omitted in which Baur engages at length with Möhler's interpretation of Gnosis in his essay. He is clearly impressed with Möhler's view that Gnosis possessed a "lively and deep religious feeling" but disagrees with his attempt of a genetic explanation of Gnosticism from within Christianity (GPK, 369–71).
[10]A full note is here omitted in which Baur explains that Möhler from the second edition adds the further parallel between Protestantism and "medieval pantheism." Accordingly, in Luther the more Gnostic-Manichean side came to the fore, whereas Zwingli adopted the "pantheistic" viewpoint. Overall, this argument finds Baur's approval although he disagrees with the identification of Luther as a Manichean (GKP, 371–2).

aforementioned link between the two must immediately be put into context: how great is the difference between Gnosticism and Protestantism that becomes apparent to us in the essentially differing concepts of evil on which they are each based?

Protestantism, just as its nature and character impel one to think, holds fast to the purely moral concept of evil. For this reason, it can only ever locate evil in sin, but sin itself in Protestantism is always a state which has developed, derived from a free, accountable deed, even where Protestants regard sin not as a current action but as a state. Gnosticism, by contrast, as is well known, assumes the seat of evil to be in matter as an autonomous principle of evil independent from God, which is why for the Gnostics, the soul's connection with the material body is the ultimate source of evil in the human being. Thus, everything that makes up the great difference between the physical and ethical concept of evil also separates Protestantism from Gnosticism. [373]

Now, the author has sought to give to his opinion on the relationship between Protestantism and Gnosticism a firmer foundation by not wanting to concede to Protestantism any concept of evil other than the gnostic-Manichaean one. But since, as we have seen, this claim is completely unfounded and impossible to prove, the purported kinship that is supposed to exist between Protestantism and Gnosticism must also be limited to the general statement that a profound consciousness of evil is expressed in both.

At this level of generality—where the contrast between the physical and the ethical concepts of evil has not yet been addressed but only the common idea in which both concepts are still one—Protestantism can have no hesitation to recognize in Gnosticism an intimation of what has come to consciousness in Protestantism itself and even before it, in the Augustinian system, which served as the basis for Protestantism in this regard.[11] When looking at the issue from this perspective, then, we have no objections to an analogy between Protestantism and Gnosticism. By the same token, however, we have also obtained the right to go further in completing the analogy by saying that Protestantism relates to Gnosticism in the same way as Catholicism relates to paganism and Judaism.

No matter how we explain its origins, Gnosticism definitely contains various elements which it borrowed from the three religions with which it came in contact at the time: paganism, Judaism, and Christianity. What connected these often mixed elements into a whole and made Gnosticism into a unique phenomenon in the domain of religious history is exactly what the present author emphasizes as a characteristic of Gnosticism: a more profound awareness of evil and, closely linked to it, a consciousness of the need for redemption. In this way, paganism and Judaism, in the form in which [374] they were connected in Gnosticism—and through the mediation of Zoroastrian dualism—made the attempt to spiritualize themselves from their position into a religious form analogous to Christianity and to attract to themselves related elements from Christianity itself.[12]

Admittedly, then, Gnosticism displays a certain kinship with Protestantism on account of its spiritualization of paganism and Judaism which finds its expression in a deeper religious life permeated by the consciousness of sin. After all, Gnosticism, like its collateral Neoplatonism, can be considered in this regard a reform of those ancient religions, especially of paganism. [If this is accepted, however,] there must be an even closer relationship between Catholicism and the form

---

[11] Cf. DCG, 553–5.
[12] It is perhaps fair to observe that Baur's explanation of the origin of Gnosis is here not entirely clear. Cf. how these ideas appear a year later: DCG, 18–24; (see Chapter 2 in this volume).

of paganism and Judaism in which these religions do not yet have the character given to them by Gnosticism.

[…]

PROTESTANTISM AS A NEW EPOCH IN THE DEVELOPMENT OF CHRISTIANITY: CATHOLIC DENIAL OF THE NECESSITY OF THE REFORMATION

[397] The natural result of everything [I have] developed thus far is that Protestants and Catholics are presented with very differing perspectives when it comes to considering the new developmental epoch of Christianity and Christian dogma induced by the Reformation. In everything that does not satisfy Protestants in Catholicism and that appears to them to contradict the original nature and character of Christianity, they can only see the urge to completely abandon the principle on which Catholicism has been founded and to put the authority of Scripture in the place of the Church's authority. They will seek, as Schleiermacher has expressed the contrast between Catholicism and Protestantism in his well-known formula, not to make the individual's relationship with Christ dependent on the Church [398] but instead to make the individual's relationship with the Church dependent on their relationship with Christ.[13] If this is indeed the case, then it must be in the interest of Catholicism to prove that hers is the only sufficient principle and that the Reformation as a new epoch can in no way carry the significance which Protestants believe they must grant it. This is the task which [Möhler's] *Symbolik* has set for itself according to its tendency and its collected content.

[…]

INVESTIGATION OF THE QUESTION OF WHETHER A FINAL RETURN OF PROTESTANTISM INTO CATHOLICISM IS TO BE EXPECTED

[412] If from a Catholic perspective, Protestantism's separation from Catholicism can only be considered in itself harmful and reprehensible, as Dr. Möhler has declared […] then it [413] also cannot be regarded as permanent. Whatever is null and untrue in itself does not carry in itself an inner condition for its permanence either. Sooner or later, it must disintegrate, and for this reason, nothing can be in store for Protestantism but its ultimate return into Catholicism.

The reason for also briefly considering here this question, in which we are once again confronting the whole difference between the Protestant and Catholic perspectives, is provided by an essay (from the *Theologische Quartalsschrift*) by A. Gengler, Professor of Theology in Bamberg, in close connection with the work we have considered so far. [The article is entitled] "Über eine angeblich zu erhoffende Indifferenzirung des Katholizismus und des Protestantismus in einem höheren Dritten" ["On the indifferentiation, allegedly to be hoped for, of Catholicism and Protestantism in a third

---

[13]Friedrich Schleiermacher, *The Christian Faith* §24, trans. Hugh Ross Mackintosh and J. S. Stewart (London: T & T Clark, 1999), 103. Baur's paraphrase stays close to Schleiermacher's words but is not a citation.

and higher reality"].[14] The author sets off from the view that Protestantism and Catholicism are both one-sided ways of understanding and developing Christianity. They must, therefore, unite and reconcile themselves in a third [reality], as is the case with all opposites. In this third reality, the [full] truth, which can partially be found on both sides, is brought together, so that the end of the struggle between Protestantism and Catholicism would result in a higher developmental level of the Christian truth, in which both, [Protestantism and Catholicism], will perish as mere moments.

The author only mentions this view, however, to describe it as the one belonging to Protestantism, which Catholicism, conscious of the necessity of its own principle, its never perishing truth and the infallible authority of its episcopacy, can never adopt. Catholicism, according to the author, will not perish, that is, cease to exist in its essence. It should, however, be developed for human consciousness; in this developmental process Catholicism realizes its true being. Protestantism is to be understood as a moment supporting Catholicism in this development without, however, destroying it.

[...]

[417] The author desires no other return of Protestantism to Catholicism than one in which the differences are truly reconciled and internally suspended. As long as the episcopacy is incapable of persuading their opposition of their error by means of reasons, it is compelled to use force in order to uphold the ecclesiastical order. Thus, ecclesiastical authority warded off the Protestantism of the twelfth and thirteenth centuries with force, until finally repeated attacks compelled the Church to release Protestantism from its midst.[15] At the Council of Trent, the Church sealed herself off within herself by restating her doctrinal conception so that its substantial truth,[16] which the episcopacy preserves at all times, would continue to be retained and not submerged in the floods of Protestant opinions. Those, therefore, who with the eye of genius have surveyed the intellectual process extending itself over the last three centuries of European history, have rightly described Catholicism as the [418] preserving and positive power.

Catholicism, according to the author, is still the substance of truth from which not even Protestantism can break away. Yet, the Catholic Church's system of doctrine[17] as articulated by the Council of Trent has not been completely developed for the subjective consciousness.[18] Therefore, the process of developing the substantial truth for human consciousness remains a task to be solved even after the release of Protestantism; indeed, it is actually the real purpose of this release. Protestantism, once released from the Church, was given the task to produce from within itself the truth that was negated in the Church. Protestantism's various attempts at representing true Christianity make up its own internal history, which is essentially the thought process directed toward finding the true concept of Christianity, continued outside the Church.

---

[14]Adam Gengler (1799–1866). Cf. Stefan Lösch, *Prof. Dr. Adam Gengler: Die Beziehungen des Bamberger Theologen zu J. J. J. Döllinger und J. A. Möhler* (Würzburg: Schöningh, 1963). The article Baur refers to appeared in *Theologische Quartalsschrift* 14 (1832): 203–53.

[15]Gengler equates Protestantism with any opposition to Catholic authority, not just the heretical movements of the high Middle Ages, but already "the first awakening of speculation among the Germanic people" in John Scotus Eriugena ("Indifferenzierung," 207–13).

[16]Substantial: here and in what follows, Baur follows Gengler in using "substance" and "substantial" [*Substanz*; *substantiell*] in a Hegelian sense in which it means the concept in itself but not yet for itself. Cf. Inwood, *Hegel Dictionary*, 285–7.

[17]*Lehrbegriff*. A popular theological term in (nineteenth century) German without an obvious English equivalent. It denotes a coherent body of teaching central for a religious tradition. See Note on Text and Translations.

[18]See Note on Text and Translations on "In itself/for itself."

The true concept of Christianity, as a result of this process, is nothing but the complete development of the substantial truth of Christianity that is nothing but the true concept of Catholicism itself. For this reason, Protestantism carries within itself the direction of once again returning to Catholicism; this is the immanent law of its movement. As Protestantism emerged out of the Church because it negated the [Catholic] Church as the true [Church], it will return into the Church if and when it will immediately convince itself and come to the realization that the truth exists within the Church.

But Catholicism also has the same task; it is the thought process continued within the Church. The Church must continue this process, partly because she could understand her essence only by becoming completely transparent to herself, and partly because she herself, once she arrives at this goal, would become capable to inwardly reconcile Protestantism with herself. Even though Protestantism carries in itself the direction for its return into the Catholic Church, it could not return into its substantial truth as such, but only into the substantial truth that has been developed into the concept. [419] This can only happen once the thought process on the objective system of doctrine within the Church has attained its result, i.e., the true concept.

In this further execution of his idea, the author maintains his presupposition that Catholicism is simply the truth, and that at the end of the historical development of Christianity all objective truth could only be contained in Catholicism, as much as that had been the case in its beginning. Nevertheless, we still see ourselves entirely thrown back onto the Protestant perspective here. What can it be but the acknowledgment of the Protestant principle—according to which in matters of faith everyone is dependent on their own conviction and not on any authority externally presented to them—when the author makes Protestantism's return to Catholicism solely dependent on the requirement that Protestants acquire the free conviction that the truth exists in the Catholic Church, that their reconciliation with her be inwardly accomplished and the contradiction not merely externally and forcefully suppressed and brought to silence?

The author cannot think of another goal for the ultimate development in the Catholic Church herself than merely the moment when Catholicism has become entirely transparent to itself. Then, the Church, through its continued thought process, will have grasped her own essence and fully developed, even for subjective consciousness, the truth she possesses. All this, however, merely articulates the truly Protestant principle that faith in authority must completely disappear and the exterior faith must become inward too. It is difficult to understand how at this level of development, the Catholic principle that individuals must unconditionally subject themselves to the authority of the Church and the episcopacy can still be maintained. As long as individuals still have the need to attach themselves to an authority with which they are externally confronted, and while the Church still applies the principle that the individual could only be placed in a truly religious relationship with Christ and God by the mediation of the Church, the episcopacy, and the priestly activity, [420] Catholicism, precisely for this reason, has not yet become fully transparent to itself. The mediating element is still in the dark, as yet waiting to become illumined, and the latter can only happen once the wall has fallen away which separates laypeople from priests and prevents Catholicism from becoming completely transparent [to itself].

[In practice, this means] that Church members are to be made equal with respect to their relationship to Christ; that every individual is guided back to their own immediate religious consciousness; and that objective truth—hitherto mediated by the Church's authority alone—is absorbed into the concept of truth gained independently by everyone. But what is this if not the priesthood of all believers in the same sense in which this basic, essential Christian idea was expressed by Protestantism from its beginning, flowing with necessity from its principle, but explicitly rejected by Catholicism at the Synod of Trent?

[Gengler] says on p. 252[19] that Protestantism should only return into a Catholicism that has become entirely transparent to itself and that Protestantism should not be reconciled with Catholicism based on an external confrontation with its truth but rather based on the recognition of Catholicism as the truth. One might call this a higher developmental stage of the subjective consciousness with respect to which the merely external embrace of Catholicism as the substantial truth on the one hand, and on the other hand the mere negation of its truth from [one's own] relative perspective—to which this truth does not *appear* as true—are subordinate moments. But the principle that gives rise to this developmental stage is the same one which Protestantism made its own from its beginning: the basic principle of the freedom of belief and conscience. By virtue of this principle, Protestants can accept as truth only independently recognized truth. For precisely the same reason, they are at no time hindered to acknowledge the real truth of Catholicism. Catholicism, however, has [in such a synthesis] [421] given up its real principle which differentiates it from Protestantism.

The author seeks to save his original thesis according to which Catholicism is simply the truth, by the following concluding claim: in this higher development of subjective consciousness, Catholicism did not perish as what was untrue in itself but was really just transfigured. But what does this transfiguration of Catholicism consist in? It can only consist in its dropping, as a temporal form, what differentiates it from Protestantism, [namely,] the authority of the Church and of the episcopacy, which cannot be maintained as the necessary mediation if the subjective consciousness is to fully develop itself. But if Catholicism drops this principle as a temporal developmental form (which it is forced to do, if only on the basis of the author's admission that the episcopacy's consciousness itself is merely human, temporally conditioned, subject at every moment in time to the possibility of error and thus in no way infallible), what remains that could essentially separate it from Protestantism? After all, with the infallibility of the episcopacy's authority the infallibility of tradition, whose carrier and organ the episcopacy is, must fall away also. But if the authority of tradition is lost, too, then both Catholicism and Protestantism are pointed to the same objective source of objective truth, and whatever falls between the beginning and the end of the development is the temporal form which separates Catholicism from Protestantism but not the truth in itself.[20]

THE ONE-SIDEDNESS OF BOTH SYSTEMS AND THE POINT FROM WHICH A RAPPROCHEMENT AND FINAL RECONCILIATION CAN PROCEED

[422] Much as we cannot share the author's opinion on the form which he assumes a final accommodation and mediation [423] of the Protestant-Catholic contrast must necessarily take, we cannot take our leave from his intelligent essay, which in many ways is appealing to Protestants, without declaring our agreement with the main idea he expresses and develops, in a way that allows us to remain as free as possible from the one-sidedness of a simply negating contrast. Protestants

---

[19]Gengler, "Indifferenzierung," 252.

[20]A full note is here omitted in which Baur comments on Gengler's apparent debt to Hegel but complains that the rigidity of his Catholic position would not ultimately be compatible with this philosophy.

must document the critical view to which they are directed by the principle of Protestantism. On this basis, it must be their task to understand the objective character of historical phenomena, especially by conceding to Catholicism, which occupies such an important position in history, its higher historical truth. That is, they must consider Catholicism from the perspective of a developmental process whose result up to this point must be of great significance for the further development of Protestantism, too.

The direction the dogmatic development of Christianity must take is prescribed by the need for both sides to avoid the particular one-sidedness toward which each systems tends. [424] In Catholicism, objectivity seeks to obtain an all too one-sided prevalence over subjectivity; in Protestantism, it is the other way around. While the former makes faith too exclusively dependent on historical knowledge, the latter is in danger of placing too little weight on historical knowledge, that is, the living connection with the development of history.

Catholics have most recently mounted the following main arguments against Protestantism. First, they point to rationalism, whose widespread predominance they feel obligated to identify as the most obvious proof for the impending dissolution of Protestantism into an arbitrary game of subjective opinions.[21] Second, they object that Protestantism with its reductionist notion of Scriptural authority [425] treats Christianity as a merely antiquarian matter. [...] [429] This view of Christianity, which, [it is alleged,] limits the true Christian reality to the time of Christ and the apostles, can only be described as "dead," whereas Catholicism, according to them, is the uninterrupted, living, and objective continuation of Christianity, the appearance which, by means of its living existence, translates itself into tradition.[22] Catholics have repeatedly alerted Protestants to their lack of a living and more comprehensive view of Christianity.[23]

It is, in fact, impossible to deny that such descriptions of the character of Protestant theology in its main features offer a rather faithful picture of a certain direction that was very common in the Protestant Church not so long ago and is still asserting itself. It is that inanimate, purely external, fearfully constraining supranaturalism, latched onto the dead letter of Scripture, biased by a one-sidedness as extensive as the rationalism that opposes it. Both systems, thus, can only exist in mutual negation. Marheineke has clearly and perceptively developed the nature of this contrast in the preface to his *Grundlehren der christlichen Dogmatik als Wissenschaft* [*Basic Doctrines of Christian Dogmatics as Science*], 2nd edition, 1827.[24] Having thus completely acknowledged the truth of the objection made from the Catholic perspective with regard to rationalism and supranaturalism, however, we also believe that every attentive observer [430] of the most recent developments in Protestant dogmatics can be expected to acknowledge that [Protestant theology] has already progressed decisively beyond the limiting opposition into which it had [previously] divided itself against itself and fallen apart.

The same phenomena that characterize this great new epoch in the Protestant system of doctrine, which always continues to develop itself with fresh vigor, also offer unmistakable evidence for an effort to reconcile the contrast between Catholicism and Protestantism by bridging, with a

---

[21]Footnote omitted.
[22]*Sich selbst überliefernde Erscheinung*. Baur here plays with the German *überliefern*, the verbal form of *Überlieferung* = tradition.
[23]Footnote omitted.
[24]Philipp Marheineke, *Die Grundlehren der christlichen Dogmatik als Wissenschaft*, 2nd edn. (Berlin: Duncker & Humblot, 1827), xi–xxvii.

mediating link, the great chasm between the written documents of Christianity and the most recent developmental stage of the religious consciousness. The desire, so vividly felt [today], to return to the orthodox[25] basis of the system of doctrine and to regard the collective consciousness, which expresses itself in the confessional documents,[26] as the developmental principle of the whole system of doctrine, can only be explained by acknowledging that individuals can only become conscious of their faith's objectivity in community with others, and that nothing works more forcefully against the subjectivity of opinions, which dissolves the unity of faith, than jointly holding on to the original foundational principle from which the Protestant system of doctrine emerged.

At the same time, one can easily see that nothing would conflict more with this newly initiated direction than such an embrace of the Church's orthodox system of doctrine that would merely renew that old, rigid, slavish attachment to the letter of the confessional documents, which has long enough enchained in hampering fetters Protestantism's free spirit and thrown it back into a formalism devoid of content. Protestants must never direct their gaze merely backwards. While they can only become aware of their ecclesial community by looking at the past, their striving must always proceed forwards.

[431] As long as Protestants only seek to seclude and entrench themselves in their old position, delimited once and for all, the same unfortunate strife will always renew itself, which makes us feel obliged to see in our opponents only the enemy who must be fought throughout, rather than a collaborator working toward the same edifice. Inasmuch as the external word of God can only be vividly known and grasped by the addition of the divine Spirit's interior operation, orthodox doctrine, too, can only obtain its true meaning and value by the mediation of the same Spirit who, as even Protestant doctrine affirms, never ceases to work within the Church.

Yet if the Christian consciousness can only produce and form itself in the Church's community of faith, it is also, on the other hand, necessary for any development of the Christian faith to be founded on a principle established above every external authority. In connection with this, we might just point out how Schleiermacher established the new developmental epoch of the Protestant system of doctrines discussed here mainly by asserting the Christian consciousness as the center of Christian dogmatics. While this consciousness could never go entirely unrecognized, it has only now been emphasized in its deeper and more encompassing dogmatic meaning. What mediates between the individual's faith and objectively given Christianity is neither the authority of the Church nor the authority of tradition; rather, it is the Christian consciousness which is above Church and Scripture.

Next to the reversal of opinion in the domain of theology itself, let us consider recent developments in philosophy which in their turn have strongly influenced theology. This philosophy has placed speculative thought in the most intimate connection with the activity of the spirit objectivized in history by considering history as the living, progressive movement of the concept, [in other words] by only allowing the absolute spirit to penetrate, and work its way up, to its own consciousness

---

[25]*Symbolisch*. Based on the confessional texts.
[26]*Symbole*. The confessional texts (here of the Lutheran Church). Cf. Johann Tobias Müller, *Die symbolischen Bücher der evangelisch-lutherischen Kirche*, 2nd edn., 2 vols. (Stuttgart: Liesching, 1848).

through [432] the mediation of history.²⁷ In this development, too, we can discern a new moment in which Protestantism and Catholicism must find a shared point of contact.

If we, then, take all these moments together, it is, in a nutshell, a purified and spiritualized concept of tradition in which Protestantism comes closer to Catholicism without, however, abandoning its principle but instead amending and organically developing it.²⁸

As far as one can judge some signs of the times, however, Catholicism cannot entirely remain a stranger either to a movement that reconciles the [previous] opposition. [433] There are voices to be heard against the ancient and conventional concept of tradition—discrete, randomly occasioned utterances, to be sure, but expressed in a very decisive tone. They do not want to know anything of a tradition that consists only in the mechanical transmission of a dead mass of dogmatic articles, but rather can find the true essence of this tradition only in a living movement and development of the Christian spirit within the Church.²⁹ These voices at the same time also enunciate [434] a new developmental epoch in Catholicism.

While we could not admit in our evaluation of the Catholic doctrine of tradition [435] that the latter concept was the common and traditional one, nor concede its application in an exclusively polemical interest, we did so only out of the conviction that a spiritualized concept of tradition must have a deeply impactful importance for the Catholic system as a whole. How much of what still separates both systems by a sharp contrast immediately falls away [as a result of this]? What an opportunity is provided for a rapprochement with the material content of the Protestant system, too? [436] For this, in fact, we have to assume in the author of the present *Symbolik* no small tendency since in this book we so often found presented as Catholic doctrine what ought more justly to be regarded as the Protestant one!

Indeed, one may even claim that Protestantism's most recent direction has had an intimate share in the more spiritual concept of tradition adopted by recent Catholic theologians. Schleiermacher's ideas have had an unmistakable influence on writings such as the one by our author, [entitled] *Unity in the Church*,³⁰ and it is equally easy to see how the same class of Catholic theologians find much of the Hegelian system compatible with their perspective and conducive to their system.³¹ Be that as it may, the impulse for a new movement, wherever it may have come from, is here, and there is no doubt about the possibility of a new, meaningful developmental epoch. What matters is only that, what has come to consciousness, be expressed without timidity and developed firmly and rigorously.

What suggests itself most vigorously to us here, at the conclusion of these investigations, is the wish that both parties might increasingly communicate with an open love of truth about their true mutual positions, unrestrained by any extraneous considerations. The struggle once begun cannot

---

²⁷Baur evidently has Hegel in mind. It is generally accepted that Baur's knowledge of Hegel's thought only dates from the posthumous publication of his *Lectures on the Philosophy of Religion* in 1832. The present text is thus the earliest evidence for Baur's new-found enthusiasm for this philosophy.

²⁸A full note is here omitted in which Baur offers evidence from Schleiermacher (*Christian Faith* §128.3, trans. Mackintosh, 593) and Marheineke (*Grundlehren*, 56) as well as some others in support of this claim.

²⁹Footnote omitted.

³⁰Möhler, *Die Einheit in der Kirche oder das Wesen des Katholicismus* (Tübingen: Laupp, 1825). English translation: *The Unity in the Church or the Principle of Catholicism*, trans. Peter C. Erb (Washington, DC: Catholic University of America Press, 2015). On Schleiermacher's influence on this work cf. Michael J. Himes, "'A Great Theologian of our Time': Möhler on Schleiermacher," *Heythrop Journal* 37 (1996): 24–46.

³¹Baur himself had observed the evidently Hegelian influence on Gengler's article discussed above.

be laid to rest; it must be fought continuously and to the end, but if it is fought with the wrong weapons, its only result can be that the struggle's ultimate outcome is deferred all the more. As long as the newly gained perspective of symbolics is repeatedly mixed up with the old, abandoned one of polemics[32]; as long as what must yet be proven is admitted without proof; as long as it is virtually assumed that only one of the two dogmatic concepts is absolutely true, fully legitimate, and of the most beautiful, inner coherence; as long as impure presentations of openly accessible teachings, false consequences, [437] bitter tirades [motivated] by irritable, excited sentiments, petty diatribes about men whose names should only be mentioned with respect, take the place of evidence and muddy the purely scholarly character of the examination; as long as only exterior power and domination are sought—as long as no progress can be made toward the future goal that is meant to unify the two sides, but only regress to the past position of separation.

---

[32]Symbolics—polemics: *Symbolik* as the discipline of comparing the dogmatic systems of individual churches was created at the turn of the nineteenth century to replace the earlier discipline of polemics which had covered similar ground during the confessional age. Cf. Philipp Marheineke, *Christliche Symbolik oder historischkritisch und dogmatischkomparative Darstellung des katholischen, lutherischen, reformirten und socinianischen Lehrbegriffs*, vol. 1/1 (Heidelberg: Mohr und Zimmer, 1810), 3: "What used to carry the colour and form of a separate theological science under the name of polemics, but by and by fought itself to death, is here resurrected in its essence but detached from its previous form, as symbolics."

CHAPTER FOURTEEN

In Defense of Critical Exegesis

FROM: AE, 208–32
TRANSLATION: CHRISTOPHE CHALAMET IN: ID. (ED.), *THE CHALLENGE OF HISTORY: READINGS IN MODERN THEOLOGY* (MINNEAPOLIS, MN: FORTRESS, 2020), 127–35

Footnotes from the original edition are prefaced by [Baur]; Chalamet's footnotes are prefaced by [CC]. All other footnotes are by the editors.

In the explosive aftermath of the publication of David Friedrich Strauss' *Life of Jesus Critically Examined* in 1835–6, Baur found himself pressed to answer for the results of his student.[1] On the one hand, Baur took issue with what he deemed the "negative" approach of Strauss, in that Strauss dismantled the regnant conceptions of the Gospel accounts of Jesus' life without erecting in their place a "positive" way of thinking of the Gospels. To this extent, Baur did not want to be charged as responsible for Strauss' conclusions, or to allow the impression to exist that the two agreed in all matters of substance. On the other hand, Baur insisted forcefully on the right of Strauss to free academic inquiry, and balked at the attempts to limit the results of criticism in advance that he perceived in Strauss' ecclesiastical detractors.

In 1835, Baur offered a report to the local Evangelischer Verein in which he made a case for the legitimacy and necessity of criticism in a spirit of free inquiry. Two years later, he took up and expanded this report into a substantial article responding to an anonymous article criticizing Baur's views in his recently published book on the Pastoral Epistles.[2] Baur's title suggests that the attack compelled him to respond. He assumed that the anonymous article had been written by the editor, E. W. Hengstenberg, but it had in reality been written by the Pietist theologian August Tholuck.[3]

Specifically, Baur attacks a protectionist stance that would curtail the freedom of "scientific" inquiry, and argues that such an approach ironically proceeds from fear rather than faith. Baur also takes affront at the attempts to render him guilty by association with Strauss. This spirited response

---

[1] For the complex relationship between Baur and Strauss, see the excellent treatment in U. Köpf, "Ferdinand Christian Baur and David Friedrich Strauss," in *Ferdinand Christian Baur and the History of Early Christianity*, 3–44.

[2] Baur, *Die sogenannte Pastoralbriefe des Apostels Paulus aufs neue kritisch untersucht* (Stuttgart and Tübingen: Cotta, 1835). Köpf points out the dependence of this article on Baur's report ("Ferdinand Christian Baur and David Friedrich Strauss," 14–22). For the text of Baur's long letter to the Evangelischer Verein, see *Ferdinand Christian Baur. Die frühen Briefe (1814–1835)*, ed. Carl Hester (Sigmaringen: Jan Thorbecke, 1993), no. 75 (129–44). The anonymous article attacking Baur and Strauss is "Die Zukunft unserer Theologie," *Evangelische Kirchenzeitung* 18, no. 36 (May 4, 1836): 281–5 and 18, no. 37 (May 7, 1836): 289–91.

[3] Ernst Wilhelm Hengstenberg (1802–69) initially studied "oriental philology" before switching to theology, succeeding de Wette to a chair in Old Testament in Berlin from 1826. Friedrich August Gottreu Tholuck (1799–1877) was a student of Neander who became a leading Pietist theologian and taught in Halle from 1826 onward. In 1837 Tholuck published a direct critique of Strauss and Baur: *Die Glaubwürdigkeit der evangelischen Geschichte, zugleich eine Kritik des Lebens Jesu von Strauß* (Hamburg: Friedrich Perthes, 1837). Hengstenberg and Tholuck, together with Ernst Ludwig von Gerlach, co-founded the *Evangelische Kirchenzeitung* in 1827.

demonstrates Baur's rhetorical flair and highlights his polemical articulation of the Protestant (Lutheran) heritage against more orthodox confessional factions in his day.

DECLARATION COMPELLED BY AND DIRECTED AGAINST AN ARTICLE OF *THE EVANGELISCHE KIRCHENZEITUNG*, EDITED BY DR. E. W. HENGSTENBERG, PROF. OF THEOLOGY AT THE UNIVERSITY OF BERLIN. MAY 1836

[208] <127>

What is, in fact, a faith which is constantly afraid and anxious that the foundation upon which its most prized and holy content rests may be taken and snatched away forever, a faith which considers every new occurrence in philosophy and theology, every critical question and inquiry which comes to the light of day about the canonical books, with the constant disquietude and apprehension that these might [209] in the long run bring its fatal end? Faith, in the authentic Protestant <128> sense, is the surest consciousness of what one holds as true. If, consequently, faith cannot exist without the Christian foundation upon which it rests, then this foundation too must rest on rock-solid grounds, and if it were possible for this foundation to be shaken and taken away from faith, then the consequence would only be the following: not that it would be the end of faith, but rather that there is yet another ground of faith, one which cannot be shaken, or that the ground of our faith which can be shaken and invalidated is still not yet the true and correct one. Whoever knows what true faith is, knows also that faith is, in its essence, what is surest and steadiest, that when everything else around it falters and dissolves, faith itself never falters and dissolves.

Therefore, where such fear and anxiety are still present within faith, when one still thinks it possible that a final stroke may be fatal to it, what is such a faith, if not faithlessness within faith, doubt which has not yet been overcome and according to which everything one believes may be completely different, and bad conscience, which such a faith bears within itself and which it cannot hide from itself or from others? As a matter of fact, the German public in recent times has not given a good witness as regards the strength of its faith, when one looks at the true panic and terror with which it has been seized since the publication of Strauss' *Life of Jesus*.[4] As if we could imagine one instant that the book of a young scholar (even if its scientific quality and significance cannot be doubted, as was recognized even by [August] Neander[5]) would rob the world of its God, of its Christ, of its all, of its final consolation[6] in time and in eternity! But this is how it always goes when faith holds fast only to the letter, that is, when, from the letter, which kills, it has not attained the Spirit, who alone enlivens.[7] Whoever clings to the mere letter [210] must in fact live in constant

---

[4] On the reception of Strauss' *Life of Jesus*, see Erik Linstrum, "Strauss's 'Life of Jesus': Publication and the Politics of the German Public Sphere," *Journal of the History of Ideas* 71, no. 4 (2010): 593–616.

[5] Neander (1789–1850) was an eminent church historian who held a chair in Berlin from 1813. Neander had been asked to conduct a review of Strauss' book and recommended that the Prussian government not censure it; see his *Erklärung in Beziehung auf einen ihn betreffenden Artikel der* Allgemeinen Zeitung (Berlin: Haude und Spener, 1836). But the next year, he published his own treatment of the life of Jesus, which was at least partially motivated by Strauss: *Das Leben Jesu Christi in seinem geschichtlichen Zusammenhange und seiner geschichtlichen Entwickelung* (Hamburg: Perthes, 1837), on which, see also Baur, CTNC 339–40.

[6] An ironic reference to the first question of the Heidelberg Catechism.

[7] Cf. 2 Cor 3:6.

agitation and worry that, with Scripture's first letters, simultaneously the last ones may be taken away from him, that the final stroke may occur, that the terrible discovery, which had been feared since the beginning, will finally be made and released publicly, namely that behind Christianity and the Christian faith there stands a really terrible and evil deceit. Where would be the joyfulness, which the Protestant faith is supposed to foster in us and in others, where would be the free and joyous faith in God and in God's eternal Word, if one were afflicted with such anxieties, and who would not think here of the Indian myth in which disbelief leads to the world's end because a leviathan has stolen the sacred scriptures and has thus deprived the world of God's Word?

This is how the matter stands, if one considers it from the standpoint of faith. But it is no different if we view it from the standpoint of science.[8] What kind of science would it be, whose only interest would be to deliver a stroke, and which, guided by this one intent, would deny the authenticity of this or that epistle, and eventually also of the entire Pauline corpus? As any person who can think would see, whoever speaks like this reveals that in him the very idea of science has not yet even begun to emerge. Only someone who does not know what science wants, and what it must want in order to conform to its nature, only someone who thinks that his personal activity and effort may be called scientific even though, far from being purely concerned with the subject matter, it serves the subject matter with a concern which is foreign to it—only such a person will presuppose that all the scientific publications which go beyond his own perspective and which obviously contradict his own agenda (and which contradict it all the more as the scientific concern which underpins these publications is purer) have something to do with dishonest and selfish [211] interests. And so what happens here is that one is projecting one's own base and menial view of science onto others.

One suspects others of being guided by impure motivations, such as the attempt to create an irritated and sour atmosphere through their publications. And since, within the field of theology, there is nothing one may be more suspicious of than disbelief, then all of the publications of this kind must be the product of disbelief: they must come from what best characterizes disbelief, namely arbitrariness and brazenness, an unfathomable frivolity, an unstable, indeed intoxicated, critical skepticism. Hence the confidence such people have that all of the publications of this sort can be disposed of in the simplest and easiest manner. They do not know that science always renews itself from itself, that it is caught up in a forward-looking, living movement. It is driven by itself, without the possibility of <129> any human power blocking its way. It always creates new paths for itself, in order to follow to its end what it has already attained and comprehended. They do not know this, and even if they knew it, this knowledge would still be insufficient. In order to participate in science's living, developing process as a real actor, one must enter in it in such a way that one is ready to give science the sacrifice it requires. One may not stipulate in advance what one wishes to receive from it, and the conditions under which one is willing to commit to it. Rather, one must be ready, when necessary, to relinquish one's subjective representations and interests in order to welcome, in return, through the rebirth of science, whatever is true and tenable about them. Here too it is necessary to kill the natural man, to die to the flesh, so that we may recognize what is not of the flesh but spiritual, so that the old may pass and all things may be new.[9] [212] No wonder, therefore, that natural man also resists science and that much about it seems inopportune

---

[8] On Baur's use of *Wissenschaft*, see Note on Text and Translations.
[9] Here Baur plays with Pauline language; cf., e.g., Rom 8:1-17.

or acrid to him, or that he simply does not wish to have anything to do with it. It is only folly to him. He cannot understand it, for it can only be understood spiritually.[10]

But he can also not completely conceal from himself the fact that there is indeed something to it; his natural sense tells him that. False, misguided, and inane science, the kind of science which does not deserve the name, never causes much worry. Worry happens only with the kind of science about which I must say to myself, in secret, that its results are not entirely made out of thin air, even if I have difficulties agreeing with them as I realize I was mistaken in my previous views (views which had become sweet habits of thoughts), as I feel hurt because my concern is being contradicted. But this conflict places natural man all the more in a state of turmoil and passion, since on the one hand he senses what takes place in science, but on the other hand he is unable, with his mind marked by the flesh, to commit to it—in order to correctly understand it—and to examine it conscientiously. Hence, what is always easiest and most convenient: natural man's accusation, his suspicion, his sentence and condemnation, his uproar and rage, his entire unruly nature, as we know it only too well. It is only on the basis of this inner contradiction that I can understand, on a psychological level, why the author of the article, alongside all the hard and offending words with which I must put up, then also adds lovely and positive comments about me—comments for which I must state my gratitude. In itself I can only see the clearest contradiction here, and I would be the greatest enigma to myself, a sort of truly Manichean two-sided being, if I were simultaneously scholarly, competent and level-headed, and arbitrarily brazen, unfathomably frivolous, unstable, and, indeed, intoxicated—and all of that to the same extent.

And so only a false faith and a false science [213] can comport themselves in such a way. Nothing of the sort happens with true faith and true science. On the contrary, the two stand in perfect harmony. Both mutually nourish and refresh each other; just as science only profits from faith, faith only profits from science. From faith, and only from faith, science learns to purify itself of anything foreign and corrupt, to dedicate itself undividedly and unconditionally to the holy reality of truth. Conversely, thanks to science, faith does not fall into sluggish quiescence, but maintains a fresh and living dynamism, becoming always more clearly and immediately conscious of its divine content. Even if science appears to be in a position of enmity with regard to faith, as science always unsettles it anew, shakes all of its foundations, and erodes the ground on which it takes root, by so doing science in fact renders it the greatest service. For the point is not how much one believes, but only what one believes and how one believes; whether one believes in such a way that one knows how to distinguish, in one's faith too, the true and the false, what is certain and what is not, what is essential and what is less so.

True faith is content with little, whereby the little it has remains a steadier and more secure possession. If one gives it only a sliver of good ground in which it may place its mustard seed, even in these conditions it becomes a tremendous tree—reaching the sky high above all the other plants of the earth—under whose shadow we may dwell.[11] One single passage of Scripture was enough for the greatest doctor of the church of ancient times to ground his faith, and to transform him into a pillar of the church. All of the doubts which the new criticism creates are extremely salutary and fruitful for faith; they must be considered a powerful educational <130> and formative instrument. For faith should never be inactive and secure, but should always grow and become stronger. How else is that possible, however—as the extensive and the intensive always stand [214]

---

[10] Cf. 1 Cor 2:13-16.
[11] See Mark 4:30-32 par.

in a reciprocal relation—unless faith learns to better distinguish between what is essential and what is less essential, between content and form; unless faith learns to separate more sharply the inner core, the very essence of the matter, from the external envelope and husk.

As faith learns to abandon and let go always more of certain particular aspects, it learns to hold on all the more, with full inner intensity and steadfastness, to what abides for it, in its unity. Science helps faith in this regard, insofar as faith must both maintain itself against science and acknowledge its legitimacy. As a living faith—that is, a faith which does not stand still, but which, in the peace it holds within itself, constantly seeks to attain an always higher certainty—became always more important to our church, our church considered the free inquiry into Scripture and about Scripture as its most inestimable gem.

Which guidance, however, does Scripture itself provide for distinguishing between what is essential to faith and what is less essential, including in relation to the historical dimension of the gospel story? Who has better articulated the whole depth and fullness of the Christian faith than the Apostle Paul in his epistles? But does he abide by the most minute details of Jesus' life history? Does he privilege certain miracles and occurrences? Does he come back, again and again, to the historical dimension of Jesus' life? Does he not presuppose, and take as his point of departure, only the most general facts of the gospel story, which everyone must recognize and presuppose in one way or another, and which after all are certain even without the gospels?

There is much to be learned, also in this respect, from Paul's understanding of the gospel, from the apostle who did not see the Lord sensuously and bodily, but who asserted most decidedly the legitimacy of his apostolic vocation against the apostles who had walked, day in and day out, with the Lord! Whether one considers this or that aspect of the gospel story as historically less reliable [215], as the product of the tradition, is irrelevant for faith. This has long been acknowledged, without qualms, by the most distinguished theologians. It has to do, ultimately, only with the relation between the historical, or original, and what comes from later traditions in the gospel story, and the balance between them. It would be a good thing to finally realize this, to limit the quarrel with the new criticism to this, in order to quarrel with what can be successfully quarrelled over, namely the question of the point at which it goes too far, instead of transforming the quarrel into a conflict over principles, which leads nowhere. Who would dare argue that, in the case of these old accounts—which go back so far in time and which have been transmitted in ways which are quite unknown to us; accounts which must always be examined according to the rules of historical criticism—the usual phenomenon did not happen, and that absolutely no trace of elements coming from the tradition have been associated with properly historical elements?[12]

---

[12][Baur] It is easy to state, as is done in the *Evangelische Kirchenzeitung*'s "Preface," on p. 43: "The NT is thoroughly based on history; all aspects of the setting in which it appeared, among which it began and developed itself, are known to us." Thus speak all who contentedly develop such a satisfying idea of human knowledge concerning historical matters generally, as well as, more specifically, of their own knowledge—a view which is quite pleasing to human vanity. As they have no idea concerning what belongs to such a knowledge, they are ready to complete what is positively missing out with matters springing out of their own arbitrariness. It is quite astonishing to dare to say, in good conscience, of any single occurrence of that time, that *all aspects of its setting are known to us*! Whoever has taken a look at these settings knows how much is unknown to us, and how it befits Christian humility to acknowledge, also here, the fragmentariness of our knowledge. Only human delusion can ignore this. But whoever, having acknowledged this, attempts to distinguish between Jesus' public life and what preceded it, or between the historical and the pre-historical, must realize how much, by so doing, is conceded to Strauss' criticism. I note this simply in order to recall how necessary it is, in every debate involving principles, to consider rigorously the implications of each of the two opposing principles.

[216] And why is such a demonstration—whereby not even the least non-historical[13] element will be granted, since this would amount to dissolving the principle which must be safeguarded—not actually made by those who take it to be an easy task? Isn't it a task which can be fulfilled—this much <131> is obvious—with a clarity and evidence which far surpass the clarity and evidence of the opponents, since the truth must let itself be demonstrated much more clearly and evidently than its opposite? The basic axiom according to which the rules of historical criticism, which otherwise apply to everything which pertains to history, find no application in this particular instance (which concerns what is most important and holy for human beings), the axiom which declares that, in this particular case and only here, the free examination which Protestantism demands is not valid: this basic axiom can only come from an *a priori* presupposition. But which presupposition can it be, if not one in which something purely arbitrary has been mixed in?

Here too let us only consider, above all, the Protestant point of view. A Protestant differs from a Catholic not only in that he does not believe in anything else than in the Word of God, but also in that he gives an account concerning the grounds of his faith. But faith itself cannot give such an account; only science, the knowledge of faith, can do it. When it is not conditioned by certain general, static truths of the religious and Christian consciousness, science is an inquiry which is never at rest; it operates without definite limits. It does not allow its results to be predetermined, for an inquiry whose results are settled in advance is not an inquiry. The difference between Protestantism and [217] Catholicism also lies in the rejection of the authority of tradition. Protestants reject tradition because, as a human construct, it falsely presents itself as the divine truth and wishes to put what emerged later on a par with what is original. Only the pure word of Scripture, rather than tradition, is valid. In the performing of the critical principle of Protestantism—a principle which aims at the strictest separation of the divine and the human—is it consistent and possible to justify, on the basis of that principle, the practice of progressing toward Scripture, but then of making a full stop in front of it, and thus to neglect to ask, also in relation to Scripture, whether here too perhaps something human and traditional may have to be separated from Scripture's divine content?

The highest principle of Protestantism does not prohibit this; on the contrary it demands it, and whoever does not abide by this Protestant critical principle, applying his best capacities, pays tribute to the Catholic "authority principle." This is the reason why in the Protestant church, since its beginning, historical and critical studies have always existed (this critical principle already comes into view, in its full significance, in Luther). And if, in recent times, these studies have led theologians whose disinterested love of truth cannot be doubted, such as Neander, to declare certain canonical books of the New Testament to be either inauthentic or at least very dubious, this, far from damaging faith, benefits it. When faith is placed in a purely human word in Scripture, it is a false faith, because the more faith ascends to a higher consideration of the word of Scripture, the more it will matter for it not to treat as God's Word what cannot be demonstrated to be such. When, with the assistance of science, faith knows how to distinguish the authentic from the inauthentic, it demonstrates its strength, its illuminating power, its penetration in the inner spirit of Scripture. Whoever [218] knows how to conduct such inquiries in a true scientific manner, that is, with motives which signal an accurate and consistent thinking and a thorough knowledge of the matter, not only is fully entitled to do so, but also adequately fulfills his task as a Protestant Christian and

---

[13][CC] In other words, following Baur's distinction between what is "historical" and what is "traditional": elements which have been created by the subsequent tradition.

theologian. Anyone who, instead of carefully examining and correcting these inquiries, obstructs them, anyone who, more mildly, seeks to curtail them on the basis of a general principle, namely the axiom according to which knowledge should not come into conflict with faith: anyone who acts in this way acts in an anti-Protestant way and pays tribute, once again, to the Catholic "authority principle"—a principle which, to put it in a Kantian way, is also the principle of lazy reason.[14]

For, indeed, why would anyone wish to let science conflict with faith? Simply because knowledge threatens *his own* faith: it does not let him rest peacefully with what he hitherto believed. The agitation in which he finds himself, instead of leading him to rid himself of this state quickly by appealing to this axiom, should have led him to see himself entrusted with the task of finding an agreement between faith and science (whose results, even if they must be circumscribed <132> and corrected in many ways as regards their details, cannot be refuted in their broad scope). Such an agreement should only be sought in the form of a higher position[15] of one's faith, instead of considering the former position as the only possible position for faith. If, on the one hand, one cannot prevent the progress of science, and if, on the other hand, one cannot adjust the result of science to *one's own* faith, then one should beware of having science carry the burden which comes in fact from the subjective incapacity of an individual person, or from the smugness of someone who is convinced that his own position must abide forever and is the only salvific one. [219] Such reactions, which have to do with the limitations of subjective standpoints and concerns, and all the anathemas which are issued by those to whom the very idea of a historical criticism is a life and death question,[16] will not prevent historical criticism from following its own way, the way which is clarified and prescribed through all the preceding stages of the development of science.

With this I believe I have provided an adequate reply to my opponent and his accusation, namely that a critical inquiry of canonical letters, such as my book on the Pastoral Epistles, will eventually lead to the full carrying out of the final stroke,[17] namely the denial of the authenticity of the entire Pauline corpus. Already in my book I have made clear what I think about such a *coup*, to use my opponent's language. The more I study the questions of the authenticity of Paul's letters, the more such ideas appear to me as totally inconsistent. If someone considers such a *coup* feasible, let him attempt to do with an unquestionably authentic Pauline epistle what I have done with the Pastoral Epistles—but let him do it in the same manner, [220] with arguments which are as historically documented as mine! Any doubt which has no basis disintegrates at once, whereas doubts which have support carry within themselves their own measure and rule—believing this belongs to the faith which is linked with science. Anyone who totally rejects in principle any doubt and inspection should explain—if his thinking is not contradictory and inconsistent—how this attitude can lead to any progress in science and to any reform in the church, how anything else follows from it than absolute standstill, the death of faith and of knowledge.

---

[14][CC] See the notion of "ignava ratio," in Immanuel Kant, *Critique of Pure Reason* A689/B717.

[15]Literally, "a higher mediation" of one's faith (*eine höhere Vermittlung*).

[16][Baur] It would be a very good thing if those who are so opposed to critical studies did not give the impression that their opposition only targets the skeptical kind of criticism, not criticism *per se*. If they wished to speak freely, they should acknowledge that such a distinction cannot be made, in itself, or, especially, in relation to their position. A criticism which may not also be skeptical is no criticism at all. Quite often, only doubt leads us to truth, and a theology which posits axiomatically that we should never doubt and inspect anything would do well to simply suppress historical criticism from the scientific fields which constitute theology.

[17]Lit. "*coup*."

The entire article from the *Evangelische Kirchenzeitung*, insofar as it deals with me, not only seeks to place my book on the Pastoral Epistles in exactly the same category as Strauss' *Life of Jesus*, so that all of the anathema which have been directed at Strauss' work in the "Preface"[18] of the *Evangelische Kirchenzeitung* may also apply to my book; it also describes me as a theologian who stands "under Strauss' influence" (a spiteful accusation, without proof, which questions my theological independence and offends my honor; an accusation which I could only qualify by using a word which I already used above[19]). And so, in addition to the rest, it is momentously announced to the public that I stand in a "friendly rapport" with D. Strauss. Here I could ask: how does the author of the article know this? Is his inquisitorial attentiveness, not just about my books, but also about my private life, so great that he deems it necessary to report about it to the public? And is he adequately informed? Since, as I have already shown, the author's truthfulness in this article, so far as I am concerned, does not appear in the best light, if I did not take up this point the public would wonder to what extent the *Evangelischen Kirchenzeitung*'s article, [221] also on this particular question, can be trusted. I make this comment only in view of other similar cases where I do not have the opportunity <133> and a reason to explain myself. I have no desire to deny conventions and relations, and I have nothing to hide about my behavior from public life. And yet a dispiriting and embarrassing sentiment overwhelms me when I consider how far the overt suspicion has gone, when one is forced to respond before all also about such personal matters. And so I do not deny at all that I stand in a friendly relation with Dr. Strauss. I wish to add that, in the long string of years in which I have learned to know him better, until now, as with other similar cases, I have not been able to discern in him the demonic nature which the editor of the *Evangelischen Kirchenzeitung*, with the unfailing eyes of his Christian love, wishes to see in him.[20]

But what may be implied by such a relation? Does it mean that I am responsible for axioms and claims I have not asserted, for books I have not written? Perhaps one will be able to draw such consequences, and account for this before God and one's conscience. To me, only one thing is worth noting, namely the confirmation of the old experience that, wherever inquisitorial attempts to brand others as heretics consolidate themselves and escalate, such attempts never remain limited to the things which are the direct objects of attention; rather, these attempts instantly extend also to all the other objects which are found to stand in looser or more distant relation with the former, primary objects. This is the old, well-documented practice whereby, *in majorem Dei gloriam*, no aspect of life is so frail and holy that it should be spared its venom. It is not the first time that, because of theological opinions, a friendship is perceived as an outrage, or a teacher is tracked with his student; for the sake of the living, even the dead [222] are not granted peace. Since I, for once, must speak of such things, I cannot omit to note that the information which is contained in the same article (p. 285), according to which the church of Württemberg has decreed the expulsion of this theologian (D. Strauss) from any ecclesial teaching post, is not quite accurate. What the author of the article, following his slogan, would have liked to have

---

[18][CC] "Vorwort," *Evangelische Kirchenzeitung* 18, no. 1 (January 2, 1836): 1–6; no. 2 (January 6, 1836): 9–14; no. 3 (January 9, 1836): 17–23; no. 4 (January 13, 1836): 25–31; no. 5 (January 16, 1836): 33–38; no. 6 (January 20, 1836): 41–5. The article to which Baur responded, "Die Zukunft unserer Theologie," also mentioned this long "Preface" ("Die Zukunft," 283).

[19][CC] Baur has the word "calumny" in mind here.

[20]That is, Hengstenberg.

occurred did not quite happen in that way. At a minimum, I do not know whether the change in the author's position, following the publication of the first part of the *Life of Jesus*, is accurately described as an exclusion, decreed by the church of Württemberg, from any ecclesial teaching position. What I know, however, is that the church of Württemberg, with regard to what is good and appropriate which it must decree and order, knows its own position well enough to embrace for itself the principles of the *Evangelische Kirchenzeitung*—principles which are inspired by the hate of heretics.[21]

Assuredly, every true friend of the Protestant church, if he is able to judge very differently such publications, having read the article on "The Future of Our Theology" as well as the "Preface" which accompanies it, will be filled with the dreariest sentiment and outlook concerning the future of our theology and of our church. Certainly, everyone must ask: what will happen, in the near future, with the Protestant church, if such axioms come to expression always [223] more unashamedly and forcefully, if they become always more commonplace? Where is the love of Christ when, as was the case with the treatment of my work, all respect is sacrificed on the altar of the hate of heretics? Where is the freedom of faith and thinking, when the circle within which a theological difference of opinion may occur always becomes narrower? Where is the faith in an invisible church, which no one can discern with one's heart amidst the visible church, when the damning judgment which is issued about actions or books, when the judging gaze, penetrate into the most interior reaches of the heart? Indeed, how can there still be, in the Protestant church, a remnant of assurance for the moral foundations of life, when those who champion the holy cause of the gospel, who dedicate themselves to their journals, who always make sure to claim how "seriously they take Christ," make such a game of the truth (as I have shown to be the case with the article under consideration, insofar as it concerns me), or when means, such as those I have shown, are <134> put to use in order to reach more surely the goal which has been set?

What this amounts to, in one word—as the honorable Neander felt compelled to state, right after having read the said "Preface," its impression on him being fresh and all the more true, and protesting in the spirit of love and freedom—is: "a *papacy*," indeed a new papacy, erected in the midst of the Protestant church, and already endowed with everything which any papacy must possess if it is not to fail in its highest and ultimate purpose.[22] I will not deny what is good about the *Evangelische Kirchenzeitung*, but no one will deny that the true spirit of Christianity cannot rule where such an impure and un-Christian principle comes to expression (were it the case only in one particular respect), as it does in the presumptuous quest to brand heretics—a quest through which the *Evangelische Kirchenzeitung* would like to suppress every free, spiritual movement in order to create a new tyranny of the spirit.

If the editor of the *Evangelische Kirchenzeitung* takes such an activity to be authentically Christian and [224] Protestant, then I can only wish, out of Christian love, that the true light may rise, at the

---

[21][Baur] *Écrasez l'infâme!* is the openly stated Christian slogan of the *Evangelische Kirchenzeitung*'s editor. On that basis, everyone is invited to decide for oneself what may in fact be said with the expression "friendly rapport" [Baur is alluding to the way in which the *Evangelische Kirchenzeitung* presents his relation to D. F. Strauss]. It seems to me to be the proper place, here, to ask the readers of these pages not to forget, anywhere in my declaration, the kind of claim to moral regard which moral principles of this kind, which are openly stated, may make.

[22][CC] For August Neander's critical comments, dated February 17, 1836, on the *Evangelische Kirchenzeitung*'s "Preface," see his *Erklärung in Beziehung auf einen ihn betreffenden Artikel*, 11–12. Also reprinted in *Evangelische Kirchenzeitung* 18, no. 30 (April 13, 1836): 233.

right time, over the terrible blindness and self-deception in which he finds himself. May he finally come to realize—he who, with the sympathizers of his *Evangelische Kirchenzeitung* alone, believes to stand so high above the spirit of the age—that this same spirit of the age, and the pernicious trajectories in which in his eyes only others are captive, hold him tightly in their arms. Doesn't his *Evangelische Kirchenzeitung* place itself at the level of some of the daily newspapers which, in his own opinion, are largely responsible for the corruption of our time, when it pays tribute in such a way to factionalism, when it so deliberately lingers with each scandal (made up or not), not in order to warn and admonish with Christian seriousness and Christian love, or to teach and refute, as is necessary, but above all in order to brand as heretic and to arouse suspicion, to judge and condemn, and to exploit every incident of this kind? Doesn't it fall to the level of the daily papers, when it sorts every person whom it has selected according to specific names, colors, and parties, when it manages to obfuscate the differences which lie under their united points of view, when it does not abstain from expressing political suspicion—including during the decisive year of 1830, which presented so many opportunities for doing so? In all this, with its way of speaking which is always excited, puffing and panting in its fervor and desire for revenge, hoping to stir up the sensuous nature in its readers, doesn't it present itself like these newspapers?

May the editor of the *Evangelische Kirchenzeitung*, if he is still ready to make "the weather of the Lord, his terrible thunderstorm, his furious and vengeful wrath,"[23] fall on the head of others, if his intent still is to frighten with the lion's roar and remind of the grave time of the judgment which is close at hand, may he, before it is too late, think about the kind of judge in front of whom he too will have to stand, accounting for all of his words. Every papacy, of whichever kind, carries with itself its own curse, the curse of [225] hybris and egomania. Sooner or later, it collapses into its own nothingness. Under a tyranny of spirit which would like to suppress a freer, spiritual life wherever it emerges, under an egomania which always only screams its "no!" (a "no" which contradicts nature) wherever there is the free and joyous love of life of the spirits—the spirits which their eternal Father, from the fullness of his life, sends out so that they may build, with invisible forces, and using the whole range of charisms of his Spirit, his kingdom, according to a plan which mortal eyes seldom notice; under such egomania no one in Germany will consent to bend one's neck, and it will not be possible that, for the sake of the project of establishing a papacy for oneself and for a few others, goes lost for the world what men such as Schleiermacher and Hegel[24] [226] have achieved, in their solemn life work, for the good of church and state and as a lasting fruit for all who, through their [227] own reflection and research, testing everything and holding fast to every good thing, know they are following in <135> their footsteps.

[228] When someone like Neander openly protests against the *Evangelische Kirchenzeitung*'s chosen standpoint, [229] that is, against an exclusive salvific dogmatics on the basis of which [230] all kinds of different schools are appraised, then the final hour of such a papacy has come. [231] And so, at this point, it cannot be concealed, quite naïvely, that the article in question[25] "has turned out to be rather dull."[26] But the consolation comes right away, with the new self-delusion that

---

[23][CC] Jer. 30:23 (Baur is quoting Luther's Bible).
[24][CC] Here Baur adds a very long footnote, which has been removed.
[25][CC] Namely: Neander's article.
[26][CC] Baur is quoting an assessment of Neander's article by A. Tholuck. See A. Tholuck, "Erklärung in Bezug auf das Sendschreiben von Prof. Weisse," *Litterarischer Anzeiger für christliche Theologie und Wissenschaft überhaupt*, no. 32 (May 24, 1836): 249.

"the esteemed man, in the Afterword of his declaration, expresses what he has to say about Strauss concerning several minor differences with greater affect than against the one who is invalidating the Christian basis, and whom he nevertheless considers as his comrade in faith and spirit,"[27] which means paying tribute to the very papacy against which he so solemnly protests. Considering the heartfelt manner in which he recently wrote about the late [Gustav] Billroth (a person I also highly esteemed) and Billroth's friend, Professor [Christian Hermann] Weisse,[28] I also cannot imagine the esteemed Tholuck[29] being of a different opinion than Neander and refusing, in our current divisions, to broadly recognize with him the unity in spirit—which is suffused with the truth of Neander's weighty words in his Declaration (p. 12): "It is easy to be consistent when one reaches conclusions and is done quickly; it is, on the other hand, hard, when one keeps one's conscience open to truth, in every direction; when, in a bitter struggle with oneself, one realizes more and more intimately that all of our knowledge is and remains fragmentary." The *Evangelische Kirchenzeitung*'s appeal, to all who take Christ seriously, to prepare themselves in all seriousness and faithfulness for the great battle of our time, for the period during which Christ's church and the kingdom of darkness will separate themselves and confront each other in greater ways than ever before: this appeal will be issued regardless. May everyone who knows what he wills, wherever he is located in such a battle, may everyone who is earnest about Christ know that [232], even if delusional human predictions are not realized in the immediate future, the Lord's divine word, on the other hand, remains eternally true: *You will know them by their fruits.*[30] May this single saying be the answer, beforehand, to whatever the *Evangelische Kirchenzeitung* might still publish about me.

---

[27][Baur] See Tholuck, "Erklärung in Bezug auf das Sendschreiben von Prof. Weisse," 249–50.

[28][CC] Gustav Billroth (February 11, 1808–March 28, 1836) was a theologian and philosopher who taught, as a lecturer, at the University of Leipzig. He was the author of *Beiträge zur wissenschaftlichen Kritik der herrschenden Theologie, besonders in ihrer praktischen Richtung* (Leipzig: Leopold Michelsen, 1831), and of a commentary on Paul's epistles to the Corinthians: *Commentar zu den Briefen des Paulus an die Corinther* (Leipzig: Weidmann, 1833). Christian Hermann Weisse (1801–66) was a professor of philosophy at the University of Leipzig. He opposed Hegel's philosophy and also wrote on theological topics, for instance, in response to Strauss: *Die evangelische Geschichte, kritisch und philosophisch bearbeitet*, 2 vols. (Leipzig: Breitkopf-Härtel, 1838). Billroth was among his students and disciples.

[29][CC] Baur was obviously unaware (and would remain so) of the fact that the anonymous article had in fact been written by August Tholuck himself!

[30][CC] Matt 7:16, 20.

BIBLIOGRAPHY

1. WORKS BY FERDINAND CHRISTIAN BAUR

a. Books

1824–5
Symbolik und Mythologie oder die Naturreligion des Alterthums. 2 parts, with 2 divisions of the 2nd part (3 vols altogether). Stuttgart: J. B. Metzler, 1824–5; reprint, Aalen: Scientia, 1979.

1827–8
Primae Rationalismi et Supranaturalismi historiae capita potiora.
Pars I. *De Gnosticorum Christianismo ideali. Dissertatio inauguralis historico-theologica, quam Deo juvante Munus Professoris Theologicae Evangelicae Ordinarii.* Tübingen: Hopferi de l'Orme, 1827.
Pars II. *Comparatur Gnosticismus cum Schleiermacheriane theologiae indole.* Tübingen: Hopferi de l'Orme, 1827.
Pars III. *Exponitur praesertim Arianismi indoles rationalis.* Tübingen: Hopfer de l'Orme, 1828.

1829
De orationis habitae a Stephano Acta Cap. VII consilio. Tübingen: Hopfer de l'Orme, 1829.

1831
Das manichäische Religionssystem nach den Quellen neu untersucht und entwickelt. Tübingen: C. F. Osiander, 1831; reprint Hildesheim and New York: Olms, 1973.
Programma: *De Ebionitarum origine et doctrina, ab Essenis repetenda.* Tübingen: Hopfer de l'Orme, 1831.
Epistula Gratulatoria ad D. Theophilum Iacobum Planck [...] Addita est brevis disquisitio in Andreae Osiandri de justificatione doctrinam, ex recentiore potissimum theologia interpretanda. Tübingen: Hopfer de l'Orme, 1831.

1832
Apollonius von Tyana und Christus, oder das Verhältniß des Pythagoreismus zum Christenthum. Ein Beitrag zur Religionsgeschichte der ersten Jahrhunderte nach Christus. Tübingen: L. F. Fues, 1832.

1834
Der Gegensatz des Katholicismus und Protestantismus nach den Principien und Hauptdogmen der beiden Lehrbegriffe. Mit besonderer Rücksicht auf Hrn. Dr. Möhler's Symbolik. Tübingen: L. F. Fues, 1834; 2nd edn. Tübingen: L. F. Fues, 1836.
Erwiderung auf Herrn Dr. Möhlers neueste Polemik gegen die protestantische Lehre und Kirche. Tübingen: L. F. Fues, 1834.
Programma: *Comparatur Eusebius Caesariensis historiae ecclesiasticae parens cum parente historiarum Herodoto Halicarnassensi.* Tübingen: Hopfer de l'Orme, 1834.

1835
Die christliche Gnosis, oder die christliche Religions-Philosophie in ihrer geschichtlichen Entwiklung. Tübingen: C. F. Osiander, 1835; reprint Darmstadt: Wissenschaftliche Buchgesellschaft, 1967. English translation: *Christian Gnosis*, ed. Peter C. Hodgson, trans. Robert F. Brown. Eugene, OR: Cascade, 2020.

Die sogenannte Pastoralbriefe des Apostel Paulus aufs neue kritisch untersucht. Stuttgart and Tübingen: J. G. Cotta'schen Verlagshandlung, 1835.

1836
Abgenöthigte Erklärung gegen einen Artikel der Evangelischen Kirchenzeitung, herausgegeben von Dr. E. W. Hengstenberg, Prof. der Theol. an der Universität zu Berlin. Tübingen: Fues, 1836.

1837
Das Christliche des Platonismus oder Sokrates und Christus. Eine religionsphilosophische Untersuchung. Tübingen: L. F. Fues, 1837.

1838
Die christliche Lehre von der Versöhnung in ihrer geschichtlichen Entwicklung von der ältesten Zeit bis auf die neueste. Tübingen: C. F. Osiander, 1838.
Ueber den Ursprung des Episkopats in der christlichen Kirche. Tübingen: Fues, 1838.

1841–3
Die christliche Lehre von der Dreieinigkeit und Menschwerdung Gottes in ihrer geschichtlichen Entwicklung.
Vol. 1: *Das Dogma der alten Kirche bis zur Synode von Chalcedon.* Tübingen: C. F. Osiander, 1841.
Vol. 2: *Das Dogma des Mittelalters.* Tübingen: C. F. Osiander, 1842.
Vol. 3: *Die neuere Geschichte des Dogmas, von der Reformation bis in die neueste Zeit.* Tübingen: C. F. Osiander, 1843.

1842
Worte der Erinnerung an Dr. Friedrich Heinrich Kern, ed. Ferdinand Christian Baur. Tübingen: L. F. Fues, 1842.

1845
Paulus, der Apostel Jesu Christi. Sein Leben und Wirken, seine Briefe und seine Lehre. Ein Beitrag zu einer kritischen Geschichte des Urchristenthums. Stuttgart: Becher und Müller, 1845; 2nd edn. 2 vols., ed. Eduard Zeller. Leipzig: Fues's Verlag, 1866–7. English translation: *Paul the Apostle of Jesus Christ*, ed. Peter C. Hodgson, trans. Robert F. Brown and Peter C. Hodgson. Eugene, OR: Cascade, 2021.

1846
Der Kritiker und der Fanatiker, in der Person des Herrn Heinrich W. J. Thiersch. Zur Charakteristik der neuesten Theologie. Stuttgart: Becher's Verlag, 1846.

1847
Kritische Untersuchungen über die kanonischen Evangelien, ihr Verhältniß zu einander, ihren Charakter und Ursprung. Tübingen: L. F. Fues, 1847.
Lehrbuch der christlichen Dogmengeschichte. Stuttgart: Becher's Verlag, 1847; 2nd rev. edn. Tübingen: L. F. Fues, 1858; 3rd edn., identical with the 2nd. Leipzig: Fues's Verlag [L. W. Reisland], 1867; reprint Darmstadt: Wissenschaftliche Buchgesellschaft, 1979. English translation: *History of Christian Dogma*, ed. Peter C. Hodgson, trans. from the 3rd Ger. edn. Robert F. Brown and Peter C. Hodgson. Oxford: Oxford University Press, 2014.

1848
Die ignatianischen Briefe und ihr neuester Kritiker. Eine Streitschrift gegen Herrn Bunsen. Tübingen: L. F. Fues, 1848.

1851
Das Markusevangelium nach seinem Ursprung und Charakter. Nebst einem Anhang über das Evangelium Marcions. Tübingen: L. F. Fues, 1851.

1852

Die Epochen der kirchlichen Geschichtsschreibung. Tübingen: L. F. Fues, 1852. English translation: *The Epochs of Church Historiography.* In *Ferdinand Christian Baur: On the Writing of Church History*, ed. and trans. Peter C. Hodgson. New York: Oxford University Press, 1968.

1853

Das Christenthum und die christliche Kirche der drei ersten Jahrhunderte. Tübingen: L. F. Fues, 1853; 2nd rev. edn. Tübingen: L. F. Fues, 1860; 3rd edn., identical with the 2nd, published under the title *Kirchengeschichte der drei ersten Jahrhunderte.* Tübingen: L. F. Fues, 1863. English translation: *Christianity and the Christian Church in the First Three Centuries*, ed. Peter C. Hodgson; trans. Robert F. Brown and Peter C. Hodgson. Eugene, OR: Cascade, 2019.

1855

An Herrn Dr. Karl Hase. Beantwortung des Sendschreibens "Die Tübinger Schule." Tübingen: L. F. Fues, 1855.

1859

Die christliche Kirche vom Anfang des vierten bis zum Ende des sechsten Jahrhunderts in den Hauptmomenten ihrer Entwicklung. Tübingen: L. F. Fues, 1859; 2nd edn., identical with the 1st. Tübingen: L. F. Fues, 1863.

Die Tübinger Schule und ihre Stellung zur Gegenwart. Tübingen: L. F. Fues, 1859; 2nd edn. Tübingen: L. F. Fues, 1860.

1860 (Baur's Death)

1861

Die christliche Kirche des Mittelalters in den Hauptmomenten ihrer Entwicklung, ed. Ferdinand Friedrich Baur. Tübingen: L. F. Fues, 1861; 2nd edn., identical with the 1st. Leipzig: Fues's Verlag [R. Reisland], 1869.

1862

Kirchengeschichte des neunzehnten Jahrhunderts, ed. Eduard Zeller. Tübingen: L. F. Fues, 1862; 2nd edn. Leipzig: Fues's Verlag [R. Reisland], 1877.

1863

Kirchengeschichte der neueren Zeit, von der Reformation bis zum Ende des achtzehnten Jahrhunderts, ed. Ferdinand Friedrich Baur. Tübingen: L. F. Fues, 1863.

1864

Vorlesungen über neutestamentliche Theologie, ed. Ferdinand Friedrich Baur. Leipzig: Fues's Verlag, 1864; reprint Darmstadt: Wissenschaftliche Buchgesellschaft, 1973, with an introduction by W. G. Kümmel. English translation: *Lectures on New Testament Theology*, ed. Peter C. Hodgson, trans. Robert F. Brown. Oxford: Oxford University Press, 2016.

1865–7

Vorlesungen über die christliche Dogmengeschichte, ed. Ferdinand Friedrich Baur.

Vol. 1/1: *Das Dogma der alten Kirche von der apostolischen Zeit bis zur Synode in Nicäa.* Leipzig: Fues's Verlag, 1865. English translation of the General Introduction in *Ferdinand Christian Baur: On the Writing of Church History*, ed. and trans. Peter C. Hodgson. New York: Oxford University Press, 1968.

Vol. 1/2: *Das Dogma der alten Kirche von der Synode in Nicäa bis zum Ende des sechsten Jahrhunderts.* Leipzig: Fues's Verlag, 1866.

Vol. 2: *Das Dogma des Mittelalters.* Leipzig: Fues's Verlag, 1866.

Vol. 3: *Das Dogma der neueren Zeit.* Leipzig: Fues's Verlag, 1867.

b. Articles and Essays

1818
Review article: "G. P. C. Kaiser, *Die Biblische Theologie, oder Judaismus und Christianismus nach der grammatisch-historischen Interpretationsmethode, und nach einer freimüthigen Stellung in die kritische-vergleichende Universalgeschichte der Religionen und in die universal Religion* (Erlangen, 1813–1814)." *Archiv für die Theologie und ihre neueste Literatur*, ed. Ernst Gottlieb Bengel. 2:3 (1818): 656–717.

1828
"Anzeige der beiden academischen Schriften von Dr. F. C. Baur: Primae Rationalismi et Supranaturalismi historiae capita potiora. Pars I. De Gnosticorum Christianismo ideali. Pars II. Comparatur Gnosticismus cum Schleiermacherianae theologiae indole. Tub. 1827." *Tübinger Zeitschrift für Theologie*, (1828), no. 1: 220–64. (*TZTh* was published without volume numbers and each issue began with new pagination).

1830
"Ueber den wahren Begriff des γλωσσαις λαλειν, mit Rücksicht auf die neuesten Untersuchungen hierüber …." *TZTh*, (1830), no. 2:75–133.

"Predigt zur Vorbereitung auf das Säcularfest der Übergabe der Augsburgischen Confession …." In *Feier des dritten Säkularfestes der Übergabe der Augsburgischen Confession auf der Universität Tübingen*, ed. Members of the Evangelical–Theological Faculty, 93–101. Tübingen: L. F. Fues, 1830.

1831
"Die Christuspartei in der korinthischen Gemeinde, der Gegensatz des petrinischen und paulinischen Christenthums in der ältesten Kirche, der Apostel Petrus in Rom." *TZTh*, (1831), no. 4: 61–206. Reprint in *Ausgewählte Werke in Einzelausgaben*, ed. Klaus Scholder. vol. 1: *Historisch-kritische Untersuchungen zum Neuen Testament*, with an introduction by Ernst Käsemann. Stuttgart and Bad Cannstatt: Frommann-Holzboog, 1963. English translation: *The Christ Party in the Corinthian Community*, ed. D. Lincicum; trans. W. Coppins, C. Heilig, L. Ogden, and D. Lincicum. Early Christianity and Its Literature. Atlanta, GA: Society of Biblical Literature, 2021.

1832
"Ueber die ursprüngliche Bedeutung des Passahfestes und des Beschneidungsritus." *TZTh*, (1832), no. 1: 40–124.

"Der hebräische Sabbath und die Nationalfeste des mosaischen Cultus." *TZTh*, (1832), no. 3: 125–92.

"Apollonius von Tyana und Christus, oder das Verhältniß des Pythagoreismus zum Christenthum. Ein Beitrag zur Religionsgeschichte der ersten Jahrhunderte nach Christus." *TZTh*, (1832), no. 4: 3–235.

1833
"Der Gegensatz des Katholicismus und Protestantismus nach den Principien und Hauptdogmen der beiden Lehrbegriffe. Mit besonderer Rücksicht auf Hrn. Dr. Möhler's Symbolik … (1832, 1833)." *TZTh*, (1833), nos. 3–4: 1–438 (published separately as a book in 1834).

1836
"Ueber Zweck und Veranlassung des Römerbriefs und die damit zusammenhängenden Verhältnisse der römischen Gemeinde. Eine historisch-kritische Untersuchung." *TZTh*, (1836), no. 3: 59–178.

"Abgenöthigte Erklärung gegen einen Artikel der Evangelischen Kirchenzeitung, herausgegeben von Dr. E. W. Hengstenberg, Prof. der Theol. an der Universität zu Berlin. Mai 1836." *TZTh*, (1836), no. 3: 179–232.

1837
"Das christliche des Platonismus oder Sokrates und Christus." *TZTh*, (1837), no. 3: 1–154 (published separately as a monograph in 1837).

"Kritische Studien über den Begriff der Gnosis. Zur Antwort auf Herrn Prof. Weisse's Kritik in den *Theologischen Studien und Kritiken*, Jahrg. 1837, 1. Heft." *TSK* 10 (1837): 511–79.

"Über den Begriff der christlichen Religionsphilosophie." *Zeitschrift für speculative Theologie* 2 (1837): 354–405.

"Der Prophet Jonas, ein assyrisch-babylonisches Symbol." *Zeitschrift für die historische Theologie* 7 = 1 Neue Folge (1837): 88–114.

1838

"Ueber der Ursprung des Episcopats in der christlichen Kirche. Prüfung der neuestens von Hrn. Dr. Rothe hierüber aufgestellten Ansicht." *TZTh*, (1838), no. 3: 1–185.

1839

"Tertullian's Lehre vom Abendmahl und Hr. Dr. Rudelbach, nebst eine Uebersicht über die Hauptmomente der Geschichte der Lehre vom Abendmahl." *TZTh* (1839), no. 2: 56–144.

1844

"Ueber die Composition und den Charakter des johanneïschen Evangeliums." *Theologische Jahrbücher* 3 (1844): 1–191, 397–475, 615–700.

1845

"Kritische Beiträge zur Kirchengeschichte der ersten Jahrhunderte." *ThJb(T)* 4 (1845): 207–314.

1846

"Begriff der christlichen Philosophie." *ThJb(T)* 5 (1846): 29–115, 183–233.

"Der Ursprung und Charakter des Lukas-Evangeliums mit Rücksicht auf die neuesten Untersuchungen." *ThJb(T)* 5 (1846): 453–615.

1847

"Bemerkungen zur johanneischen Frage, besonders in Betreff des Todestage Jesu und Passahfeier der ältesten Kirche. Gegen Herrn Dr. Bleek." *ThJb(T)* 6 (1847): 89–136.

"Ueber Princip und Charakter des Lehrbegriffs der reformirten Kirche in seinem Unterschied von dem der lutherischen, mit Rücksicht auf A. Schweizer's Darstellung der reformirten Glaubenslehre." *ThJb(T)* 6 (1847): 309–89.

"Kritische Studien über das Wesen des Protestantismus." *ThJb(T)* 6 (1847): 506–81.

1848

"Charakter und Bedeutung des calixtinischen Syncretismus." *ThJb(T)* 7 (1848): 163–97.

"Das johanneische Evangelium und die Passafeier des zweiten Jahrhunderts." *ThJb(T)* 7 (1848): 264–86.

"Die johanneischen Briefe. Ein Beitrag zur Geschichte des Kanons." *ThJb(T)* 7 (1848): 293–337.

"Noch ein Wort über das Prinzip des reformirten Lehrbegriffs." *ThJb(T)* 7 (1848): 419–43.

1848–9

"Zur Geschichte des protestantischen Mystik." *ThJb(T)* 7 (1848): 453–528; 8 (1849): 85–143.

1849

"Die evangelisch-theologische Fakultät vom Jahr 1777 bis 1812," and "Die evangelisch-theologische Fakultät vom Jahr 1812 bis 1848." In *Geschichte und Beschreibung der Universität Tübingen*, K. Klüpfel (ed.), 216–47, 389–426. Tübingen: L. F. Fues, 1849.

"Zur neutestamentlichen Kritik. Uebersicht über die neuesten Erscheinungen auf ihrem Gebiet." *ThJb(T)* 8 (1849): 299–370, 455–534.

1850–1

"Die Einleitung in das Neue Testament als theologische Wissenschaft. Ihr Begriff und ihre Aufgabe, ihr Entwicklungsgang und ihr innerer Organismus." *ThJb(T)* 9 (1850): 463–566; 10 (1851): 70–94, 222–53, 291–329.

1850–2

"Beiträge zur Erklärung der Korintherbriefe." *ThJb(T)* 9 (1850): 139–85; 11 (1852): 1–40, 535–74.

1851
"Das Wesen des Montanismus." *ThJb(T)* 10 (1851): 538–94.
"Ehrenrettung Calvins gegen eine katholische Verunglimpfung." *ThJb(T)* 10 (1851): 595–8.

1852
"Kritik der neuesten Erklärung der Apokalypse." *ThJb(T)* 11 (1852): 305–400, 441–69.

1853
"Rückblick auf die neuesten Untersuchungen über das Markusevangelium." *ThJb(T)* 12 (1853): 54–94.
"Über die Philosophumena Origenis." *ThJb(T)* 12 (1853): 152–61.
"Die Hippolytus Hypothese Bunsens." *ThJb(T)* 12 (1853): 428–42.

1854
"Die johanneische Frage, und ihre neuesten Beantwortungen (durch Luthardt, Delitzsch, Brückner, Hase)." *ThJb(T)* 13 (1854): 196–287.
"Caius und Hippolytus." *ThJb(T)* 13 (1854): 330–66.

1855
"Das Princip des Protestantismus und seine geschichtliche Entwicklung, mit Rücksicht auf die neuesten Werke von Schenkel, Schweizer, Heppe und die neuesten Verhandlungen über die Unionsfrage." *ThJb(T)* 14 (1855): 1–137.
"Die beiden Briefe an die Thessalonicher, ihre Aechtheit und Bedeutung für die Lehre von der Parusie Christi." *ThJb(T)* 14 (1855): 141–68.
"Die reichsgeschichtliche Auffassung der Apokalypse." *ThJb(T)* 14 (1855): 218–314.
"Über die Stelle Jak. 4, 5." *ThJb(T)* 14 (1855): 573–6.

1856
"Das System des Gnostiker Basilides und die neuesten Auffassungen desselben." *ThJb(T)* 15 (1856): 121–62.
"Der erste petrinische Brief, mit besonderer Beziehung auf das Werk ... von Dr. Bernh. Weiss." *ThJb(T)* 15 (1856): 193–240.

1857
"Ueber Zweck und Gedankengang des Römerbriefs, nebst der Erörterung einiger paulinischer Begriffe, mit besonderer Rücksicht auf die Commentare von Tholuck und Philippi." *ThJb(T)* 16 (1857): 60–108, 184–209.
"Zur johanneischen Frage, 1) über Justin d. M. gegen Luthardt, 2) über den Passahstreit gegen Steitz." *ThJb(T)* 16 (1857): 209–57.
"Das Verhältniss des ersten johanneischen Briefs zum johanneischen Evangelium." *ThJb(T)* 16 (1857): 315–31.
"Die Lehre vom Abendmahl nach Dr. J. L. Rückert ... " *ThJb(T)* 16 (1857): 533–76.
"Rede bei dem Eintritt der Blaubeurener Promotion am 18. Oktober 1857 (Ansprache im Evangelisch-theologischen Seminar in Tübingen)." Offprint of the *Monatsschrift für die Kirchliche Praxis. Zeitschrift für praktische Theologie*, Neue Folge 35 (1904): 152–61.

1858
"Bemerkungen über die Bedeutung des Wortes Κανών." *ZWT* 1 (1858): 141–50.
"Seneca und Paulus, das Verhältniss des Stoicismus zum Christenthum nach den Schriften Seneca's." *ZWT* 1 (1858): 161–246, 441–70.
"Entgegnung gegen Seitz zum Paschastreit." *ZWT* 1 (1858): 298–312.

1859
"Die Lehre des Apostels Paulus vom erlösenden Tode Christi ... " *ZWT* 2 (1859): 225–51.

1860
"Die Bedeutung des Ausdrucks: ὁ υἱὸς τοῦ ἀνθρώπου." *ZWT* 3 (1860): 274–92.

c. More Recent Editions

Ausgewählte Werke in Einzelausgaben, ed. Klaus Scholder. 5 vols. Stuttgart-Bad Cannstatt: Friedrich Frommann Verlag (Günther Holzboog), 1963–75.
Vol. 1: *Historisch-kritische Untersuchungen zum Neuen Testament*, with an introduction by Ernst Käsemann (1963). Contains "Die Christuspartei in der korinthischen Gemeinde," "Ueber Zweck und Veranlassung des Römerbriefs," "Abgenöthigte Erklärung," and "Ueber den Ursprung des Episkopats."
Vol. 2: *Die Epochen der kirchlichen Geschichtsschreibung* (1852), Dogmengeschichtliche Vorreden aus den Jahren 1836–1858, with an introduction by Ernst Wolf (1963).
Vol. 3: *Das Christentum und die christliche Kirche der drei ersten Jahrhunderte* (2nd edn., 1860), with an introduction by Ulrich Wickert (1966).
Vol. 4: *Kirchengeschichte des neunzehnten Jahrhunderts* (1862), with an introduction by Heinz Liebing (1970).
Vol. 5: *Für und wider die Tübinger Schule* (1975). Contains Baur's *An Herrn Dr. Karl Hase* (1855) and *Die Tübinger Schule* (2nd edn., 1860), along with articles by Hase, Uhlhorn, Ritschl, and Zeller.
Briefe. Part 1: *Die frühen Briefe (1814–1835)*, ed. Carl E. Hester. Sigmaringen: Thorbecke, 1993.
"Dokumentation einiger Predigten." In Christian Andreae, *Ferdinand Christian Baur als Prediger: Exemplarische Interpretationen zu seinem handschriftlichen Predigtnachlaß*. Arbeiten zur Kirchengeschichte 61. Berlin: de Gruyter, 1993, 399–554.
Ursula Streckert, "Der Briefwechsel Ferdinand Christian Baurs mit Ludwig Friedrich Heydt – die Introspektion." *Journal of the History of Modern Theology* 23 (2016): 56–129, 236–72.

d. Unpublished Manuscripts

Geschichte des Alterthums. Unpublished lecture manuscript. Undated [prior to 1826]. Tübinger Universitätsbibliothek, Mh II 166q.
Kirchengeschichte. Unpublished lecture manuscript. Undated [1827?]. Tübinger Universitätsbibliothek, Mh II 166 h.
Klaus Schuffels. "Der Nachlaß Ferdinand Christian Baurs in der Universitätsbibliothek Tübingen und im Schiller-Nationalmuseum Marbach/Neckar." *ZKG* 111 (1968): 375–84.

2. SECONDARY LITERATURE

NB: This part of the bibliography is strictly limited to items cited in the *Reader*.

a. Ancient Sources

Augustine of Hippo. *De trinitate*, ed. W. J. Mountain and F. Glorie. 2 vols. CCSL 50/50A. Turnhout: Brepols, 1968 and 2001. English translation: Arthur West Haddan. *Nicene and Post-Nicene Fathers* (NPNF), First Series, vol. 3, ed. Philipp Schaff. Buffalo, NY: Christian Literature Publishing, 1887. Revised and edited for New Advent by Kevin Knight. Online: https://www.newadvent.org/fathers/1301.htm. Accessed on August 19, 2021.
Basil of Caesarea. *De spiritu sancto*, ed. Benoit Pruche. 2nd edn. *Sources Chrétiennes* 17 bis. Paris: Éditions du Cerf, 1968.
Cicero. *Academica*. In *On the Nature of the Gods. Academics*, trans. H. Rackham. Loeb Classical Library 268. Cambridge, MA: Harvard University Press, 1933.
Clement of Alexandria. *Stromata*, ed. Otto Stählin et al. 2 vols. *Clemens Alexandrinus' Werke*. vols. 2–3. Berlin: de Gruyter, 2011 and 2013. English translation: Clement of Alexandria. *Stromateis*, trans. John Ferguson. Washington, DC: The Catholic University of America Press, 1991.

Cyril of Jerusalem. "*Catecheses ad illuminandos.*" In *Cyrilli Hierosolymorum archiepiscopi opera quae supersunt omnia,* ed. W. C. Reischl and J. Rupp. 1 vol., 1–321. Munich: Lentner, 1848 and 1860.
Epiphanius. *Panarion*, ed. Karl Holl and Jürgen Dummer. *Epiphanius Werke.* vols. 1–3. Berlin: de Gruyter, 2011–13. English translation: Frank Williams, *The Panarion of Epiphanius of Salamis.* 2 vols. Leiden: Brill, 2008 and 2013.
Eusebius of Caesarea. *Historia ecclesiastica*, ed. Eduard Schwartz et al. 3 vols. 2nd edn. *Eusebius Caesariensis Werke.* vol. 2 in 3 parts. Berlin: de Gruyter, 1999.
Eusebius of Caesarea. *Contra Marcellum*, ed. Erich Klostermann and Günther Christian Hansen. 3rd edn. Berlin: de Gruyter, 1991.
Gregory of Nyssa. *Epistulae*, ed. G. Pasquali. *Gregorii Nysseni Opera.* vol. 8/2. 2nd edn. Leiden: Brill, 1959.
Josephus, *De bello iudaico*. Flavius Josephus. *Translation and Commentary*, ed. Steve Mason. vol. 1B: *Judean War 2.* Leiden: Brill, 2008.
Marcus Aurelius. *Ad se ipsum*, ed. Jan Henrik Leopold. Leipzig: Teubner, 1908.
Origen. Contra Celsum, ed. Paul Koetschau. 2 vols. *Origenes' Werke.* Vols. 1–2. Leipzig: Hinrich'sche Buchhandlung, 1899. English translation: Henry Chadwick. *Origen: Contra Celsum*, trans. with an introduction and notes. Cambridge: Cambridge University Press, 1953.
Philo of Alexandria. *Quod omnis probus liber sit*, ed. Thomas Mangey, *Philonis Iudaei Opera Quae Reperiri Potuerunt Omnia.* vol. 2, 445–70. London: William Bowyer, 1742.
Philo of Alexandria. *De vita contemplativa*, ed. Thomas Mangey, *Philonis Iudaei Opera Quae Reperiri Potuerunt Omnia.* vol. 2, 471–86. London: William Bowyer, 1742.
Socrates, *Historia ecclesiastica*, ed. Pierre Maraval and Pierre Périchon. 4 vols. Paris: Éditions du Cerf, 2004–7.

b. Modern Literature

Adams, Nicholas. *The Eclipse of Grace: Divine and Human Action in Hegel.* London: Wiley Blackwell, 2013.
Alkier, Stefan. "Belief in Miracles as the Gateway to Atheism: Theological-Historical Remarks about Ferdinand Christian Baur's Critique of Miracles." In *Ferdinand Christian Baur and the History of Early Christianity*, ed. M. Bauspiess, C. Landmesser, and D. Lincicum, trans. P. C. Hodgson and R. F. Brown, 261–86. Oxford: Oxford University Press, 2017.
Anonymous [= August Tholuck]. "Die Zukunft unserer Theologie." *Evangelische Kirchenzeitung* 18, no. 36 (May 4, 1836): 281–5 and 18, no. 37 (May 7, 1836): 289–91.
Augusti, Johann Christian Wilhelm. *Lehrbuch der christlichen Dogmengeschichte.* 4th edn. Leipzig: Dyk'sche Buchhandlung, 1835.
Aulén Gustaf. *Christus Victor: An Historical Study of the Three Main Types of Atonement*, trans. A. G. Hebert. Eugene, OR: Wipf and Stock, 2003.
Bähr, Karl, Wilhelm Christian Felix. *Die Lehre der Kirche vom Tode Jesu in den ersten drei Jahrhunderten.* Sulzbach: Seidel'sche Buchhandlung, 1832.
Barth, Karl. *History of Protestant Theology in the Nineteenth Century: Its Background and History.* New edn. London: SCM, 2001.
Bauer, Bruno. *Kritik der evangelischen Geschichte des Johannes.* Bremen: Schünemann, 1840.
Bauer, Bruno. *Kritik der evangelischen Geschichte der Synoptiker.* 3 vols. Leipzig: Wigand, 1841–2.
Baumgarten-Crusius, Ludwig. *Lehrbuch der christlichen Dogmengeschichte.* 2 vols. Jena: Im Verlag der Crökerschen Buchhandlung, 1832.
Bauspiess, Martin. "The Essence of Early Christianity: On Ferdinand Christian Baur's View of the Synoptic Gospels." In *Ferdinand Christian Baur and the History of Early Christianity*, ed. M. Bauspiess, C. Landmesser, and D. Lincicum, trans. P. C. Hodgson and R. F. Brown, 177–205. Oxford: Oxford University Press, 2017.
Bauspiess, Martin, Christof Landmesser, and David Lincicum (eds). *Ferdinand Christian Baur and the History of Early Christianity.* Oxford: Oxford University Press, 2017.

Beck, Christian Daniel. *Commentarii historici decretorum religionis Christianae et formulae Lutheriae*. Leipzig: Dyck'sche Buchhandlung, 1801.

Benes, Tuska. *In Babel's Shadow: Language, Philology, and the Nation in Nineteenth-Century Germany*. Detroit: Wayne State University Press, 2008.

Bengtsson, Jan Olof. *The Worldview of Personalism: Origins and Early Development*. Oxford: Oxford University Press, 2006.

Billroth, Gustav. *Beiträge zur wissenschaftlichen Kritik der herrschenden Theologie, besonders in ihrer praktischen Richtung*. Leipzig: Leopold Michelsen, 1831.

Billroth, Gustav. *Commentar zu den Briefen des Paulus an die Corinther*. Leipzig: Weidmann, 1833.

Boyarin, Daniel. *A Radical Jew: Paul and the Politics of Identity*. Berkeley: University of California Press, 1994.

Costache, Doru. "Christian Gnosis: From Clement of Alexandria to John Damascene." In *The Gnostic World*, ed. Garry W. Trompf et al., 259–70. London: Routledge, 2019.

Cotta, Johann Friedrich. "Dissertatio quarta, historiam doctrinae de redemptione ecclesiae, sanguine Jesu Christi facta, exhibens." In Johann Gerhard. *Loci Theologici*, ed. J. F. Cotta. vol. 4, 105–32. Tübingen: Cotta, 1765.

Creuzer, Friedrich. *Symbolik und Mythologie der alten Völker, besonders der Griechen*. 4 vols. Leipzig and Darmstadt: Leske, 1810–12 (4th edn. 1837–42).

Dähne, August Ferdinand. *Geschichtliche Darstellung der jüdisch-alexandrinische Religionsphilosophie*. Halle: Waisenhaus, 1834.

Danz, Christian. "Geschichte als fortschreitende Offenbarung Gottes: Überlegungen zu Schellings Geschichtsphilosophie." In *System als Wirklichkeit: 200 Jahre Schellings "System des Transzendentalen Idealismus,"* ed. Id., Claus Dierksmeier, and Christian Seysen, 69–82. Würzburg: Königshausen & Neumann, 2001.

De Wette, Wilhelm Martin Leberecht. *Kurzgefasstes exegetisches Handbuch zum Neuen Testament*. 2 vols. in 9. Leipzig: S. Hirzel, 1837–47.

Drecoll, Volker Henning. "Ferdinand Christian Baur's View of Christian Gnosis, and of the Philosophy of Religion in His Own Day." In *Ferdinand Christian Baur and the History of Early Christianity*, ed. Martin Bauerspiess, Christof Landmesser, and David Lincicum, 116–46. Oxford: Oxford University Press, 2017.

Dubois, Jean-Daniel. "Basilides and the Basilidians." In *The Gnostic World*, ed. Garry W. Trompf et al., 156–61. London: Routledge, 2019.

Elliott, Mark W. "Christology in the Seventeenth Century." In *The Oxford Handbook of Christology*, ed. Francesca Aran Murphy, 297–314. Oxford: Oxford University Press, 2015.

Erbacher, Hermann. "Bähr, Karl." *Neue Deutsche Biographie* 1 (1953): 520. Online: https://www.deutsche-biographie.de/pnd11937515X.html#ndbcontent. Accessed on August 19, 2021.

Fackenheim, Emil. "Kant's Concept of History." In *The God Within: Kant, Schelling, and Historicity*, ed. J. W. Burbidge, 34–49. Toronto: University of Toronto Press, 1994.

Feuerbach, Ludwig. *Gesammelte Werke*, ed. Werner Schuffenhauer. vol. 1: *Frühe Schriften, Kritiken und Rezensionen*. East-Berlin: Akademie Verlag, 1963. English translation: Ludwig Feuerbach. *Thoughts on Death and Immortality, from the Papers of a Thinker, along with an Appendix of Theological-Satirical Epigrams, Edited by One of His Friends*, trans. James A. Massey. Berkeley: University of California Press, 1980.

Fraedrich, Gustav. *Ferdinand Christian Baur der Begründer der Tübinger Schule als Theologe, Schriftsteller und Charakter*. Gotha: Perthes, 1909.

Frey, Jörg. "Ferdinand Christian Baur and the Interpretation of John." In *Ferdinand Christian Baur and the History of Early Christianity*, ed. M. Bauspiess, C. Landmessern, and D. Lincicum, trans. P. C. Hodgson and R. F. Brown, 206–35. Oxford: Oxford University Press, 2017.

Gengler, Adam. "Über eine angeblich zu erhoffende Indifferenzirung des Katholizismus und des Protestantismus in einem höheren Dritten." *Theologische Quartalsschrift* 14 (1832): 203–53.

Georgii, Ludwig. "Die neuesten Gegensätze in Auffassung der alexandrinischen Religionsphilosophie, insbesondere des jüdischen Alexandrinismus." *Zeitschrift für die historische Theologie* 9, nos. 3 and 4 (1839): 3, 1–98; 4, 1–98.

Gieseler, J. K. L., *Dogmengeschichte*, ed. E. R. Redepenning. Bonn: A. Marcus, 1855.

Hagenbach, Karl Rudolf. *Lehrbuch der Dogmengeschichte*. 2 vols. Leipzig: Weidmann 1840–1. 4th rev. edn. 1857. English translation: *A Text-Book of the History of Doctrines*, trans. C. W. Buch, rev. Henry B. Smith. New York: Sheldon & Co., 1861–2.

Harris, Horton. *The Tübingen School*. Oxford: Oxford University Press, 1975.

Hase Karl von. *Kirchengeschichte: Lehrbuch zunächst für akademische Vorlesungen*. 3rd edn. Leipzig: Breitkopf und Härtel, 1837.

Hase, Karl von. *Die Tübinger Schule: Ein Sendschreiben an Herrn Dr. Ferdinand Christian von Baur*. Leipzig: Breitkopf und Härtel, 1855.

Hasse, Friedrich Rudolf. "Review of F. C. Baur, *Die christliche Gnosis oder die christliche Religions-Philosophie in ihrer geschichtlichen Entwicklung*." *Zeitschrift für speculative Theologie* 1, no. 1 (1836): 209–44.

Hegel, Georg Wilhelm Friedrich. *Vorlesungen über die Philosophie der Religion, nebst einer Schrift über die Beweise vom Dasein Gottes*, ed. Philipp Marheineke. *G. W. F. Hegel' Werke, herausgegeben durch einen Verein von Freunden des Verewigten*. vols. 11–12. Berlin: Duncker & Humblot, 1832.

Hegel, Georg Wilhelm Friedrich. *Vorlesungen über die Philosophie der Geschichte*, ed. Eduard Gans. *G. W. F. Hegel' Werke, herausgegeben durch einen Verein von Freunden des Verewigten*. vol. 9. Berlin: Duncker & Humblot, 1837. (Partial) English translation: *The Philosophy of History*, trans. J. Sibree. New York: Dover, 1956.

Hegel, Georg Friedrich Wilhelm. *Vorlesungen über die Philosophie der Religion*, ed. Walter Jaeschke. 3 vols. in 4. Hamburg: Meiner, 1983–85. English translation: *Lectures on the Philosophy of Religion*, ed. Peter C. Hodgson, trans. R. F. Brown, P. C. Hodgson, and J. M. Stewart. 3 vols. Oxford: Oxford University Press, 1985.

Hegel, Georg Friedrich Wilhelm. *Vorlesungen über die Philosophie der Weltgeschichte*, ed. Bernadette Collenberg-Plotnikov. 4 vols. in 5. Hamburg: Meiner, 2015–2020. English translation: *Lectures on the Philosophy of World History*. vol. 1, ed. Peter C. Hodgson, trans. Robert F. Brown and Peter C. Hodgson. Oxford: Oxford University Press, 2011.

Hegel, Georg Friedrich Wilhelm. *The Phenomenology of Spirit*, trans. Terry Pinkard. Cambridge: Cambridge University Press, 2018.

Hengstenberg, Ernst Wilhelm. "Vorwort." *Evangelische Kirchenzeitung* 18, no. 1 (January 2, 1836): 1–6; no. 2 (January 6, 1936): 9–14; no. 3 (January 9, 1836): 17–23; no. 4 (January 13, 1836): 25–31; no. 5 (January 16, 1836): 33–8; no. 6 (January 20, 1836): 41–5.

Henke, Ernst. "Baumgarten-Crusius, Ludwig Friedrich Otto." *Allgemeine Deutsche Biographie* 2 (1875): 162–4. Online: https://www.deutsche-biographie.de/pnd116091568.html#adbcontent. Accessed on August 19, 2021.

Hilgenfeld, Adolf. *Die clementinische Recognitionen und Homilien*. Jena: J. G. Schreiber, 1848.

Hilgenfeld, Adolf. *Kritische Untersuchungen über die Evangelien Justin's*. Halle: C. A. Schwetschke und Sohn, 1850.

Hilgenfeld, Adolf. *Die Evangelien nach ihrer Entstehung und geschichtlichen Bedeutung*. Leipzig: Hirzel, 1854.

Hilgenfeld, Adolf. *Die jüdischen Apokalyptik in ihrer geschichtlichen Entwicklung*. Jena: Mauke, 1857.

Himes, Michael J. "'A Great Theologian of our Time': Möhler on Schleiermacher." *Heythrop Journal* 37 (1996): 24–46.

Hodgson, Peter C. *The Formation of Historical Theology: A Study of Ferdinand Christian Baur*. New York: Harper & Row, 1966.

Hodgson, Peter C. "F. C. Baur's Interpretation of Christianity's Relationship to Judaism." In *Is There a Judeo-Christian Tradition: A European Perspective*, ed. Emmanuel Nathan and Anya Topolski, 31–52. Berlin: de Gruyter, 2016.

Hodgson, Peter C. "Preface to the English Edition." In *Ferdinand Christian Baur and the History of Early Christianity*, ed. Martin Bauspiess, Christof Landmesser, and David Lincicum, v. Oxford: Oxford University Press, 2017.

Hoffmann, Heinrich. "Literatur zum Neuprotestantismus." *Zeitschrift für Theologie und Kirche* 32 (N. F. 5) (1924): 382–406.

Hofmann, Michael. *Theologie, Dogma und Dogmenentwicklung im theologischen Werk Denis Petaus*. Bern: Peter Lang, 1976.
Holtzmann, Heinrich. "Münscher, Wilhelm." *Allgemeine Deutsche Biographie* 23 (1886): 22. Online: https://www.deutsche-biographie.de/pnd124728030.html#adbcontent. Accessed on August 19, 2021.
Inwood, Michael. *A Hegel Dictionary*. Oxford: Blackwell, 1992.
Jonas, Hans. *The Gnostic Religion: The Message of the Alien God and the Beginnings of Christianity*. 3rd edn. Boston, MA: Beacon Press, 2001.
Kant, Immanuel. *Critique of Pure Reason*, ed. and trans. Paul Guyer and Allen W. Wood. Cambridge: Cambridge University Press, 1998.
Kany, Roland. *Augustins Trinitätsdenken: Bilanz, Kritik und Weiterführung der modernen Forschung zu "De trinitate."* Tübingen: Mohr Siebeck, 2007.
Kelley, Shawn. *Racializing Jesus: Race, Ideology, and the Formation of Modern Biblical Scholarship*. London: Routledge, 2002.
Kippenberg, Hans. *Discovering Religious History in the Modern Age*, trans. Barbara Harshav. Princeton: Princeton University Press, 2002.
Klenz, Heinrich. "Ziegler, Werner Karl Ludwig." *Allgemeine Deutsche Biographie* 45 (1900): 190–2. Online: //www.deutsche-biographie.de/pnd116988134.html#adbcontent. Accessed on August 19, 2021.
Köpf, Ulrich. "Ferdinand Christian Baur und David Friedrich Strauss." In *Ferdinand Christian Baur and the History of Early Christianity*, ed. Martin Bauspiess, Christof Landmesser, and David Lincicum, 3–44. Oxford: OUP, 2017.
Köstlin, Karl Reinhold. *Der Ursprung und die Composition der synoptischen Evangelien*. Stuttgart: Mäcken, 1853.
Krafft, W. "Hasse, Friedrich Rudolf." *Allgemeine Deutsche Biographie* 10 (1879): 754–5. Online: https://www.deutsche-biographie.de/pnd101740824.html#adbcontent. Accessed on August 19, 2021.
Landmesser, Christof. "Ferdinand Christian Baur as Interpreter of Paul: History, the Absolute, and Freedom." In *Ferdinand Christian Baur and the History of Early Christianity*, ed. Martin Bauspiess, Christof Landmesser, and David Lincicum, trans. Robert F. Brown and Peter C. Hodgson, 116–46. Oxford: Oxford University Press, 2017.
Lentz, Carl Georg Heinrich. *Geschichte der christlichen Dogmen in pragmatischer Entwickelung*. 2 vols. Helmstedt: Fleckeisensche Buchhandlung, 1834–5.
Lieu, Judith. *Marcion and the Making of a Heretic: God and Scripture in the Second Century*. Cambridge: Cambridge University Press, 2015.
Lincicum, David. "Ferdinand Christian Baur and the Theological Task of New Testament Introduction." In *Ferdinand Christian Baur and the History of Early Christianity*, ed. Martin Bauspiess, Christof Landmesser, and David Lincicum; trans. Peter C. Hodgson and Robert F. Brown (Oxford: Oxford University Press, 2017), 83–95.
Linstrum, Erik. "Strauss's 'Life of Jesus': Publication and the Politics of the German Public Sphere." *Journal of the History of Ideas* 71, no. 4 (2010): 593–616.
Lösch, Stefan. *Prof. Dr. Adam Gengler: Die Beziehungen des Bamberger Theologen zu J. J. J. Döllinger und J. A. Möhler*. Würzburg: Schöningh, 1963.
Lücke, Friedrich. "Kritik der bisherigen Untersuchungen über die Gnostiker, bis auf die neusten Forschungen darüber von Herrn Dr. Neander und Herrn Prof. Lewald." *Theologische Zeitschrift* 2 (1820): 132–71.
Lücke, Friedrich. *Einleitung in die Offenbarung des Johannes*. Bonn: E. Weber, 1852.
Marheineke, Philipp. *Christliche Symbolik oder historischkritisch und dogmatischkomparative Darstellung des katholischen, lutherischen, reformirten und socinianischen Lehrbegriffs*. 3 vols. Heidelberg: Mohr und Zimmer, 1810–13.
Marheineke, Philipp. *Die Grundlehren der christlichen Dogmatik als Wissenschaft*. 2nd edn. Berlin: Duncker & Humblot, 1827.
Markschies, Christoph. *Gnosis: An Introduction*, trans. John Bowden. London: Bloomsbury, 2003.
Mason, Steve. "Jews, Judaeans, Judaizing, Judaism: Problems of Categorization in Ancient History." *JSJ* 38 (2007): 457–512.

Möhler, Johann Adam. *Die Einheit in der Kirche oder das Wesen des Katholicismus.* Tübingen: Laupp, 1825. English translation: *The Unity in the Church or the Principle of Catholicism,* trans. Peter C. Erb. Washington, DC: Catholic University of America Press, 2015.
Möhler, Johann Adam. "Versuch über den Ursprung des Gnosticismus." In *Beglückwünschung seiner Hochwürden [...] D. Gottlieb Jac. Planck [...] zur Feier seiner 50-jährigen Amtsführung, am 15. Mai 1831, dargebracht von der katholisch-theologischen Fakultät Tübingen.* Tübingen: Hopfer de l'Orme, 1831.
Möhler, Johann Adam. *Symbolik oder Darstellung der dogmatischen Gegensätze der Katholiken und Protestanten nach ihren öffentlichen Bekenntnisschriften.* Mainz: Kupferberg, 1832; 2nd edn. 1833.
Mosheim, Lorenz von. *Versuch einer unparteiischen und gründlichen Ketzergeschichte.* Helmstedt: Weygand, 1748.
Müller, Karl Otfried. *Geschichte hellenischer Stämme und Städte.* 3 vols. Breslau: Max, 1820–4.
Müller, Johann Tobias. *Die symbolischen Bücher der evangelisch-lutherischen Kirche.* 2nd edn. 2 vols. Stuttgart: Liesching, 1848.
Münscher, Wilhelm. *Handbuch der christlichen Dogmengeschichte.* 4 vols. Marburg: In der neuen akademischen Buchhandlung, 1797–1809.
Münscher, Wilhem. *Lehrbuch der christlichen Dogmengeschichte,* ed. Daniel von Coelln. 3rd edn. 2 vols. Kassel: Krieger, 1832–4.
Neander, August. *Genetische Entwickelung der vornehmsten gnostischen Systeme.* Berlin: Dümmler, 1818.
Neander, August. *Allgemeine Geschichte der christlichen Religion und Kirche.* 11 vols. Hamburg: Perthes, 1826–52. English translation: *General History of the Christian Religion and Church,* trans. Joseph Torrey. London and Boston: Crocker and Brewster, 1849–51.
Neander, August. *Erklärung in Beziehung auf einen ihn betreffenden Artikel der Allgemeinen Zeitung.* Berlin: Haude und Spener, 1836 (= *Evangelische Kirchenzeitung* 18, no. 30 [April 13, 1836]: 233).
Neander, August. *Das Leben Jesu Christi in seinem geschichtlichen Zusamenhange und seiner geschichtlichen Entwickelung.* Hamburg: Perthes, 1837.
Neander, August. *Die christliche Dogmengeschichte,* ed. J. L. Jacobi. vol. 1. Berlin: Wiegandt und Grieben, 1857.
Nitzsch, Friedrich. "Augusti, Johann Christian Wilhelm." *Allgemeine Deutsche Biographie* 1 (1875): 685–6. Online: https://www.deutsche-biographie.de/pnd116381086.html#adbcontent. Accessed on August 19, 2021.
Nüssel, Friederike. "Semler, Johann Salomo." *Religion Past and Present.* Consulted online on August 13, 2021. http://dx.doi.org.proxy.library.nd.edu/10.1163/1877-5888_rpp_SIM_124819
Palmer, Christian. "Cotta, Johann Friedrich." *Allgemeine Deutsche Biographie* 4 (1876): 526–7. Online: https://www.deutsche-biographie.de/pnd116689676.html#adbcontent. Accessed on August 19, 2021.
Pattison, George. "Hegelian Augustinianism: Philipp Marheineke." In *The Oxford Guide to the Historical Reception of Augustine,* ed. Karla Pollmann and Willemien Otten. Oxford: OUP, 2013. Online version (2014). Online: https://www.oxfordreference.com/view/10.1093/acref/9780199299164.001.0001/acref-9780199299164-e-360#. Accessed on August 17, 2021.
Pétau, Denys (Dionysius Petavius). *Opus de theologicis dogmatibus.* 4 vols. in 5. Paris: Cramoisy, 1644–50.
Plitt, Gustav Leopold (ed.). *Aus Schellings Leben in Briefen.* 3 vols. Leipzig: Hirzel, 1869–70.
Ramelli, Ilaria. *Bardaisan of Edessa: A Reassessment of the Evidence and New Interpretation.* Piscataway, NJ: Gorgias Press, 2009.
Rasimus, Tuomas. *Paradise Reconsidered in Gnostic Mythmaking: Rethinking Sethianism in Light of the Ophite Evidence.* Leiden: Brill, 2009.
Ritschl, Albrecht. "Ueber die Essener." *Theologische Jahrbücher* 14 (1855): 315–56.
Ritschl, Albrecht. *Die Entstehung der altkatholischen Kirche.* Bonn: A. Marcus, 1850; 2nd edn. Bonn: A. Marcus, 1857.
Ritschl, Albrecht. "Über die beiden Principien des Protestantismus (1876)." In *Gesammelte Aufsätze,* ed. Otto Ritschl, 234–47. Freiburg: J. C. B. Mohr, 1893.
Ritter, Carl. *Vorhalle der europäischen Völkergeschichten vor Herodotus um den Kaukasus und um die Gestade des Pontus: Eine Abhandlung zur Altertumskunde.* Berlin: Reimer, 1820.

Rudolph, Kurt. *Gnosis: The Nature and History of Gnosticism*, trans. Robert McLachlan Wilson. Edinburgh: T&T Clark, 1983.

Schelling, Friedrich Wilhelm Joseph. "System Des Transcendentalen Idealismus (1800)." In *Sämmtliche Werke*, ed. K. F. A. Schelling. vol. I/3, 327–634. Stuttgart: Cotta, 1858. English translation: *System of Transcendental Idealism*, trans. Peter Heath. Charlottesville, VA: University of Virginia Press, 1978.

Schelling, Friedrich Wilhelm Joseph. "Vorlesungen über die Methode des akademischen Studiums (1803)." In *Sämmtliche Werke*, ed. K. F. A. Schelling. vol. I/5, 207–311. Stuttgart: Cotta, 1859. English translation: *Lectures on University Study*, trans. Ella S. Morgan. *The Journal of Speculative Philosophy* 11 (1877): 92–100, 160–77, 225–44, 363–70; 12 (1878): 205–13; 13 (1879): 190–8, 310–19; 14 (1880): 145–53; 15 (1881): 1–8, 152–8.

Schleiermacher, Friedrich Daniel Ernst. *Über den sogenannten ersten Brief des Paulos an den Timotheos. Ein kritisches Sendschreibung an J.C. Gass*. Berlin: Realschulbuchhandlung, 1807 [= Schleiermacher, Friedrich Daniel Ernst. *Schriften aus der Hallenser Zeit (1804–1807)*, ed. Hermann Patsch. *Kritische Gesamtausgabe*. vol. I/5, 153–242. Berlin: de Gruyter, 1995].

Schleiermacher, Friedrich Daniel Ernst. *Der christliche Glaube. 1821/22*, ed. Hermann Peiter. 2 vols. Berlin: de Gruyter, 1984.

Schleiermacher, Friedrich Daniel Ernst. *Hermeneutics: The Handwritten Manuscripts*, ed. Heinz Kimmerle, trans. Jack Forstman and James Duke. Atlanta, GA: Scholars, 1986.

Schleiermacher, Friedrich Daniel Ernst. "Über die Glaubenslehre: Zwei Sendschreiben an Lücke" (1829). In *Kritische Gesamtausgabe*. vol. I/10, ed. Hans-Friedrich Traulsen and Martin Ohst, 307–94. Berlin: de Gruyter, 1990.

Schleiermacher, Friedrich Daniel Ernst. *The Christian Faith*, trans. H. R. Mackintosh and J. S. Stewart. London: T & T Clark, 1999.

Schleiermacher, Friedrich Daniel Ernst. *On the Doctrine of Election*, trans. Iain G. Nicol and Allen G. Jorgenson. Louisville, KY: John Knox Press, 2012.

Schumacher, Lydia. *Divine Illumination: The History and Future of Augustine's Theory of Knowledge*. Oxford: Wiley Blackwell, 2011.

Semler, Johann Salomo. *Abhandlung von freier Untersuchung des Kanon*. 4 vols. Halle: Carl Hermann Hemmerde, 1771–5.

Shaffern, Robert W. "The Medieval Theology of Indulgences." In *Promissory Notes on the Treasury of Merits: Indulgences in Late Medieval Europe*, ed. Robert N. Swanson, 11–36. Leiden: Brill, 2006.

Stäudlin, Karl Friedrich. *Geschichte und Literatur der Kirchengeschichte*, ed. Johann Tychsen Hemsen. Hannover: Hahn'sche Hofbuchhandlung, 1827.

Stanley Jones, F. (ed.). *Rediscovery of Jewish Christianity: From Toland to Baur*. History of Biblical Studies. Atlanta, GA: Society of Biblical Literature, 2012.

Steffens, Heinrich. *Christliche Religionsphilosophie*. 2 vols. Breslau: Max und Komp, 1839.

Strauss, David Friedrich. *Das Leben Jesu kritisch bearbeitet*. 2 vols. Tübingen: Osiander, 1835–6. English translation: *The Life of Jesus Critically Examined*, trans. Maryann Evans [= George Eliot] 3 vols. London: Chapman brothers, 1846 (ed. Peter C. Hodgson. Philadelphia: Fortress, 1972).

Tschackert, Paul. "Stäudlin, Carl Friedrich." *Allgemeine Deutsche Biographie* 35 (1893): 516–20. Online: https://www.deutsche-biographie.de/pnd100276318.html#adbcontent. Accessed on August 19, 2021.

Tholuck, August. "Erklärung in Bezug auf das Sendschreiben von Prof. Weisse." *Litterarischer Anzeiger für christliche Theologie und Wissenschaft überhaupt*, no. 32 (May 24, 1836): 249–51.

Tholuck, August. *Die Glaubwürdigkeit der evangelischen Geschichte, zugleich eine Kritik des Lebens Jesu von Strauß*. Hamburg: Friedrich Perthes, 1837.

Thomassen, Einar. "Valentinus and the Valentinians." In *The Gnostic World*, ed. Garry W. Trompf et al., 162–9. London: Routledge, 2019.

Wagenmann, Julius August. "Rettberg, Friedrich Wilhelm." *Allgemeine Deutsche Biographie* 28 (1889): 273–4. Online: https://www.deutsche-biographie.de/pnd116449837.html#adbcontent. Accessed on August 19, 2021.

Weisse, Hermann Christian. *Die evangelische Geschichte, kritisch und philosophisch bearbeitet*. 2 vols. Leipzig: Breitkopf-Härtel, 1838.

Wendte, Martin. "Ferdinand Christian Baur: A Historically Informed Idealist of a Distinctive Kind." In *Ferdinand Christian Baur and the History of Early Christianity*, ed. Martin Bauspiess, Christof Landmesser, and David Lincicum, 67–80. Oxford: Oxford University Press, 2017.

Williamson, George S. *The Longing for Myth in Germany: Religion and Aesthetic Culture from Romanticism to Nietzsche*. Chicago: Chicago University Press, 2004.

Wolff, Christian. *Theologia naturalis scientifica pertractata*. 2 vols. Frankfurt: Renger'sche Buchhandlung, 1736-7.

Wolfson, Elliot R. *Through a Speculum That Shines: Vision and Imagination in Medieval Jewish Mysticism*. Princeton: Princeton University Press, 1994.

Zachhuber, Johannes. "Baur, Ferdinand Christian." In *The Oxford Guide to the Historical Reception of Augustine*, ed. Karla Pollmann and Willemien Otten. Oxford: OUP, 2013. Online version (2014), https://www.oxfordreference.com/view/10.1093/acref/9780199299164.001.0001/acref-9780199299164-e-167?rskey=ljLWfK&result=60. Accessed on August 17, 2021

Zachhuber, Johannes. *Theology of Science in Nineteenth-Century Germany: From F. C. Baur to Ernst Troeltsch*. Oxford: Oxford University Press, 2013.

Zachhuber, Johannes. "Theology and History in the Controversy between Albrecht Ritschl and Eduard Zeller." In *Theology, History and the Modern University*, ed. Michael DeJonge and Kevin Vander Schel, 125–47. Tübingen: Mohr Siebeck, 2021.

Zeller, Eduard. *Die Philosophie der Griechen*, 2nd edn. 3 vols. Tübingen: Fues, 1844–52. (*Die Philosophie der Griechen in ihrer geschichtlichen Entwicklung*). 3 vols. in 5. Tübingen: Fues, 1856–68.

Zeller, Eduard. "Ueber den Zusammenhang des Essäismus mit dem Griechenthum." *Theologische Jahrbücher* 15 (1856): 401–33.

Zeller, Eduard. "Ferdinand Christian Baur" (1861). In *Vorträge und Abhandlungen geschichtlichen Inhalts*, 354–434. Leipzig: Fues, 1865.

Ziegler, Werner Karl Ludwig, "Historia dogmatis de redemptione." Göttingen 1791. In *Commentationes Theologicae,* ed. Johann Kaspar Velthusen et al. vol. 5, 227–99. Leipzig: Barth, 1798.

GENERAL INDEX

absolute, the 8, 22, 26–7, 62, 67, 108, 135, 139
    absolute beginning 5, 36–7, 158
    absolute idea (*See under* idea)
    absolute religion (*See under* religion)
    absolute spirit (*See under* spirit)
Alexander the Great 159, 168
Alexandria, Alexandrian 29, 32, 63, 168–9
allegory 30, 63
antithesis 12, 28, 59–61, 132, 145–8
apologists 158
appearance (*Erscheinung*) 19, 27, 36–7, 39–42, 47–8, 71, 158 n. 1
archetype (*Urbild*) 37, 88
atonement (*See* reconciliation)
Augustinianism 82–4
autonomy 60, 152

Beatitudes, the 173–4
Bible (*See* Scripture)
biblical theology (*See under* theology)
bishop, bishops, (*See also* epicopacy) 150, 196–8
Blaubeuren, Protestant (Lutheran) Seminary 2, 17

canon (*See also* New Testament) 98–9, 128, 130–2, 187
Catholicism/Catholic (*See also* Early Catholicism) 60–1, 81–2, 145, 148, 150, 152–4, 187–8, 191–202, 208–9
Charlemagne 150
Christian consciousness (*See under* consciousness)
Christology 6, 8, 38, 127, 138 n. 25, 149–50
church, the 54, 60, 62–3, 147–55, 187, 195–202
    Church History (*See also* ecclesiastical historiography) 5, 13–14, 54–5, 62, 146–9
    visible and invisible church 86, 148, 151–3, 211
collective consciousness (*See under* consciousness)
concept (*Begriff*) 10, 19, 27–9, 37–9, 41, 47–8, 54–9, 66–75, 79–83, 123, 133, 167–9, 197, 200–1
    concept of religion (*Religionsbegriff*) 28, 31, 34, 43, 46–8, 66, 71
consciousness

Christian consciousness 116–18, 132–9, 149, 173–6, 200
collective consciousness 19, 22, 57, 67, 162, 200
God-consciousness 38, 67–8, 164, 166–7
individual consciousness 19, 61
moral consciousness 72, 162, 165, 167, 170, 173–4, 177–9
religious consciousness 30, 53, 61, 67, 69, 71, 107, 109, 127, 132, 149–53, 160–3, 168, 173, 179, 197, 200
self-consciousness 53, 59–61, 63, 70, 72–3, 84–5, 89, 135–8, 164–7, 174
subjective consciousness 59, 63, 68, 72–3, 88, 109, 136, 145–6, 197–8
Council of Nicaea 61–2
Council of Trent 196, 198
creation 28, 192
criticism 11, 95–101
    gospel criticism 102–7, 128, 185–9
    historical criticism 144, 154–5, 206–9
    New Testament criticism 98–9, 106, 188

damnation 193
death of Christ 39–43, 69–70, 107–10, 113–14, 133–4, 181–2
devoid of presupposition, presuppositionless 104, 128
Docetism, docetic 32–3, 35–7, 40
dogma 9–11, 46–9, 55–64, 71–5, 96, 149–50, 153–4
dogmatics 54–7, 199–200

early catholicism 12, 157
Ebionites, Ebionitism (*See also* Jewish-Christian) 34, 122, 187
ecclesiastical historiography (*See also* church history) 143–55
eclecticism 165–6
Egypt, Egyptian 20–2, 32–3, 124, 168–9
Epicureanism 164–6
episcopacy (*See also* bishop, bishops) 196–8
epoch (*See* period)

Essenes 169–70
ethical (*See* moral)
etymology 22
evil 26, 192–4

faith
   Christian faith 38, 46, 86, 134, 149, 182, 200, 205, 207
   faith and knowledge 41–2, 60, 209
   faith and science 206, 209
   Protestant faith 205
Father 88, 90, 108–11, 127, 134–5
finite, finitude 26–9, 40, 63, 65–7, 72–3, 77, 88, 91, 108–9, 129, 136–9, 161, 163, 173, 177
flesh (σάρξ)
forgiveness of sin (*See under* sin)
freedom 36–7, 46, 59–61, 71–4, 82–4, 129, 134, 136–8, 152–3, 198, 211

Galilee 112, 119, 124, 181
Gnosticism/Gnosis 3, 6, 25–43, 186, 191–5
God-consciousness (*See under* consciousness)
God-man (Christ) 38–43, 66, 68–73, 78, 82, 154
grace 31, 66, 69, 82, 108–9, 133–4, 174
Greece 21
Greek philosophy 63, 163–8
Greek religion (*See under* religion)
Griesbach theory 12, 101, 172 n. 32
guilt 31, 67–72, 193

Hegelian philosophy 38, 41–2, 79, 90 n. 37
Hegelianism 79–86
historical theology (*See under* theology)
historiography (*See* ecclesiastical historiography)
history
   history of dogma 9–11, 46, 49, 53–64, 78, 149
   world history 19, 38, 40–1, 62, 158–60, 164, 167, 170

idea 21, 26–7, 36–7, 40, 42, 47, 63, 68, 89, 133–4, 144–5, 147–55
   absolute idea 49, 63, 113, 117, 138
   idea of God 38, 63, 68–9, 78, 82, 88, 177
   Messianic idea 133–4, 179–81
Image [of God] 19, 89–91
Incarnation 40, 78, 110, 171
individual, individuality (*See also* particular, particularity) 18–22, 37, 40, 57, 67–9, 85, 105–6, 145–6, 152, 154, 159, 162, 164–6, 176–7, 197
   individual consciousness (*See under* consciousness)
   universal individual 40

infinite 25, 28, 29, 65, 77, 84, 88, 91, 139, 153 n. 10
Innocent III 150

Jerusalem 111–13, 117, 119, 121–2, 125, 157, 180
Jewish-Christian, Jewish Christianity (*See also* Ebionites) 11–12, 101–2, 112–14, 186–7
Judaism 25–6, 29–30, 32–4, 48, 63, 67–8, 107, 109–13, 118, 123, 126–7, 132–8, 167–70, 179–82, 193–5
justification 136, 192

kērygma 55
Kingdom of God 157, 173, 176–8

Law 11–12, 67, 107–9, 126–7, 174–7
   law-giver [in Kant's philosophy] 72
   Mosaic law 55, 111, 122, 175
   Sabbath law 175
Logos [Christ] 101, 107, 109–13, 149, 171
   Logos in Philo of Alexandria 29

Manichaeism 25
manifestation 27, 132, 145, 147 n. 5, 148, 150–5
matter 25, 28–33, 35–7
mediation (*Vermittlung*) 27, 30, 34, 39, 42, 59–60, 66–7, 70, 103–4, 107–8, 197–8, 200
Memoria, intelligentia, voluntas or *caritas* or *dilectio* [in Augustine] 88–90
Messiah, Messianism 107, 109–10, 113, 121–3, 125, 133–4, 179–82
metaphysics, metaphysical 26, 69, 109
Middle Ages, medieval 53, 61, 80–1, 84, 150–3
miracles 113, 120, 158, 170–2, 180–2, 207
Monad 34
moral religion (*See under* religion)
morality, moral, ethical 26, 30–1, 67, 70, 72, 109, 112, 122, 157, 164–7, 174–9, 193–4, 211
   moral consciousness (*See under* consciousness)
Mosaic law (*See under* law)
myth, mythical 67, 120, 128, 188, 205
   mythical interpretation of the gospels 104–5, 120–1, 188
mythology [*Mythologie*, the study of myth] 17–23

nation, national 63, 67, 108, 110, 119, 123, 126–7, 159–61, 168, 179–81
natural religion (*See under* religion)
natural theology (*See under* theology)
nature 28, 31, 67, 77, 164, 166, 193
   nature religion (*See under* religion)
necessity 28, 31, 61–2, 71–2, 103–4, 147 n. 5, 152, 195–8

Neoplatonism 167
New Testament 11–14, 41, 55–6, 99, 124, 187–8, 208
　New Testament canon (*See* canon)
　New Testament criticism (*See under* criticism)

objective 9–10, 38–41, 58–60, 67–73, 80–5, 134–5, 144, 197–9
Old Testament 109–13, 121–7, 167–9, 174–8
organism 19, 31

paganism 25–6, 32–5, 48, 66–8, 109–13, 161, 163, 167, 193–5
papacy, pope 150–4, 211–13
parable, parables 120, 125, 157, 173, 177–8
particular, particularity (*See also* individual, individuality) 57, 61–3, 88, 118, 145–6, 159–60, 170, 176–7
Pastoral Epistles 131–2, 186–7, 209–10
Paul the Apostle 69, 107, 127, 129–39, 186–7, 207
Pauline Christianity, Paulinism 102, 132, 172, 187
Peace of Westphalia 154
Pelagianism 82–4
period, epoch 48–9, 61–2, 71–4, 148–55, 159, 164, 186–8, 195, 199–201
Pharisees 111–12, 119, 122–3, 125, 169, 174–5
philosophy of religion 20, 27, 29–31, 37–43, 45–9, 63–4, 72, 169
Platonism 164
Pneumatic (*See also* spirit) 37–8, 108, 139
polemics [theological discipline] 202
pope, the (*See* papacy, pope)
positive religion (*See under* religion)
poverty, the poor 170, 173–4
practical reason 72
predestination 84 n. 20
principle
　Catholic principle 197
　　Protestant principle 60–1, 79, 145, 153, 197, 199, 208
prophet, prophets, prophecy 68, 109, 121 124–5, 174, 176
Protestantism/Protestant 60–1, 79–80, 83–4, 145, 148, 152–4, 192–202, 204–5, 208, 211

rationalism 20 n. 10, 83, 145, 199
reconciliation (*Versöhnung*), atonement 40, 61, 65–75, 78, 80–2, 108, 134, 149, 162, 197–8
redeemer 36–7, 68–70
redemption 36–7, 66, 68–9, 149, 164, 174, 194
Reformation 60–5, 72–3, 77, 80–4, 148, 150–1, 195

religion
　absolute religion 5, 8, 10, 41, 47–8, 63, 65, 68, 134, 161–7
　Greek religion 8, 22, 163
　moral religion 165, 179
　natural religion 46
　nature religion (*Naturreligion*) 19, 31
　positive religion 26, 46
religious consciousness (*See under* consciousness)
representation 63, 67, 150–1
　vicarious representation (*Stellvertretung*) 69
resurrection [of Christ] 40, 43, 117, 119, 133, 157, 181–2
　Lazarus' resurrection 113
revelation 30, 46, 63, 109, 112, 149, 162, 164, 167
　self-revelation 28,
Rome, Roman Empire 158–60, 163 n. 11

Sabbath law (*See under* law)
sacrifice, sacrificial 65, 68, 70, 71, 106, 154, 205
Sadducees 169
salvation 28, 31, 36–7, 82, 109–11, 152–3, 167 n. 22, 179
Sanhedrin 111
satisfaction 161, 163, 165
　theory of satisfaction 59, 71–4, 80–2
scholasticism, scholastic 53, 60–2, 77, 151
science, scientific 19–23, 38, 54, 57, 78, 84, 86, 96, 99, 204–9
Scripture, Bible 79–80, 83, 99, 104, 117, 168, 195, 199–200, 206–8
self-bifurcation (*Selbstentzweiung*) 27
self-consciousness (*See under* consciousness)
self-determination 89
self-emptying (*Entäußerung*) 38
self-knowledge 89
sense-certainty (*sinnliche Gewissheit*) 42
Sermon on the Mount 121, 126–7, 172–4, 176–8
sin 31, 36, 66, 68–71, 82–3, 108–9, 174, 192–4
　forgiveness of sins 107–8, 177
Skepticism 165–6
Socinianism 154
Socrates 38, 164–5
Son of David 113, 123
Son of God 107–8, 133, 158, 160, 162, 180
Son of Man 180, 182
source, sources 19, 78, 104, 122, 144, 146, 150, 162, 167–9, 171–2, 189, 198
speculative theology (*See under* theology)
spirit (*Geist*)
　absolute spirit 28–9, 38–40, 42, 66, 72, 91, 134, 136, 200
　divine spirit, spirit of God 19, 71, 134–6, 200

Holy Spirit 82, 150
human spirit 19, 22, 54, 58, 83, 86, 91, 135
state (*See also* nation) 67, 152–3, 159, 161, 212
Stoicism, Stoic 164–7
subject, subjective 38, 59–60, 61, 65, 69–70, 72–3, 80–5, 89, 96–7, 107, 127, 134–7, 152–4, 165–7, 176–8, 198–9, 205, 209
   absolute subject 138
   subjective consciousness (*See under* consciousness)
sublate (*aufheben*) 28, 40, 43, 66–7, 89
supranaturalism 2–3, 6–7, 191, 199
symbolism, symbolics (*Symbolik*) 20, 201–2
Synoptic Gospels, synoptics 101, 105, 107–8, 112–16, 128, 171–2, 180, 187–8
system 20–1, 22, 27, 32–4, 36–7, 41, 57, 63, 149–51, 154, 164, 192, 194, 201
   system of doctrine (*Lehrbegriff*) 196–7, 199–200,

tendency (*Tendenz*) 12, 105–7, 112, 114, 116, 118, 126, 188
theocracy 168–9, 178
theology
   biblical theology 56
   historical theology 78
   natural theology 46, 166–7
   speculative theology 45, 48, 86
theory, theories 69, 71–3, 80–1, 165
Therapeutae 169
tradition 60, 116, 120–3, 148, 153, 157, 172, 188, 198–201, 207–8
Trinitarian relationship 87, 89
Trinity 77–8, 88, 90, 149
Tübingen 2–3, 17, 191
Tübingen School 4, 185–9

union (*Einswerdung*), unity (*Einheit*) 19, 27, 38, 40–3, 57–9, 66–71, 78–80, 88–90, 102, 110–11, 147–55, 159
universality 18, 39–40, 61, 63, 90 n. 37, 127, 147 n. 5, 159

visible and invisible church (*See under* Church)

Word, the (*See also* Logos) 178, 208
world history (*See under* history)

Zoroastrian 194

INDEX OF ANCIENT SOURCES

Augustine
De civitate dei
XI.24 — 91

De trinitate
X.11.17–18 — 88
XI.5.8 — 91
XIV.8.11 — 91
XV — 87
XV.1.1 — 91
XV.21.40 — 88
XV.21.40–1 — 88
XV.21.41 — 89
XV.22.42 — 90
XV.23.43 — 89, 90

Basil of Caesarea
Liber de spiritu sancto
27.66 — 55

Cicero
Quaestiones academicae
2.9 — 55

Clement of Alexandria
Stromata
III.5.3 — 34

Cyril of Jerusalem
Catecheses ad illuminandos
4.2 — 55

Epiphanius
Panarion
30.17.5 — 122
30.2.2 — 122
30.26.1–28.7 — 122
42.9 — 131

Eusebius
Contra Marcellum
1.4.15–16 — 55

Ecclesiastical History
3.25 — 130
3.39.16 — 172
4.26 — 159

Gregory of Nyssa
Epistula
24.2 — 55

Irenaeus
Adversus Haereses
I.24.4 — 36

Josephus
Bellum Judaicum
2.8.3 [2.122–3] — 170

Marcus Aurelius
Meditations
2.3 — 55

Origen
Against Celsus
1.42 — 104
2.30 — 159, 160

Philo of Alexandria
De vita contemplativa
13 — 170

Quod omnis probus liber sit
75 — 170

Seneca
Epistulae morales ad Lucullium
94 — 55

Socrates
Historia ecclesiastica
2.44.4 — 55

INDEX OF MODERN AUTHORS

Abelard 80 n. 8
Adam, Nicholas 38 n. 39
Alkier, Stefan 172 n. 31
Anselm of Canterbury 71, 73, 80–3
Augusti, Johann Christian Wilhelm 74
Aulén, Gustaf 80 n. 8

Bähr, Karl Wilhelm Christian Felix 74
Barth, Karl 1
Bauer, Bruno 45, 103 n. 5, 187
Bauer, Ludwig 8 n. 31
Baumgarten-Crusius, Ludwig 57 n. 7, 75
Baur, Emilie, née Becher 2
Baur, Jakob Christian 2
Bauspieß, Martin 1 n. 2, 4 n. 15, 8 n. 35, 31 n. 17,
    95 n. 1, 101 n. 2, 129 n. 3, 172 n. 31–2, 186 n. 3,
    203 n. 1
Beck, Christian Daniel 75 n. 19
Benes, Tuska 22 n. 19
Bengel, Ernst Gottlob 2, 4 n. 17, 103 n. 5
Bengtsson, Jan Olof 90 n. 37
Billroth, Gustav 213
Boeckh, August 23 n. 21
Boehme, Jacob 25, 29 n. 9
Bowden, John 26 n. 2
Boyarin, Daniel 129 n. 2
Brown, Robert F. 14, 40 n. 42, 53, 56 n. 6, 63 n. 12,
    95 n. 1, 101 n. 2, 129, 163 n. 11, 172 n. 31, 185,
    186 n. 3, 203 n. 1
Burbidge, J. W. 7 n. 27

Chemnitz, Martin 103 n. 5
Coelln, Daniel von 74 n. 17
Coppins, Wayne 113 n. 46, 186 n. 6
Costache, Doru 32 n. 24
Cotta, Johann Friedrich 74
Credner, Karl August 103 n. 5
Creuzer, Friedrich 3, 17–18, 20–1

Dähne, August Ferdinand 170 n. 28
Danz, Christian 8 n. 32
de Wette, Wilhelm Martin Leberecht 95, 103 n. 5,
    106, 130 n. 5, 137, 203 n. 3

Delitzsch, Franz 95
Dierksmeier, Claus 8 n. 32
Dilthey, Wilhelm 14
Dorner, Isaak August 10
Drecoll, Volker Henning 31 n. 17, 32 n. 23
Dubois, Jean-Daniel 32 n. 18
Duke, James 98 n. 7

Ebrard, Johann Heinrich August 103 n. 5
Eichhorn, Friedrich 78 n. 2
Eichhorn, Johann Gottfried 103 n. 5, 130 n. 5
Elliott, Mark W. 154 n. 13
Erb, Peter C. 201 n. 30
Erbacher, Hermann 74 n. 11
Eschenmayr, Carl August 2

Fackenheim, Emil 7 n. 27
Ferguson, John 34 n. 32
Feuerbach, Ludwig 41 n. 45
Fichte, Immanuel Hermann 90 n. 37
Forstman, Jack 98 n. 7
Frey, Jörg 101 n. 2, 109 n. 25

Gass, J. C. 11 n. 45, 130 n. 5
Gengler, Adam 195–8, 201 n. 31
George Eliot (Maryann Evans) 4 n. 12, 104 n. 11,
    185 n. 1
Georgii, Ludwig 168 n. 24
Gerhard, Johann 74 n. 9
Gerlach, Ernst Ludwig von 203 n. 3
Gerson, Jean 103 n. 5
Gieseler, Johann Karl Ludwig 32 n. 23, 56 n. 6, 62
    n. 10, 103 n. 5
Guyer, Paul 96 n. 3

Hagenbach, Karl Rudolf 62 n. 10
Hammer-Purgstall, Joseph Freiherr von 21
Harnack, Adolf 11
Harris, Horton 1 n. 2, 9 n. 37
Harshav, Barbara 23 n. 21
Hase, Karl von 148 n. 6, 150 n. 8, 154
Hasse, Friedrich Rudolf 45, 47–8
Heath, Peter 19 n. 9

Hebert, A. G. 80 n. 8
Hegel, Geord Wilhelm Friedrich 7–10, 25, 27–9,
   37–43, 53, 63 n. 11, 65, 72, 78–9, 86, 134 n. 15,
   153 n. 10, 163 n. 11, 191, 201, 212
Heilig, Christoph 113 n. 46, 186 n. 6
Hengstenberg, Ernst Wilhelm 203–4, 210 n. 20
Henke, Ernst 75 n. 19
Herder, Johann Gottfried 17
Hermann, Gottfried 18 n. 4
Hester, Carl E. 3 n. 7, 20 n. 10, 203 n. 2
Hilgenfeld, Adolf 169 n. 27, 171 n. 29,
   181 n. 50,
Himes, Michael J. 201 n. 30
Hodgson, Peter Crafts 1, 14, 30 n. 14, 40 n. 42, 53,
   56 n. 6, 63 n. 12, 95 n. 1, 101 n. 2, 104 n. 11,
   106 n. 12, 129, 143–4, 157, 163 n. 11, 172 n. 31,
   185, 186 n. 3, 203 n. 1
Hoffmann, Heinrich 154 n. 12
Hofmann, Michael 74 n. 15
Holtzmann, Heinrich 74 n. 17, 95
Hug, Johann Leonhard 103 n. 5
Hupfeld, Hermann 95

Inwood, Michael 27–8, 38 n. 39, 42 n. 46, 47 n. 3,
   99 n. 8, 132 n. 11, 196 n. 16

Jacobi, Justus Ludwig 56 n. 6
Jonas, Hans 193 n. 8
Jones, Frederick Stanley 122 n. 89
Jorgenson, Allen G. 84 n. 20

Kaiser, Gottlieb Philipp Christian 4–5
Kant, Immanuel 7, 65, 72–3, 77, 96 n. 3, 166 n. 19,
   169 n. 27, 209
Kany, Roland 87–8
Käsemann, Ernst 113 n. 46
Kelley, Shawn 30 n. 14
Kimmerle, Heinz 98 n. 7
Kippenberg, Hans 23 n. 21
Klenz, Heinrich 74 n. 10
Köpf, Ulrich 4 n. 15, 101 n. 3, 104 n. 9, 186 n. 4,
   188 n. 17, 203 n. 1
Köstlin, Karl Reinhold 171–2
Krafft, W. 47 n. 5

Landmesser, Christof 1 n. 2, 4 n. 15, 8 n. 35,
   31 n. 17, 95 n. 1, 101 n. 2, 129 n. 3, 172 n. 31,
   186 n. 3, 203 n. 1
Lentz, Carl Georg Heinrich 75
Lieu, Judith 32 n. 25, 36 n. 36
Lindgren, Uta 21 n. 16

Lösch, Stefan 196 n. 14
Lücke, Friedrich 3, 31 n. 16, 95, 171 n. 30
Luther, Martin 38 n. 39, 80 n. 8, 83, 151, 193 n. 6,
   n. 10, 208

Mackintosh, H. R. 37 n. 37, 55 n. 2, 68 n. 6, 166
   n. 19, 195 n. 13, 201 n. 28
Marheineke, Philipp 3 n. 6, 7 n. 26, 27 n. 6,
   41 n. 45, 47 n. 5, 87 n. 29, 191, 199, 201–2
Markschies, Christoph 26 n. 2
Mason, Steve 112 n. 40
Massey, James A. 41 n. 45
McLachlan Wilson, Robert 26 n. 4
Möhler, Johann Adam 2–3, 8, 11, 25, 80 n. 6,
   84 n. 20, 191–202
Morgan, Ella S. 7 n. 28
Mosheim, Lorenz von 31 n. 16
Müller, Karl Otfried 21 n. 18
Münscher, Wilhelm 57 n. 7, 74
Murphy, Francesca Aran 154 n. 13

Nathan, Emmanuel 30 n. 14
Neander, August 13, 29, 31 n. 16, 33–4, 56 n. 6,
   62 n. 10, 75 n. 19, 103 n. 5, 106, 162 n. 9, 186,
   203 n. 3, 204, 208, 211–13
Nicol, Iain G. 84 n. 20
Niehoff, Maren J. 29 n. 10
Nitzsch, Friedrich 74 n. 16
Nüssel, Friederike 98 n. 6

Ogden, Lucas 113 n. 46, 186 n. 6
Osiander, Andreas 103 n. 5
Otten, Willemien 87 n. 26, 87 n. 29

Palmer, Christian 74 n. 9
Patsch, Hermann 11 n. 45
Pattison, George 87 n. 29
Peiter, Hermann 20 n. 10
Pétau, Denys 10, 74
Plitt, Gustav Leopold 78 n. 2
Pollmann, Karla 87 n. 26, n. 29

Ramelli, Ilaria 32 n. 22
Rasimus, Tuomas 32 n. 20
Redepenning, Ernst Rudolf 56 n. 6
Rettberg, Friedrich Wilhelm 79–85
Ritschl, Albrecht 1, 4, 10, 83 n. 16, 169 n. 27,
   174 n. 35
Ritter, Carl-Georg 20–1
Rudelbach, Andreas Gottlob 95
Rudolph, Kurt 26 n. 4, 32 nn. 18–22

INDEX OF MODERN AUTHORS

Schelling, Friedrich Wilhelm Joseph 2, 7–8, 17, 19 n. 9, 25, 29 n. 9, 53, 77–8, 86, 90 n. 37, 147 n. 5, 165 n. 19, 191
Schelling, Karl Friedrich August 7 n. 28
Schleiermacher, Friedrich Daniel Ernst 1, 3, 7–8, 11, 17, 20, 25, 29 n. 9, 37 n. 37, 39 n. 41, 42, 55, 68, 72, 80 n. 6, 84 n. 20, 86, 95, 98, 103 n. 5, 130 n. 5, 134 n. 15, 162 n. 9, 166 n. 19, 169 n. 27, 191, 195, 200–1, 212
Scholder, Klaus 113 n. 46
Schuffenhauer, Werner 41 n. 45
Schumacher, Lydia 88 n. 31
Semler, Johann Salomo 98 n. 6
Seysen, Christian 8 n. 32
Shaffern, Robert W. 81 n. 11
Sibree, John 153 n. 10
Stäudlin, Karl Friedrich 146 n. 4
Steffens, Heinrich 90 n. 37
Stewart, J. Michael 40 n. 42, 63 n. 12
Stewart, J. S. 37 n. 37, 55 n. 2, 68 n. 6, 166 n. 19, 195 n. 13
Storr, Gottlob Christian 103 n. 5, 188 n. 17
Strauss, David Friedrich 1, 4, 11–12, 65, 97 n. 4, 101, 103–6, 114–16, 120 n. 79, 185–9, 203–4, 207 n. 12, 210, 213
Swanson, Robert N. 81 n. 11

Tholuck, Friedrich August Gottreu 203, 212–13
Thomassen, Einar 32 n. 19
Topolski, Anya 30 n. 14
Torrey, Joseph 162 n. 9
Troeltsch, Ernst 1, 154 n. 12
Trompf, Garry W. 32 nn. 18–19, 32 n. 24
Tschackert, Paul 146 n. 4

Velthusen, Johann Kaspar 74 n. 10
Voss, Johann Heinrich 18 n. 4

Wagenmann, Julius August 79 n. 3
Weisse, Christian Hermann 90 n. 37, 103 n. 5, 212 n. 26, 213
Welzig, Werner 21 n. 15
Wendte, Martin 8 n. 35, 186 n. 3
Wieseler, Karl Georg 103 n. 5
Wilke, Christian Gottlob 103 n. 5
Williamson, George F. 18 nn. 3–4, 21 n. 13, n. 19
Wolff, Christian 46
Wolfson, Elliot 138 n. 25
Wood, Allen 96 n. 3

Zeller, Eduard 1–4, 129, 165 n. 15, n. 17, 167 n. 22, 169 n. 27
Ziegler, Werner Karl Ludwig 74
Zwingli, Ulrich 193 n. 10

INDEX OF BIBLICAL PASSAGES

Exodus		3:3	124
34:29-35	136	4:14	124
		4:15-16	124
Psalms		4:23	121
8:3	125	5:3	170, 173
22:15	126	5:3-12	173
22:18	126	5:13-16	174
78:2	125	5:17	122, 126, 174
		5:18	175
Isaiah		5:48	177
6:9	125	6:12	177
7:14	124	6:19-24	176
9:1	124	7:12	176–7
29:13	125	7:16	213
40:3	124	7:20	213
42:1	125	8:17	121, 125
53:4	125	9:14	175
61:2	181	9:16	176
64:4	135	9:16-17	176
		9:27	123
Jeremiah		11:27	127
30:23	212	12:1-14	175
31:15	124	12:18-21	125
32:6	126	12:23	123
		13:1-9	178
Hosea		13:14-15	125
11:1	124	13:35	125
		13:45-46	178
Micah		15:1	175
5:2	124	15:8	125
		15:13	175
Zechariah		15:22	123
9:9	125	15:24	123
11:12	126	18:3	178
13:7	126	19:1	119
		20:30	123
Matthew		20:31	123
1:22	124	21:15	123
2:6	124	21:23	119
2:13-15	124	21:9	123
2:15	124	22:37-9	176
2:18	124	22:41-5	123
2:23	124	23:1-3	175

INDEX OF BIBLICAL PASSAGES

23:3	122, 175	7:21	111
23:4	175	7:22	111
23:23	175	7:38	110
23:37-39	119	7:39	118
24	121	7:42	113
24:1-2	121	8:17	111
24:29	182	8:56	110
26:31	126	10:15	110
27:35	126	10:34	111
27:53	121	11:8-10	117
27:9	126	11:16	117
28:10	119	11:51	110
28:16	119	11:52	110
28:19	123	12:14-15	110
		12:16	117
Mark		12:24	110
4:1-9	178	12:38-39	110
4:30-32 par.	206	12:41	110
		12:52	110
Luke		13:8	116
4:19	181	13:24	110, 114
6:20	173	14:5	117
8:4-8	178	14:8	117
		14:22	117–18
John		16:9	117–18
1:1-13	109	16:17	117–18
1:9	110	16:29	117–18
1:11	111	17:3	109
1:14	113	18:10-11	116
1:42	115	18:15-16	114
1:43	115	18:26-27	116
2:17	110	19:26-27	114
2:19	117	19:28	110
2:22	117	19:36	110
2:23	117	20:1-9	115
3:14	110	20:2-3	115
3:14-15	110	20:24	118
3:21	109	21	113–14
4:12	110	21:3-8	115
4:21	111	21:15-19	116
4:22	109	21:22-23	113
4:24	162	21:23	114
4:30	110		
4:31-34	117	Acts	
4:42	109	1:21-22	118
5:5-6	117	3:19-21	133, 182
5:46	109	16:4	55
6:5-14	117	17:7	55
6:32	110		
6:45	110	Romans	
6:67	118	1:3	113
6:68-69	115	1:4	108
6:70-71	118	2:25-9	175

7:7-13	108	3:13-16	137
8:1-17	205	3:14	137
8:5-17	108	3:14-16	137
8:14	135	3:17	136–7
8:14-16	135	3:18	137–88
8:15-16	134	5:14-15	69
8:16	134	5:15-16	133
		5:15-17	133
1 Corinthians		5:16	181
1	138		
1:19-31	138	Galatians	
2:6-16	138	3:2	134
2:9	135	3:2-3	134
2:9-12	135	3:10-14	108
2:13-16	206	3:20	67
3:21-23	138	4:4	135
15:45	108	4:6	135
15:47	108	5:2-6	175
15:47-49	108	5:17	108
15:56	108		
15:8	133	Ephesians	
		2:15	55
2 Corinthians			
2	136	Philippians	
2:14-15	139	2:7	38
3	136		
3:6	136, 204	Colossians	
3:6-16	136	2:14	55
3:10-11	136		
3:12	137	Revelation	
3:12-13	136–7	11:1-2	121
3:13	137	11:13	122

www.ingramcontent.com/pod-product-compliance
Lightning Source LLC
Chambersburg PA
CBHW080936300426
44115CB00017B/2835